MW01596343

THE MUSHARRAF REGIME AND THE GOVERNANCE CRISIS: A CASE STUDY OF THE GOVERNMENT OF PAKISTAN

THE MUSHARRAF REGIME AND THE GOVERNANCE CRISIS: A CASE STUDY OF THE GOVERNMENT OF PAKISTAN

DR. SOHAIL MAHMOOD

Nova Science Publishers, Inc.
Huntington, New York

Senior Editors: Susan Boriotti and Donna Dennis
Coordinating Editor: Tatiana Shohov
Office Manager: Annette Hellinger
Graphics: Wanda Serrano
Book Production: Matthew Kozlowski, Jonathan Rose and Jennifer Vogt
Circulation: Cathy DeGregory, Ave Maria Gonzalez and Raheem Miller
Communications and Acquisitions: Serge P. Shohov

Library of Congress Cataloging-in-Publication Data
Available Upon Request

ISBN 1-59033-135-4.

Copyright © 2001 by Nova Science Publishers, Inc.
227 Main Street, Suite 100
Huntington, New York 11743
Tele. 631-424-NOVA (6682)   Fax 631-425-5933
E Mail: Novascience@earthlink.net

Printed in the United States of America

CONTENTS

SECTION I

Chapter 1

INTRODUCTION: A BRIEF POLITICAL HISTORY

Soon after independence in 1947, Pakistan moved from a parliamentary system to a presidential one and then finally reverted to the original parliamentary system. Pakistan's political system remains fragile. To understand the complexity of the crisis it is necessary to comprehend the historical background and context of the problem. First, the historical aspects are considered. The Pakistan Muslim League (PML) led by Quaid-e Azam Muhammad Ali Jinnah had founded Pakistan. Unfortunately for Pakistan, Jinnah died in 1948 and his chief lieutenant Liaqat Ali Khan in 1951. The PML lost its most capable leaders. The succeeding party leadership did not have the stature or the capability of the earlier party leaders. The party floundered as a result. The first parliamentary period stretching from 1947-1958 was conspicuous for a musical-chair of sorts in the national capital where a number of successive governments came and went. Political instability and the weakening of the PML marked the period. In 1958, General Ayub seized power through a bloodless coup. Later, he used the PML as a prop to his regime. He was to rule until 1969 when he abdicated in favor of the Army chief, General Yahya Kahn. The Yahya interregnum lasted until December 1971 when the rulers were forced to resign having lost East Pakistan and the humiliation of over 90,000 Pakistani troops having to surrender to the Indian military. East Pakistan seceded to become Bangladesh. Zulfiqar Ali Bhutto took power in January 1972 right after the debacle in East Pakistan. Zulfiqar Ali Bhutto had once served in Ayub Khan's cabinet as his foreign minister but had left him to establish his own party in 1967. Bhutto's PPP swept the polls in West Pakistan in the first general elections of 1970. Bhutto was a gifted populist who introduced a new people's style of politics in the country. In the beginning, he was immensely popular with the people and his socialist vision was a great hope of the country's impoverished masses. However, Bhutto was not able to deliver as per expectations of the people. He turned dictator from populist and even abandoned the left orientation of his PPP. General elections were held in March 1977 the results of which were contested by the Pakistan National Alliance – an electoral alliance of nine parties opposed to the PPP – which resulted in violent protests. Bhutto clamped down hard. Finally, General Zia ousted him on July 5, 1977. He was executed two years later. Once again, the PML was used by the military regime to legitimize its rule. After the party-less general elections of December

1985, General Zia chose a PML leader – Junejo – to become his premier. General Zia ousted Junejo in July 1988. Zia ruled the country for eleven long years promising a return to democracy and meanwhile raising the slogan of Nizam-i-Mustafa (Islamization).[1] Zia exploited Islam the most to maintain his own power. He died in a mysterious airplane crash on August 17, 1988. Zia was a remarkable man and was very devote and humble. However, at the same time very cunning and manipulative. Just like his rival Zulfiqar Ali Bhutto, he has also left a powerful legacy in Pakistan. Zia's son Ijaz ul-Haq, a senior vice president of the PML, was trying to galvanize his fathers political constituency into a rival political force. Hence, there is an emphasis on celebrating Zia's death anniversary in a big way. Zia was certainly not the only one who used Islam to legitimize his authority. Such was the power of Islam in Pakistan that all leaders espouse Islamic ambitions. Even the Quaid-i-Azam talked of making Pakistan into a "fortress of Islam" and a "laboratory of Islam". Muhammad Ali Jinnah had founded Pakistan in 1947. He was a great leader who is loved by all Pakistanis. The PML was more of an independence movement that a political party. Although Pakistanis believe that had not the Quaid-i-Azam died, so early in 1948 he might have built a powerful democratic political party. Unfortunately, his beloved and trusted successor, Liaqat Ali Khan, was killed in 1951. After the premature deaths of the two leaders, the PML degenerated into "a coalition interested only in gaining power".[2] The party leadership indulged in intrigues and ignored the essential requirements of nation building. Malik contends that the PML aligned itself with the unelected ruling elites who have employed its name. It was only that General Zia took this to the extreme. The problem was that our leadership has failed to go further down the road of actually building a modern Islamic state. Obviously pious sentiments and rhetoric are insufficient to change ground reality. General Zia died in August 1988 in a mysterious airplane crash. Meanwhile, the military's premier intelligence outfit - ISI - had cultivated a young Punjabi executive – Nawaz Sharif – to enter the political fray under the mantle of the PML. Nawaz Sharif had served briefly as a finance minister in General Jiliani's cabinet in Punjab during the Zia era. General elections were held in November 1988, which were won by the Pakistan People's Party (PPP), and Benazir Bhutto became chief executive. Earlier, Benazir had successfully taken over the leadership of her father's party. She was seen to be a new style politician - progressive and a reformer. Benazir was the first women chief executive of a Muslim country. The people expected Benazir to lead Pakistan into a new era of economic progress and social and cultural modernity. She failed to deliver, however. In turn, Nawaz Sharif became chief minister of Punjab. President Ghulam Ishaq Khan dismissed Benazir on corruption charges in 1990. General elections were again held in which the IJI – an election coalition dominated by the PML - won power. Nawaz Sharif became prime minister for the first time in 1990 but could not complete his term and was dismissed in 1992. After winning the general elections, Benazir replaced him as chief executive in 1993. President Farooq Ahmed Legahri dismissed her in November 1996. This was the second time Benazir had

---

[1] Malik, Iftikhar, *State and Civil Society in Pakistan: Politics of Authority, Ideology and Ethnicity*, (London: Macmillan Press, 1997), 52.

[2] Malik, *State and Civil Society in Pakistan*, 31.

been dismissed on identical charges of corruption. This time it was all the more ironic because Legahri was her choice as President. He had earlier served the PPP as its secretary general. Elections were again held and PML came back to power in February 1997. By now Pakistan's multi-party system had moved towards a two-party system composed of the PML and PPP. The two parties had emerged as the biggest political forces in the country and the two main rival contenders of power. The two-party system failed to deliver, however. By mid 1999, the system had been largely discredited in popular perception.

Since the death of General Zia in August 1988, the country has had four governments because of four general elections based on adult suffrage. The crisis of governance in Pakistan mainly stems from an inadequate, failing federal setup, and over centralization of power in the central government. What are the problems in our political system and why? Pakistan moved from a parliamentary system to a presidential one and then finally reverted to the original parliamentary system. Whatever the form of government, Pakistan has always been governed in a highly centralized manner. Some name it the vice regal system as witnessed in the colonial British Raj era. The question was whether centralization of power and the structure of the federal setup have anything to do with good governance. The current political crisis in Pakistan is largely because of Benazir Bhutto and Nawaz Sharif's failures. He has not been able to handle power wisely or properly. Najam Sehti argues that when Nawaz came into office in February 1997 he had everything going for him. Most Pakistanis were willing to give him the benefit of the doubt because they were "sick and tired of instability, longed for good governance"[3]. Although he kicked off his second term on populist schemes like collecting public donations to repay the country's debt but somehow failed to sustain them. Inconsistency became a habit with him. Meanwhile, the same old faces turned up in his cabinet. The budget allocated Rs 2.18 billion for the prime minister's and president's houses in Islamabad while only Rs 1.98 billion had been allocated for the country's entire social sector. People were disappointed. Sethi reports that Nawaz Sharif made decisions on his whims. A case in point was food riots in April attributed also to bad planning in Government. Sethi argued hat the premature formal recognition of the Taliban government in Kabul had antagonized Pakistan's neighbors that had resulted the Afghan policy in shambles. The Thirteenth Constitutional Amendment was passed in a single day on April 1, 1997. This happened without any meaningful debate in the parliament. The famous article 58 (2) b was scrapped. The manager in which the amendment was undertaken has been severely criticized.[4] It was alleged that Nawaz Sharif had established a new style of "bulldozing" legislation in a docile parliament. The controversial Anti-Terrorist Act Nawaz was passed on August 13, 1997 in such a hasty manner. Many people argued that the manner in which the bill was passed was unwarranted. Regardless of the merits or demerits of the bill, the people expected that a full-fledged debate should take place on perhaps the most important public issue of the day. It was later that Khalid Anwar, Law Minister was doing much of the explaining on television. This was not

---

[3] Najam Sehti, *The Friday Times*, August 14-21, 1997.
[4] Ibid.

called for. The proper way was to do all the explanations and clarifications during the parliamentary debate and not afterwards. Similarly, the Fourteenth Amendment was bulldozed through Parliament on the same lines as the earlier constitutional amendment. In one brazen incident, Nawaz Sharif conducted a raid and punished senior government officials in the full glare of the media by ordering their arrest and even handcuffs were put on them in public. This all happened after he had supposedly conducting his own private investigation. Where was due process of law? Obviously the believe that a person was innocent until and unless proven guilty and that to by a court of law was discarded. All agreed that it was very inappropriate and uncalled for the prime minister to carry out summary justice in this fashion. Let the judiciary do its job. Nawaz Sharif's impatience was obvious and understandable. The country was in a mess and he knew it. In sum, the governing style of Nawaz Sharif was very inappropriate for a truly democratic leader. Undoubtedly, Pakistan's leadership has failed the country. Earlier, many critics had pointed towards the hollowness of this democratic era. Newberg was unsparing of the situation and argued that Pakistan had a titular democracy which was hamstrung by politicians "who equate personal ambition with national interest" profiting from their position while the poor remain disfranchised. The elite lived a life of luxury in a society in which there are gross inequalities".[5] In 1995, the international weekly newsmagazine, The Times, had asked the telling question whether the country was any longer governable by Benazir or any one else. There was complete confusion in the ranks of the top leaderships. Incompetence, sheer callousness, and reckless attitude of the federal ministers, and petty jealousy in the cabinet ranks had reduced the whole exercise of collective responsibility to a farce. Bickering over petty matters was the rule of the day. There was a lack of direction on the part of the two chief executives. Both Nawaz Sharif and Benazir Bhutto had turned into egomaniacs. They lived in a world of self-delusion. The scene at the highest level became comic, if not tragic. Cronies were awash with praise at their slightest "achievement". More and more state efforts are made under their names. Pakistanis had the Chief executives run a relentless election campaign from day one. It seemed absurd and uncalled for. Like Benazir, Nawaz Sharif too had proved to be a failure. In the end, it seemed that he simply could not handle the requirements of his office. Seemingly, Nawaz Sharif had a pleasant personality but was not very intelligent. The sheer complexity of leading Pakistan seemed to overwhelm him. Much like his rival, - Benazir - Nawaz Sharif also became obsessed with his image, got used to sycophancy, and finally had lost touch with reality. Pakistan's multi-party system had moved towards a two-party system composed of the PML and PPP. The two parties have emerged as the biggest political forces in the country and the two main rival contenders of power. The two-party system failed to deliver, however. In fact, whatever the form of government the country had been governed in a highly centralized manner. Some name it the vice regal system as understood in the colonial British Raj era. Since independence in 1947, Pakistan had witnessed an unprecedented period of internal strife, lawlessness, high crime rates, poor leadership, and bad governance at all levels. Both Benazir Bhutto and Nawaz Sharif had taken turns at running the government. Pakistan's constitution has been

---

[5] Paula Newberg, "The Two Benazir Bhuttos", *New York Times*, Nov. 2, 1995.

amended several times for the benefit of only the rulers. The country had suffered tremendously because of past misrule. Resultantly, Pakistan had been weakened from within. The situation has become very complex, to say the least. During this democratic era, spanning at least eleven years, all civilian government had failed to deliver. Matters had grown worse with time. The Pakistani state was indeed malfunctioning. Many analysts pointed out that poor governance was the primary reason of this malfunction. Undoubtedly, the country had faced a crisis of governance. In addition, democracy had failed to deliver in Pakistan. Obviously, the rulers were themselves largely responsible for the failure. That is certain. Nevertheless, the system has to be blamed as much as the rulers themselves. In order to understand the political crisis in the country it must be appreciated where the country had been in the last half a century. Pakistan was faced with a complex multiple dimensional crisis of immense proportions. The state had failed to deliver and the poor people had suffered enough. Pakistan had stomached enough periods of instability, corruption, and bad governance that lasted for more than a decade. The problems had piled up over time. Pakistan faced a number of major challenges, both external and internal. The crisis of governance in Pakistan mainly stemmed from an inadequate and failing federal setup and concentration of power in the central government. What were the problems in Pakistan's political system and why? Pakistan moved from a parliamentary system to a presidential one and then finally reverted to the original parliamentary system. Whatever the form of government, Pakistan has always been governed in a highly centralized manner. Some name it the vice regal system as understood in the colonial British Raj era. Pakistan had a federal and parliamentary system of government. The last constitution adopted in 1973 created this system. There had been significant changes since then. Since the death of General Zia in August 1988, the country had had four governments because of four general elections based on adult suffrage. Benazir Bhutto and Nawaz Sharif had taken turns at running the government. Pakistan's constitution had been amended several times for the benefit of only the rulers. The country had suffered because of misrule. Pakistan had been weakened from within. The situation had become very complex, to say the least. During this democratic era, spanning at least eleven years of civilian government had failed to deliver. Matters had grown worse with time. The Pakistani state was malfunctioning. Many would point out that poor governance was the primary reason of this malfunction. Undoubtedly, the country had faced a crisis of governance. Bad governance at every level was a stark fact. Malfunction had been the norm and not the exception in Pakistan. By late September 1999, many people felt that a military coup was inevitable and so it happened. Finally, General Musharraf ousted the Nawaz Sharif Government in a bloodless coup on October 12, 1999. The people of Pakistan welcomed the coup. After a more than thirteen-year stint of frail democracy from 1985-1999, the military had returned to power. Initially there was immense public support for the new military regime. On March 15, 2000, the regime clamped a countrywide ban on all political meetings at public places, strikes and processions. General Musharraf made a solemn commitment to the restoration of a responsible democratic order. He said that the country had witnessed intense and frequent conflicts, disorder, indiscipline, and breakdown of institutions. The result had been the creation of a fractious society and incalculable damage to the economy. The General might have been right in his assessment of the situation. Meanwhile, General Musharraf got the desired support from the Supreme Court of Pakistan. The May 10, 2001 Supreme Court verdict had given the regime the legitimacy it desired, on the one hand, and also fixed the time-table for the Army's return to the barracks as three years after conducting elections. Immediately, the Musharraf regime, as expected, stated that it would respect the Supreme Court verdict. The military regime saw the Supreme Court verdict as a legitimization of its extra-constitutional entry to the corridors of power in Pakistan. The Musharraf regime has promised to focus on rebuilding the economy, strengthening the federation, uplifting the masses, improving governance, and laying the foundations of true democracy. However, no timetable is given for the accomplishment of the task. It is commonly expected that the Army will rule the country for several years. The Musharraf regime was trying to tackle them in a disciplined and systematic manner. However, tangible results are limited as yet. The regime faced a serious governance challenge that could not be easily overcome. On June 20, 2001, General Musharraf dissolved the Parliament and became President of Pakistan. The Chief Justice of Pakistan, Irshad Hasan Khan administered the oath to him. General Musharraf shall continue to hold the office of the Chief Executive and the Army chief as well. President Musharraf said that:[6]

> My major concern for Pakistan is the stability and harmony for this country. I have also been saying that I would like to place proper checks and balances on the supreme structure of the political environment. I have always also been saying that I will ensure and guarantee the continuity and the sustainability of all the reforms, all the restructuring that I and my government are doing. And I have also finally been saying that national interest I will ensure will remain supreme over any personal or political interests....But above all (other considerations) this decision has been taken in the supreme national interests. I feel in all humility that if I have a role to play for this nation I will not shirk, I will not hesitate, I will not back down. So whatever decision whether it involved the embarrassment of a personal decision for my self I hold national interest supreme. I personally in all sincerity, in all sincerity think, in all honesty think that I have a role to play in this nation. I sincerely think that I have a job to do here and therefore I cannot and I will not let this nation down. So, therefore, the decision to become the President.

Apparently, Pakistan has entered another long spell of military rule. Surprisingly, there was little opposition to the seizure of complete power by General Musharraf. It was commonly expected that the Army would rule the country for several years. How the Musharraf regime dealt with these challenges would determine Pakistan's future. The military regime's task of solving them was indeed very daunting. There were no easy answers to Pakistan's problems. However, proper planning, determination, and a single-minded resolve of the nation could see the country through the present crisis. A new era had begun in the country's life. Circumstances had put tremendous responsibility on the shoulders of the military regime. The nation hoped and prayed for its success. Given Pakistan's fragility it could not tolerate more rules of bad governance. The country would

---

[6] See text of President, Chief Executive General Pervaiz Musharraf statement in *Pakistan Observer*, June 21, 2001, 11.

surely collapse if it happened again. Therefore, the Musharraf regime should not fail to deliver. A cautious note of hope is in order.

How do you explain this phenomenon of repeated military rules in Pakistan? More importantly, what went wrong in Pakistan? Why has the political system failed? Firstly, the political leadership had failed the country. Unfortunately, Pakistani leaders had no vision, commitment, or caliber. Matters had grown from bad to worse. Secondly, democracy was not given a reasonable chance to grow roots in the country. It has been argued that political parties were weak simply because they were never given a chance to take roots in Pakistani political soil. Pakistan had been ruled by the military for nearly half of its history. There were two significantly long spells of military rule - General Ayub Khan (58-68) and General Zia's rule (77-88). Both are commonly considered as failures. General Musharraf's coup had interrupted the growth of the political system yet once again. There is some weight in the argument. The counter-argument is that the military intervened only when the country was threatened from within and that the Army was a reluctant ruler of Pakistan. It was true this time also with General Musharraf seized power in October 1999. Nevertheless, the military had cast a long shadow on political party system in Pakistan. Most political parties owe their existence to the Army's Intelligence services. Such is the power of the Army that its support is widely thought to be indispensable for the establishment and continuation of political parties in the country. An underlying authoritarian culture in Pakistan makes this significant for politics. In other words, the democratic institutions of which the political parties are one significant element have never established themselves as they have done elsewhere, say India.

The political parties in Pakistan are in a crisis. Generally, political parties in Pakistan are generally weak and poorly organized. Participation of citizens in selecting in selecting their representatives lies at the heart of democratic politics. Political parties are crucial in the effort of ordinary citizens shape public policies. Periodic and contested elections reward or punish these parties through gain or loss of office. Essentially a political party aims to capture power and a sound party structure facilitates this quest. A party in a democratic polity must necessarily involve maximum opportunity for participation by ordinary citizens. The party tradition was weak in Pakistan as compared to the one in Europe. Most political parties have not much social welfare work at the local level. Grassroots support can only be strengthened by concrete work for the welfare of the masses. The purpose was to involve the local community and at the same time earn good will for the party. Any such activity, if undertaken enthusiastically and sincerely, will generate appreciation for the party. Community acknowledgment will surely result in tangible electoral benefits. Such activity was also a means to strengthen grass-roots support for the parties. It needs to be understood clearly by the political parties leadership that politics as usual will not work in the future. After all, the political parties are in politics not for the short haul but the long one. The political parties must make an improvement, no matter how small, in the lives of lives of the people today and not just feed them on rhetoric and future promises. Increasingly people are getting disgusted by all politicians who they suspect are manipulating them to achieve their own designs. Generally, the political parties do not have a solid base of public support all over Pakistan. Pakistanis earnestly believe that the political parties can achieve a significant redirection and a change for the better for Pakistan provided they are ready to provide bold leadership. Pakistan deserved better leadership then provided by the political parties yet. Decision-making was highly centralized in nearly all Pakistan's political parties. No internal elections are held despite the claims of democracy. In short, political party system in Pakistan was itself extremely weak. By now, the two-party system was in a shambles. Nawaz Sharif was living in exile in Saudi Arabia and Benazir had been out of the country for several years leaving the PPP in a leadership void. The failures in Pakistan are obviously much more than that of its rulers. After all, the people of Pakistan had chosen them as their leaders and should therefore share the blame for their failures. It is a universal maxim that you get the leadership you deserve. The Prophet Muhammad (peace be upon him) also taught us this principle.

Some argue that the Pakistanis are a weak nation as compared to say the Chinese, Turks, Americans, British, French or the Germans. Maybe in the half-century, the Pakistanis will indeed become a strong nation. Time will tell. Yet, it has still not adequately resolved the important question of a distinct national identity. Was Pakistan a nation state? An answer to the question requires an understanding of the concept. National identity was considered the heart of the nation-state concept. The longing and determination of a people to live together inside given territorial boundaries, having "a sense of a common past and a common future" establishes national identity. Individuals may sense this national identity because of lasting feeling of common cultural ties. The people may also feel an identity because of economic ties and the conviction that authority was derived from the people. Individuals may think that the nation deserved their loyalty because they themselves made its laws and government system. For example, each citizen of America, France, Germany, and Great Britain has developed a strong sense of national identity. Pakistanis in Pakistan have not. The root cause of Pakistan's political crisis was very basic in some ways. Pakistanis have failed at nation building and the acquisition of a strong national identity. The main reasons are: rhetoric of ideology; dearth of capable and popular leadership; strong political parties; oligarchic elates and their mislaid preferences; and neglect for constitutionals.[7] Rose and Evans argue that Pakistan has "a long way to go before it can be said to have achieved full national integration, but disintegration along ethnic lines is less of a danger than it ever has been".[8] The two most significant separatist movements of the 1970s, among Pathans in NWFP and Baluchis in Baluchistan have stopped to function as separatist movements, even though both remain as powerful political forces art the provincial level.[9] The problem it seems was that Pakistanis as a nation have not decided as to what exactly they aspire to collectively. Most of us have come to doubt the viability of all political systems. Pakistan's Islamic destiny has become murky given the confusion in its ranks. Take the example of the religious political spectrum. Some Ulema and other lay Muslims consider nationalism to be the negation of the ideas of Ummah-i-Islamia where a transnational Islamic community exists in place of independent sovereign states. Some even question

---

[7] Iftikhar Malik, *State and Society in Civil Society in Pakistan: Politics of Authority, Ideology and Ethnicity* (New York: St. Martin's Press, 1997) 13.
[8] Rose & Evans, *Pakistan's Enduring Experiment*", op. cit., 23.

the idea of elections, parliaments and political parties, and a constitution. It was not by chance that a section of the Ulema and some other Islamic groups cooperated with General Zia ul-Haq dismissing the very notion of electoral politics as unIslamic.

It was also not surprising that Nawaz Sharif employed grandiose Islamic rhetoric on occasion to bolster his popularity in the Islamic communities. It was never easy or unproblematic to operationalize Islamic values in state and society of Pakistan. A fundamental problem with Islamists was that of their intellectual failure in coming up with alternate viable models of government and economics. The issue was critical and needs to be discussed. Undoubtedly Pakistan had failed as a community to live according to Islamic dictates of brotherhood, social justice, egalitarianism and fairness. The employment of just sentiments was not enough to make a strong nation. Pakistanis incorrectly believed once that Islam was a sufficient condition to keep the country united. Unfortunately, the country disintegrated in 1971 and Bangladesh was born. The people of the remaining Pakistan were in shock over the tragedy. The event still shapes our perceptions of our own perpetual insecurity on the one hand and that of Indian aggression on the other.

The people have suffered because of the shortcomings of the political system. Apparently, there is a deep desire and longing for a real change. Given the past grave failures of all governments in our history, the Musharraf regime is still being given the benefit of the doubt. We need to understand that though the two- party has failed to deliver yet the institution of political party-system cannot and should not be discarded. It is agreed that politicians and also political parties do not command the respect they might otherwise had commanded in circumstances that were more positive. Nevertheless, it does not make any sense to throw out the baby with the bathwater. The regime must understand that the political party system is an institution needing urgent repairs. The task is formidable for any one. By their very nature, political parties are tedious to build. The sooner we begin the better for the country. Strong political parties are seen as essential institutions in any modern democracy. Next time around, let us such parties compete against each other in a more sophisticated manner. The question is that can we afford to wait until they are built and then call for general elections. Obviously, building strong political leadership and political parties will take years not months. What is to be done? The regime must do its best in the time allocated to it. Meaning hold elections as planned and then gracefully pull out. Remember there are no great saviors or "a great general on horseback" any more. Men who always knew everything or could do everything better. Given the complexity of the age, a single leader cannot lead the nation to triumph. No single person can even understand the complexity, let alone have a solution for it. For modern societies, the concentration of power in one person or an uncontrolled elite is extremely dangerous. Since wrong decisions are more probable. Therefore, we urge the military regime to restore democracy in Pakistan sooner than its stipulated three-year period. In the eventually Pakistan shall progress better under an Islamic democratic system. Why has General Musharraf decided not to allow participation of political parties in the forthcoming local government elections? No satisfactory explanation has been

---

[9] Ibid.

given as yet. Exclusion of political parties from the election process is a very big mistake. The country shall suffer from it. Remember that political parties are crucial to the whole exercise of building true democracy through a "bottom-up" strategy. They cannot and should not be ignored. Political parties are useful mechanisms for the practical conduct of democracy. They fulfill essential functions to promote democracy in the nation. They recruit; mobilize public opinion for their cause. Parties educate public opinion and provide venues for its systematic orchestration. Most importantly, political parties provide platforms where serious discussion about political matters takes place and a consensus policy arrived at. Remember conflict in politics is inherent. The question is whether ideological conflict waged by political parties is any worse than conflict based on ethnic, tribal, biradari, or other loyalties. The regime be warned that local government elections conducted on non-political basis will further fan the worst forms of ethnic and biradari conflicts in the country. The country cannot afford such a situation from building up. Therefore, it would be more prudent to allow political parties to participate in the coming elections. One of the primary reasons for the failure of the democratic experiment in Pakistan can be attributed to the failure of its political parties. We need to rectify this shortcoming. What better place to begin than the Local Government. Pakistan badly needs strong political parties that can deliver what they promised. Today Pakistan has a very weak political party system. Political parties, with very few exceptions, are undemocratic establishments with personalistic politics being the norm. Leadership is not chosen in democratic fashion nor is internal democracy practiced in any significant manner. There is mere lip service to democracy. Once in power they acted with authoritarian impulses and weakening internal democracy even further. Moreover, patronage politics and massive corruption in party ranks had eroded popular faith in the party system itself. Most seriously, parties in power had failed to deliver according to the expectations of the people, including their own ranks. Thus, politicians had political parties generally do not command the respect they might otherwise had commanded in circumstances that are more positive. Enforce democratic norms in all political parties. In fact, very few political parties are democratic internally. When there is no meaningful practice inside the parties, then how can we expect them to behave in democratic fashion once in power? They should be required by law to practice what they preach. At the minimum, we must forbid parties that do not practice what they preach. These must be suspect and therefore shunned. That is also an Islamic dictum. The irony is that all the major political parties in the country, PPP and PML included, are bereft of internal democracy. The contradiction in what they said and did was too apparent. Hence, the failure to deliver any meaningful democracy. Let all our parties be required to practice democratic values in their operation. It should be required that all political parties elect their party leadership in yearly elections. In addition, the elections should be held in a fair and transparent manner. The example of Quaid-i-Azam is before us. He being a true democrat insisted in contesting the post of president of the Muslim League as per constitutional requirements of the party. This was even when the nation had reposed in his person their complete and unflinching loyalty and support. To him these internal elections were the essence of democratic behavior. We must today emulate his examples. His spirit at building a disciplined party machine needs to be recreated once again. The spirit of working g for a great and noble cause must be rekindled. Let us join hands to build strong parties and thereby build strong institutions for the nation. Let our parties slowly and surely build democratic norms and values in themselves. Let them become the vehicles of the required transformation. Only then, will they be allowed to contest general elections. Otherwise, law will forbid them. It be understood clearly that strong vibrant political operates are crucial to putting the democratic experiment back on track. Again, the sooner we begin the better for us all

The Musharraf regime is trying to tackle the governance crisis in a disciplined and systematic manner. However, tangible results are limited as yet. The regime faces a serious governance challenge that cannot be easily overcome. Pakistan has grave systematic failures and structural faults in its political and economic systems. These faults remained prevalent for too long. Therefore, the system has seriously malfunctioned as a result. The political and economic situation in the country can only be described as serious, if not dismal. Before the coup last October, Pakistan had witnessed an unprecedented period of internal strife, lawlessness, high crime rates, and bad governance at lower levels. All these developments have led to a general sense of malaise and disillusionment with the ability of the state system to deliver, even erosion of government authority and even somewhat loss of state legitimacy. General Musharraf promised to eradicate corruption, revive the economy and open the way for "true democracy". However, he has made little advancement with the economy or corruption and has postponed the return of democracy until October 2002. General Musharraf had announced plans for a new political system calculated to support his own power base by excluding the senior politicians. *The New York Times* article said:[10]

> That would compound Pakistan's problems. A speedier timetable for restoring democracy is urgently needed. Pakistan's democratic governments have been flawed. However, its military dictatorships have blighted its economic and political development and gravely damaged its international reputation. General Musharraf's administration has proved no different. Military rulers claim they can push through reforms because they do not have to make deals with entrenched political interests. Nevertheless, they are beholden to Pakistan's single most powerful interest group the military and its related intelligence services.

Today, the press in Pakistan was free and vibrant a rare success story. While most state structures and institutions, are in a mess some parts of the private sector like private banking and English-medium educational institutions are thriving. Pakistan was a country full of contradictions. Even in the current democratic setup, the military retains enormous influence. Unlike India, Pakistanis still cannot fully rule out the possibility of a military coup. However, the chances of that happening are very remote. Again, unlike neighboring India the Pakistan military never developed the professional aloofness from politics that one could assume would be the case given the common British Raj origin. Military apologists argue that the military take-over were by default. The politicians were too inept and corrupt to handle state responsibilities and hence had to be relieved of the

---

[10] Military Misrule in Pakistan" in *The New York Times* dated August 28, 2000.

burden. Ironically, there was some truth in this argument. Nevertheless, Pakistan's tragedy does not stop here. The military regimes - Ayub, Yahya and Zia - were also failures. Few would doubt this stark reality. Today the military seems to have learnt its lesson and prefers to exercise power from behind the scenes. This again was more a statement of the civilian leadership's failure than the raw ambition of the military brass. At least this was what a section of the public believes to be the case. No one can dispute the fact that the cause of democracy in Pakistan has suffered tremendously because of military rule. Rose and Evans have argued that an obvious restraint in Pakistan's democracy was the continued deficiency of civilian control over the military. In September 1995, Benazir bowed to Army pressure to get the man favored by the brass appointed for post of Inter Services Intelligence chief which she did not favor. She had become more pragmatic towards the reality of the Army's influence. In addition, the Army was determined to retain its control over some key areas of policy declared as "out of bounds" to civilian government, especially areas that touch national security. A case in point was the Army's control over the country's nuclear weapons program. In addition, the Pakistani government does not have much room in cutting military expenditure.[11]

Income and wealth present intense contrasts in Pakistani society. At the top are a small number of wealthy families. Below them, a much larger group, are relatively well off. At the bottom of the class structure are the millions of poor who live in desperate conditions. Pakistan has had a number of constitutional experiments. The last of which in 1973 was the most notable and enduring. The military has ruled for nearly half of the country's existence. After nearly fifty-four years of existence, Pakistan faces a multidimensional crisis of immense magnitude. The military government is trying its best to turn the country around for the better. The people demand nothing less than bold revolutionary steps are taken to make Pakistan what it was destined to be - a great and prosperous Muslim country. The following reform proposals, if taken together, will usher the country into a new era of greatness and worldwide respect. We can certainly become an Asian tiger in the not too distant a future if, and that is a big if, the Nawaz Government undertakes the bold reform measures necessary to achieve whatever it takes to realize the ambition. Time is of the essence as Pakistan has wasted enough of it. Fifty-four years is a long period. Many felt that Pakistan had been left far behind in the development race and must catch up fast. Pakistan need not be the tragedy that it is. We envisage an across the board national consensus to see the exercise through. Without the peoples, participation the dream of becoming an Asian Tiger cannot be realized. The Government owes it to the unfortunate but brave Pakistanis to try to the best of its capabilities. The people ask for nothing more and nothing less.

What are Pakistan's primary challenges? Today, important challenges included divisive political issues, weak economy, and development failures. The major challenges were economic decline, poverty increase, reinventing the government system, restructuring the federation, accountability and integrity in the public sector, greater public participation requirements, decentralization and devolution of power. One of the

---

[11] Leo E. Rose & D. Hugh Evans, "Pakistan's Enduring Experiment", *Journal of Democracy* reprinted in *The Friday Times*, May 30-June, 1997, 21-22.

greatest failures in Pakistan was its growing poverty and corresponding low human development. The incidence of poverty was very high in Pakistan. The GOP's Human Development and Poverty Reduction Strategy, 1999 stated that Pakistan ranked 138 among 174 developing countries in the quality of life index. The document says that the bottom line was that poverty is rising in Pakistan. The GOP estimated that at least 36 million people fell below the poverty line. The quality of life indicators like education, health and nutrition showed no appreciable development. Poverty remained prevalent. In reality, the poor had become poorer. This confirms the observation that rapid growth in GNP and income does not guarantee a sufficient degree of fulfillment of the basic needs for everyone in the country.

Pakistan has grave systematic failures and structural faults in its political and economic systems. These faults remained prevalent for too long. Therefore, the system has seriously malfunctioned as a result. The political and economic situation in the country can only be described as serious, if not dismal. Before the coup last October, Pakistan had witnessed an unprecedented period of internal strife, lawlessness, high crime rates, and bad governance at lower levels. All these developments have led to a general sense of malaise and disillusionment with the ability of the state system to deliver, even erosion of government authority and even somewhat loss of state legitimacy. The military regime's task of solving the governance crisis is indeed very daunting. The people have suffered because of the shortcomings of the political system. Apparently, there is a deep desire and longing for a real change. Given the past grave failures of all governments in our history, the Musharraf regime is still being given the benefit of the doubt. People feel that Pakistan badly needs stability for the economic reforms to take place.

General Musharraf promised to eradicate corruption, revive the economy and open the way for "true democracy". However, he has not made little advancement on the economic revival front nor has dented corruption in any meaningful way. Meanwhile, he has postponed the return of democracy to October 2002. General Musharraf had announced plans for a new political system calculated to support his own power base by excluding the senior politicians. A New York Times article said that:[12]

> General Pervaiz Musharraf overthrew Pakistan's democracy, promising to eradicate corruption, revive the economy and open the way for "true democracy". He pledged to restrain nuclear weapons development and pursue peaceful diplomacy with India. Ten months later, he has made little progress with the economy or corruption and has put off the return of democracy until at least 2003…Now General Musharraf has announced plans for a new political system designed to buttress his own power by excluding the country's top politicians. That would compound Pakistan's problems. A speedier timetable for restoring democracy is urgently needed. Pakistan's democratic governments have been flawed. Nevertheless, its military dictatorships have blighted its economic and political development and gravely damaged its international reputation. General Musharraf's administration has proved no different. Military rulers claim they can push through reforms because they do not have to make deals with entrenched political interests. However, they are beholden to Pakistan's single most powerful interest group

---

[12] "Military Misrule in Pakistan", *The New York Times*, August 28, 2000.

the military and its related intelligence services. Military spending absorbs more than a quarter of Pakistan's yearly budget, diverting resources needed for education and development...The International Monetary Fund is also unhappy with the slow pace of promised economic reforms. General Musharraf should acknowledge that he is worsening Pakistan's problems and therefore should accelerate the return to democratic rule.

Although Pakistan is under military rule, the top military leadership is still squeaking clean and committed. General Musharraf and his colleagues seem to understand that the country has been left behind in its development march. The military regime is trying its best to turn around Pakistan. Previously, the country seemed to be muddling through in its politics. It had become a country where dramatic change was highly unlikely. Today the country faces a multidimensional crisis the most important of which was that of governance. Another failure was at successful nation building. The magnitude of the crisis was realized by most ardent observers of the country. Pakistan has not come up to the expectations of its own citizens and friends outside. More than a half century ago, it seemed that Pakistan was born to become a great, just, tolerant and prosperous Muslim country. Our founding fathers made the citizens believe in the dream of Pakistan. The spirit was high then. In Jinnah, known fondly as the Quaid-i-Azam, Pakistanis had a great leader. Today it was different. Why had Pakistan's past leadership failed? Could Pakistan ever become a powerful and respected nation? Most Pakistanis believe that their country could certainly attain greatness in the not too distant a future if, and that was a big if, the Musharraf Government undertakes the bold reform measures necessary for the purpose. Time is of the essence as Pakistan has wasted enough of it. Fifty-four years is a long period. Unfortunately, Pakistan has been left behind in the development race. Pakistan need not be the tragedy that it is. Without the uplift of the people and their wholehearted participation, the dream of becoming a developed country cannot be realized. The Government and the ruling elite owe it to our unfortunate, but brave, people to try to do their best. The people ask nothing more and nothing less. The question was whether it was likely to happen. The answer is a sad negative. Pakistanis earnestly hope that history would eventually prove this apprehension was misplaced and wrong. The failure at national integration and the establishment of political order is in some ways the failure of the Pakistan's political parties. Currently, it seems that a more sincere and competent leadership is at the helm of affairs in Pakistan. The Musharraf regime faces a serious challenge in reforming Pakistan's political and economic system. Soon after coming into power, it promised to focus on rebuilding the economy, the federation, building democracy, and improving efficiency, transparency and accountability of the government. Then the reform agenda announced by the regime had received wide public support. On October 17, 1999, General Musharraf announced his seven point agenda, namely:[13]

1.   Rebuild national confidence and morale.

---

[13] *The News* International, Oct. 18, 2000.

2. Strengthen the federation, remove inter-provincial disharmony and restore national cohesion.
3. Revive the economy and restore investor confidence.
4. Ensure law and order and dispense speedy justice.
5. Revamp state institutions.
6. Devolution of power to the grass-root level.
7. Ensure swift and across the board accountability.

Some skeptic observers had pointed out that, given the capacity of the military regime, the implementation of the new agenda remained problematic. Pakistan's governance crisis was a complex multi-dimensional one of staggering proportions. Undoubtedly, the country faced bad governance at every level. Governance would imply issues of government effectiveness, accountability, transparency and adherence to the rule of law. Good governance was also to be understood as having a normative connotation and includes the hopes, aspirations and predilections of the governed. It was agreed that a state must achieve a high level of good governance because lack of capacity to carefully monitor and implement, otherwise good policy designs, will hamper and distort development. Achieving objectives of good governance requires a long-term political commitment to make the system work. As administrative systems have become increasingly complex, procedures and structures have created red tape and inefficiency. Reinventing government was needed simply to keep up with the rapid change. Essentially, it involves a broad restructuring of public service systems. Organizational structures, purposes, incentive systems, accountability procedures, authority distribution patterns, even culture was changed in the process. To achieve efficiency and effectiveness, change undertaken must ensure that the development process remains unhampered by lapses and shortcomings in current structures. Thus, governance would be best in a society with an effective production and delivery of jobs and services in an efficient way and in legitimate conditions.

Having realized that there was no magic bullet or quick fix to Pakistan's governance problem, the GOP had decided to tackle the issue in a serious and systematic manner. Years of neglect are not easily ended. The central plank of good governance efforts was the reform of the public service system. However, public service reforms are notoriously difficult to undertake. The GOP was cognizant of the fact that the very best plan or budget system was of little utility, if there are no expeditious and precise mechanisms to follow them through to the very end. Certainly, a country's development was thwarted because of poor governance. Thus, the issue of governance had taken center stage in the development debate. The Musharraf regime had promised to focus on rebuilding the economy, the federation and building true democracy by primarily was focusing on governance issues. It had also promised to improve efficiency, transparency and accountability of the GOP agencies. General Musharraf has repeatedly assured us that he is completely committed to the timetable for elections in 2002 given to him by the Supreme Court of Pakistan and that he cannot visualize staying on beyond that deadline. Also, he has often talked about the need of a "checks and balance" on any future prime minister to prevent him or her from abusing power. The quality of politicians needs to be improved, as they had been a "dismal failure", said General Musharraf. According to him, Pakistan had in the past last eleven or twelve years gone down in all important areas, and all institutions were in "total disarray" and had been "politicized and corrupted". Many people were strongly convinced that Pakistan should create an effective third tier of government. For the common man in Pakistan, like elsewhere in the region, the local government was critical and it was a level that he or she interacted most. The third tier of government would help fill a large gaping hole in the availability of state services to the people. Pakistanis need to openly debate on such questions and arrive at a consensus for the sake of the country. Pakistan's religion teaches us to work based on Shura and Ijma, the requirement of which was consensus as wide as possible. On issues of governance, Islam would desire the input of the public in issues affecting their lives. Pakistanis must practice Islam and not just cherish it. The point was that any model of government must necessarily have the support of the people. Pakistanis had argued for the case of creating a third tier of government and decentralization of authority in Pakistan. The issue needs to be discussed further. The Musharraf regime envisaged nothing less than re-inventing the administrative machinery in Pakistan. The Musharraf regime had promised a new local government system to be inaugurated on august 14, 2001. It was cognizant of the fact that the third tier of government was vital for true democratization and sound development. It had to be rebuilt after a lapse of several years. The regime had taken a new initiative of institution building at the local government level. It had allocated a sizeable sum for poverty alleviation for a two-year period. The plan was to target money to infrastructure development through local government. The regime initiated a new program of local development through a decentralized mechanism of local government.

THE GOVERNMENT OF PAKISTAN SYSTEM

Pakistan has a federal and parliamentary system of government. The last constitution adopted in 1973 created this system. There have been significant changes since then. The head of state is the President, who is elected for a renewable, five-year term jointly by an Electoral College composed of the National Assembly, Senate and the four provincial assemblies. The presidency is originally a titular post, but following the famous Eighth Amendment of March 1985, the office holder is given authority to dissolve the National Assembly, and appoint and dismiss the Prime Minister, the cabinet and provincial governors. The president, therefore, emerged as a dominant political figure. Later, the comparative significance of the office has been eroded due to the last constitutional amendments. Today, the president is a mere figurehead as the military rules the country.

The federation of Pakistan is comprised of four provinces: Punjab, Sindh, NWFP and Baluchistan. The federal design signified division of powers between a national government and constituent units. Such a division is given in the constitution. Governors are appointed by the central government but served as figureheads only. Local governments are constituted by elected Provincial Assemblies and headed by Chief Ministers. There are also tribal areas administered by the federal government, like FATA and FANA, and the NWFP provincial government. Responsibility for the subjects of health, labor, education, agriculture, social welfare, industry and roads is entrusted to the provinces. However, principal power resides with the central government. Pakistan has a bicameral legislature - the National Assembly and the Senate. The National Assembly was the most significant political body. The leader of the political party with the most seats in the National Assembly becomes the prime minister. The prime minister and his cabinet control much of government's daily functioning. The National Assembly has 207 members, directly elected for five-year terms by universal adult suffrage, plus 20 women chosen by the National Assembly and 10 separately elected religious minority members. The Senate has 87 members, elected, a third at a time, for six-year terms by provincial assemblies, and tribal areas, in accordance with a quota system. The National Assembly was the more powerful of the two chambers, having exclusive jurisdiction over financial affairs. To become law, bills must be passed by both chambers and must be approved by the President, who has the power of veto. The presidential veto may, however, be overridden by a simple majority of both houses.

Previously, the chief of government was the Prime Minister, drawn from the National Assembly. The Prime Minister chooses the cabinet ministers from the parliament and determines their number and responsibilities. He lays the guidelines of government policy and is accountable to he parliament along with his cabinet. The Prime Minister can be removed by the parliament through a "vote of no confidence". However, no premier has been removed through this method. Nawaz Sharif, the last prime minister, was widely believed to be Pakistan's most powerful national leader because of the fact that the Pakistan Muslim League won more than three-fourth of the National Assembly seats in the February 1997 general elections. The PML had captured all but a few seats in Punjab and Shabaz Sharif, younger brother of Nawaz, became chief minister. The PML shared power with its allies in Sind, NWFP and Baluchistan.

The second tier of government is the province. The Governor is the constitutional head of the province and is appointed by the central government. A provincial government is constituted by the elected Provincial Assemblies and headed by Governors. Today, the Governors act as chief executives of the administrative machinery. Primarily the Governors and the provincial cabinet conduct the government policy-making in a province. The cabinet is composed of several Ministers each heading a particular department like Agriculture, Finance, Forestry, Home, Industries, Information, Irrigation, Communication & Works, Law, Local Government & Rural Development, Physical Planning & Housing, Health, Planning and Development, Law, Education, Transport, etc. The Provincial Secretariats are the principal seat of the provincial governments where all policy-making takes place. To facilitate administrative work, the provinces have been divided into 20 divisions and then sub-divided into 106 districts.[14] A Commissioner heads each division while a Deputy Commissioner heads each district. Perhaps the single most important administrative unit in the country is the district. The

---

[14] The Government of Baluchistan has decided to decrease the number of districts in the province by two. The decision is taken in or about January 2001. Similarly, the Government of NWFP is contemplating to decrease the number of districts by perhaps a total of one, as reported in the press at the end of 2000.

Deputy Commissioner, as head of the district, holds powers of the district magistrate and is responsible for revenue collection, coordination, protocol, law, and order. The provincial departments, e.g. communication, education, health, agriculture, irrigation, etc. are controlled by their respective heads called Secretaries, reporting to their respective Ministers. In the provinces, the Local Government and Rural Development Department together with the elected institutions form the local government system. The department has been involved in technical functions of planning, contracting, supervision, and monitoring of development schemes. Serving as an executive branch of the local government the department oversees the operation of the local councils. Under the ordinance, the local government members are not allowed to contest national elections. The ordinance provides direct elections of the Chairman of all councils for a term of four years, and limits the role of the councils to non-political local governance and rural development. The union council is the lowest tier, with an elected membership based on universal adult franchise. The Chairman is elected by majority vote of the members and receives a monthly honorarium from the government.

Theoretically, the local governments are considered as the third tier of government in Pakistan. In reality, they have been missing for the most time and otherwise extremely weak. The Musharraf regime had suspended the few existing local governments in the country. However, they are increasingly being seen as vital for Pakistan's democratization, sustainable development and empowerment of the people. It has to be rebuilt after a lapse of several years. The Musharraf regime is in the process of creating a strong third tier in the country. Elections to the local government elections were staggered from December 2000 to July 2001. The new local government system shall be in place by August 14 this year. The restructuring of the system of government is the need of the hour. Pakistan needs a better administrative setup to fulfill the demands of sustainable development for the benefit of the people.

The civil service is organized as a two-tier system. The central government controlled the Central Superior Services (CSS), which are classified into 14 groups, such as Foreign, police, district management, secretariat, accounts, etc. The selections to the CSS are made by the Federal Public Service Commission. The four provincial governments had their own Provincial Public Service Commissions such as Punjab Public Service Commission, Sind Public Service Commission, etc. The recruitment to the provincial civil services is done by these Commissions. There is no lateral entry in the CSS. Each division is headed by a Secretary. There are 30 divisions in all. A very few specialists are taken as Advisors to the various Ministries who are not from the CSS. The entry to the civil service, at both the central and the provincial levels, is done through a competitive examination system. Over the years, various reform commissions and committees had submitted recommendations for the revamping of the civil service. What is wrong with the civil service? The civil service had an overly centralized organizational structure. It is slow, ineffective, rigid and unimaginative. Discipline is lax and rules are not evenly enforced. Internal mechanisms of accountability had weakened over time. External accountability via parliament and legal system had become ineffective. With time, professionalization had eroded. Politicization of the civil service, and political interference had reduced the effectiveness of state machinery. The performance of the state bureaucracy is not as expected because of some existing structural flaws and bad working practices acquired over time. Honesty, integrity, and hard work are not sufficiently rewarded. Moreover, sloppiness, and poor work habits are tolerated and no action taken against bad officers. Therefore, performance had suffered. Establish a new and better civil service by introducing new management techniques and organizational structures. In future, the staff will be better skilled and better trained. A wide range of reforms and re-engineering of the public administration system is required. The implementation of the reform program involved comprehensive planning and a reasonable gestation period. Emphasis is placed not on creating new institutions but on improving standing structures and mechanisms, and finding more effective ways of enforcing these mechanisms.

Presently, the military is firmly in control of Pakistan. There is no challenge to its rule for the time being. Currently, the government administrative system is a mixture of both civilian and military sub-systems. However, the military is clearly superior and being in charge so to speak. General Musharraf had decided not to impose martial law and instead built an exterior military monitoring structure controlled by the military brass itself. Overlying the administrative structure of the GOP is a system of Army Monitoring Teams that are divided into divisional-level structures that are then further sub-divided into district-level structures. These are manned entirely by military officers who report to their own senior military command. The nine Corps Commanders are very effectively overseeing all the government machinery. They report directly to General Musharraf, the President, Army Chief and Chief Executive of Pakistan. Thus, the military has its own elaborate system of monitoring and evaluation of the entire provincial civil machinery. According to some sources, the dual system has caused some confusion in normal bureaucratic reporting and authority patterns. The Musharraf regime had introduced major changes in the government system. At the apex of the government shall soon stand the National Security Council (NSC) consisting of the President, COAS, CJASC, provincial governors and some civilian members. This shall be an advisory body only. Today the regular cabinet that consists of about twenty members. A National Reconstruction Bureau (NRB) has been established in the Chief Executive's Office for planning the reforms. The NRB is working on a practical plan to overhaul the entire administrative machinery. The work of the NRB is still shrouded in mystery. The NRB has been asked to ensure that unnecessary duplication of government tasks would end. Mergers of various divisions would be initiated immediately. A beginning was made when the military regime announced its intention of merging three divisions into one. Later it also decided to merge some federal commercial agencies[15]. Thus, the military

---

[15] The Water & Power, Petroleum & Natural Resources, Industries & Production divisions were to be merged into a new Ministry of Fuel & Energy. The proposed ministry of Fuel and Energy had existed once before Partition but was later bi-furcated into Water & Power and Petroleum. The regime decided that the telecommunications division was transferred into the Science and Technology ministry and a new Information Technology division was to be established in the Science & Technology Ministry.[15] In addition, the Gas Regulatory Authority (yet to be established) was to be merged with *The Nation*al Electric Power Regulatory Authority, NEPRA as a single regulatory of the energy sector.[15] The regime decided to merge the Federal Chemical & Ceramics Corporation (FCCCL) and Ghee Corporation Pakistan (GCP) into

regime was moving in the right direction. It was expected to gradually cut the accumulated fat that had accumulated over the decades. The regime was clear in its intention to end waste through corruption and mismanagement. Anecdotal evidence suggested that billions of rupees could be saved because of strict measures. It was increasingly felt that bold measures were urgently needed to cut the size of the GOP. How many cuts were feasible? The matter was being currently debated. General Musharraf had complained of overstaffing in government departments. The military regime was cautious about downsizing, however. It took it as a public relations problem to be handled carefully. Today the situation was very complex and there was available no easy solution to Pakistan's many predicaments. Even more the requirement for greater deliberations, research and study. Sound planning was required.

The National Accountability Bureau (NAB) is headed by a serving Lt. General of the Army and is responsible to carry out the crusade against corruption in the country. It has regional bureaus setup for the purpose.

General Musharraf does seem to have the resolve and commitment to turn around Pakistan. No matter what the noble intentions, the military cannot do it alone, however. The military regime seemed sincere in tackling some of Pakistan's most basic problems. Whether the military regime succeeds or not depends on many factors, including assistance from the West. Critics of the military government argue that the military rule is part of the problem in Pakistan, and therefore can never become part of the solution. At best, General Musharraf can do his part by sorting out the mess in the government system, make peace with India, and then leave. In the end, only an enlightened civilian leadership can rule over Pakistan. There are no "great men" any more. Men who always knew everything or could do everything better. For modern societies, the concentration of power in one person or an uncontrolled elite is extremely dangerous. Since wrong decisions are more probable. Pakistan's main objective is to urgently train government officials who could help create the conditions, which shall assure Pakistan's appropriate response and adaptability to new and unforeseen changes looming across the horizon. Pakistan cannot not fail in this venture. The people hope General Musharraf and his colleagues understand this vital fact of our age. Pakistan cannot fail in this venture.

The National Fertilizer Corporation. Most of the operating units under the FCCCL and GCP were to be privatized.

Chapter 2

EXTERNAL CHALLENGES

Today, the Musharraf regime is faced with a host of challenges, both external and internal that profoundly affect it governance policy. The major external challenges are globalization, Information Technology (IT) Revolution, and the emphasis on democratic governance.

GLOBALIZATION

The first major challenge was the globalization of the world economy and the accompanied shifts. The trend was occurring partly because of the reduction in communications and transport costs in recent decades. Globalization had increased capital flows and trade worldwide. Some developing countries that opened their economies appropriately had been successful in achieving prosperity in less time. Since 1990, capital flows to developing countries had increased six-fold, according to the World Bank. This development had been linked with another important global change – a paradigm shift towards development of a global knowledge economy. The two coupled were perhaps the single most significant change of our times. We were living in an era that was characterized by rapid change due to various technological, economic and social changes. Countries had jumped from poverty to world economic power in a single generation. Technological advances in telecommunication and computers proliferate in an ever-increasing stride. Great changes had come about as a massive transformation of the global economy was taking place right before eyes. History was being squeezed as never before, so to speak.

Rapid development of telecommunications and global trade had created a global economy of truly staggering proportions. Markets had gone global lately. Unquestionably, on a diversity of dimensions, the world economy had become far more integrated in the past few decades than it used to be. Trade was one such measure. In USA, the share of exports in national income had nearly doubled, from 4% in the 1950s to 7% in the 1990s. Since the USA was a continental-trading zone in its own right, which indicates a relatively low share of international trade, that increase was already grand.

Integration through flows of capital had grown even faster than integration through trade and goods. The enlargement of international finance had been extraordinary, and all the most impressive for taking place over a relatively short period. International transactions in equities and bonds and daily turnover on the foreign-exchange market had both risen at an amazing rate over the past 20 years. It was now a well-known fact that daily turnover on the currency markets frequently surpasses the global stocks of official foreign-exchange reserves. The issue was whether central banks could any more influence exchange rates by buying and selling currency in the markets. Flows of foreign direct investment had also risen swiftly, although nothing like as rapidly as transactions in securities and currency. The World Economic Survey notes that the demand of economics shape both culture and politics. It argued that perhaps the nation state had come to a turning point. In future, the need for communication and mobility between economies shall gain importance. This need shall create an increasingly homogenous global culture that in turn would promote economic integration and gradually fog the political frontiers between countries. [1]

The future trend of regionalization was sure to grow. Countries were coming together in an integrating their economies to achieve economies of scale and other advantages. A successful experiment was unfolding in front of our eyes in the shape of European Unions. North America was coming together under the umbrella of NAFTA. It was speculated that a new form of arrangement should be made at the regional level. Instead of normal competition, countries seek various options through which they share resources and join hands in countless ways. Supranational institutions were in the making. At times, it was referred to as "government by cartel". The World Economic Survey argued that states were "pooling power in order to retain and increase it, in just the same way that a firm in a cartel gives up the freedoms to sell all it could in order to gain share in the group's fatter monopoly profits. So far the state's freedom of actions had barely been touched by the global market; should it become more circumscribed, expect more rule by cartel".[2]

There were other profound changes taking place worth mentioning. Technological advances in telecommunication and computers proliferate in an ever-increasing stride. Great changes had come about as a massive transformation of the global economy was taking place right before eyes. History was being squeezed as never before, so to speak. Surely, a new industrial revolution was under way. Advances in computer technology and telecommunications were moving rapidly on, eroding national boundaries, shrinking distances and extending the domain of the global economy. Increasingly, this reconstruction was rendering states as "mere servants of international markets". These technological changes were also bringing about "a transformation in the realm of ideas, starting towards the end of the 1970s and reaching its climax ten years later with the collapse of communism. That destroyed the system not only in the form practiced in communist countries but, more important for those in the West who never experienced it directly, as a sustaining Utopian myth. Judged as propaganda, 1989 did for big

---

[1] "The World Economic Survey", *The Economist*, 1997.
[2] Ibid.

government what 1929 did for laisser-faire"[3]. There was an on-going debate about "globalization". Was it a good thing or a bad thing? Do we embrace it or resist it? However, every one agrees that international market forces had indeed emerged as powerful. Rapid development of telecommunications and global trade had created a global economy of truly staggering proportions. Consider some developments: The Internet would both double its numbers of users and increase its number of uses. By 2002, 18.5% of all domestic telephone traffic would be carried over the Net. Sales of gateway services, a piece of hardware making it easier to telephone via the Net, were expected to rise from $160 million in 1997 to $1.26 billion by 2000. Fax traffic by Internet was another growth sector. For example, the $25 billion market for international fax traffic was seeing profound changes. The cost of a fax from New York to London, currently about 30 cents, could fall to around 6 cents when routing transmissions over the Internet becomes widespread. The processing power of fiber optics would increase. Networks were going to operate at higher speeds and higher capacity.

How would these changes affect countries like Pakistan? Would the world economy growth benefit or hurt us? It all depends on how Pakistanis handle the complex issues. There were two views on the subject: the optimist majority and the pessimist minority. Let us first understand the gist of their arguments. The optimists display intense faith in science, technology, and western capitalist and democratic systems. They believe that technology would usher into a new utopia of material affluence for all. Unprecedented changes were around the corner. Western civilization would greatly benefit from these technology-led changes. If the developing countries choose, they could also join the bandwagon of the West so to speak. It was for them to decide. In sum utopia was around the corner.

The pessimists disagree. Things were not so simple they argue. Firstly, they agree that market forces, for reasons of technology and ideology, had lately gained the upper hand. This development was deeply disturbing. The gains from globalization were far smaller than supposed, and the drawbacks much greater. In addition, such benefits, as there may be, would be divided unfairly within society. This critical issue is sometimes ignored. The new global capitalism shall certainly enrich many but workers would suffer. The worst sufferers would be the unskilled. Globalization would extend inequality, intensify poverty and increasingly lead to alienation. These costs would increase at a time when the capacity of states to respond was declining. Their failure to act would weaken the foundations of the democratic states. The prosperity of Pakistan and, ultimately, the success of the country in an expanding global in market were dependent upon the performance of its government. As sophistication in communications grows, capital, technology and jobs were moving to whichever countries offer a competitive edge. To compete, Pakistan needs to harness technological and scientific advances to best effect in commerce and industry and in service delivery, within both private and public sectors.

Pakistan suffers tremendously from its small economic size. It could be argued that Pakistan was no longer economically viable. It was too small an economy at about $70 billion and even very high growth rates, at above 6% per annum, would not transform the

---

[3] Ibid.

economic size into a respectable economy. It would take decades for Pakistan to become a developed country. Therefore, we had to seriously work at integrating Pakistan's economy into a regional block. Others had done it so could we? The EU, ASEAN, NAFTA were role models for us to study and copy. The EU was a remarkably successful experiment in regionalization and integration. Pakistan must study the models of successful regionalization and try to copy their path. Pakistan should chart its future destiny in a regional block comprising of Islamic countries in the Middle East and Southwest Asia region, most likely the ECO, but not SAARC as it was dominated by India, a non-Muslim country. Pakistan being an Islamic state must strive to operationalize the value of Ummah-i-Islami into reality. Although, the realization of a unified Ummah was in the far distant we had still to take some concrete steps now. We could and should work hard to realize Pakistan's cherished values in some manner of concrete reality. Let us transform Pakistan's values into practical reality. Generally, the imperatives of good governance were understood. We do not have to re-invent the wheel. Solutions could be readily incorporated into or reform process with some systematic effort. Implementation remains problematic. It needs political would.

We disagree with the common argument that the developing countries should adopt only "Third World Solutions to Third World problems". It needs to be stressed that knowledge, being universal, does not belong to any one region it belongs to all. There were solutions found in the developed world that were readily available and adaptable to Pakistan's situation. There were known management tools that could increase productivity and enhance performance in Pakistan. Pakistan should adopt techniques and solutions regardless of source or place of origin. Only then could we catch up something that we desperately want and were non-controversial.

In sum, globalization was there to stay and we could not avoid it. However, Pakistan could make the most of it provided it had the will to do so. The best international practices needed to be adapted for the country's specific circumstances. For example, Pakistan could and should learn from success stories like Singapore, South Korea, and Malaysia, etc. Successful implementation of good governance practices would result in better economic performance. Pakistan achieved high growth rates previously and could surely repeat the performance. Good governance policies that countries like Malaysia had successfully adapted could be easily repeated here. The opportunity available could not be missed. Pakistan must be determined to reach out and grab it immediately. The Musharraf regime must first seek adequate understanding of the globalization process. It must initiate research and accept responsibility for determining the impact of globalization process upon Pakistan's country. It is clearly understood that we had already lost time. Pakistan was not what it was supposed to be. Successive leaderships had failed to use the potential of the people. In addition, the tide of history waits for no one, including us. The rate of current global change, both economic and social, was breathtaking and largely unprecedented. There was both opportunity and threat present in the contemporary era. The Musharraf regime needs to be pro-active rather than just reactive. Pakistan could not miss the bus yet again. The future of the country depended upon the regime's capacity to successfully tap the most of the globalization opportunity present over the horizon. The people expect the military regime to deliver on this score. It could only miss the opportunity at Pakistan's peril.

INFORMATION TECHNOLOGY (IT) REVOLUTION

Pakistan was faced with the challenge of the Information Technology (IT) Revolution. People everywhere acknowledged some with enthusiasm, some with doubt, that the world was being much transformed, often in unexpected ways, by IT. The personal computer had joined the ranks of other tools – most notably video, TV and the telephone – to create a vast and growing global network that people used to converse, argue, teach, learn, hold meetings, buy or sell things, send and receive information of virtually all kinds. This was, among other things, an enormous new industry. The information and communications section was expanding twice as the rest the world economy. In the industrialized nations, people and organization were adapting to the new information environment. Government bureaucracies are transformed into "cyberocracies", with information traveling across conventional boundaries, after (to the disarray of some) becoming widely available inside and outside official channels.

Political scientists had recognized that "information power" was becoming just as important in international affairs as a country's other strengths like military, economic, social and political. Meanwhile, corporations were going through a managerial revolution of their own as they apply new information technology to all stages of production and distribution. Some transform themselves into "virtual corporations" that were essentially networks rather than classical hierarchical organizations. Individuals and NGOs too were becoming "netizens" or a new information-based civil society that was funding ways to harness IT for more participatory, open democracy. However, the world was changing quickly and unexpectedly, it was changing events. For the past twenty years, IT had developed in a way unparalleled in history. The only certainty was that more change was over the horizon. In the 21st century, no aspect of human activity would be able to escape the influence of the new global technology. It would eventually alter scientific knowledge and maybe cultural activity too. This would happen everywhere. First, we need to comprehend what was happening at the global level. The Information Age was different in many ways. It was surely affecting our lives also in countless ways. It must be understood what was changing and why? Crawford explained the essential characteristics of the Information Age as:[4]

> Knowledge was expandable and self-generating: The raw goods of an industrial economy were finite resources. Unlike physical things, knowledge increases as it was used. In using ones knowledge to improve a task, one improves his knowledge and expands his understanding of the task. In a Knowledge Economy, a scarcity of resources was replaced by an expansion of resources.
> Knowledge was shareable: The transfer of knowledge to other people does not prevent its use by the original holder. The knowledge economy differs from its predecessors in its

---

[4] Richard Crawford, *In the Era of Human Capital* (Harper Business/Harper Collins Publishers, 1991), 11.

emphasis on developing knowledge through formal research and development efforts and on transmitting abstract knowledge to individuals through formal education and training. In agriculture and industrial economics, most knowledge was acquired through experience. People learned through doing. The son learned farming by following his father and the daughter learned how to make clothe by following the master weaver. In the Knowledge Economy, people must learn basic subjects like reading and mathematics and advance subjects like physics and accounting in the classroom before they could participate in the Knowledge Economy.

Knowledge was substitutable: It could and did replace land, labor and capital. For example, a farmer who could grow more food on a specific piece of land using new farming techniques does not need additional land to increase production.

Knowledge was transportable: In today's electronic society, knowledge moves at the speed of light. In a few seconds, one could fax to Taiwan a schematic for a new computer chip that represents months of intensive engineering work.

Because of the trend, the world economy had become more integrated, with more basic heavy industry based in the developing world while the historically industrialized countries move into the advanced sectors. It was estimated that by the year 2000 some 30% of all manufactured goods would be produced in the developing world. This trend was particularly evident in East Asia. East Asia would be the dominant area of world growth because of its heavy concentration of rapidly advancing countries.[5]

Along with the transition to the Knowledge Economy comes the collapse of what was known as information float throughout the world. Information float was the advantage that a country had in international trade because of arriving there before other countries were able to develop or borrow that technology. Historically, the economic advantage of developing a new technology lasted a long time. England was able to dominate the world's economy for almost a century from 1815 to 1914 because it was the first to develop many of the basic technologies of the Industrial Revolution, such as the steam engine. Today, this form of domination was not possible. Modern communications technologies and computers had created powerful new systems for instantaneously transmitting information worldwide. A worldwide communication network had now been developed and used for global telecasting. The result of the advance was that technological breakthrough was no longer a long-term advantage to the country that generates the advance. Within a few months of an improvement in personal computer technology by a US firm like IBM, electronic firms in Korea, Hong Kong or Taiwan had reverse engineered the technology and were making clones of the product for the world market.

The development of the Information Age was truly baffling. All national leaderships acknowledge that they must be able to tap into data networks of the "electronic highways" of the global economy. They were the infrastructure of a world information economy newly forming. Leaders of developing countries were convinced that they had to play catch-up very fast. They could not afford to be complacent any more. Would information technology "leap" developing countries in this century? More importantly,

---

[5] Ibid. 20.

what would happen to countries that were left behind? How could they possibly catch up? These questions needed to be earnestly debated in public forums.

DEMOCRATIC GOVERNANCE

People everywhere were demanding a greater share in power than ever before. A good method to achieve it was through decentralization and devolution mechanisms. Empowering of local government was a global trend. They had been empowered in many countries in Latin America, Asia, and the Middle East and Africa. Europe and North America already had a tradition of decentralized structures in many countries. The question to be asked was why was this happening. The issue of decentralization and devolution had attracted considerable attention lately. Out of seventy-five developing countries that had a population of more than five million, sixty-three developing countries were engaged in decentralization. Many countries consider decentralization as "a highly promising method of solving their many problems and using available potential". Advancement of local development could be full of promise when it was coordinated with the expressed needs of the citizens. A decentralized structure of government bureaucracy was advantageous. In several countries, with centralized systems, the local level had been neglected. Despite allocation of money and many attempts of reforms, several governments had not been able to provide quality and consistent services at the local level required to improve the standard of living of the people. The comparative nearness to the citizens permits the naming of relevant local problems that were considered of being of high priority. These problems were included in a development program and solutions were found in partnership with local organizations. Such a methodology had a dispensation for adequate groundwork and dynamic participation of affected local people in the implementation phase. From the perspective of the ordinary people what do we do that would make a real difference in their lives? How do you bring them the fruits of good governance in a most effective manner? We were strongly convinced that we could do this by creating an effective third tier of government. This tier had to be provided sufficient resources and capacity to meet public needs.

Forms of Decentralization

Decentralization had various forms. The literature makes the following distinctions:

- Delegation: Defined responsibilities transferred to national regional, and ordinarily semiautonomous units of government frequently practiced in the transportation, telecommunication, and energy sectors.
- Deconcentration: Given functions carried out by the field offices of a central government organization. For example, field offices of state departments who on

the permission of the central government assume the control of certain responsibilities distant to the central office.

- Devolution: Meaning the transfer of resources and certain powers to legitimate local governments. For example, provinces, districts or municipalities were all responsible to act on national policy.

- Economic decentralization: Meaning the deregulation of central government control, and the carrying out of strategies to build the private sector and the strengthening of partnerships between government and the private sector.

What was wrong with highly centralized systems? Centralized systems fail because of a number of factors. First, the problem faced was that of low response by the people. The government activity had been directed from above rather than from demand below. It was common that the local people reject these gifts from the central government simply because they had not been involved in the decision-making process and therefore do not feel that they own these projects. Second, officials employed by the federal government lack knowledge about local problems and needs. They do not understand differences in local needs and conditions because the knowledge happens to be thinly distributed across the entire community was not available to the central planning agency. Even the greatest central planning agency could not decide whether, in a particular local village case, improving the irrigation system or expanding schooling was more significant at a specific time. Only the local government could decide these things.[6] From the perspective of the ordinary people what could the state do that would make a real difference in their lives? How do you bring them the fruits of good governance in a most effective manner? For the common man in Pakistan, like elsewhere in the developing countries, the local government was critical and it was the level that he or she interacts most and his most frustrated. Kalin gives four reasons for strengthening local government. They were:

1. A local body was more accessible and quicker in response. Local services and programs could be more easily adapted to a specific local need

2. The allocation of state resources could be done most efficiently the responsibility for each outlay was given to the level of government, which was the most close to beneficiaries.

3. Local development assists in reducing costs. If the locals feel that the money was theirs then the local people were more likely to be watchful over expenditures and to utilize money more efficiently. In addition, it provides more opportunity for public contributions to augment a local project.

4. Development programs undertaken with public participation permit local adaptation to specific needs. People were ready to give money if they were able to participate in the decision-making process and feel that the specific project benefits them directly. Involvement of locals increases sense of ownership and responsibility for the program. The public becomes stakeholders in the success of the program. Therefore, they were more likely to invest their resources and time

---

[6] Ibid. 20.

into advancing the goals of the program. In turn, these assists in producing superior outcomes rather than if the development programs were decided from distant government agencies. Thus, beneficiaries who possess ownership of a program were also more likely to ensure sustainability. The fact that the locals were involved in the early planning encourages careful monitoring and protection of the results of the planning exercise.

The federal government often lacked knowledge about local problems and needs. They do not understand differences in local needs and conditions because the knowledge happens to be thinly distributed across the entire community was not available to the central planning agency. It was at the local level that people contact government departments most for meeting their every day life. For ordinary people the federal government was far away from their own every day life personal experiences and their needs. The local level matters for they individual and their families. In several countries, with centralized systems, the local level had been neglected. Despite allocation of money and many attempts of reforms, several governments had failed to provide quality services on a regular basis at the local level. This failure was not so much because of a lack of money; rather, rather, it had resulted because of ineffective employment of available money and other resources.

Local governments were concerned essentially with providing services for the local communities like municipal services, primary education and health care, These services were obviously very essential and local governments were given elected councils so that the citizens could had open access to them and get the services they desire. Local problems were best handled locally. The governments need to apply the subsidiary principle in government. The principle simply says that decision-making should happen at the lowest level possible. In other words, decisions should not go to an upper level (provincial government, or even worse the federal government) than necessary. It was argued that decentralization was a tested way to solve acute governance problems in developing countries like Pakistan. Intense centralization and lack of delegated authority at lower levels had created a mess of government in several developing countries like Pakistan. The debate about the merits and demerits of decentralization and devolution of power continued. Were the benefits of decentralization and devolution apparent and superior to centralization tendencies? Decentralization was a global trend and local governments had been empowered in many countries in Latin America, Asia, and the Middle East and Africa. Europe and North America already had a tradition of decentralized structures in many countries. The question to be asked was why was this happening. For ordinary people the federal government was far away from their own every day life personal experiences and their needs. The local level matters for they individual and their families. In several countries, with centralized systems, the local level had been neglected. Despite allocation of money and many attempts of reforms, several governments had failed to provide quality services on a regular basis at the local level. This failure was not so much because of a lack of money; rather, rather, it had resulted because of ineffective employment of available money and other resources.

Centralized systems fail because of a number of factors. First, the problem faced was that of low response by the people. The government activity had been directed from above rather than from demand below. It was common that the local people reject these gifts from the central government simply because they had not been involved in the decision-making process and therefore do not feel that they own these projects. Second, officials employed by the federal government lack knowledge about local problems and needs. They do not understand differences in local needs and conditions because the knowledge happens to be thinly distributed across the entire community was not available to the central planning agency. Even the greatest central planning agency could not decide whether, in a particular local village case, improving the irrigation system or expanding schooling was more significant at a specific time. Only the local government could decide these things.

From the perspective of the ordinary people what do we do that would make a real difference in their lives? How do you bring them the fruits of good governance in a most effective manner? We were strongly convinced that we could do this by creating an effective third tier of government. This tier had to be provided sufficient resources and capacity to meet public needs. Unfortunately, this tier was missing for the moment in Pakistan. The third tier of government would help fill a large gaping hole in the availability of state services to the people. Pakistanis need to openly debate on such questions and arrive at a consensus for this was an Islamic requirement. Pakistan's religion teaches us to work based on Shura and Ijma, the requirement of which was consensus as wide as possible. On issues of governance, Islam would desire the input of the public in issues affecting their lives. Pakistanis must practice the tenants of Islam as they made ample sense in their lives. The point was that any model of government must necessarily have the support of the people. We have argued for the case of creating a third tier of government and decentralization of authority in Pakistan. This issue needed to be discussed further.

What is governance in the first place? The simplest meaning would be the ability to translate state policies into ground reality so that it makes a difference in the betterment of society. The term implies broadly issues of government effectiveness, accountability, transparency and adherence to the rule of law. The idea of governance was a broader than that of government. The primary characteristics of government included first the constitution, then the government itself, meaning the three basic wings which were legislature, executive and judiciary, while governance involved established connections between these formal institutions and the broader civil society. Good governance was also to be understood as having a normative connotation and included the hopes, aspirations and predilections of the governed.

The concept of governance means the activities, manner and management through various modes of exercising the power of government Simply put, the government was the authority and the governance was the process through which the policies of the government was executed and implemented. Like all enterprises, government had to be managed properly. Policies had to be implemented as desired by top management. The question was does the enterprise do its job well. Do we have the means to check the effectiveness of a particular section of the enterprise and changing it if we do not like what we get? These issues were obvious when we think enterprises. They should be also when we talk about government. Thus, governance becomes a primary issue here also. Running the government was the job of the civil service directed at the highest levels by the elected political leadership. Government could expand or contract its scale of activities like a business. Of course, there were some very basic differences between a business and a government. For example, the bottom-line (in terms of profit and income) was not the primary consideration of government. Other considerations were more important most of the time. Nevertheless, we would like to imagine that government could be as efficiently led as a business. One should remember that government was not just some abstract thing to look from a distance. It had been established to serve the people, and this was something that the people and the Government should not forget.[7] Today, the world was caught in a new era that was characterized by high rate of change. All governments had to keep pace with the great sea of changes enveloping them. These changes were taking place everywhere. These changes, highly complex in nature, had created enormous problems for all systems of governance, especially in the developing countries. Government systems could age and become irrelevant for solving current problems, or in benefiting from opportunities available. Pakistan was one such political system.

All governments aim at creating public services that not only fulfills the demands of common man but also was also capable of meeting the requirements of the coming century. A wide range of reforms and re-engineering of the public service was thus required. The task was not easy, however. The implementation of the reform programs required comprehensive planning and a reasonable gestation time. The main emphasis is on improving standing mechanisms and finding more effective ways of enforcing them. There was no single model or form of good governance, nor was there a single structure or set of structures. It was a broad, dynamic, complex process of interactive decision-making that constantly evolved and responded to changed circumstances. Although bound to respond to the specific requirements of different issues governance was an integrated approach to questions of human survival and prosperity. Recognizing the systemic nature of these issues, it must promote systemic approaches in dealing with them. There was increasing worldwide emphasis on restructuring of government because of its failure to deliver, according to expectation of citizens. What is needed to strengthen the ability of government to perform effectively, efficiently and responsively? Answers to the question have changed overtime. Previously, there had been emphasis on institutional strengthening, development management and institutional development. Overtime, the emphasis on building capacity has grown to include the linkage and processes between the public sector, the market, and the civil society.[8] It is felt that capacity building should mainly focuses on management, structures and personnel. These three dimensions of governance are inter-related and that effort to improve effectiveness, efficiency and responsiveness of the government must address all of them.

---

[7] Derbyshire and Derbyshire, *The Business of Government*, (Edinburgh: Chambers, 1987), 6.

Government sponsored governance initiatives are the key to reform anywhere.

People, nearly everywhere, complain that bureaucracies are behaving in an eccentric and haphazard manner. Sometimes, departments were unnecessarily responsible for a single activity. The system of bureaucracy had developed incrementally the world over, and each step was logical in itself, but the resulting arrangements now consist of overlapping responsibilities, duplication of efforts, and competition among departments. These features were in contrast to the basic ideal bureaucratic model and seldom result in efficiency of operations. Thus, in many parts of the world, reorganization of civil bureaucracy had become an urgent need. However, it was not easy. Political forces supporting organizational status quo were usually stronger than those favoring the reorganization effort were. Generally, bureaucrats and politicians defend their turf and are reluctant to give up power and status. Another problem for administrations, especially in the developing countries, was the widening gap between governors and governed and between the administrators and administered. Following the law of increasing entropy, governmental and administrative systems had become increasingly complex. Their procedures and structures had created red tape and inefficiency. More importantly, a distance between the rulers and ruled was being created. This was essentially a problem of legitimacy in the public sector. This had been partly solved by a traditional answer: decrease the level of complexity of society in general and of the public services in particular. Deregulation not only had a positive potential for flexibility and thus for inefficiency. It also intends to narrow some disparities of excess bureaucracy. This may cause an improvement in legitimacy of government services. Public services at different levels had important problems in common. The statement refers to the problem of ungovernability of the state and a failure in controlling developments of society. These problems become visible in the field of finance where budget deficits occur and in management where efficiency and effectiveness decrease. The problem was also felt in the notion of democracy where a legitimacy deficit could occur. By efficiency was meant the relationship of input to output. Effectiveness was a relationship of output and effects. Legitimacy was the degree of acceptance of authority by those who had to accept the authority.

One of the peculiar characteristics of our age is the near universal growth of the public sector reflective of an increase in expectations of government performance. The administration of the state had extended over diverse functions and activities both economic and social. Generally, state budgets had also increased as a percentage of GDP. In West Europe state budgets increased from around 10% of GDP at the beginning of the century to about 35% in the 1950s. Budgets further increased to about 45% in the 1980s.[9] In the countries of the former Soviet Union, the average government spending in 1992 is 45% of GDP but fell to an average of 29% in 1995.[10] In the West, a shift in focus towards sharing responsibilities between public and private sector was being increasingly felt.

---

[8] Merilee Grindle. "The Good Government Imperative: Human Resources, Organization, and Institutions", *Getting Good Government: Capacity building in the public sector of developing countries*, ed., Merilee Grindle (Harvard Institute of International Development/Harvard University Press, 1997), 8.

[9] Percy Allum, *State and Society in Western Europe* (Cambridge, MA: Polity Press, 1995), 359.

[10] "Temporarily tight in Tbilisi", *The Economist*, Aug. 3, 1996, 70.

Rather than doing it alone, the focus was now on the interaction aspects of governance, which were emphasized by looking into aspects that were other than a one-dimensional analysis of the sui generis sectors. It was necessary to pay attention to the better match between requirements of governance and capabilities to govern. In many places, governance was proving ineffective in controlling the law and order situations, crime, urban decay, poverty, and high level of corruption and mismanagement in government bureau and terrorism. The problems were multiplying as never before and seemingly beyond the reach of the state. People were worried and increasingly becoming disgusted with this state of affairs. People demand actions. There was a general apprehension that good governance requirements were not being met. Governments in many countries were trying very hard to improve efficiency, transparency and accountability of their personnel and agencies. What were the causes of government failures? How best to improve governance? These issues be debated earnestly the world over. In an age of scarcity, good governance had become the issue of today. Good governance was the major challenge of our times. The essential components of a good government were:

- Good governance, which was dependent upon the existence of a participatory process and the consent of the people.
- Accountability of the government for its actions, which was dependent upon the availability of information, transparency of decision-making and the presence of effective mechanisms to call individuals and institutions to account.
- Competence of the government, which was the capacity to formulate appropriate policies, make sound and timely decisions, and perhaps most importantly implement them effectively.
- Rule of law and respect for human rights. The government had to guarantee groups and individuals their security and their basic human rights. It had to provide an enabling framework for economic and social activity and to permit and encourage all types of individual participation.

What was good governance? The essentials of good governance were also well known: a well trained, properly remunerated civil service, the free flow of information, transparency, voice, and a commitment to fight corruption. In addition, ownership was always an important consideration. Governments must be in a position of leadership; the people must be consulted and involved. For sustainable development to occur public participation must be ensured. In an age of scarcity, good governance had become the issue of our times. Governance would imply issues of government effectiveness, accountability, transparency and adherence to the rule of law. Good governance was also to be understood as having a normative connotation and included the hopes, aspirations and predilections of the governed. It was agreed that a state must achieve a high level of good governance because lack of capacity to carefully monitor and implement, otherwise good policy designs, would hamper and distort development.

Achieving objectives of good governance requires a long-term political commitment to make the system work. As administrative systems had become increasingly complex, procedures and structures had created red tape and inefficiency. Reinventing government was needed simply to keep up with the rapid change. Essentially, it involved a broad restructuring of public service systems. Organizational structures, purposes, incentive systems, accountability procedures, authority distribution patterns, and culture were changed in the process. To achieve efficiency and effectiveness, change undertaken must ensure that the development process remains unhampered by lapses and shortcomings in current structures. Thus, governance would be best in a society with an effective production and delivery of jobs and services in an efficient way and in legitimate conditions.

Governance played a consequential role in enhancing productivity levels and better income distribution. It was dependent on the well functioning of public institutions. Setting the right priorities, formulation of appropriate policies and their effective and efficient implementation for public welfare was elementary to good governance. It was a given that only an effective, responsive, transparent, participatory and efficient public administration structure could possibly secure favorable implementation of government policies.

The central plank of good governance efforts was the reform of the civil service system. Essentially, this was seen as prerequisite for public sector reforms. However, civil service reforms were notoriously difficult to undertake. In the developing countries, many international donors' agencies had emphasized reform in this were. These multilateral agencies emphasized that governance was the essential issue in project aid. For example, USAID had noted "the finest planning and budgeting system in the world were of little use, if there were not quick and accurate means to track progress and to know the relationship between the planned events and actual events".[11]

How could the public sector be made more efficient and effective? These issues be debated earnestly the world over. The contemporary challenge was to formulate a reform strategy in which sequencing and prioritization were carefully laid out in advance. For example, goals, objectives and performance criteria of government agencies must be elaborated before any structural change was incorporated in the design of the system. Then, only a few critical agencies had to be taken up for detailed reforms. Early success, though modest, was critical for building credibility of government reforms measures. A primary business of Government pertains to development, both societal and economic. The challenge was to translate sound development goals into effective plans and then implement them. We were talking of good governance here. The issue to be debated was why our development goals not achieved. What was behind our failure? How to translate sound development goals into concrete and effective plans? How to spend the capital of our economy to improve people's lives on a sustained basis. Where had we gained? Why was good governance not achieved? Questions like the above needed be to be addressed. Good governance must vary from case to case.

For proper development, appropriate knowledge base and management skills had to be acquired. Countries, like Japan, had arisen because of attaining excellent management

---

[11] *The Effectiveness of Aid to Pakistan*" (Islamabad: Economic Affairs Division, GOP and UNDP, 1990), A.9.

skills. For Japan, lack of capital or even physical resources did not pose an insurmountable obstacle on the path of development and prosperity. The ability to skillfully manage existing resources was the key to success. Pakistan was deficient in good managerial skills. The Government must meet this vital requirement. Only then would Pakistan's dreams come true. This was not going to be easy. We must note that what works elsewhere was not necessarily suitable for us. It might work, and then it might not. We could only find out by trying it after some careful analysis. Experimentation of various models was the key to Pakistan's success.

Governance has become a central issue of our times. All international institutions and governments everywhere employ the rhetoric of good governance. The literature on governance is available in abundance. Intrinsically the concept of governance relates to government but it means much more. The primary characteristics of government include first the constitution, then the government itself, meaning the three basic wings, which are legislature, executive and judiciary, while governance involves established connections between these formal institutions and the broader civil society. The simplest meaning of governance is the ability to translate state policies into ground reality so that it makes a difference in the betterment of society. The term implies broadly issues of government effectiveness, accountability, transparency, and adherence to the rule of law. The concept of governance means the activities, manner, and management through various modes of exercising the power of government. Simply put, the government is the authority and the governance is the process through which the policies of the government is executed and implemented. Thus, the term of government implies the exercise of authority in managing and controlling the functions of the members of the body politic and directing the total affairs of the state for promoting the causes of common welfare. In any democratic country, elected representatives of the people reflect the wishes and aspirations of the people in the governance of the country. The basic concept of governability means the permanent balance between needs of governance on the one hand and capacities to govern others. There is no single model or form of good governance, nor is there a single structure or set of structures. Governance is a broad, dynamic, complex process of interactive decision-making that is constantly evolving and responding to changing circumstances. Increasingly, among international organizations, governance is used both as a concept to provide a broad overview of society and describes the way it manages itself. Governance has also been described and dealt with in terms of how to improve the functioning of the actual political and administrative system extant in a particular country. The term used has been "good governance." This has typically meant concern about civil service reform; the encouragement of efficient governmental organization (which frequently means the downsizing of government bureaucracies); and the strong encouragement of transparency and accountability in government. Good governance has a normative connotation also that includes the hopes, aspirations, and predilections of the governed. Although bound to respond to the specific requirements of different issue areas, governance must take an integrated approach to questions of human survival and prosperity. A serious problem for administrations, especially in the developing countries, is the widening gap between governors and governed and between the administrators and administered. Following the law of increasing entropy, governmental and administrative systems have become increasingly complex. The procedures and structures have created red tape. More importantly, a distance between the rulers and ruled is being created. This is essentially a problem of legitimacy in the public sector. There is increasing worldwide emphasis on restructuring of government because of its failure to deliver according to expectation of citizens. People complain that bureaucracies are behaving in an eccentric and haphazard manner. Sometimes, departments unnecessarily share responsibility for a single activity. The system of bureaucracy has developed incrementally the world over, and each step is logical in itself, but the resulting arrangements now consist of overlapping responsibilities, duplication of efforts, and competition among departments. These features are in contrast to the basic ideal bureaucratic model and seldom result in efficiency of operations. Thus, in many parts of the world, reorganization of civil bureaucracy has become an urgent need. However, it is not easy. Political forces supporting organizational status quo are usually stronger than those favoring the reorganization effort are. Generally, bureaucrats and politicians the world over defends there turf and are reluctant to give up power and status. Governance plays a consequential role in enhancing productivity levels and better income distribution. It is dependent on the well functioning of public institutions. Setting the right priorities, formulation of appropriate policies and their effective and efficient implementation for public welfare is elementary to good governance. It is a given that only an effective, responsive, transparent, participatory and efficient public administration structure can possibly secure favorable implementation of government policies. In any democratic country, elected representatives of the people are meant to reflect the wishes and aspirations of the people in the governance of the country. Governments must be in a position of leadership; the people must be consulted and involved. For sustainable development to occur public participation must be ensured. It is agreed that a state must achieve a high level of good governance because lack of capacity to carefully monitor and implement, otherwise good policy designs, will hamper and distort development. The essentials of good governance are:

(1) Accountability

Everywhere better accountability is commonly seen as the most vital key to better governance. How to strengthen the ability of government to perform effectively, efficiently, and responsively? Answers to the question have changed overtime. Previously, there has been emphasis on institutional strengthening, development management, and institutional development. Issues of good governance have considerable implications for public administration in the developing countries. Achieving objectives of good governance requires a long-term political commitment to make the system work. Accountability of the government for its actions is dependent upon the availability of information, transparency of decision-making and the presence of effective mechanisms to call individuals and institutions to account. Competence of the government, which is the capacity to formulate appropriate policies, make sound and timely decisions, and perhaps most importantly implement them effectively. Public officials must be held responsible for their actions.

(2) Rule of Law and Respect for Human Rights

The legal framework for the conduct of the government should be well defined. It should contain elaborate sets of rules, known in advance, that are enforced. Conflicts be resolved by independent judicial bodies and there should exist mechanisms for amending rules when they no longer serve their purpose.[12] In addition, the government has to guarantee groups and individuals their security and their basic human rights. It has to provide an enabling framework for economic and social activity and to permit and encourage all types of individual participation.

(3) Voice and Democratic Governance

All over the world, the demand for voice is becoming increasingly recognized. Nobel laureate Amartya Sen said that:[13]

"while democracy is not as yet universally practicable nor indeed uniformly accepted in the general climate of world pinion, democratic governance has now achieved the status of being taken as generally right" Democracy promotes good governance. Democracy though with varied meaning, is yet having some distinguishable characteristics like: leadership chosen by citizens in free and fair elections, all citizens having the legal right to vote and run for office, opposition to government to be tolerated and freely expressed, functioning political parties, accountability of the government to the people, parliament and judiciary, and a free press. Joseph, Kesselman, and Krieger argue that no one confuses the democratic character of the Indian or French governments with the dictatorial rule of Nigeria's military regime or the Chinese Communist Party. Twenty years ago democracies constituted a small minority of countries in the world. In comparison today they are a majority.[14] All ingredients of democracy mentioned above are conducive to the development of good governance. In addition, good governance requires the existence of a participatory process indicating the consent of the people. One should remember that government is not just some abstract thing to look from a distance. The government is established to serve the people, and this is something that the people and the government itself should not forget.[15]

---

[12] Sources: ODA (Overseas Development Administration) (1993) *'Good Government', Technical Note no. 10* (London: ODA); World Bank (1992) *Governance and Development* (Washington D.C.: World Bank).

[13] Shahid Yusuf, "The Changing Development Landscape", *Finance and Development*, IMF, December 1999, 16.

[14] William Joseph, Mark Kesselman & Joel Frieger, Eds. *Third World Politics at the Crossroads* (Lexington, MA: D.C. Heath, 1996), 7.

[15] Derbyshire & Derbyshire, *The Business of Government*, (Edinburgh: Chambers, 1987), 6.

(4) Transparency

The business of government is conducted in a transparent manner. There is publicly available information for policy analysis and debate. In addition, information on efficiency of state machinery is available. Thus, transparency by itself can become a formidable means of preventing corruption. [16]

(5) Government Ownership of the Reform Process

The governments must be in a position of leadership. Without the government's leadership, a serious reform process can never take off. In addition, the people must be consulted and involved. For sustainable development to occur public participation must be ensured.

(6) Effective Public Sector Management

Like all enterprises, government has to be managed properly. Policies have to be implemented as desired by top management. Running the government is the job of the civil service directed at the highest levels by the elected political leadership. The government can expand or contract its scale of activities like a business. We ask the question: does the enterprise do its job well? These issues are obvious when we think enterprises. They should be also when we talk about government. Thus, governance becomes a primary issue here also. Of course, there are some very basic differences between a business and a government. For example, the bottom-line (in terms of profit and income) is not the primary consideration of government. Other considerations are more important most of the time. Nevertheless, we would like to imagine that government could be as efficiently led as a business. A primary business of government pertains to development, both societal and economic. The challenge is to translate sound development goals into effective plans and then implement them. We are talking of good governance here. A well-trained, properly remunerated civil service is an absolute must for sustainable development. The government must manage its personnel and financial resources effectively through appropriate reporting, budgeting, and accounting systems and eradicate inefficiency. [17]

Today we are living in an era that is characterized by a very high rate of change. Governments have to keep pace with the great sea of changes enveloping them. These changes are taking place everywhere. These changes, highly complex in nature, have created enormous problems for all systems of governance, especially in the developing countries. Government systems can age and become irrelevant for solving current

---

[16] Sources: ODA (Overseas Development Administration) (1993) 'Good Government', Technical Note no. 10 (London: ODA); World Bank (1992) Governance and Development (Washington D.C.: World Bank).
[17] Ibid.

problems, or in benefiting from opportunities available. There are many such political systems in our part of the world. Re-structuring of the entire systems is the need of the hour. We can learn from mistakes committed by others. Many countries have progressed remarkably in the march of re-engineering government systems. Experiments in altering public sector institutions have employed different institutional models. Re-engineering government involves restructuring public organizations and systems. Organizational sizes, purposes, incentive systems, accountability procedures, authority distribution patterns, even organizational culture is changed. In order to achieve efficiency, effectiveness and fairness in public organizations change is required. It is also undertaken to ensure that the development process remains unhampered by lapses and shortcomings in administration structures.

Public services at different levels have important problems in common. The statement refers to the problem of ungovernability of the state and a failure in controlling developments of society. These problems become visible in the field of finance where budget deficits occur and in management where efficiency and effectiveness decrease. The problem is also felt in the notion of democracy where a legitimacy deficit can occur. By efficiency is meant the relationship of input to output. Effectiveness is a relationship of output and effects. Legitimacy is the degree of acceptance of authority by those who have to accept the authority. Thus, governance would be best in society with "an effective production and delivery of jobs and services in an efficient way and in legitimate conditions taking into account the degree of dynamics, complexity, diversity and risk".[18]

In short, a paradigm shift towards good governance has meant the sharing responsibilities between public and private sector is being increasingly felt in the developed countries. Rather than doing it alone, the focus is now on the aspect of interaction, which are emphasized by looking into bearings that are other than a one-dimensional analysis of the sui generis sectors. It is necessary to pay attention to the better match between requirements of governance and capabilities to govern.

In many places, governance is proving ineffective in controlling the law and order situations, crime, urban decay, poverty, and high levels of corruption and mismanagement in government bureaus. The problems are multiplying as never before and seemingly beyond the reach of the state. People are worried and increasingly becoming disgusted with the present state of affairs. People everywhere demand action. There is a general apprehension that good governance requirements are not being met. Governments in many countries are trying very hard to improve efficiency, transparency, and accountability of their personnel and agencies. What are the causes of government failures? How best to improve governance? How can the public sector be made more efficient and effective? Another problem for administrations, especially in the developing countries, is the widening gap between governors and governed and between the administrators and administered. Following the law of increasing entropy, governmental and administrative systems have become increasingly complex. Their procedures and

---

[18] Geert Bouckaert, "Governance between Legitimacy & Efficiency Citizen Participation in the Belgium Fire Services". *Modern Governance: New Government Society Interactions*, ed. by Jan Kooiman (London: Sage, 1993), 146.

structures have created red tape and inefficiency. More importantly, a distance between the rulers and ruled is being created. This is essentially a problem of legitimacy in the public sector. This has been partly solved by a traditional answer: decrease the level of complexity of society in general and of the public services in particular. Deregulation not only has a positive potential for flexibility and thus for inefficiency. It also intends to narrow some disparities of excess bureaucracy. This may cause an improvement in legitimacy of government services.[19] Thus, the issues pertaining to good governance are earnestly being debated the world over. In an age of scarcity, good governance has become the issue of today.

There is a strong consensus, both inside and outside of developing countries, that a restructuring of the entire management system of public services is badly needed. How can it be done? Each country must learn from mistakes committed by others. Some countries, like New Zealand, USA and Great Britain, had progressed remarkably in the march of reinventing government systems. Experiments in altering public sector institutions had employed different institutional models, however. What is then the governance philosophy best suitable for each country? The answer has to be found after patient deliberations. There are no easy solutions or shortcuts readily available. What is required, at the minimum, is that a scientific approach be adopted which requires careful analysis, systematic efforts, and a commitment for practical solutions. In addition, a high level of political commitment is obviously concerned. In many developing countries, there is usually a glaring lack of political commitment to see the reforms through. This problem must be overcome quickly.

---

[19]*Modern Governance: New Government - Society Interactions*, ed. by Jan Kooiman (London: Sage, 1993), 146.

SECTION II

INTERNAL CHALLENGES

The Musharraf regime is faced with a host of challenges, both external and internal that profoundly affect it governance policy. The major external challenges are globalization of the world economy; the Information Revolution; greater public participation requirements, decentralization and devolution of power, and the quest for reinventing government. Internal challenges include:

- Public Accountability
- Economic Decline, Poverty Increase and Unsustainable Development
- Fragile Political System
- Dysfunctional Public Services

Chapter 3

PUBLIC ACCOUNTABILITY

Public accountability is the demand of the times. It is essential for maintaining public confidence in government, justifying state activities and ensuring the overall legitimacy of the state. However, the means and modes of such accountability may vary among different societies depending on their historical background, culture and ideology. Accountability could be explained in terms of its administrative, political and economic dimensions. Mauro, an economist with IMF, explains that economic theory had given quite a bit of insight into causes of corruption and its consequences. An essential principle was that corruption could occur where rents exist, most often resulting from government regulation, and another condition was met that public officials had discretion in allocating them. The classic example of a state restriction, which resulted in rents and rent-seeking behavior, was that of an import quota. In addition, the associated licenses that civil servants gave to businesses promoted bribes. Examples of availability of rents included price controls, multiple exchange rate practices, and foreign exchange allocation schemes, trade restrictions (such as tariffs), favoritism industrial policies (such as tax deduction and subsidies), and government controlled provision of credit. We had all the above in Pakistan. The availability of rents makes the possibility of corrupt behavior. You reform the economy, de-regulate it gradually, and decrease the availability of rent and the decrease in corruption behavior would follow. This was the economic argument. Corruption happens only when the circumstances and structural arrangements make it possible. Alter the structure corruption would decrease. Thus, prevention was better than cure. The logic was simple yet powerful. Given the circumstances, both political and economic, this was a tall order indeed. It was not easy to implement these reform measures today.

Economic theory has given quite a bit of insight into causes of corruption and its consequences. A key principle is that corruption can occur where rents exist, most often resulting from government regulation, and another condition is met that public officials have discretion in allocating them. The classic example of a state restriction, which results in rents and rent-seeking behavior, is that of an import quota. In addition, the associated licenses that civil servants give to those businesses that are willing to bribe. Examples of availability of rents include price controls, multiple exchange rate practices, and foreign exchange allocation schemes, trade restrictions (such as tariffs), favoritism industrial policies (such as tax deduction and subsidies), and government controlled provision of credit. We have all the above in Pakistan. The availability of rents makes the possibility of corrupt behavior. You reform the economy, de-regulate it gradually, and decrease the availability of rent and the decrease in corruption behavior will follow. This is the economic argument. Corruption happens only when the circumstances and structural arrangements make it possible. Alter the structure and corruption will decrease. Thus, prevention is better than cure. The logic is simple yet powerful. Given the circumstances, both political and economic, this is a tall order indeed. It is not easy to implement these reform measures today

Corruption distorts resource allocation and the performance of governments, civil society, and the private sector. The causes of corruption are varied. Many factors lead to corruption incidences, such as:

- Poverty and income inequality.
- Low public sector remuneration.
- Lack of a formal system of incentives
- Weak public administration.
- Institutional failures.
- Lack of accountability, transparency.
- Lack of community feeling and social cohesion.

There is no single or easy solution to contain and remove corruption. However, a comprehensive national anti-corruption strategy, if followed earnestly, can make a difference. The success of the anticorruption program depends on their design.

It is important to tackle the issue head on because it undermines the very legitimacy of a political system. That is dangerous to say the least.

EFFECTS OF CORRUPTION

Different kinds of corruption are not equally harmful. Corruption that undermines the rules of the game, for example, property rights, credit and banking, or the justice system – destroys political and economic development. In comparison, giving bribes to access public services is less damaging. The extent of corruption is also significant. In countries where corruption becomes the norm, the effects are incapacitating. Such systematic corruption, like in Pakistan, is one of the primary reasons why the country is in the category of developing nations.

Economic Costs of Corruption

Corruption has enormous costs to the nation. Some of which are:

Bribery Raises Transaction Costs and Uncertainty

Bribery usually leads to inefficient economic outcomes. It obstructs long-term domestic and foreign investment. It distorts technology choices and sector priorities. For example, it can create incentives for contracting of large defense projects rather than rural health clinics specializing in preventive care. It pushes companies underground, outside the formal sector. Corruption undercuts the country's ability to raise revenues, and leads to higher taxes on fewer and fewer taxpayers. This, in turn, reduces the government's capacity to provide essential public goods, including the rule of law.

Corruption as a System

One will tend to find corruption when a person has monopoly power over a service or good, has then discretion to decide who will get it and how much, and is not accountable. Corruption is also a crime of calculation. In cases where bribes are big, the chances of being caught slim, and the punishment if caught slight, many officials will succumb to the temptation of corruption. Therefore, fighting corruption begins with designing better systems.

Corruption is to be seen as a symptom of other underlying problems rather than an independent variable. In other words, corruption is the symptom of basic political, institutional, and economic causes. Addressing corruption effectively means tackling the underlying causes of the phenomenon.

Many Faces of Corruption

Corruption has many faces. We need to point out several structural features that create incentives for corruption in government service. In other words, it is useful to consider what private parties "purchase" from a bureaucrat or politician by bribery:

1) Public Revenues

Bribes lower costs for those who are ready to pay them. Private individuals and corporations seek to lower their cost of taxes, regulations, and duties imposed on them by government.

2) Government Contracts

Bribes may confer high financial rewards to private individuals through, privatization, contracts, and concessions. Bribes affect the allocation of scarce resources.

3) Bribes as Incentive Payment

Public officers have little incentive to do their jobs as required because of low pay and inadequate monitoring.

4) Bribe as Substitute for Legal Forms of Political Influence

Bribery by politicians buys votes and bribery of politicians buys influence.

5) Influencing Outcome of the Legal and Regulatory Process

Bribes can buy judicial decisions and alter the regulatory process. The government either fails to stop illegal activities (such as drug dealing) or unduly favors one party over another in court cases.

6) Time Savings and Regulatory Avoidance

Bribes can expedite government decisions and permissions to carry out legal activities.

Public accountability is essential for maintaining public confidence in governance, justifying state activities and ensuring the overall legitimacy of the state. However, the means and modes of such accountability may vary among different societies depending on their historical background, culture, and ideology. Accountability can be explained in terms of its administrative, political, and economic dimensions. In the developing world, the colonial origin of the bureaucracy makes it too advanced or "overdeveloped" in relation to the political and economic realms of society. After independence instead of fundamental change the bureaucratic set up the power of the bureaucracy is expanded further. It now undertook social and economic development. The power of bureaucracy is expanding further due to its technical expertise, coercive authority, and control over information and resources. As a result, the bureaucracy is so overwhelmingly powerful that it is difficult to ensure accountability of the bureaucracy by the relatively weak political institutions. In fact, the bureaucracy has intervened in national politics and established control over the political institutions in many countries. In the final analysis, accountability depends on the capacity of citizens to articulate and exercise power.

However, this requires an existence of a vibrant civil society and strong democratic political culture. In most developing countries the pre-requisite of people's power is either relatively weak or absent. The prevalence of colonial political and administrative legacy discourages the development of a strong civil society, which includes associations, organizations and groups emerging which are independent from the state and ruling party. In the context of weak civil society, while the common people are largely content with the immediate family and ethnic concerns and pre-occupied with patron-client issues, it is the state bureaucracy that remains the most organized and powerful related to this absence of dynamic civil society is the lack of deep-rooted democratic political culture in many developing countries, which directly constraints realization of accountability at the national level. [1]

Accountability means measuring performance against tangible targets for efficiency, service quality, or output. It is becoming apparent that administrative accountability is meaningless without proper political accountability. The benefits of democratization are beyond doubt. Benefits are felt in specific aspect of governance, such as facilitation of orderly changes of government and the protection of personal rights to realize its potential. Formal democratization must be deepened through more meaningful public participation in politics.[2] Better accountability is commonly seen throughout the world as the key to better governance. However, the past decade many approaches have been pursued in attempts to tighten the reins of accountability within government and between government and the public. The new approach to political accountability has been democratization that is taken up with vigor in many developing countries. However, the results have been disappointing. Democratization at the level of institutions is not necessarily accompanied by the necessary changes in attitudes and behavior among both governors and the governed. Our own case warns us against taking it for granted that changes in governments through periodic elections will necessarily or automatically lead to better governance. Where democratization disappoints, it is common to see civil society as the missing ingredient.[3]Successful accountability depends on the capacity of citizens to articulate and exercise power. Expecting a military government to promote democratic governance may be a contradiction in terms. Yet given the complexity of our situation this is exactly what we hope shall happen. No matter what the contradiction the people of Pakistan are willing to give the Musharraf regime the benefit of the doubt. The people are willing to let the military regime chart a new course of politics for the country. This speaks not about the capacity of the military to deliver but about the incapacity of the civilian leadership to make any difference, given their chance. Also, it needs to be perfectly clear that there is no quick fix solution to the problem, no matter how earnestly desirable.

---

[1] M. Shamsul Haque, "Local Governance in Developing Nations", *Regional Development Dialogue*, Vol. 18, No. 2, autumn 1997. Published by United Nation Center for Regional Development, Nagoya, Japan. Page-iv to xiv.

[2] Polidano and David Hulme, No Magic Wands, Accountability and Governance in Developing Countries, *Regional Development Dialogue*, Vol. 18, No. 2, autumn 1997, page-vi.

[3] Op. cit. pp. 13-14.

Comparative analysis suggests that corruption happens only when the circumstances and structural arrangements make it possible. Alter the structure corruption will decrease. Thus, prevention is better than cure. The logic is simple yet powerful. Given the circumstances, both political and economic, this is a tall order indeed. It is not easy to implement these reform measures today. Public accountability is essential for maintaining public confidence in governance, justifying state activities and ensuring the overall legitimacy of the state. An individual performs best in an organizational culture that is rewarding, and fair. Today, the most important issue in the public mind is that of public accountability. The reason is simple. The country has suffered horrendous corruption at the highest level. It had become notorious for graft and kickbacks throughout the machinery of government. It is widely acknowledged that the corrupt politicians, in league with bureaucrats, had pocketed most of the money meant for public services. Ample anecdotal evidence is available about kickbacks in big-item military purchases. Thus, the top military brass in Pakistan is also not clean. Undoubtedly, there exists a staggering magnitude of corruption in Pakistan. Estimates of corruption vary. The entire civilian era of the 1980s and 1990s is commonly described as one where there is massive corruption in the state apparatuses. Corrupt officials, according to one estimate, pocketed nearly half of the appropriations. It has been estimated that a staggering $100 billion of stolen money has left the country for safe havens around the world. A few years ago, Pakistan was considered one of the most corrupt countries in the world. When the Musharraf regime came to power it promised to pursue a practical strategy to fight corruption in the country and to tackle the problem of corruption in Pakistan on a war footing. It established a very powerful agency - the National Accountability Bureau (NAB) headed by a serving Lt. General of the Army. The NAB has initiated an accountability process designed to expose previous wrongdoing, recoup ill-gotten gains, and restore public confidence in government institutions. The immediate objective was to improve cash recovery position. According to international financial institutions, total size of stuck-up loans, including all the public, private and commercial banks, was Rs 208 billion (about $4 billion) last year. There must be a marked improvement in this area. The National Accountability Bureau (NAB) had recovered about 10 billion by end of 1999, which many saw as a good start. Yet, the NAB has recovered about Rs 50 billion of stolen money. Critics also point out that the current workload of NAB includes cases against only politicians, businesspersons, and bureaucrats. No serving military official or member of the higher judiciary has yet been apprehended by NAB. Now it seems that NAB has finally bowed under relentless public criticism of even-handedness in the accountability drive. It has decided to investigate several shadowy defense deals involving retired military chiefs. Media reports disclose that the defense ministry entered into defense deals worth six billion dollars in the last ten years. Some of the deals are shadowy and involved kickbacks worth at least one billion dollars. It has been alleged that millions of dollars have been paid in illegal commissions to secure these defense contracts. Recently, the notoriously corrupt former Naval Chief, Mansoor ul-Haque is arrested with the help of the US government. He is wanted by the NAB in corruption charges regarding the famous Agosta submarine deals. Mansoor will be soon brought back to the country to stand trial. He is yet the highest-ranking military man to have been arrested for corruption crimes.

The Musharraf regime needs to revamp the entire GOP. It must aim at creating public services that not only fulfills the demands of common man but also is also capable of meeting the requirements of the coming century. A wide range of reforms and re-engineering of the public service is thus required. The task is not easy, however. The implementation of the reform programs required comprehensive planning and a reasonable gestation time. The main emphasis is on improving standing mechanisms and finding more effective ways of enforcing them. There is no single model or form of good governance, nor is there a single structure or set of structures. Good governance should be understood as a broad, dynamic, complex process of interactive decision-making that is constantly evolved and responded to changed circumstances. Although bound to respond to the specific requirements of different issues, governance is essentially an integrated approach to various issues. The GOP should recognize the systemic nature of these issues. Therefore, it must promote systemic approaches in dealing with these issues. There is a strong consensus, both inside and outside of Pakistan, that a restructuring of the entire management system of public services is the need of the hour. How could it be done? What is the governance philosophy best suitable for Pakistan? The answer has to be found after patient deliberations. There are no easy solutions or shortcuts readily available. What is required, at the minimum, is that the adoption of the scientific approach. This requires careful analysis, systematic efforts, practical solutions and sustained efforts, plus a high level of political realism and commitment by all concerned. The Musharraf regime wishes to break the inertia. Although reorganization of civil bureaucracy has become an urgent and felt need, it is not easy. Political forces supporting organizational status quo are usually stronger than those favoring reforms are. Generally, bureaucrats the world over defends their turf and are reluctant to give up power and status. Another problem for administrations, especially in the developing countries, is the widening gap between governors and governed and between the administrators and citizens. A distance has resulted between the rulers and ruled. This is essentially a problem of legitimacy in military rule. The Musharraf regime faces an obvious legitimacy deficit situation. Many international donors' agencies have repeatedly emphasized reform in this area. They emphasized that governance was the essential issue in project aid. For example, the UNDP, CIDA, Asian Development Bank, and the World Bank have noted that planning and budgeting systems are of little use, if the GOP does not have a quick and accurate means to track progress and to know how to quickly alter the discrepancies between the plan and the actual reality. For this a committed and smart public service is needed. Therefore, stress on building one.

The Musharraf regime was convinced that it was possible to make systematic improvements by pursuing a practical strategy to fight corruption in the country. The relatively weak political institutions in Pakistan can only be strengthened with timely action, and determined effort. Recommendation for an improved anticorruption strategy include:

- Punish some major offenders: A successful strategy must begin by "frying a few big fish". In Pakistan, where the rich and powerful engage in corruption with impunity, the only method is to convict and punish major corrupt figures. Thus, corrupt politicians, senior bureaucrats, both civilian and military, and officials of the higher judiciary must be hauled up and given exemplary punishment. The GOP must quickly identify a few big tax evaders, a few high-level government bribe takers, and a few bribe givers. Since a campaign against corruption can easily turn into a campaign against the opposition, the first big fish to be fried must also include people from the military itself.

- Lead by personal example: The Musharraf regime should realize that a lack of proper accountability and weak rule of law has led to nourishment of numerous corrupt practices. Therefore, the military rulers must set an example for others to follow.

- Implement civil service reform: It bears repetition that a well-trained, properly remunerated civil service is an absolute must for sustainable development. The Musharraf regime must manage its personnel and financial resources effectively through appropriate reporting, budgeting, and accounting systems and eradicate inefficiency. An individual performs best in an organizational culture that is rewarding, and fair. Hence, work hard to create this culture. Therefore, the Musharraf regime must earnestly implement civil service reforms. Trained and efficient civil service will help reduce corruption. Thus, indirectly reform of overall government structures will have an affect on incidence of corruption. Reform of the entire bureaucratic system will help end corrupt practices.

- Adhere to the rule of law: The military regime must promote a rule of law culture in the country. Only the adherence to a culture of law can possibly end corruption in the country. This is a long-term solution, however. Perhaps the single biggest public concern is the issue or rule of law. Countries that claim to be democracies pride themselves on living under the rule of law. The idea of respecting the law, as opposed to the will of an individual, can be traced back centuries. In our case, it originated with Prophet Muhammad (upon whom be peace) and the notion of Shariah. The Prophet Muhammad (upon whom be peace) was adamant is asserting the law over all individuals, including himself and his family. The concept of rule of law is well established and cannot be challenged. In Islam, no one, and whatever his rank or position in society, is above the law. In other words, there is not one law for the rich and another for the poor or one law for the officials and another for the people. The concept of rule of law is also well established in the western tradition. For example, Dicey, an eminent constitutional lawyer, has also identified the concept as an essential feature of western concepts of constitution and judicial process. The problem of the notion of rule of law is not the law itself; we have fair laws for the most part, but the fact that they are not applied fairly. The problem is selective application of rules. The real problem with rules, in countries like Pakistan, is their selective enforcement. The rich and powerful are above rules. This is tragic. Rules are rules and are meant for everyone rich and powerful, poor and weak, alike. This is a fundamental Islamic belief that desperately needs to be operationalized in Pakistan. Rules must be universal in application. Lack of it breeds corruption, disillusionment, and apathy in society. We highlight the issue because we strongly feel that Pakistan must make strident efforts to develop into a powerful, modern Islamic state where there is equality, justice, security, and equal opportunity for all not just the few. We have to operationalize Islamic values into our political system. The concept rule of law is one such cardinal value of Islam that cannot be ignored anymore.

- Focus on prevention by repairing corrupt systems: A successful anti corruption efforts fixes corrupt systems. A strategy which would include the following:
  - Collect information in order to raise the probabilities of corruption being detected and punished.
  - Increase the social consequences of corruption. Educate the people against the evil of corruption. Ostracize them so that they feel outcasts of society. Boycott them so that they feel left out. Educate people that money is not everything in life. We have to produce role models in Pakistan. Easier said then done, however. We can only try harder.
  - Involve the people in diagnosing corrupt systems. Successful campaigns against corruption must involve the public. Citizens can be of invaluable sources of information about where corruption is occurring. Consult them. How do we do that? Setting up citizens' oversight bodies for public agencies. Involve professional organizations like the Pakistan Medical association, Chambers of Commerce & Industry, Bar Council, etc. Consult with local village councils in the rural areas and ward council leadership in the urban areas. Call-in radio and television shows and educational programs can be employed for the purpose. In order for this consultation to be successful, it is essential that participating individuals must participate with protection of anonymity.
  - Make bribery a risky behavior by emphasizing exposure. A vibrant media can help control bribery by exposing graft in government offices. Such investigative reporting must be encouraged and rewarded by the GOP. The media can become an ally in the fight against corruption.
- Political will: Creating the political will to fight corruption is of paramount importance. Combating corruption is a daunting task and therefore finding pockets of political support is crucial. There are some reform-minded leaders whose leadership, and public support, is crucial at the time.
- Rule-bound government machinery: Simply making rules more transparent, fair and simple limit opportunities of corruption. For this to happen, a sea change in the attitude of our ruling elite has to take place. Unfortunately, evidence indicates that this is unlikely to happen in any dramatic manner in the near future. We as a nation are poorer for it.

- Democratization and constitutionalism as a political process: Further development of the complex process of democratization and that of constitutionalism will help eradicate corruption in Pakistan. Strong legal and open government institutions can assist in controlling corruption to a considerable extent.
- Proper functioning of all state institutions can forcefully check arbitrary behavior of public officials. There is a need to decrease the discretionary control of public officials Procedures be clear-cut, clarified, and streamlined. Official discretion needs to be reduced in carefully well thought out and pragmatic fashion. The people who are likely to be affected must understand and cooperate in the exercise. Payoffs will naturally be reduced.
- Simply making rules more transparent limits opportunities for corruption. The problem with rules in countries in Pakistan is that they are selectively enforced. The rich and powerful do not like government rules to be applied on them. Rules are rules and no one should be an exception in its regulation. A sea change of attitude, especially in Pakistan's ruling elite, is needed to get this point across. Education is the key to help make the powerful realize their shortcomings.
- Economic measures enhancing deregulation and privatization: In general, any reform measures that increase competitiveness in the economy will reduce incentives for corrupt behavior. A monopoly service-provider or business enterprise gives no choice or an alternative for the consumers to exercise. The GOP should therefore break such giant monopolies. Fostering deregulation, if careful undertaken, can help eradicate corruption. Privatization itself has to be transparent and open. Mauro, an economist with IMF, explains that economic theory has given quite a bit of insight into causes of corruption and its consequences. A key principle is that corruption can occur where rents exist, most often resulting from government regulation, and another condition is met that public officials have discretion in allocating them. The classic example of a state restriction, which results in rents and rent-seeking behavior, is that of an import quota. In addition, the associated licenses that civil servants give to those businesses that are willing to bribes. Examples of availability of rents include price controls, multiple exchange rate practices, and foreign exchange allocation schemes, trade restrictions (such as tariffs), favoritism industrial policies (such as tax deduction and subsidies), and GOP controlled provision of credit. [4] We have all the above in Pakistan. The availability of rents makes the possibility of corrupt behavior. Reform the economy, de-regulate it gradually, and decrease the availability of rent and the decrease in corruption behavior will follow. This is the economic argument. Corruption happens only when the circumstances and structural arrangements make it possible. Alter the structure corruption will decrease. Thus, prevention is better than cure. The logic is simple yet powerful. Given the circumstances, both political and economic, it is not easy to implement

[4] Paulo Mauro, "Corruption: Causes, Consequences, and Agenda for Further Research", *Finance 7 Development*, Mar. 1998, 11.

these reform measures today. Economic measures enhancing deregulation and privatization are helping by themselves. In general, any reform measures that increases competitiveness in the economy is reducing incentives for corrupt behavior. A monopoly service-provider or business enterprise gives no choice or an alternative for the consumers to exercise. Thus, WAPDA and Pakistan Railways, both state monopolies, are highly ineffective. The entry of private power producers in the game had changed the situation. Likewise, PTCL (Telephone Company) is a state monopoly and therefore corruption incidence is high. With the telecommunications market opening up, and the entry of private service providers, choices had increased. Thus, the monopoly of PTCL is being dented and if this continues, surely corruption in PTCL could only decrease. The Musharraf regime is keen to break such giant monopolies and foster deregulation. It is geared to accelerate the program of privatization of state assets. The entire privatization process is completely transparent, open and above board. The proceeds of privatization are spent on debt retirement purposes only.

- Strengthen the regulatory bodies established so far like the National Electric Power Regulatory Authority (NEPRA), Pakistan Telecom Agency (PTA), etc. must ensure that in the new era of competition the rights of the ordinary consumers are not hurt. Likewise, the Securities and Exchange Commission that was established to oversee the proper functioning of stock exchange market should especially protect the interests of the small investors.

- Show commitment to privatize all the commercial activities now under the public sector. It is hoped that the GOP will be able to sell some of its financial institutions at a reasonable price. The GOP must only perform the most essential functions leaving the rest to the private sector and the civil society.

- Promote and strengthen civil society: A meaningful dent at corruption necessarily requires an existence of a vibrant civil society and strong democratic political culture that will take time to develop. Given the situation of military rule in Pakistan, it is not going to happen overnight. Leaders must see that it is possible to make systematic improvements by pursuing a practical strategy to fight corruption in the country.

- Promises to better the lot of the public servants attract little notice. No one believes them anymore. Therefore, refrain form rhetoric. Put your money where your mouth is. The public servants deserve better treatment. Their neglect is now bordering on the criminal. Public sector wages are so low in Pakistan that survival has become impossible. It should be no surprise that corruption flourishes under such conditions. Therefore, an appropriate pay increase for the civil service is required in the next budget. Therefore, the wage structure of the public sector employees is revised. From next year, onwards a Cost of Living Allowance (COLA) is given to the entire public service every year. COLAs are common in many countries.

- A trained and efficient intelligence service could reduce corruption. The numerous Intelligence outfits are consolidated into just two agencies: civilian and military. The civilian agency – the Federal Intelligence Agency – should be strengthened to investigate white-collar crime and sophisticated corruption at the highest levels. Thus, current investigation efforts need to be consolidated immediately. In addition, unnecessary duplication of efforts should be curtailed, as resources are very scarce.

- Strong legal and open government institutions help in controlling corruption. Proper functioning of all state institutions can forcefully check arbitrary behavior and corrupt practices. With a strong public check on behavior of officials through institutions like the higher judiciary, corruption will decrease.

- Trained and efficient public service will help reduce corruption and as such, the reform of overall government, structures will indirectly have an impact on incidence of corruption. The Federal Intelligence Agency will be strengthened and involved more aggressively in fighting corruption.

- Promote the media's "watch-dog" function. A vibrant media could help control bribery by exposing graft in government offices. Such investigative reporting be encouraged and rewarded by the military regime. The media could become an ally in the fight against corruption.

- Revamp government auditing services. The auditing services are being revamped and after the strengthening of the Auditor General office reports will be available for timely action and as such, the normal accounting and legal arm of the State should become a potent instrument to fight corruption.

- Revamping the police services, courts, and civil society will help eradicate corruption.

- Revamping of the Central Board of Revenue (CBR). Tax administration is a key area and is a fundamental prerequisite for success of the tax initiatives taken recently especially, when the tax rates had been lowered in the hope that more tax revenues will be collected. Identify a few big tax evaders, corrupt officers, and give them exemplary punishment.

- Clear political will show to fight corruption as it is entrenched in the system and could not be eradicated overnight. Finding pockets of political support is crucial. Therefore, a broad public coalition to institutionalize the crusade is established. Previously, the Army had launched a campaign against ghost schools and fake appointments. It had revealed that about 15,000 teachers were involved in the rackets. Similarly in the Railways and WAPDA, the military authorities were able to mount a successful crackdown on corruption.

THE ISSUE OF INSTITUTIONALIZATION OF ACCOUNTABILITY THROUGH THE JUDICIARY

The Pakistani public is strongly demanding that the Musharraf Government carry out an impartial process of accountability and that corruption be eliminated from the body politic of the country. All political parties and groups are united in response to this stringent public outcry against the rot in the country's political system. Previously, both the PPP and PML governments were rightly dismissed for their insensitivity, bad governance and gross corruption. The issue of corruption is very complex, to say the least. Corruption cannot be eliminated overnight and there are no quick fixes to the menace. Can the military government turn the tide of official corruption? We do not think so. Some level of corruption is inevitable in Pakistan simply because it is built into the political and economic system itself. This does not mean that we either condone it or that the country has the luxury to be complacent. Corruption can only be tackled by building a strong and fair political and socio-economic system and quicken reform of governmental management structures. Where does the military government begin? The most important check to corruption is the fear of punishment, the so-called long arm of the law eventually catching upon you. Punishment must be made as sure as death and taxes and that too for every one including the highest government officials and political bosses. This can only be done by powerful and independent investigation and prosecuting agencies in the executive and most of all by an independent, powerful and competent higher judiciary. The correct path to follow is to reform and overhaul both the executive and judiciary. The Musharraf Government is warned that it is answerable to the public. The public outcry for an end to high corruption and demand for justice is real. In numerous other countries, a powerful and independent judiciary has been seen as the fundamental key to the popular battle against official corruption. Recently the Indian Supreme Court took under its wing the premier investigation agency in the country - the Central Bureau of Investigation (CBI) from the control of the office of the prime minister because of a possible conflict of interest. The CBI was directed to investigate the Hawala case, which had led to the indictment of several central ministers in the last Congress government, and the ex-Premier was himself a suspect. Later Narishma Rao was arrested on a fraud charge. He is the first prime minister in Indian history that is undergoing trial for corruption. A first in the subcontinent's legendary corrupt politics. Many consider it a landmark in the country's history. This development is being welcomed by the Indian public, which like its counterpart in Pakistan is also wary of political corruption in high places. The Supreme Court's move to wrest control of CBI in India was indeed smart. Why cannot the Supreme Court in Pakistan follow the example of its counterpart in India? In the current circumstances, we all know it cannot. That is precisely the point. The Supreme Court, even sitting at the apex of the judiciary, does not have the authority or the will to take such drastic action. That is a pity. The country must endeavor to strengthen the judiciary in comparison to the executive and only then accountability of officials and politicians be realized. There is a valid point in the argument that it is for the courts to punish officials for corruption in the normal way of doing things, meaning that due process of law cannot and should not be sacrificed at the alter of expediency or politics. It is an old maxim that justice should not only be done but seen to be done. This makes sense in our case also. Moreover, this is also an Islamic requirement. Selection of competent and high caliber judges on merit alone is a universal principle of good governance and an also a basic requirement of Islam. In addition, the Musharraf regime must remember that much better performance is expected from the military regime than shown so far. In reality, the overall performance of NAB has been less than spectacular. It is still possible for the Musharraf regime to make systematic improvements in the corruption crusade by systematically pursuing a practical strategy to improve integrity and accountability in the public service. The Musharraf regime must recall that public accountability is its very raison d'etre. It shall make or break with public perceptions regarding performance on this very score.

Chapter 4

ECONOMIC DECLINE, POVERTY INCREASE AND UNSUSTAINABLE DEVELOPMENT

Since independence, Pakistan has achieved an economic growth averaging about 5% annually. The country has shown impressive economic improvement from 1976 to 1986. Per capita income grew by an average of 3.46% per annum and the total GNP grew by an average of 6.50% per annum during the period. Pakistan has shown impressive economic improvement from 1976-77 to 1986 information through their committee. Per capita income grew by an average of 3.46% per annum and the total GNP grew by an average of 6.50% per annum during the same period. However, Pakistan was not included in the World Bank's category of "Highest-Growth Economies" which includes countries like Thailand, South Korea, China, Singapore, Chile and Malaysia. All these countries have a GNP per capita growth rate of at least 5.7% during the period 1985-1993.[1] During the last three years, India has shown remarkable economic growth at an average of 7% per year making it among the ten fastest growing economies in the world.[2] The GDP per capita of Pakistan was $430 in 1993, which rose to $460 by 1995. In comparison, the GDP of India in 1994 was $295 billion while the per capita GDP for the same year was $320.[3] Pakistan's GDP per head increased to $490 in 1998.[4] The real GNP per capita, after controlling for inflation, increased by only 125% during the 1950-97 period. This was because of the rapid increase in Pakistan's population from 43 million to 135 million in 1997. Today Pakistan is the seventh largest country in the world with a population size of 150 million and the size of it's economy is only Rs 4 trillion or $64 billion estimated on conventional terms. Real GDP calculated on the purchasing power parity basis is $237 billion. Given Pakistan's large population, the current per capita income is about $492 only. The GNP is also calculated on the preferred Purchasing Power Parity (PPP) basis. On the PPP basis, India's GNP in 1999 was over $ 2 trillion. While India ranked 153 in

---

[1] Russet & Starr, 355.

[2] *The Economist*, March 18, 1997, 29.

[3] *Global Economic Prospects and the Developing Countries 1996* (Washington, D.C.: World Bank, 1996), pp. 76-77.

[4] The World in 1998 (London: *The Economist* Intelligence Unit, 1997), 84.

the world, Pakistan's ranking was lower at 159. The following table ranks per capita income on the PPP basis:[5]

Country	Per Capita Income $ (PPP)
India	2,149
Iran	5,163
Honduras	2,254
Guatemala	3,517
Pakistan	1,757

Pakistan's economic growth rate in the last five years or so has been uneven. In 1995-96 real GDP growth rates at constant factor cost is a healthy 6.8%; in 1996-97, it decreased to only 1.9%; in 1997-98 it increased to 4.3%; in 1998-99 it again decreased to 3.1%. The target for 1999-2000 was 5%.[6] The actual growth rate in 1999-2000 was only 4.8%. Initially, the 2000-2001 year's target was 5%, which was later reduced to 4.5%. However, the actual growth was only 2.6%.[7] In comparison, the current growth rate of India is about 5%, for both China and Turkey about 8%, and Malaysia 6.5%.[8] During the last three years, India had shown remarkable economic growth at an average of 7% per year making it among the ten fastest growing economies in the world.[9] In comparison, Pakistan's record is poor. The following table compared Pakistan's economic performance with some other countries.[10]

The fundamentals of Pakistan's economy are very weak. Consider:

1. The size of Pakistan's economy is only about $62 billion. For the sake of comparison, the economy of India is over $450 billion.
2. The economic growth rate in Pakistan has decreased in the last few years. In the 1960s, it was 6.77% and in the 1980s, it was 6.45%. In the 1990s, it decreased to 4.59% only.[11] In March 2001, the GOP revised the GDP growth rate from 4.5% to 3.8% due to the prolonged drought situation. The actual growth rate was only 2.6% in 2000-2001. For the sake of comparison, the current GDP growth rates for the region are given below.[12]
3. The GOP (and the IMF) envisaged an economic growth of only 5.5% by 2002-3.[13]
4. Given the large population size, Pakistan's per capita income is about $400 only.
5. The black economy is estimated at about 50-75% of the actual economy.

[5] *Dawn*, May 28, 2001.
[6] See Annual Report of the State Bank of Pakistan, 1998-99 reprinted in *The News*, Dec. 20, 1999.
[7] See the Economic Survey 2000-2001, Government of Pakistan, Economic Affairs Division, June 2001, in *Pakistan Observer*, June 17, 2001, 1.
[8] "Bottomline", *Asiaweek*, April 20, 2001, 52.
[9] *The Economist*, March 18, 1997, 29. The figure for Pakistan cited from *The News*, Jan. 8, 2000.
[10] Ibid. pp. 79-86.
[11] Sultan Ahmed, "Higher growth or more taxes?" *Dawn*, Dec. 21, 2000.
[12] *Asiaweek*, April 20, 2001, 52.
[13] *Dawn*, July 26, 2000.

Country	GDP $ Billions	GDP per Capita
France	1,374	$23,910
Germany	2,159	$26,400
Italy	1,225	$21,380
Switzerland	246	$34,750
Turkey	186	$2,800
Canada	648	$21,220
USA	8,431	$31, 230
UK	1,317	$22,300
Australia	424	$21,380
China	1,098	$880
Hong Kong	195	$29, 890
India	412	$420
Indonesia	233	$1, 150
Japan	4,545	$35,906
Malaysia	87	$4,000
Philippines	87	$1,200
Singapore	101	$32, 020
Thailand	149	$2,400
Brazil	803	$4, 970
Egypt	93	$1,460
Israel	101	$16, 940
Saudi Arabia	148	$7, 470

Country	GDP Growth Rate (%)
India	6.0
Malaysia	6.5
Turkey	8.3
China	8.2
Indonesia	5.1

6. Foreign exchange reserves are at $2.85 billion only as of June 20, 2001[14]. India, in comparison, has reserves of over $40 billion and China about $150 billion.

7. More than 80% of the country's national revenue is spent on debt servicing and defense alone.[15] In the budget, Pakistan has to meet the foreign debt liability of $4.5 billion by end of the current fiscal year.

Tackle the very serious problem of debt expansion. In the year 2000-2001, debt servicing payments are projected to increase by 7.9% to Rs 4,1632 million or by 2.7% of GDP by end of June 2001.[16]The 2001-2002 budget an astronomical amount of Rs. 329.18 billion has been set aside for debt servicing, which is 40% of the total outlays of Rs 752 billion.[17]

---

[14] *PO,* June 20, 2001, 11.
[15] Zahid Hussein, *"A Nation of Tax Resisters",* op. cit., 23.
[16] See Economic Survey 2000-2001 (Islamabad: GOP, EAD, June 2001) in *PO,* June 17, 2001.
[17] See Budget 20001-20002 (Islamabad: GoP, Finance Division, June 2001) in *PO* June 19, 2001.

Poverty has doubled in the last decade or so. In fact, if the economy does not show significant improvement, overall poverty is projected to further increase in the current decade.

Spending on social services in Pakistan remains very low. Pakistan's Human Development Index ranking, as reported by the United Nations Human Development Report 2000, is a very low 135 out of 174 countries surveyed. For the sake of comparison, India is 128 on the international scale, China is 99, Sri Lanka is 84, and Myanmar is 125.[18] Recently, General Musharraf quoted the country's position as 138 among 174 poor countries.[19]

Exports remained stagnant at $8.5 billion for several years.[20] In 2000-2001, exports barely touched $ 9 billion only. Compare this with Singapore and Hong Kong that have exports of over $100 billion per annum.

A very low flow of Foreign Direct Investment (FDI) into the country. The FDI peaked in 1996 to $922 million and declined to $370 million in 1999.[21] Another report says that FDI amounted to around $600 million in 1999; the figure is based on the difference between the amount of FDI stocks in 1998 ($9.2 billion) and 1999 ($9.8 billion). However, this constituted 0.21 per cent of FDI global flows ($4.7 trillion). FDI stocks in Pakistan in 1999 represented 4.4 per cent of its GDP.

The two fundamental challenges faced by Pakistan are the severe debt crisis and the fiscal deficit problem.

THE DEBT CRISIS

Today, Pakistan is faced a debt crisis of an immense magnitude. The country is facing hardship in meeting international obligations like debt servicing. More than two-thirds of the budget is taken by debt servicing and defense expenditures. Why did this happen? The problem is that successive governments in the country had increasingly relied on borrowing from domestic as well as foreign sources. While the total amount of debt kept on steadily, increasingly successive governments seemed to be least bothered. No substantial plans are made to reduce them. Pakistan had now reached the stage where it needs loans to repay loans. Pakistan faces a debt crisis with no easy solution in sight. By 1995, the external debt situation had become very serious because it had enlarged to approximately half Pakistan's GNP. The situation if not corrected could spell disaster to Pakistan's fragile economy. See table below for a comparison. Only Indonesia and Egypt had higher figures while India, China, Turkey and Malaysia are below Pakistan. See table below:[22]

[18] *Khaleej Times* (daily), July 14, 2000.
[19] *Pakistan Observer*, Aug. 30, 2000.
[20] See "Bottom Line", *Asiaweek*, Nov. 17, 2000, 51 and *The Nation*, Nov. 27, 2000.
[21] *The News*- Business section, April 11, 2001.
[22] Source: *World Development Report, 1997*, pp.246-47 and *The Economist*, Nov. 27-Dec. 3, 1999, 99.

Country	External Debt as % of GNP (Year)		
	1980	1995	1999
India	11.9	28.2	20
Pakistan	42.4	49.5	52
China	2.2	17.2	15
Egypt	89.2	73.3	-
Indonesia	28.0	56.9	81
Turkey	27.4	44.1	50
Thailand	-	-	60
Philippines	-	-	60
Taiwan	-	-	9
Russia	-	-	88
Malaysia	28.0	42.6	50

Associated with the poverty issue is that of rapidly growing population. The World Bank estimates that Pakistan's population is currently growing at a rate of 3%, and is projected to double in the next two decades. The country's fertility rate is 65% higher than the average for all low-income countries. However, Pakistan made some progress in the area of human development from the early 1970s to early 1990s. Despite the progress, the country still lags far behind the average for low-income countries.[23] Pakistan's Human Development Index ranking, as reported by the United Nations Human Development Report 2000, is a very low 135 out of 174 countries surveyed.[24] The adult literacy rate of Pakistan is only 44% while that in India is 55%. The education enrolment ratio in Pakistan is only 43%, while that in India is 54%. The population with access to safe drinking water in Pakistan is 79% while that in India is 81%. There are 50 million adult illiterates in Pakistan today.[25] The poor in Pakistan continue to suffer. The astronomical rise in electricity charges, increase in postal rates, telephone, gas, etc. meant the disposable income of the people belonging to the lower and middle classes had been curtailed. The GOP had failed to tame inflation, which was running in the double digits. The net result was that the poor classes were worse off than before. The great tragedy with Pakistan is that the quality of life indicators like education, health and nutrition showed no development. Poverty remained prevalent. In reality, the poor became poorer. This confirms the observation that rapid growth in GNP and income does not guarantee a sufficient degree of fulfillment of the basic needs for everyone in the country.[26] The World Bank says that Pakistan's economic performance in the last two decades has been characterized by relatively fast GDP growth driven by an enterprising private sector, agriculture and cotton-based manufacturing. In 1988, the country began to reorganize its social and economic policies to promote private sector investment, energize public finances and improve its extremely poor social indicators. Though structural reforms

---

[23] *Dawn*, Feb. 5, 1996.

[24] *Khaleej Times* (daily), July 14, 2000.

[25] Figures are from UNDP's Human Development Report, 2000, in *Dawn* Jan. 8, 2001.

[26] K. Balasubramaniam, "Privatization of Health and Its Impact on the People of South Asia", *Dominance of the West Over the Rest* (Penang, Malaysia: Just World Trust, 1995), 170-71.

have been mixed, Pakistan made important advances in privatization and in attracting private investment in the energy sector.[27]

Clearly, the country's debt crisis had reached an alarming stage. This could and should not be allowed to continue. Pakistan's position is better understood when compared with others. The external debt figures of several countries for 1995 are given below:[28]

Country	Total External Debt (billion $), 1980	Total External Debt, (billion, $), 1995
India	20.5	93.7
Pakistan	9.9	30.1
China	4.5	118.0
Egypt	19.1	34.1
Indonesia	20.9	107.8
Turkey	19.1	73.5
Malaysia	6.6	34.3

By 1996, the country's total debt, both foreign and domestic, amounted to $51 billion. This figure was now equivalent to 90% of GDP, or over six times total revenues from exports in 1985.[29] Pakistan's foreign debt was $26.1 billion in 1996. By September 1997, the foreign debt of Pakistan was reported to have reached $39 billion. By 1997, the total debt outstanding was close to 88% of GDP. Of the total debt about $28 billion, some 46%, was foreign and $24 billion domestic.[30] By fiscal 1996-97, the total debt had risen to Rs 780 billion and foreign debt, expressed as percentage of GDP, was then above 44%. The figure rose to 48% in 1997-98.[31] Pakistan's total domestic debt rose from Rs 58 billion in fiscal 1980-81 to Rs 381 billion in fiscal 1989-90. In 1995-96, domestic debt expressed as percentage of GDP was 42%, which by 1998-99, had increased to 45% of GDP.[32] By end of June 1998, the foreign debt of Pakistan had reached $22.6 billion, which further increased to $23.1 billion by end of June 1999. Pakistan's total outstanding external debt had increased to $30.3 billion at the end of June 1999 indicating a rise of $1.65 billion or 5.7% during 1998-99. At this level, the debt constituted nearly 52% of the country's GDP.[33] In June 1999, debt service payments were almost 1.5 times the size of the country's foreign exchange reserves.[34] More importantly, Pakistan had already technically defaulted when the Nawaz Government had frozen $11 billion in local foreign exchange accounts on the night of May 28, 1998 to prevent a dollar run on the banks. This GOP action led to a public outcry then. The action is commonly regarded as

[27] *Dawn*, Dec. 5, 1996.
[28] Source: *World Development Report, 1997*, pp.246-47. For Pakistan's 1999 figure severe Eastern Economic Review-*Asia 1999 Yearbook*, 179.
[29] *The Nation*, Dec. 22, 1996.
[30] *Dawn*, March 17, 1997.
[31] Ibid.
[32] Ibid.
[33] *The Nation*, Dec. 20, 1999 and *The News*, Jan. 8, 2000.
[34] *The News*, Jan. 8, 2000.

responsible for the shattering of business and investor confidence.[35] The State Bank of Pakistan had later openly criticized the Nawaz Government for this action. Foreign exchange reserves stood at $1.4 billion on May 16, 1998 decreased to $930 million in June to $500 million by August 1998. In November 1998, they had decreased to the lowest level of $410 million only.[36] In 1998-99, the total national debt increased by Rs 441.9 billion (7.8%) to Rs 2,927 billion. The debt that was 90.8% of GDP as on June 30, 1998 climbed to 96.7% as on June 30, 1999.

By 1995, the external debt situation had become very serious because it had enlarged to approximately half Pakistan's GNP. The situation if not corrected could spell disaster to Pakistan's fragile economy. The GOP has sought support from its creditors through the Pakistan Development Forum to implement an ambitious reform agenda to deal with its fundamental structural problems. A number of initiatives are being planned. The GOP seeks new soft loans of about $6 billion to come out of its debt crisis.[37] Pakistan is faced with a serious debt crisis. The total external debt of Pakistan is now 54% of GDP.[38] The 1999-2000 budget total expenditure outlay is Rs 526 billion out of which Rs 287 went for debt servicing alone. Nearly 56% of the budget is going to debt servicing alone.[39] Thus, Pakistan is caught in a vicious debt quagmire from where there seems little hope of escape. Luckily, debt-servicing payments declined from $4.7 billion in 1997-98 to $2.6 billion in 1998-99. The significant decline was due to the re-scheduling of payments of $2.89 billion by December 13, 1999. This was part of an exceptional financial arrangement, which Pakistan has negotiated with the IMF in January 1999. It has been decided by the Paris Club creditors to re-schedule $3 billion to give Pakistan some breathing space till the end of December 2000. Pakistan's financing gap in 1999-2000 has been estimated as $5.4 billion, which has been fully covered by these exceptional financing arrangements.[40] Meanwhile, the country was facing possible default by the end of 2000. The IMF bailed out Pakistan through a $596 million facility package. The breather qualified Pakistan to secure loans from other multilateral agencies such as the Asian Development Bank and a rescheduling of loans of about $1.6 billion from the London Club, which was due in February 2001. The IMF set strict conditionality for its assistance that includes: devaluation, broadening the tax base, and strengthening tax administration.[41] The GOP has to meet the foreign debt liability of $4.5 billion by end of June 2001.[42] The Musharraf regime claims that it is determined to tackle the economic crisis in a systematic manner and turn around the economy as quickly as possible. Recently, General Musharraf claimed that:[43]

---

[35] Far Eastern Economic Review-*Asia 1999 Yearbook*, 179.
[36] See State Bank Report, *The News*, Dec. 14, 1999.
[37] *Pakistan Observer*, March 14, 2001.
[38] *Dawn*, Jan 8, 2001.
[39] *The News*, Jan. 8, 2000.
[40] *The News*, Dec. 13, 1999.
[41] Pakistan & Gulf Economist, Dec. 11-17, 2000, 27.
[42] *The News*, Sept. 4, 2000.
[43] *Pakistan Observer*, June 8, 2001, 11.

The country has established very strong credentials with the donors. "They now think that we are no longer a one tranche country. We are no longer accused of faking and fudging".... (Explaining the fiscal problems emanating from debt servicing)... "After debt-servicing, defense, and establishment cost, we have no money left. Therefore, I say it is a question of survival, where prudence dictates not to borrow, realities dictate otherwise. It is a catch 22 situation. It is a dilemma. To overcome these problems we need breathing space from debt-servicing and in this space, work towards the revival of the economy...hope that Pakistan would get the breathing space through the Poverty Reduction Growth Facility (PRGF) and it will then be up to us how best we utilize the breathing space. In these 3-5 years we need to register growth, increase our GDP, increase exports, privatize, increase revenues – these are the for acts we have to perform.

Meanwhile, Pakistan was faced with a critical debt-servicing problem. In 1996, foreign debt as percentage of GDP had already crossed 87% of GDP.[44] The debt servicing liability had also increased accordingly from $1.70 billion in 1992-93 to $2.44 billion in 1997-98 showing an annual compound rate of 7.4%.[45] In fiscal 1996-97, debt servicing consumed Rs 198 billion, rising to Rs 248 billion in fiscal 1997-98. This entailed an increase of 24.9%. Debt servicing alone had eaten up 54% of expenditures in fiscal 1997-98, and another 29% had gone to defense. Taken together, defense and debt servicing, had swallowed 83% of the budget outlay.[46] The 1999-2000 budget total expenditure outlay was Rs 526 billion out of which Rs 287 billion went for debt servicing alone. Thus, nearly 56% of the budget went to debt servicing alone.[47] The external debt as percentage of exports had risen from 1980 instead of decreasing like in Turkey and Malaysia. See the table below for comparison of Pakistan's position with that of some other countries:[48]

Country	External Debt as % of Exports of Goods & Services	
	1980	1995
India	136.0	201.2
Pakistan	208.7	257.9
China	---	77.3
Egypt	207.7	208.1
Indonesia	---	202.9
Turkey	333.1	177.8
Malaysia	44.6	40.8

The foreign debt figures for various countries in 1997 are given in the table below: [49]

---

[44] Figures taken from the *Annual Report of the State Bank of Pakistan*, 1998-99.
[45] *Memorandum For the Pakistan development Forum 1999-2000* (Planning Commission, Government of Pakistan, April 1999), 3.
[46] Hasan Iqbal Jafri, "Sink or Swim?" *The Herald*, (monthly) July 1997, 136.
[47] *The News*, Jan. 8, 2000.
[48] Source: *World Development Report, 1997*, pp. 246-47.
[49] *The Economist*, Mar. 18, 1997.

Country	Total Foreign Debt (billion $)
USA	681
Japan	Zero
Saudi Arabia	16
Malaysia	27
Iran	21
Egypt	41
Pakistan	38

Today, Pakistan's external debt is about $38 billion. Eleven years ago, it was only about $14 billion. Today debt servicing alone consumes about 33% of the state expenditures.[50] The GOP has sought support from its creditors through the Pakistan Development Forum to implement an ambitious reform agenda to deal with its fundamental structural problems. A number of initiatives are being planned. The GOP seeks new soft loans of about $6 billion to come out of its debt crisis.[51] Pakistan is faced with a serious debt crisis. The total external debt of Pakistan is now 54% of GDP.[52] Pakistan is caught in a vicious debt quagmire from where there seems little hope of escape. The 1999-2000 budget total expenditure outlay is Rs 526 billion out of which Rs 287 went for debt servicing alone. Thus, nearly 56% of the budget is going to debt servicing.[53] Luckily, debt-servicing payments declined from $4.7 billion in 1997-98 to $2.6 billion in 1998-99. The significant decline was due to the re-scheduling of payments of $2.89 billion by December 13, 1999. This was part of an exceptional financial arrangement, which Pakistan has negotiated with the IMF in January 1999. It has been decided by the Paris Club creditors to re-schedule $3 billion to give Pakistan some breathing space till the end of December 2000. Pakistan's financing gap in 1999-2000 has been estimated as $5.4 billion, which has been fully covered by these exceptional financing arrangements.[54] Meanwhile, the country was facing possible default by the end of 2000. The IMF bailed out Pakistan through a $ 596 million facility package. The breather qualified Pakistan to secure loans from other multilateral agencies such as the Asian Development Bank and a rescheduling of loans of about $1.6 billion from the London Club, which is due in February 2001. The IMF set strict conditionality for its assistance that includes: devaluation, broadening the tax base, and strengthening tax administration.[55] The GOP has to meet the foreign debt liability of $4.5 billion by end of the current fiscal year.[56] Tax revenues were to grow by 15.4% from Rs 363 billion in 1997-98 to Rs 418 billion in 1998-99.[57] The previous Government's reform measures, like sharp decreases in tax rates, failed to address the greater problems of the economy of

---

[50] *The News* International, April 11, 2001.
[51] *Pakistan Observer*, March 14, 2001.
[52] *Dawn*, Jan 8, 2001.
[53] *The News*, Jan. 8, 2000.
[54] *The News*, Dec. 13, 1999.
[55] *Pakistan & Gulf Economist*, Dec. 11-17, 2000, 27.
[56] *The News*, Sept. 4, 2000.
[57] *Memorandum For the Pakistan Development Forum, 1999-2000*. Op. Cit., 18.

Pakistan like increasing tax revenue.[58] Pakistan is faced with a serious debt crisis. The total external debt of Pakistan is now 54% of GDP.[59] Today, 57% of the budget goes into debt servicing. Pakistan's financing gap in 1999-2000 of $5.4 billion had been fully covered by these exceptional financing arrangements.[60] The IMF bailed out Pakistan through a $ 596 million facility package. The breather qualified Pakistan to secure loans from other multilateral agencies such as the Asian Development Bank and a rescheduling of loans of about $1.6 billion from the London Club, which is due in February 2001. The IMF set strict conditionality for its assistance that includes: devaluation, broadening the tax base, and strengthening tax administration.[61] The GOP has to meet the foreign debt liability of $4.5 billion by end of the current fiscal year.[62]

The Economic Survey 2000-2001, the most reliable government document in such matters, states that total public debt grew from Rs 155 billion in 1980 to Rs 802 billion in 1990 and jumped to Rs 3.19 trillion by mid 2000. In other words, the public debt grew at an average rate of 16% per annum over the last two decades. Consequently, the public debt burden increased from 66% of GDP in 1980 to almost 100% by mid 2000. The outstanding figure for public debt was roughly 400% of government revenue in 1980 but increased to 624% by mid 2000.[63]

A significant problem with Pakistan's economy is that a substantial portion of the loans the country receives is consumed by debt servicing and the share of net transfers had been on the decline over the years. Net transfer is the actual money in the hands of the government after the agreed installments of principle and interest on the debt had been serviced. The share of net transfers, out of gross disbursements, had been reduced significantly over the years. This meant that only a small amount is left over for the purposes of development. This situation spells disaster. All past governments are at fault. Pakistan needs to reduce its external debt burden from the current $38 billion to a more manageable level. Pakistan had to export significantly more. The current budget 2001-2002 has allocated debt-servicing figure as Rs 329.2 billion, which is 40% of current expenditures at Rs 621.7 billion. This is the biggest item in current expenditure. The next biggest expenditure is that of defense at Rs 131.6 billion, and the third biggest item is that of running the civil government, which is Rs 80.6 billion. Together the three biggest items add up to a colossal Rs 541.4 billion [64]

In fiscal 1999-2000, total revenue receipts were projected at Rs 356 billion. Against this, debt servicing swallowed up Rs 287 billion and defense Rs 142 billion. The total added up to Rs 429 billion. Revenue fell short by Rs 73 billion in funding just these two expenditures. Meeting other expenditures like running the government and development meant further public debts. Added together, debt servicing and defense expenditures exceed Pakistan's total national income.

[58] *The Economist*, Sep. 13, 1997.
[59] *Dawn*, Jan 8, 2001.
[60] *The News*, Dec. 13, 1999.
[61] *Pakistan & Gulf Economist*, Dec. 11-17, 2000, 27.
[62] *The News*, Sept. 4, 2000.
[63] See Economic Survey, 2000-2001 (Islamabad: GOP, June 2001), in *Pakistan Observer*, June 17, 2001.

FISCAL DEFICIT CRISIS

As elsewhere, Pakistan's federal budget has also increased considerably over the decades. In the case of Pakistan, the federal budget has also increased considerably over the decades. The figure for fiscal 1992-93 was Rs. 292 billion. In 1993, the GNP of Pakistan was \$43.3 billion and the budget expenditure totaled \$8.3 billion.[65] The state budget being 19.16% of GNP in that year. In 1995, the federal budget increased to Rs. 434.7 billion. In the fiscal year of 1996-97, the federal budget totaled Rs 500.2 billion. It has since been reduced. In the 1998-99 budget of Rs. 500.2 billion government revenues are projected to rise from Rs. 452.2 billion (16.3% of GDP) in 1997-98 to Rs. 522.9 billion (16.8% of GDP). Government expenditure rose from Rs 599.6 billion in 1997-98 to Rs 666.1 billion in 1998-99. It further increased to about Rs 698 billion in 1999-2000. The budget for the year 2001-2002 is Rs 752 billion, up by Rs 54 billion from last year.[66]

Added together, debt servicing and defense expenditures exceed Pakistan's total national income. Tax revenues in 1996-1997 amounted to Rs 268 billion; in 1997-1998, which increased to Rs 286 billion, and further increased to Rs 380 billion in 1998-99. In 1999-2000, the revenue increased further to Rs 351.6 billion. The 2000-2001 fiscal year's target for tax collection by the Central Board of Revenue (CBR) was Rs 417 billion, out of which only Rs 277 billion has been collected in the first three quarters of the fiscal year. By the fiscal year's end (June 2001) only Rs 390 had been collected. The CBR had once again missed its given target. The fiscal situation has become very difficult in Pakistan. In fiscal year 2000-2001, the fiscal deficit decreased to 5.3% of GDP from 6.5% of GDP in fiscal 1999-2000. In monetary terms, the figure had declined from Rs 206.8 billion in the 1999-2000 fiscal year to Rs. 185.7 billion in fiscal year 2000-2001. This was the lowest fiscal deficit in the past 18 years.[67] Public deficits had reached a point where interest payments on debt, around 33% of current government expenditures, were impinging on the provision of needed public services and development expenditures.[68]

The Musharraf regime had pledged to reduce the budget deficit. In order to reduce the budget deficit further, the military regime wanted to raise additional billions in taxes. Revenue. The problem is that Pakistan's gross revenue and taxes, as percentage of GDP, was comparatively very low. In fiscal year 1992-93 and 1993-94, the gross revenue, as percentage of GDP, was 18.6%, which decreased in 1994-95 to 17.4%, and in 1995-96, it slightly increased to 17.6%. In 1996-97, the figure rose to 18.2% but again decreased to 16.3% in 1997-98. In 1998-99, gross revenue and taxes as percentage of GDP rose slightly to 16.8%. What was Pakistan's position as regards the tax/GDP ratio in

---

[64] See Budget 2001-2002 (Islamabad: Government of Pakistan, Finance Division, June 2001) in *Pakistan Observer*, June 19, 2001.

[65] "Basic Facts", *Contemporary Issues in Pakistan*, Saeed Shafqat, ed., (Lahore: Gautam Publishers, 1995), 11.

[66] See Budget 20001-2002 (Islamabad: Government of Pakistan, Finance Division, June 2001) on *Pakistan Observer*, June 17, 2001.

[67] See Economic Survey of Pakistan (Islamabad: Government of Pakistan, Economic Affairs Division, June 2001) on *Pakistan Observer*, June 17, 2001.

comparison with similarly situated developing countries? The figure was given as around 18-20%. In the decade of the 1980s, the tax/GDP ratio averaged 13.4%. In fiscal year 1992-93, tax as percentage of GDP was only 13.0%, in 1993-94 up slightly to 13.2. It remained at this level in 1994-95 and in 1995-96 increased to 14.5%, then decreased to 13.1% in 1997-98. It increased slightly in 1998-99 to 13.5%. The revenue-GDP ratio had declined from 18.6% to 17.6% in 1995-96. During the entire 1990s, the ratio was 13.8% only.

Fiscal Year	Gross Revenue as Percentage of GDP
1992-93	18.6
1993-94	18.6
1994-95	17.4
1995-96	17.6

(Government of Pakistan, Finance Division)

Fiscal Year	Tax as Percentage of GDP
1992-93	13.0
1993-94	13.2
1994-95	13.2
1995-96	13.2
1996-97	14.5

(Government of Pakistan, Finance Division)

The problem in Pakistan is that gross revenue and taxes as percentage of GDP are very low. The tax to GDP ratio has remained stagnant in the range of 11 to 14% over the last two decades. The current tax to GDP ratio is low at 15%, which is one of the lowest in the developing world. The tax/GDP ratio in similar developing countries, as regards the stage of development, is 18-20. Obviously, this needs to be improved.

In 2000-2001, fiscal year total tax revenue collected was Rs 390 billion, reflecting an increase of Rs 43 billion as compared to 1999-2000. The current years target has been set as Rs 457 billion.[69] The Musharraf regime has pledged to reduce the budget deficit. More than 80% of the country's national revenue is spent on debt servicing and defense alone.[70] The defense spending in 2000-2001 was Rs 170 billion. The GOP figures show a lower defense spending simply because the amount of military pensions, at least Rs 26 billion, has been shifted to the civilian category.

The budgetary deficit as percentage of GDP is 3.3% in 1999-2000 slightly down from 3.4% in 1998-99. The deficit had hit a high of 5.6% of GDP in 1997-98, and still higher 6.4% in 1996-97.[71] The budgetary target for fiscal year 2000-2001 was set at 5.3% of GDP, which was met. Earlier, the GOP had made a commitment with IMF to contain

---

[68] *The News-* Business section, April 11, 2001.

[69] *Pakistan Observer*, July 8, 2001, 12.

[70] Zahid Hussein, "*A Nation of Tax Resisters*", op. cit., 23.

[71] Figures taken from the Annual Report of the State Bank of Pakistan, 1998-99 reported in *The Nation*, December 20, 1999.

the budget deficit within this limit. Previously, it had been lowered from 7-8% to 6.5% of GDP (Rs 206.8 billion) in 1999-2000.[72]

Successive governments in Pakistan, including the present military regime, have increasingly relied on borrowing from domestic as well as foreign sources. While the total amount of debt kept on steadily, increasing successive governments seemed to be least bothered. No substantial plans were made to reduce them. Pakistan has now reached the stage where it needs loans to repay loans. The GoP's reform measures, like sharp decreases in tax rates, were welcomed but failed to address the greater problems of the economy of Pakistan like increasing tax revenue.

In the current 2001-2002 budget net revenue receipts is estimated as Rs 453.8 billion, which indicate an increase of 16.9% over the revised estimates for fiscal 2000-2001, and an increase of 10.1% over the original budget estimates for fiscal 2000-2001.[73] The problem is that successive governments in Pakistan, including the present military regime, have increasingly relied on borrowing from domestic as well as foreign sources. While the total amount of debt kept on steadily, increasing successive governments seemed to be least bothered. No substantial plans were made to reduce them. Pakistan has now reached the stage where it needs loans to repay loans. The GoP's reform measures, like sharp decreases in tax rates, were welcomed but failed to address the greater problems of the economy of Pakistan like increasing tax revenue. The tax system of the country suffers from several endemic problems. Firstly, the tax base of the country remains very small. The total taxpayers in the country are only 1.9 million.[74] Secondly, the CBR is notoriously corrupt. Thirdly, the tax laws are cumbersome to follow. Fourthly, Pakistan's gross revenue and taxes, as percentage of GDP, are comparatively very low. The tax/GDP ratio was 13.8% only. Finally, Pakistan has been living well beyond its means. Successive governments in Pakistan, including the present military regime, have increasingly relied on borrowing from domestic as well as foreign sources. Pakistan has now reached the stage where it needs loans to repay loans. Added together, debt servicing and defense expenditures exceed Pakistan's total national income. While the total amount of debt kept on steadily, increasingly successive governments seemed to be least bothered. No substantial plans are made to reduce them. Pakistan had now reached the stage where it needs loans to repay loans. Pakistan faces a debt crisis with no easy solution in sight. The Musharraf regime is expected to better in the area. In order to reduce the budget deficit further, the Musharraf regime will have to raise additional billions in taxes.

In April 2001, General Musharraf said that Pakistan would be approaching the World Bank to seek rescheduling of its outstanding loans to get some "breathing space" for at least three years, and spare funds for development. He said that in three to four years, Pakistan would be able to meet its debt servicing liability and get out of the debt trap. All resources were consumed by debt servicing and defense, leaving little for development. General Musharraf stated that no development project could be launched without getting

---

[72] See Economic Survey 2000-20001 (Islamabad: GOP, June 2001) in *Pakistan Observer*, June 17, 2001, 1.

[73] See Budget 2001-2002 (Islamabad: Government of Pakistan, Finance Division, June 2001) in *Pakistan Observer*, June 19, 2001, 1.

more foreign loans and more loans meant adding to the already huge debt burden. Describing it as a catch-22 situation, General Musharraf said that the approach about foreign loans needed to change to rid Pakistan of the burden of loans and initiate development activities. The solution lay in economic revival that would be possible only with augmented emphasis on promotion of IT and agriculture.[75] Many independent observers doubt the claims of General Musharraf and question his ability to pull Pakistan out the economic crisis.

THE MUSHARRAF REGIME'S ECONOMIC REFORM AGENDA

At the very beginning, the crisis and economic slowdown was acknowledged by the Musharraf regime. Shaukat Aziz, the Finance Minister, said in December 1999 that there is "no easy exit from the existing economic quagmire".[76] Soon after coming to power, the Musharraf regime quickly announced a broad-based economic revival strategy to tackle the fundamental problems. It seems to be determined to move swiftly ahead at reforming the political economy. The primary components of the economic crisis in the country's economy were described as economic slowdown, rising debt, and fiscal deficit.

General Musharraf vowed to make all out efforts to improve the deteriorating economic conditions in order to eradicate poverty and hunger in the country.[77] In December 1999, the State Bank of Pakistan warned that the "sluggish" growth in economy activity witnessed in 1998-99 continued and that Pakistan could "postpone the solution of these problems at a great risk". If left "unattended" they could "become yet another constraint on the development effort".[78] The central bank emphasized the need to have policies that could facilitate an economic turn around, in terms of improved trade position, better savings, increased investment, and more production. The bank defined essential problem areas where urgent action is needed as:[79] (1) Build investor confidence; (2) Structural change in fiscal policy; (3) Reduction in budget deficit to more sustainable level; (4) Address the national debt servicing issue; (5) Improve exports; (6) Population control; and (7) Improve human capital.[80] Meanwhile, there is a very low flow of Foreign Direct Investment (FDI) into the country. The FDI peaked in 1996 to $922 million and declined to $370 million in 1999.[81] Another report says that FDI amounted to around $600 million in 1999; the figure is based on the difference between the amount of FDI stocks in 1998 ($9.2 billion) and 1999 ($9.8 billion). However, this constituted 0.21 per cent of FDI global flows ($4.7 trillion). FDI stocks in Pakistan in 1999 represented 4.4 per cent of its GDP. Experts agree that Pakistan can increase FDI inflows only if its

[74] *The Economist*, Sep. 13, 1997.
[75] *Dawn*, April 20, 2001.
[76] *The News* International, Dec. 17, 1999.
[77] Ibid.
[78] See State Bank of Pakistan report in *The News*, Dec. 14, 1999.
[79] Ibid.
[80] *Pakistan Observer*, March 14, 2001.
[81] *The News*- Business section, April 11, 2001.

policy of offering incentives is consistent with its macro-economic policy, taxation framework, a consistent investment policy, besides establishing a framework for property rights and dispute settlement. The military regime desired to quickly revive the economy. The military regime wanted a quick economic turnaround. For the purpose, a number of strategic measures were planned. For the purpose, the Planning Commission is working on a 2025 Plan broken up into segments that of five, ten, fifteen, twenty and twenty five years. Future Five Year Plans shall be integrated in the 2025 Plan. Recognition that fiscal discipline, scientific mechanisms for checks and monitoring and judicious control over all state spending is a basic requirement of good governance in the financial area. The regime wanted to rebuild investor confidence shattered by past actions. The Musharraf regime believed in pursuing policies consistently and not changes them as frequently as done in the past. Good governance is the main requirement for rebuilding the lost confidence. Therefore, more emphasis shall be placed in this area. The GoP plans to take steps to curtail the black economy. It believes that it can be eliminated by strict enforcement of existing laws, rooting out corruption in the CBR, and gradual introduction of modern taxation methods. Critics argued that not enough had been done. The Musharraf regime should prioritize the greater documentation of the economy. Effective internal controls and a system of incentives and rewards are gradually improving the working of the taxation system. Ensure taxation officials did not harass taxpayers. Critics also argued that not enough steps had been taken to deregulate the economy. Economic measures enhancing deregulation and privatization can help control corruption in the country. In general, any reform measures that increases competitiveness in the economy is reducing incentives for corrupt behavior. A monopoly service-provider or business enterprise gives no choice or an alternative for the consumers to exercise. It is not surprising that WAPDA and Pakistan Railways being monopolies are highly corrupt institutions. The entry of private power producers in the game should and had changed the situation. Likewise, PTCL (Telephone Company) is a state monopoly and therefore corruption incidence is high. With the telecommunications market opening up, and the entry of private service providers, choices had increased. Thus, the monopoly of PTCL is being dented and if this continues, surely corruption in PTCL could only decrease. The Musharraf regime should therefore break such giant monopolies and foster deregulation. It should accelerate the program of privatization of state assets. The entire privatization process is completely transparent, open and above board. The proceeds of privatization were to be spent on debt retirement purposes only. To the credit of the military regime, it had already taken initiatives in the direction of serious reform. This agenda was composed of the following objectives:[82]

- Reduction in mark-up (interest rates) by 2%.
- Another amnesty for undeclared assets. The purpose was to bring about an early elimination of the underground economy.
- A very serious effort to end endemic corruption in the country.

---

[82] See *The Nation*, Dec. 17, 1999 and *The News*, Dec. 13 & 17, 1999.

- Increase the revenue collection by broadening the tax base. Carrying out a systematic program to revamp and improve the taxation system is being implemented.
- The imposition of income tax on agriculture and General Sales Tax (GST) at the retail level
- Steps to ensure greater documentation of the economy, effective internal controls and a system of incentives and rewards to gradually improve the working of the taxation system
- Eradicate the confusion and complexity in tax payment. The Finance Minister had said that federal taxes will be cut from the current more than two dozen heads to just three heads (income, sales and customs).[83] Earlier, government announced measures to reduce 22 provincial taxes to just seven.
- Delinquent taxpayers are being hauled up in the newly set up Accountability Courts. They should face jail sentences for not paying state taxes.
- Steps to curtail the black economy estimated at about 50-75% of the actual economy (estimate Rs 3 trillion). For the first time in history, the Army is going to be involved in denting the huge black economy in Pakistan. The GOP believed that it could eliminate the black economy by strict enforcement of existing laws, rooting out corruption in the CBR, and gradual introduction of modern taxation methods.
- Modernization of the system by strengthening the IT system, and planned integration of all the tax records into a unique Common Tax Identification Number. It had already developed the system but it needs further modernization and refinement. Introduce better management practices. The discretionary powers of the CBR officials are to be curtailed. Powers are to being defined clearly. Relaxation of rules is too common in the past. Such unwarranted behavior of officials had now halted. The abuse of the SRO system in granting undue concessions will be further curtailed.
- Steps to broaden the tax base, reduce the number of taxes, slash their rates, bring tax delinquents to book and induct the Army to undertake the documentation of the economy. The GOP had taken steps to strengthen the IT system, and planned gradual integration of all the tax records. It also planned to introduce better management practices. The discretionary powers of the CBR officials are to be curtailed and powers are to being defined clearly.
- Strengthen the financial and fiscal systems, create a favorable investment climate to attract foreign investment, and improve resource allocation mechanisms. Financial sector reform is already in progress, and included giving greater autonomy and powers to the State Bank of Pakistan and the Corporate Law Authority, better monitoring and regulation of the banking sector by both the State Bank of Pakistan and the Finance Ministry, the strengthening of stock exchange regulatory mechanisms, better devices to mobilize savings by the

---

[83] *Dawn*, February 25, 2000.

institution of mandatory pension schemes, and the increase of government savings through overall stringency measures pertaining to budgetary expenditure.

- Tackle the twin problems of debt expansion and current account imbalance by simultaneously taking three measures: (i) generate additional export surplus in the manufacturing and agriculture sectors; (ii) attract foreign direct investment (FDI) as well as domestic investment; (iii) privatize public sector enterprises like KESC, WAPDA, SNGPL, Pakistan Railways, Pakistan Steel, etc. which had been in the red for a long time.
- Greater emphasis on poverty alleviation and provision of relief to the poorer sections of society.
- Stress on the promotion of small and medium industries.
- Establishment of a new micro-credit bank of the famous Grameen type to be called the Khushali Bank.
- Seeking new soft loans of about $6 billion to come out of its debt crisis.

The agenda has received wide public support and there is enthusiasm that the economy is on the road to recovery. However, some skeptic observers point out that, given the capacity of the military regime, the implementation of the new agenda remains problematic. The question is why has Pakistan's economic performance remained poor. What is the reason for the slow growth? Most importantly, why has the state failed to deliver? The answer is complex and beyond the scope of the present essay. However, policy makers agreed on a number of primary reasons: political instability, poor governance, corruption, and lack of consistent state policies.[84] The Asian Development Bank, in particular, has linked offer of soft loans to good governance practices in the decision-making mechanisms of the GOP. Delays occur and projects are not properly implemented because of such bad practices, says the ADB.[85] In a recent visit to Pakistan, some senior World Bank officials had called for a speedier implementation of the GOP's structural reforms program. The World Bank has also asked for the "building internal as well as external support for reforms through more thorough and sustained communication both at home and abroad".[86]

The World Bank said that Pakistan's economic performance in the last two decades had been characterized by relatively fast GDP growth driven by an enterprising private sector, agriculture and cotton-based manufacturing. In 1988, the country began to reorganize its social and economic policies to promote private sector investment, energize public finances and improve its extremely poor social indicators. Pakistan made important advances in privatization and in attracting private investment in the energy sector.[87] While it is true that the country had experienced continuous growth of the economy, it is also true that it suffers from gross inequitable distribution of wealth.

---

[84] *Dawn*, April 1, 2001.
[85] *Dawn*, Mar. 28, 2001.
[86] *Dawn*, Mar. 27, 2001.
[87] *Dawn*, Dec. 5, 1996.

Available data indicates that the iniquity in the income distribution is getting worse.[88] The Musharraf regime must bring about real change for the better for the people of Pakistan. The continuation of past practices and usual status quo politics will be a disaster for the nation. The nation must believe in the establishment of an egalitarian Islamic order.

In addition, the Musharraf regime should cut defense spending to release money for other vital areas like removing poverty and stopping environmental degradation. Defense spending consumes 6% of Pakistan's GNP and is 125% of social spending on health and education. The proponents of heavy defense spending in Pakistan have considerable influence. Given Pakistan's enmity with India over the Kashmir dispute, this pressure for higher defense spending is formidable. In addition, the military government itself has a stake in greater military spending. The cost of military spending in terms of human development is very high. Ajay Singh argues, "The quest for military superiority has escalated into a dangerous, and expensive race in one of the world's poorest regions". More money spent upon defense is not equivalent to better national security. The Pakistani military, like any other in the world, will always try its best to protect its allocations. Pakistan being one of the poorest countries of the world, as regards social well-being, cannot afford a big military. Previous civilian governments had shamelessly followed a policy of appeasement of the politically powerful Army interests. A fundamental change of direction is needed in Pakistan. The defense spending should be cut and savings realized should be transferred to education and health development. The social sector needs to be emphasized along with that of national security. Hunger, poor health and illiteracy pose an internal threat to the security of the nation and cannot be ignored by the military regime. The public, we ardently believe, must call for a bigger defense cut. It needs to be pointed out that bigger state spending does not automatically mean better defense. Anecdotal evidence suggests that allocated money is wasted in the defense sector. The privileged and indulgent lifestyle of the military brass must also end with that of its civilian counterpart. After all, there is nothing special about the military in Pakistan. However, the people in Pakistan are afraid to criticize the military rulers. Pakistanis do not have any protection from human rights abuses and arbitrary action of the military regime currently ruling the country. We continue to believe that one of the basic principles of democracy is the establishment of civilian supremacy over the military and that this principle be constituted in Pakistan at the earliest. Military rule is a very sensitive subject on which few people would like to express themselves. The reasons are obvious.

---

[88] Ibid. 171.

REFORM AGENDA: THE AGRICULTURE SECTOR

Pakistan's economy is heavily dependent upon agriculture, which accounts for 25% of its GNP and employs nearly three-quarters of the country's population. In the recent past, the greatest segment of economic growth has come from the agriculture sector. Pakistan's economy is heavily dependent upon it. Agriculture accounts for nearly 25% of its GNP and employs nearly three-quarters of the country's population. Wheat is the main food crop, followed by rice, millet, maize, barley and pulses. Cotton is by far the most important cash crop and accounts for employment of five percent of population. High quality Basmati rice is also a major export. Other crops include sugar cane, oil seeds (mustard, rape, sesame, linseed and castor), and tobacco, fruit, vegetables, chilies and fodder crops. In the recent past, the greatest segment of economic growth has come from the agriculture sector. Given the great significance of agriculture, the GOP has focused on sustained agriculture growth as one of the most vital segments of its economic revival strategy. The GOP is evolving a strategy to increase the production of five major crops including tea, edible oil, wheat, cotton and rice. For the first time in history, Pakistan exported wheat last year. Chief Executive, General Musharraf said that since rice and cotton are major crops for earning foreign exchange their production should be increased in the country. He said that the country wanted to save $700-$800 million through import substitution by local cultivating of tea. Pakistan spends about $1.5 billion on import of edible oils and tea alone. Therefore, the GOP is emphasizing the production of these five crops so to save foreign exchange.[89]

In the recent past, the greatest segment of economic growth has come from the agriculture sector. Notwithstanding government claims, the sector has been neglected. The agriculture sector is suffering because of an unprecedented drought situation in the country. For the first time in many years, the agriculture sector has registered a decline. The agriculture sector is suffering because of an unprecedented drought situation in the country. The GOP states that around Rs 92 billion losses has already occurred due to the drought situation.[90] Wheat output shall decline from a record 21 million tons last year to about 17.5 million tons this year. Later, the GoP announced that the loss was much lower at Rs 25 billion while estimated balance of payments loss was at $927 million.[91] Not all of Pakistan's problems are an act of God, some are definitely man-made. Notwithstanding past GOP claims, the agriculture sector has been neglected. What are the problems of the agriculture sector? The following are the commonly expressed problems in the country's agriculture sector.

1. Low use of advanced production technology.
2. Inadequate use of inputs in the form of higher and balanced doses of fertilizers, use of quality seeds, and integrated pest management

---

[89] *Pakistan Observer*, March 26, 2001.
[90] *The News* International, April 3, 2001.
[91] See Economic Survey 2000-2001, (Islamabad: GOP, Economic Affairs Division, June 2001), in *PO*, June 17, 2001.

3. Expected rise in costs as the General Sales Tax (GST) is levied on farm inputs. As per the conditionality of the IMF and World Bank.
4. Inadequate institutional credit for farm activity, especially for subsistence and medium-sized farms that are 93% of the total farming community.
5. Poor delivery of state services, especially agriculture extension.

An Agriculture Strategy was announced on April 7, 2001 by the federal government. Some important features of which are:[92]

1. Increase the production of five major crops including tea, edible oil, wheat, cotton and rice. For the first time in history, Pakistan exported wheat last year. Since rice and cotton are major crops for earning foreign exchange, their production will be increased in the country. The country plans to save $700-$800 million through import substitution by local cultivating of tea. Pakistan spends about $1.5 billion on import of edible oils and tea alone.
2. Improvement of water courses, field water application as well as drainage are essential for making optimum use of the available water and preventing a decline in the productivity of the Indus Basin due to water-logging and soil salinity.
3. Gradual induction of private sector into the wheat business. Currently, the procurement, storage, and marketing of whet are dominated by the public sector.
4. The current allocation from the Public Sector Development Plan (PSDP) for agriculture development projects is 0.45% only, which is less than Rs 500 million. The allocation will be increased to 4% next fiscal year.
5. An allocation of Rs 7 billion will be provided to the provinces for different irrigation projects
6. Alter cropping patterns so that water-intensive crops like rice and sugarcane are gradually phased out. Cotton and sugar beet is to be introduced
7. Construction of four water reservoirs.
8. The installation of 10,000 tube wells in the country. Provincial governments to decide the location.
9. Efficient water conservation technologies will be encouraged and provinces shall adopt techniques to save water like brick lining of canals, watercourse management, leveling of land. The provinces shall submit the water projects to the Planning commission and Rs 6 billion shall be provided for the purpose.
10. An additional credit facility of Rs 100 million will be made available for efficient water utilization techniques, including drip, sprinkler and other methods
11. Increase in operational research and decrease in establishment charges. The ratio of operational vs. establishment charges will be 60:40. This will be established by various measures, including the rightsizing of different departments.
12. Export processing zones and cold storages will be established to encourage the export of fruits, vegetables, etc.

---

[92] *Dawn* and *The Nation*. April 8, 2001.

13. The cultivation of olive oil will be encouraged; (m) a successful wheat productivity model program financed by the Food and Agriculture Organization (FAO) in Sargodha shall be replicated in other districts.
14. Production of milk, meat and tobacco shall be increased.
15. A policy on corporate framing is being discussed. This will help the agriculture sector to grow swiftly. The industrial status will enable the sector and investors to avail of all those facilities currently available to industrialists. The law will be amended to remove any ceiling on land holdings to attract big investors. Some tax concessions shall also be given for the purpose.

Recently, the GoNWFP also adopted an Agriculture Development Strategy, the main features of which are:[93]

1. Regional emphasis shall be given to development of various crops in the NWFP in accordance with the following plan: (a) Horticulture and off-season vegetables in the northern region (Hazara and Malakand), (b) Cash crops in central region (Peshawar and Mardan valleys, and (c) Cereal crops like wheat and gram in southern region.

2. A Farm Service Center (FSC) shall be established in each of the 25 districts of the NWFP. The functions of an FSC are:(a) Provide essential agriculture inputs by bringing Agriculture Extension wing closer to the farming community, (b) farmer enrollment for which there shall be an enrollment fee of Rs 100 and a membership fee of Rs 500. The GoNWFP shall provide a matching grant to each FSC. The control of the FSC would be only transferred to the farming community when the membership exceeds 2000. The registration of the FSC would be under the Cooperative Act. The general body, management and financial committees would run the FSC. The rules and by-laws have been formulated.

3. Distribution of 10,000 tons of certified seeds to the farmers. Last year only 1,000 such seeds were distributed. This year the seeds shall be distributed by: Agriculture Research and Agriculture Extension wings, Nuclear Institute for Food and Agriculture (NIFA), and the Pakistan Oilseed Development Board (PODB). Each organization has been given a separate distribution target.

The Agriculture University, Peshawar would be responsible for out-reach with the help of professors in general and officers in particular. All university professors and final year students will be required to spend 30% of their time with the growers at the FSC to assist in technical matters as required under TIPON Ordinance, 1985.

The field officers of Pakistan Oilseed Development Board (PODB) would be attached to the FSCs to assist in the technical matters on oilseed crops. Agriculture projects, which are financed trough the regular Annual Development Plan, would be integrated into the system of FSCs in due course of time. These are projects of

---

[93] *The News* International, April 25, 2001.

horticulture promotion, on-farm water management, cultivation of tea gardens, olive plantations, and oil seed crops.

Similarly, other provinces have also come up with their development strategies.

THE INFORMATION TECHNOLOGY (IT) EMPHASIS

The IT field is one of the very few areas where there has been genuine progress. Rapid spreading of Internet connections across the country. An investment of Rs 12 billion in the IT field. [94] A new IT division established in the Science & Technology Ministry. Recently, the GOP announced an IT Policy and Action Plan. The GOP will spend Rs 15 billion on IT this year out of which 60% will be spent on human resource development. Today there are 110 licensed Internet Service Providers in the country out of which 63 are operating. The number of users has climbed to 0.25 million.[95] The GOP has made remarkable progress in extending the Internet facility in the country. By June 2001, the facility will have extended to 400 cities and villages. The GOP is establishing Internet cafes at various district post offices and gas stations throughout the country. [96] The GOP is to provide a large skilled work force to meet the local and export needs. The policy envisages the establishment of four new IT universities, and Accreditation Services, Educational Intranet and strengthening of existing IT institutes. The GOP is set to launch projects like Government Online, Electronic Governance Project, and E-Commerce Network.[97]

THE REVAMPING OF THE TAXATION SYSTEM

The GOP is aware that a fundamental problem in the tax system is that it had a very narrow base. Thus, a very small section of the population pays income tax. The Musharraf regime is in the process of creating a broad-based tax structure to remove the shortcomings. The regime had already decided to levy agriculture income tax and across-the-board GST. It believed that it is a requirement of basic fair play and equity that all income regardless of source be taxed. There are only 1.6 million tax assesses in 1999 slightly up from 1.4 million from 1998.[98] The ratio of tax payees to total population in Pakistan is one of the lowest in the developing world. The tax to GDP ratio had remained stagnant in the range of 15%, which needs to be improved. Currently, it is about 13.5% only.[99] In the fiscal year 1998-1999, Rs 308 billion in taxes are collected. The target fixed for the 1999-2000 fiscal year is Rs 356 billion. A chronic problem is the shortfall in announced targets for the CBR. Therefore, it is imperative that the current target be met.

---

[94] *Pakistan Observer*, Jan. 7, 2001.
[95] *The News*, August 27, 2000.
[96] *Pakistan Observer*, Aug. 28, 2000.
[97] *The News*, August 24, 2000.
[98] *The Nation*, Feb. 19, 1999.

No downward revisions are allowed in the target, as is done in previous years. The sting is that the rich feudal and business communities did not pay their taxes. This is shameful indeed. The regime plans to take tough measures to force these rich people to pay what is due the nation. The current target to increase the number of taxpayers to 2 million must be achieved. The regime shall ensure that all segments of society, regardless of source, pay their fair share of taxes. One of the peculiarities of Pakistan's tax system is the large number of exemptions granted to the rich and powerful. The withdrawal of these exemptions is going to add a staggering amount of Rs 115 billion according to one estimate.[100] Therefore, no exemptions are allowed under normal circumstances. Spread the tax net everywhere. Tackle the fundamental problem of a very narrow base of the tax system. The universal principle that anyone able to pay must pay regardless of source need be followed, (d) Simplification of the tax system. Plan to eradicate the confusion and complexity in tax payment. Previously, the Federal Chambers of Commerce & Industry (FCCI) had come up with a decent proposal to shorten tax heads to just five that will include federal, provincial local direct and indirect. Currently, taxpayers are paying under more than two dozen heads. This is ridiculous and a waste of time and energy. The Musharraf regime had promised to look into the matter. The Punjab Government announced measures to reduce 22 provincial taxes to just seven.[101] (e) Lower the tax rates. In 1997, the GOP had announced a program to revive the economy. Personal income tax rates are reduced from 10% to 35% to only 5% to 20%. However, the GOP later imposed two new tax rates on salaried persons. Salaried persons earning more than Rs. 500, 000 are taxed at 25%, and those earning Rs. 700, 000 are taxed at 30%. Thus, the previous four slab rates had been extended to six, which is a departure of past pronouncements of the Nawaz Government. Taxation of the public corporate sector is lowered to 30% from 33% and other companies from 43% to 35%. Taxation for banking companies is lowered from 58% to 55%. Tariff rates are brought down from a maximum of 65% to 45%.[102] Many observers welcomed revision of tax rates in this sector. Some analysts are concerned that the GOP will face a revenue loss of some Rs. 50-60 billion because of these cuts, (f) Introduction of a more equitable tax system.

A major problem with Pakistan's taxation system is that it relied on indirect taxation, which are regressive in nature, hurting more the poor as opposed to the rich. Direct taxation, which is fairer; contributed only 26% of the total tax collected. The average rate in other countries is 35%. In the 1998-99 budget, the total tax revenue is given as Rs. 308 billion out of which direct taxes are only Rs. 114.8 billion, while indirect taxes are Rs. 223.4 billion. Thus, currently there is a tilt towards indirect taxes. Taxation increases must come from widening the net of income tax, a direct tax, and simultaneously cutting it like done elsewhere. To the credit of the previous government, it had increased the net collection form direct taxes from 6.6% over last year, from Rs. 103 billion to Rs. 110 billion. Customs duty declined from Rs. 74 billion to Rs. 65 billion, showing a decline of 12%.

[99] *The News*, Nov. 29, 1999.
[100] *Financial Times*, April 1996.
[101] *The News International*, Jan. 1, 2000.

In sum, the military government must overhaul the taxation system with emphasis on reform of the Central Board of Revenue (CBR). Improve tax administration. Tax evasion is rampant because of lax administration and corruption in the revenue departments. It should use an iron hand to deal with endemic corruption in the CBR.

THE NEW EMPHASIS ON THE EXPORT SECTOR

The Musharraf regime has stressed the development of Pakistan's export base. There was an urgent eemphasis on increasing exports. Earlier, the GOP has fixed the target for exports for 2000-2001 at $10 billion. There is an increase of 11.3% in exports in the first half of the current fiscal year, giving hope that the annual target will be met.

Emphasize increasing exports on a high priority-basis. The second Nawaz Government desired to initiate a reform agenda that was to emphasize the following strategic directions:(a) Create a culture of export and quality in society, and including civil society institutions. Media institutions, professional associations, community development organizations, educational and research institutions, and NGOs, shall had to be involved in creating such a culture, (b) The Commerce Ministry should provide up-to-date market intelligence, support for marketing expenses of firms establishing links with buyers in growing economies, providing technical transfer especially in management skills and methods to trade related industry, support for background research in export potential, improve the efficiency of the duty drawback scheme, (c) Accomplish rapid institutional change for the creation of a supportive environment conducive to increased trade, (d) Focus on changing market conditions, trends and opportunities made available in the new global economy, (e) Make best use of the liberalization underway because of the new WTO regime, (f) Take broad measures to improve Pakistan's overall competitive position in global markets. For example, it should further promote brand names already well established in the international markets and introduce "Made in Pakistan" labels as marks of national pride and excellence, (g) Minimize regulations concerning exports. It may also facilitate exporters by removing procedural complications, avoiding unnecessary and frequent changes in rules and regulations, and pursue consistent policies, (h) Ensure adequate supplies of raw materials for export industries on competitive rates, (i) Accomplish rapid institutional change for the creation of a supportive environment conducive to increased trade, (j) Focus on changing market conditions, trends and opportunities made available in the new global economy, (k) Promulgate an Export Insurance Scheme to safeguard new exporters, (l) Harmonize tariffs with ASEAN and develop a mechanism for exchange of information, (m) Explore ASEAN markets for non-traditional exports. The country may enter barter trade of some goods with ASEAN, (n) Pursue aggressive marketing tactics, improve quality, price products in a realistic manner, and participate in trade fairs, (o) Better involvement of the Commerce Ministry in strengthening the trade sector. The ministry be fully aware of the implications of developments in the WTO regime and should assist in better tapping the huge potential

---

[102] *Dawn*, July 14, 1997.

for trade expansion. It should make the country better prepared to make use of the opportunities available. Simultaneously, steps are taken as part of an overall strategy, under Commerce Ministry guidance, to meet the requirements of WTO and be in a state of greater preparedness to deal with the concerns of Pakistan global customers, (p) More emphasis on increased trade in services and making better use of special treatment currently available to Pakistan as a developing country, (q) Incentives provided to export industries to increase value-added production. Increased emphasis on Total Quality Management and productivity should become the topmost priority in Pakistan's production and service sectors, ® Establishment of more Export Processing Zones (EPZs) in the country like in Lahore and Rawalpindi in proximity to the newly set up industrial zones. Organize of the EPZA along modern and professional lines in order to provide better services to foreign investors, (s) an extensive and aggressive marketing campaign to lure foreign direct investments should be launched immediately.

The following measures have been taken to increase Pakistan's exports: (a) Lowering of the maximum customs duty from 35 to 30% from July 1, 2001, (b) Reducing of tariff slabs from 5 to 4 with minimum duty on raw materials and machinery and maximum on finished goods

THE ISSUE OF POVERTY INCREASE
AND UNSUSTAINABLE DEVELOPMENT

Perhaps the most serious issue in the country is increasing poverty. Pakistan faces the challenge of a weak economy and increasing poverty. In the last ten years or so, the poverty level has more than doubled from 16% to around 35%.[103] In 1991, the estimated figure was 34%.[104] Recent government reports indicate that the figure has actually further risen to 40%.[105] There is no doubt that poverty has increased in the country. The total number of people living in poverty number 40 million, out of which 27 million live in extreme poverty.[106] Earlier, the GOP stated in January 2000 that 35% of Pakistanis lived below the poverty line.[107] According to the Basic-Need Approach, it is 46.0% and according to the Calorie-Based Approach, it is 27.3%. A Dawn editorial in December 199 stated that during the 1990s, poverty had increased in Pakistan and some 25-30% of the population, some 30 million, are affected.[108] Shaukat Aziz, the Finance Minister had acknowledged, "Poverty is posing a serious threat to the social cohesion and peace of civil society".[109] Shahid Javed Burki, a respected author, estimated that the incidence of poverty in Pakistan had risen to around 36% today up from 18% in the 1980s.[110] At least

---

[103] *The Nation*, July 13, 2000.
[104] *<http://CIA/the World Fact Book, 1999/ Pakistan/ Fact book home page/Pakistan.htm>*.
[105] Zahid Hussein, "A Nation of Tax Resisters", *Newsweek*, July 17, 2000, 23.
[106] *The News*, July 7, 2000.
[107] *The Nation*, January 23, 2000.
[108] See editorial, *Dawn*, December 17, 1999.
[109] *Dawn*, Dec. 17, 1999.
[110] *The News*, Jan. 16, 2000.

36 million people or 6 million households fall below the poverty line. More households have become potentially vulnerable, and may fall into the poverty trap, as structural adjustment started in the beginning of 1990s continues, and necessary reforms are launched without cushioning their impact on the poor. Javed Jabbar, ex-Advisor to the Chief Executive on National Affairs and Information said in January 2000 that 35% of Pakistanis live below the poverty line.[111] Earlier, the GOP's Human Development and Poverty Reduction Strategy 1999 stated that: [112]

The bottom line is that poverty is rising in Pakistan. At least 36 million people or 6 million households fall below the poverty line. More households have become potentially vulnerable, and may fall into the poverty trap, as structural adjustment started in the beginning of 1990s continues, and necessary reforms are launched without cushioning their impact on the poor.

The Social Development Policy Center's latest report indicates that 15 million more people could fall below the poverty line in the next three years if Pakistan was compelled to make a balance of payments adjustments in the short run due to severe foreign exchange reserves.[113] Recently, the European Union (EU) had recommended the inclusion of Pakistan in the list of those poor countries of the world that will be getting cash assistance of around $1 billion this year for poverty alleviation. The Relief Commissioner of the EU has based his contention on the report of special representative of the World Bank who had stated that one fourth of the population of Pakistan is living below the poverty line and "if immediate assistance is not provided its security and sovereignty will be jeopardized".[114] According to the Basic-Need Approach, it is 46.0% and according to the Calorie-Based Approach, it is 27.3%. A *Dawn* editorial in December 199 stated that during the 1990s, poverty had increased in Pakistan and some 25-30% of the population, some 30 million, are affected.[115] Shaukat Aziz, the Finance Minister had acknowledged, "Poverty is posing a serious threat to the social cohesion and peace of civil society".[116] Shahid Javed Burki, a respected author, estimated that the incidence of poverty in Pakistan had risen to around 36% today up from 18% in the 1980s.[117] The bottom line is that poverty is rising in Pakistan. At least 36 million people or 6 million households fall below the poverty line. More households have become potentially vulnerable, and may fall into the poverty trap, as structural adjustment started in the beginning of 1990s continues, and necessary reforms are launched without cushioning their impact on the poor. Today Pakistan ranks as the seventh most populated country in the world. The population growth rate is a high 2.2%. Therefore, by the year 2050 the

---

[111] *The Nation*, January 23, 2000.
[112] *Human Development and Poverty Reduction Strategy*, April 1999 (Planning Commission, Government of Pakistan), 2.
[113] See report "A National Poverty Reduction Strategy and the Role of Donors" by Social Policy Development Center cited in *Pakistan Observer*, May 6, 2001.
[114] *Pakistan Observer*, July 10, 2000.
[115] See editorial, *Dawn*, Dec. 17, 1999.
[116] *Dawn*, Dec. 17, 1999.
[117] *The News*, Jan. 16, 2000.

population of the country will have climbed to 300 million.[118] The European Union has recommended the inclusion of Pakistan in the list of those poor countries of the world that will be getting cash assistance of around $1 billion this year for poverty alleviation. The Relief Commissioner of the EU has based his contention on the report of special representative of the World Bank who has stated that one fourth of the population is living below the poverty line and if immediate assistance is not provided Pakistan's security and sovereignty will be put at risk.[119] One of the greatest failures in Pakistan is its low human development. Earlier, the GOP's Human Development and Poverty Reduction Strategy 1999 stated that Pakistan ranked 138 among 174 developing countries in the quality of life index. The country's current Human Development Index ranking, which is constructed using nine indicators related to education (e.g., primary, secondary, and tertiary enrollment- total and female) and health (e.g., doctors, infant survival rate, and hospital beds) as calculated by the UNDP annually and reported by the United Nations Human Development Report 2000, is 135 out of 174 countries surveyed. For the sake of comparison, India is 128 on the international scale, China is 99, Sri Lanka is 84, and Myanmar is 125.[120] Like so many other developing countries, Pakistan today needs help of the international donor community. In fact, if the economy does not show significant improvement, overall poverty is projected to further increase in the current decade. The problem with Pakistan's economy is the small spending on social services. More than 80% of the country's national revenue is spent on debt servicing and defense alone.[121]

Unfortunately, the poor in Pakistan continue to suffer. The astronomical rise in electricity charges, increase in postal rates, telephone, gas, etc. meant the disposable income of the people belonging to the lower and middle classes had been curtailed. The GOP had failed to tame inflation, which was running in the double digits. The net result was that the poor classes were worse off than before. The great tragedy with Pakistan is that the quality of life indicators like education, health and nutrition showed no development. Poverty remained prevalent. In reality, the poor became poorer. This confirms the observation that rapid growth in GNP and income does not guarantee a sufficient degree of fulfillment of the basic needs for everyone in the country.[122] The World Bank says that Pakistan's economic performance in the last two decades has been characterized by relatively fast GDP growth driven by an enterprising private sector, agriculture and cotton-based manufacturing. In 1988, the country began to reorganize its social and economic policies to promote private sector investment, energize public finances and improve its extremely poor social indicators. Though structural reforms

---

[118] *The Nation*, July 13, 2000. For figure for population growth rate see "Bottom Line", *Asiaweek*, Nov. 17, 2000, 51.

[119] *Pakistan Observer*, July 10, 2000.

[120] *Khaleej Times* (daily), July 14, 2000.

[121] Zahid Hussein, "*A Nation of Tax Resisters*", op. cit., 23.

[122] K. Balasubramaniam, "Privatization of Health and Its Impact on the People of South Asia", *Dominance of the West Over the Rest* (Penang, Malaysia: Just World Trust, 1995), 170-71.

have been mixed, Pakistan made important advances in privatization and in attracting private investment in the energy sector.[123]

While it is true that the country has experienced continuous growth of the economy, it is also true that it suffers from gross inequitable distribution of wealth. The rich have become richer while the poor have become poorer. Data below indicates the tragic reality of skewed income in Pakistan.

Distribution of Household Incomes of the Poorest 20% and Richest 20% of the Population Expressed as a Percentage of the Total GNP in Five South Asian Countries

Country	Percentage share of GNP of the poorest 20%	Percentage share of GNP of the richest 20%	Ratio of income between the poorest 20% and the richest 20%
Bangladesh	6.6	46.3	7.0
Nepal	5.0	50.4	10.1
India	3.1	64.5	20.8
Pakistan	6.9	46.7	6.8
Sri Lanka	5.9	49.8	8.4

In Pakistan, the share of lowest 20% decreased from 8.2% of the total in 1970-71 to 6.9% in 1984-85 while the share of then richest 20% increased because of the relatively rapid growth in the income of the richest 10% of the population.

Distribution of Household Incomes of the Poorest 20% and the Richest 20% of the Population in Pakistan in 1970-71 and 1984-85

Year	Percentage of share of GNP of the poorest 20% of the population	Percentage share of GNP of the richest 20% of the population	Ratio of income of the richest and poorest 20%
1970/71	8.2	41.4	5.0
1984/85	6.9	46.7	6.8

In the country, recent evidence indicates, as disclosed by Balasubramaniam, that the iniquity in the income distribution is getting worse.[124]

The adult literacy rate of Pakistan is only 44% while that in India is 55%. The education enrolment ratio in Pakistan is only 43%, while that in India is 54%. The population with access to safe drinking water in Pakistan is 79% while that in India is 81%. There are 50 million adult illiterates in Pakistan today.[125] Earlier, the Human Development Report 1994, UNDP states that public expenditure on education is only

---

[123] *Dawn*, Dec. 5, 1996.
[124] Ibid, 171.
[125] Figures are from UNDP's Human Development Report, 2000, in *Dawn* Jan. 8, 2001.

3.4% of GNP while public expenditure on health is only 1.8% of GNP. Rural population with access to sanitation is only 30%.[126]

Pakistan had achieved some improvement in the health sector. The rates of immunization of children had almost doubled from 1988-1998. Knowledge of family planning had become widespread. However, some health indicators are improving very slowly. The World Bank estimated that in 1998, one in every 38 women died from causes related to pregnancy, and infant mortality rate was at 90 per 1,000 live births. The average for low-income countries was 64 then.[127] Today Pakistan's infant mortality rate is 88, slightly down from 1998. In comparison, India current infant mortality rate is 71.[128] Latest data indicated that Pakistan is falling behind some of its neighbors and other Muslim countries.[129] The facts speak for themselves. The average life expectancy in the developing countries is 63 while it is only 50 years in the least developing countries. The average life expectancy in the developed countries is 75.[130] The current life expectancy in Pakistan is 63 years while that in India is 62.[131] It is apparent from available data that Pakistan is doing very badly in the vital areas of development and social well being, with the exception of number of doctors available to provide medical services. Unfortunately, the quality of medical care is still very low in Pakistan despite the comparatively large number of doctors available. Perhaps sheer numbers of doctors available do not make that much of a difference. The view that Pakistan's medical services are of low quality is based on personal observation and anecdotal evidence and not on a scientific study.

Pakistan's current Human Development Index ranking, as reported by the United Nations *Human Development Report 2000*, is a low 135 out of 174 countries surveyed. For the sake of comparison, India is 128 on the international scale, China is 99, Sri Lanka is 84, and Myanmar is 125. Coupled with the poverty problem is the country's population explosion. There exists a strong relationship between population growth and poverty increases. Today Pakistan ranks as the seventh most populated country in the world. The population growth rate is a high 2.2%. Therefore, by the year 2050 the population of the country will have climbed to 300 million.[132] The stark reality is that unless the population growth rate is brought under control, Pakistan will not be able to provide for the basic needs of its teeming millions; food, water, energy, even fresh air in cities. Moreover, the scarcity of food and water will cause the breakdown of law and order and make the country difficult to govern. Pakistan's family planning program needs to be re-energized immediately. It cannot afford failure on this score.

One of the biggest problems faced by Pakistan is its rapidly growing population. The World Bank estimates that our population is currently growing at a rate of 3%, and is

---

[126] *World Development Report 1997*, (UNDP), pp. 224-25.

[127] See Country Brief, *"Pakistan" South Asia Brief*, (Washington & Islamabad: The World Bank Group), Sep. 1998.

[128] *Asiaweek*, April 20, 2001, 52.

[129] "Vital Signs", *Asiaweek* June 21, 1996, 66.

[130] Bruce Russet and Harvey Starr, *World Politics: The Menu for Choice*, 5th ed. (new York: Freeman & Co., 1996), 350.

[131] *Asiaweek*, April 20, 2001, 52.

[132] *The Nation*, July 13, 2000. For figure for population growth rate see "Bottom Line", *Asiaweek*, Nov. 17, 2000, 51.

projected to double in the next two decades. The country's fertility rate is 65% higher than the average for all low-income countries. However, Pakistan made some progress in the area of human development from the early 1970s to early 1990s. Despite the progress, the country still lags far behind the average for low-income countries.[133] The United Nations Human Development Index of social well-being ranks the country 132 out of 173. The Human Development Report 1994, UNDP states that public expenditure on education is only 3.4% of GNP while public expenditure on health is only 1.8% of GNP. Rural population with access to sanitation is only 30 %.

The Musharraf regime claims that eradication of poverty is one of its foremost tasks. Everyone agrees that this is a daunting challenge that must be met at all costs. The country depends upon success in this area. The GOP must spend more on the social sector by increasing the allocations for the Public Sector Development Programs (PSDP). These PSDPs are financed out of the annual budget. However, the reality is different. Over the years, the PSDP has decreased rather than grown. In 1991-92 budget the development expenditure was only 7% of GDP, which was further lowered to 5% in 1992-93. It was again further lowered to 3.3% in 1997-98, and 3.2% in 1998-99. Later, it is increased to 3.4% in 1999-2000. The current development budget is 3% of the GDP. In monetary terms, the PSDP in 1997-98 is allocated only Rs 90 billion.[134] The development budget for 1996-97 was allocated at Rs 104 billion versus Rs 96 billion in 1997-98 fiscal year. Since the rate of inflation was high, the development budget in real terms had been reduced.[135] The officially stated figure for inflation last year was 13%, and said to be 11% this year.[136] The target for 1996-97 was to lower it to a single digit of 8%.[137] For 1998-99, the PSDP was allocated Rs 110 billion but is reduced to Rs 98 billion in October 1998. For 1999-2000, Rs 116 billion was allocated for the PSDP.[138]

The poor in Pakistan are leading a terrible existence. They are becoming disillusioned with government promises of better days to come. Pakistan has become a tragedy in this respect. Certainly, more monetary resources must immediately flow to augment the share of national wealth received by the poor and lower middle-income classes to prevent them from sinking further down the economic ladder. Apparently, economic indicators provide enough evidence of Pakistan's poor performance in the most vital areas of socio-economic development. Please refer to the comparative data given in the tables above.

This state of affairs is intolerable in an Islamic state that calls for social and economic justice. The assumption of capitalism is that as the growth of the economy brought national prosperity every one would benefit. The rising tide would lift all boats, they would have us believe. It bears repeating that a growing economy benefiting everyone is not necessarily the case. The old theory of "trickle down economics" has been discredited. Poverty is not reduced just because the economy is growing. The current

---

[133] *Dawn*, Feb. 5, 1996.
[134] Hasan Iqbal Jafri, "Sink or Swim?" *The Herald* (monthly), July 1997, 136.
[135] *Nation*, June 17, 1996, 7.
[136] *Dawn*, June 22, 1996.
[137] Frontier Post, May 19, 1996.
[138] *Public Sector Development Program: New Initiatives 1999* (Planning Commission, Government of Pakistan, n.d.), 2.

supply-side economics of the GOP cannot deliver to the very poor. The state cannot abdicate its responsibility to its most hapless citizens. The state is responsible to transfer wealth or, at least, afford decent economic and employment opportunities to the weaker segments of society. This is an Islamic requirement. We have failed to translate this ideal into practice, unfortunately. Progress and development must translate into better quality of life for not only a small elite but also the masses. Any thing less is unfair, deplorable and a gross injustice. The political parties must make the establishment of an egalitarian society- a central plank of their election manifestos. Egalitarianism is a cardinal Islamic value and the GOP must embrace it wholeheartedly and practice it firmly. The continued practice of supply-side economics will be taken as an act of betrayal of public trust. All political parties and interests are expected to stand up for real change and not status quo politics. We must convince ourselves first and then the world that as Pakistanis we believe in the establishment of an egalitarian Islamic order.

More than 80% of the country's national revenue is spent on debt servicing and defense alone.[139] The adult literacy rate of Pakistan is only 44% while that in India is 55%. The education enrolment ratio in Pakistan is only 43%, while that in India is 54%. The population with access to safe drinking water in Pakistan is 79% while that in India is 81%. There are 50 million adult illiterates in Pakistan today.[140] Earlier, the Human Development Report 1994, UNDP states that public expenditure on education is only 3.4% of GNP while public expenditure on health is only 1.8% of GNP. Rural population with access to sanitation is only 30%. See tables below:[141]

Country	Adult illiteracy % Female	Adult illiteracy % Male
Nepal	86	59
Bangladesh	74	51
Nigeria	53	33
India	62	35
Pakistan	76	50
China	27	10
Sri Lanka	13	7
Egypt	61	36
Indonesia	22	10
Morocco	69	43
Syria	44	14
Jordan	21	7
Turkey	28	8
Malaysia	22	11

Source: World Development Report 1997, pp. 226

[139] Zahid Hussein, "*A Nation of Tax Resisters*", op. cit., 23.
[140] Figures are from UNDP's Human Development Report, 2000, in *Dawn* Jan. 8, 2001.
[141] *World Development Report 1997*, (UNDP), pp. 224-25.

Country	Adult literacy rate (%)
Malaysia	83
Turkey	82
Iran	72
Egypt	51
Pakistan	38
Nigeria	57
Bangladesh	38
Indonesia	84

Source: World Development Report, 1996

Country	Percentage of Total Population with Access to Healthcare	
	1980	1993
Bangladesh	80	74
India	50	-
Pakistan	65	85
Egypt	100	99
Jordan	-	90
Malaysia	-	88

Source: World Development Report 1997, pp. 224-25

Country	Percentage of Total Population with Access to Safe Water	
	1980	1994-95
Bangladesh	-	83
India	-	63
Pakistan	38	60
Egypt	90	84
Jordan	89	89
Turkey	67	92
Malaysia	-	90
USA	-	90

Source: World Development Report 1997, pp. 224-25

Country	Percentage of Total Population with Access to Sanitation	
	1980	1995
Bangladesh	-	30
India	-	29
Pakistan	16	30
Egypt	70	-
Jordan	76	30
Turkey	-	94
Malaysia	75	94
USA	98	85

Source: World Development Report 1997, pp. 224-25

The Benazir Government had somewhat increased allocations for the social sectors in the 1996-97 budget. The allocation of the education sector had received a four-fold raise, going up to Rs 1,625 million from Rs 434 million in 1993. Expenditure on health had gone up to Rs 3,219 million as against Rs 329 in 1993, representing almost a ten-fold increase. Allocations for population welfare sector were Rs 2,000 million as against Rs 829 million in 1993. The water sector received Rs 16,061 million up from Rs .6,681 million in 1993. Allocation for rural development was also doubled.[142]

Pakistan had achieved some improvement in the health sector. The rates of immunization of children had almost doubled from 1988-1998 Knowledge of family planning had become widespread. However, some health indicators are improving very slowly. The World Bank estimated that in 1998, one in every 38 women died from causes related to pregnancy, and infant mortality rate was at 90 per 1,000 live births. The average for low-income countries was 64 then.[143] Today Pakistan's infant mortality rate is 88, slightly down from 1998. In comparison, India current infant mortality rate is 71.[144] Latest data indicated that Pakistan is falling behind some of its neighbors and other Muslim countries.[145] The facts speak for themselves. The average life expectancy in the developing countries is 63 while it is only 50 years in the least developing countries. The average life expectancy in the developed countries is 75.[146] The current life expectancy in Pakistan is 63 years while that in India is 62.[147] It is apparent from available data that Pakistan is doing very badly in the vital areas of development and social well being, with the exception of number of doctors available to provide medical services. Unfortunately, the quality of medical care is still very low in Pakistan despite the comparatively large number of doctors available. Perhaps sheer numbers of doctors available do not make that much of a difference. The view that Pakistan's medical services are of low quality is based on personal observation and anecdotal evidence and not on a scientific study.

---

[142] *Dawn* June 25, 1996, 5.

[143] See Country Brief, *"Pakistan" South Asia Brief*, (Washington & Islamabad: The World Bank Group), Sep. 1998.

[144] *Asiaweek*, April 20, 2001, 52.

[145] "Vital Signs", *Asiaweek* June 21, 1996, 66.

[146] Bruce Russet and Harvey Starr, World Politics: The Menu for Choice, 5th ed. (new York: Freeman & Co., 1996), 350.

[147] *Asiaweek*, April 20, 2001, 52.

Pakistan's current Human Development Index ranking, as reported by the United Nations Human Development Report 2000, is a low 135 out of 174 countries surveyed. For the sake of comparison, India is 128 on the international scale, China is 99, Sri Lanka is 84, and Myanmar is 125. Coupled with the poverty problem is the country's population explosion. There exists a strong relationship between population growth and poverty increases. Today Pakistan ranks as the seventh most populated country in the world. The population growth rate is a high 2.2%. Therefore, by the year 2050 the population of the country will have climbed to 300 million.[148] The stark reality is that unless the population growth rate is brought under control, Pakistan will not be able to provide for the basic needs of its teeming millions; food, water, energy, even fresh air in cities. Moreover, the scarcity of food and water will cause the breakdown of law and order and make the country difficult to govern. Pakistan's family planning program needs to be re-energized immediately. It cannot afford failure on this score.

One of the biggest problems faced by Pakistan is its rapidly growing population. The World Bank estimates that our population is currently growing at a rate of 3%, and is projected to double in the next two decades. The country's fertility rate is 65% higher than the average for all low-income countries. However, Pakistan made some progress in the area of human development from the early 1970s to early 1990s. Despite the progress, the country still lags far behind the average for low-income countries.[149] The United Nations Human Development Index of social well-being ranks the country 132 out of 173 countries.

Latest data indicates that Pakistan is falling behind some of our neighbors and other Muslim countries. The tables below clearly indicate the situation. Data for the USA is given for information purposes only and not for the sake of comparison.[150] The facts speak for themselves.

The average life expectancy in the developing countries is 63 while it is only 50 years in the least developing countries. The average life expectancy in the developed countries is 75.[151]

Pakistan's infant mortality rate (the number of children who die during the first year out of every 1,000 live births) was above the average 99 in the least developed countries in 1992. The average infant mortality rate was 11 in developed countries. See table below:[152]

---

[148] *The Nation*, July 13, 2000. For figure for population growth rate see "Bottom Line", *Asiaweek*, Nov. 17, 2000, 51.

[149] *Dawn*, Feb. 5, 1996.

[150] "Vital Signs", *Asiaweek* June 21, 1996, 66.

[151] Bruce Russet and Harvey Starr, *World Politics: The Menu for Choice*, 5th ed. (new York: Freeman & Co., 1996), 350.

[152] Todaro, *Economic Development*, 44.

Country	Infant Mortality Rate
Afghanistan	172
Central African Rep.	141
Bangladesh	120
Nigeria	114
Pakistan	109
India	91
Zambia	76
Brazil	69
Kenya	62
Mexico	47
Venezuela	24
USA	9
Japan	5

Source: Population Reference Bureau, 1992 World Population Data sheet (Washington, D.C.: Population Reference Bureau, 1992)

The latest figures available are given below:

Country	Infant mortality rate (per 1,000 live births), 1995
USA	8
Malaysia	12
Iran	38
Egypt	56
Turkey	48
India	68
Pakistan	90
Bangladesh	79
Japan	31

Source: World Development Report, 1997, p.224-25.

It is apparent from the tables above that Pakistan has fallen behind Bangladesh in reducing infant mortality rates. This is pitiable.

Apart from the problem of comparatively low GNP growth Pakistan suffers from one of the highest population growth rates in the world, which is major reason why the per-capita GNP of Pakistan remains miniscule. In October 1997, Pakistan's population had reached 137.4 million and the population growth rate remained at a very high 2.9%. For the sake of comparison the population of some countries is given below:[153]

---

[153] *Asiaweek*, October 17, 1997.

Country	Rate of Population Growth	Total Population (million)
USA	1.0	269.2
Turkey	2.1	64.0
India	2.1	953.7
Egypt	2.2	61.1
Malaysia	2.4	21.7
Iran	3.4	62.9
Pakistan	2.9	137.4
Germany	0.7	82.6
Japan	0.3	126.1
France	0.6	58.7
Britain	0.3	58.6
Canada	1.3	30.3
China	1.2	1,232.1
S. Korea	0.9	45.9
Taiwan	1.0	21.8
Mexico	1.9	93.9
Russia	0.4	149.8
Malaysia	2.4	21.7
Australia	1.2	18.5
Thailand	1.5	61.4
Brazil	1.9	162.8
Indonesia	1.6	200.0
India	2.1	953.7
Turkey	2.1	64.0
Iran	3.4	62.9
Philippines	2.3	71.8
Nigeria	2.9	104.4
Egypt	2.2	61.1
Sri Lanka	1.2	18.3
Bangladesh	2.2	125.8
Nepal	2.3	22.0

Pakistan is far behind other countries in the region as far as various measures of development and progress are concerned. See tables below:

Country	People per Telephone
USA	1.3
Malaysia	6.6
Iran	14.8
Egypt	20.8
Pakistan	62.7
India	85.0

Country	People per Television
USA	1.2
Turkey	4.3
Malaysia	4.7
Egypt	8.6
Iran	15.9
India	21.2
Pakistan	45.2

Country	People per Doctor
Turkey	955
Egypt	1,316
Pakistan	2,000
Malaysia	2,063
India	2,063
Iran	3,140

Country	Calorie Intake
USA	3,671
Turkey	3,429
Egypt	3,336
Iran	3,181
Malaysia	2,884
Pakistan	2,377
India	2,243

Country	Prevalence of Malnutrition (% Under 5), 1995
Bangladesh	84
India	63
Pakistan	40
Egypt	9
Japan	17
Malaysia	23

Source: World Development Report, 1997, pp. 224-25

It is apparent from the above tables that Pakistan is doing very badly in the vital areas of development and social well being, with the exception of number of doctors available to provide medical services. Unfortunately, the quality of medical care is still very low in Pakistan despite the comparatively large number of doctors available. Perhaps sheer numbers of doctors available do not make that much of a difference. The view that our medical services are of low quality is based on personal observation and anecdotal evidence and not on any scientific study.

Pakistan suffers form a sustainable development crisis of staggering proportions. It has failed to undertake a sensible development path that might have led to material prosperity for all and at the same time not damaging the country's environment. Instead of a pragmatic approach based on participatory management, a bottom-up strategy and the democratic governance paradigm, Pakistan has followed an overly centralized, top-down, and bureaucratized approach with little or no citizen involvement. The country failed to develop as a result. Unfortunately, Pakistan's economic growth has not benefited the poor people of the country. In fact, the fruits of growth did not trickle down sufficiently notes the GOP's Debt Reduction Management Committee report issued in March 2001.[154]

REFORM AGENDA

The eradication of poverty is one of the foremost tasks of the Musharraf regime. This is a daunting challenge that must be met. There is some recognition in the UN and other international agencies that much more needs to be done for countries like Pakistan. Gustave Speth, Administrator, UNDP says that poverty cannot be eradicated without environmental security, among other things.[155] The Musharraf regime has planned that by the year 2003 Pakistan's poverty rate will go down to 26% and the population rate to 2.1%.

The Musharraf regime claims that eradication of poverty is one of its foremost tasks. Everyone agrees that this is a daunting challenge that must be met at all costs. The country depends upon success in this area. The GOP must spend more on the social sector by increasing the allocations for the PSDP, which are financed out of the annual budget. However, the reality is different. Over the years, the PSDP has decreased rather than grown. In 1991-92 budget the development expenditure was only 7% of GDP, which was further lowered to 5% in 1992-93. It was again further lowered to 3.3% in 1997-98, and 3.2% in 1998-99. Later, it is increased to 3.4% in 1999-2000. The current development budget is 3% of the GDP. In monetary terms, the PSDP in 1997-98 was allocated only Rs 90 billion.[156] The development budget for 1996-97 was allocated at Rs 104 billion versus Rs 96 billion in 1997-98 fiscal year. Since the rate of inflation was high, the development budget in real terms had been reduced.[157] The officially stated figure for inflation last year was 13%, and said to be 11% this year.[158] The target for 1996-97 was to lower it to a single digit of 8%.[159] For 1998-99, the PSDP was allocated Rs 110 billion but was reduced to Rs 98 billion in October 1998. For 1999-2000, Rs 116

[154] *Dawn*, March 26, 2001.
[155] See Forward, Global Public Goods, *UNDP web page*.
[156] Hasan Iqbal Jafri, "Sink or Swim?" *The Herald* (monthly), July 1997, 136.
[157] *Nation*, June 17, 1996, 7.
[158] *Dawn*, June 22, 1996.
[159] *Frontier Post*, May 19, 1996.

billion was allocated for the PSDP.[160] Today, Pakistan faces an environmental degradation crisis of staggering proportions. All available evidence indicates that the overall situation of Pakistan's environmental challenges is very serious. Thus, the problem of environmental degradation in the country is getting worse not better. In addition, there is ample evidence to suggest that Pakistan has failed to stem the tide of environmental degradation in any significant manner. Despite the rhetoric, the GOP has miserably failed to ensure adequate protection and sustainable use of the county's natural resources. A recent official report says that resulting from increasing impoverishment and absence of any alternatives an increasing number of poor and landless persons are putting "unprecedented pressure" on the country's natural resource base because of their survival struggle. In the next few decades, the most pressing challenge shall come from environmental degradation, poverty, and lack of agriculture planning. Besides it will induce health hazards due to lack of access to sanitation facilities and clean water, indoors pollution from biomass stoves, severe soil degradation, and deforestation.[161] Among others, the World Bank notes that poor natural resource management and population growth have has a negative impact on the country's water, land, and agricultural resource base. Pollution and environmental degradation are having an affect on public health and agricultural productivity and other economic sectors. This is holding back economic growth. More or less, all surface water is being contaminated by pollution from agricultural runoff, domestic and industrial waste. Overgrazing, water logging, wind and water erosion, and salinization, have degraded almost 42% of the land in the country. Air pollution levels are escalating and are already above World Health Organization standards in Karachi and Lahore.[162] Some of Pakistan's natural resources like water for irrigation purposes and forests are facing increasing pressure. Like so many other developing countries, Pakistan today needs help of the international donor community. In fact, if the economy does not show significant improvement, overall poverty is projected to further increase in the current decade. More poverty shall translate into more pressures on the natural resources of the country. There is some recognition in the UN and other international agencies that much more needs to be done for countries like Pakistan. . We cannot achieve sustainable human development without reversing the depletion of fresh water, clean air, and soils. [163]

The GOP has pledged that by the year 2003 the poverty rate will go down to 26% and the population rate to 2.1%. The strategy says that increased public expenditure has the potential to reduce poverty by undertaking the following actions:[164] (a) Provide cash and food transfer to the most vulnerable and disadvantaged population, (b) Allocate more resources to the development of basic infrastructure needed by for farmers, (c) Provide micro-credit to entrepreneurs establishing labor-intensive small and medium industrial

---

[160] Public Sector Development Program: New Initiatives 1999 (Planning Commission, Government of Pakistan, n.d.), 2.

[161] *The Nation*, June 19, 2000.

[162] *Country Brief: Pakistan.* Html, (World Bank Group Home web page, News, Publications, Topics in Development- Countries and Regions, IBRD | IDA | IFC | MIGA).

[163] See Forward, Global Public Goods, <http: www UNDP web page>.

[164] *Dawn*, July 26, 2000.

enterprises, (d) Improve the efficiency and enhance the level of public expenditures directed towards safe water supply and sanitation facilities, basic healthcare and primary education. The Food Support Program was launched on August 29, 2000. Under the program, monetary assistance will be provided to millions poor people. The Khushal Pakistan Program, previously known as the Poverty Alleviation Program, was launched last year with an allocation of Rs 35 billion. By end last year, a total of 6365 development schemes had been approved, out of which 3058 schemes had already been completed while another 2,476 are to be completed by the end of this year. The national program will provide jobs to about 0.5 million people.[165]

The country faces the staggering twin challenge of increasing poverty and environmental degradation. Just recently, the European Union (EU) has recommended the inclusion of Pakistan in the list of those poor countries of the world that will be getting cash assistance of around $1 billion this year for poverty alleviation. The Relief Commissioner of the EU has based his contention on the report of special representative of the World Bank who has stated that one fourth of the population is living below the poverty line and if immediate assistance is not provided Pakistan's security and sovereignty will be put at risk.[166] Explaining the reason for Pakistan's backwardness, General Musharraf claims that: "During the last fifty years, the country could not march towards the path of development, despite availability of rich mineral resources. The past governments could have made efforts to remove poverty, but their wrong policies further aggravated the situation".[167] He vowed that his government will "make all out efforts to improve the deteriorating economic conditions in order to eradicate poverty and hunger in the country".[168]

FAILURES AND ACHIEVEMENTS OF THE MUSHARRAF REGIME

Why has Pakistan's economic performance remained poor? Policy makers agree on a number of primary reasons: political instability, poor governance, corruption, and lack of consistent state policies. As Pakistan's population is rapidly increasing, it must increase the economic growth rate just to stay at the same level. Failing to do so would further increase poverty in the country. The economic crisis was acknowledged by the Musharraf regime. However, it claims that because of some vital steps, the economic slide has been checked and the country has been put on the road to sustained growth. Meanwhile, the World Bank has placed Pakistan with Congo and Ethiopia. While the debt burden increased, the GNP declined from $63.5 billion to $ 58.8 billion in 1999. The debt indicators for Pakistan have worsened and it has joined the severely indebted group of low-income countries, according to Global development Finance of the World Bank.[169] Given the fact that the primary problem in Pakistan is the implementation of policy, one

---

[165] *Pakistan Observer*, March 10, 2001.
[166] *Pakistan Observer*, July 10, 2000.
[167] *Pakistan Observer*, Aug. 30, 2000.
[168] Ibid.

may ask what is the ground reality. In other word, how well has the military really managed the economic affairs of the country? General Musharraf claims that the country has been put "on the road to economic recovery".[170] Does the claim hold any weight? The reality is different from what the General Musharraf's rhetoric would suggest. Consider the following performance failures:

1. Tackle the very serious problem of debt expansion. In the year 2000-2001, debt servicing payments are projected to increase by 7.9% to Rs 4,1632 million or by 2.7% of GDP by end of June 2001.[171]The 2001-2002 budget an astronomical amount of Rs. 329.18 billion has been set aside for debt servicing, which is 40% of the total outlays of Rs 752 billion.[172]

2. Decrease the budget deficit. The budget 2001-2002 has given a deficit of Rs 186.9 billion or 4.9% of GDP.[173]

3. Tackle the problem of current account imbalance by simultaneously taking three measures: (i) generate additional export surplus in the manufacturing and agriculture sectors; (ii) attract foreign direct investment (FDI) as well as domestic investment; (iii) privatize public sector enterprises which have been in the red for a long time.

4. Put sufficient emphasis on poverty alleviation and provision of relief to the poorest sections of society. Inn fact, the poverty alleviation programs and development expenditures have been cut.[174]

5. Bring down the population growth rate to a satisfactory level. The population growth rate continues to be a high 2.6% per year while India's growth rate has decreased to 1.9%.[175] Independent analysts point out that the real population growth rate in Pakistan is about 3% per year and not the lower figure of 2.6% given by the GOP.[176]

6. Establish of an enabling environment for economic growth by following good governance practices and sound planning.

7. Improve the savings and investment, which have fallen to 11% of GDP, the lowest for a long time.[177]

8. Undertake bold action to tackle the horrendous task of documentation of the economy and elimination of smuggling.

9. Revive and sustain a high level of economic growth. The State Bank of Pakistan's recent third quarterly report for current fiscal year said that the GDP

---

[169] *The News-* Business section, April 11, 2001.
[170] *The Economist*, May 26, 2001, 30.
[171] See Economic Survey 2000-2001 (Islamabad: GOP, EAD, June 2001) in *PO*, June 17, 2001.
[172] See Budget 20001-20002 (Islamabad: GoP, Finance Division, June 2001) in *PO* June 19, 2001.
[173] *PO*, June 20, 2001, 1.
[174] See editorial, "lies and damned lies", *The Friday Times,* vol. Xiii, no. 15, June 8-14, 2001, 1.
[175] See Bottomline, *Asia week*, Nov. 17, 2000, 51.
[176] See editorial, "lies and damned lies", *The Friday Times,* vol. Xiii, no. 15, June 8-14, 2001, 1.
[177] Ibid.

growth would remain below 3%. Last year the growth rate was 4.5%.[178] The actual growth in fiscal 2000-20001 is estimated to be only 2.6%.[179]

10. Introduce better debt management. Reduce the total debt, both domestic and foreign, on a credible and sustainable basis.

11. Bring a dent to rising unemployment rates.

12. Improve human development indicators and the PQLI (Physical Quality of Life Indicators) as measured by UN agencies.

13. Levy a reasonable General Sales Tax (GST) and agriculture income tax. The present GST at 15% is very high.

14. Sufficiently decrease the "underground economy" or black economy", which is estimated somewhere between 50-70% of the regular economy. A number of general amnesty schemes have failed to make a meaningful dent in the "underground economy", for a limited time, had been given already

15. Meet the export target. Earlier, the target for exports for 2000-2001 was set at $10 billion. There was an increase of 11.3% in exports in the first half of the current fiscal year, giving some hope that the annual target would be met. However, the State Bank of Pakistan's third quarterly report for current fiscal year said that the annual exports are likely to be about $9.3 billion only.[180] The country's actual exports during 2000-20001 were about $9 billion. In comparison with some other developing countries, the performance of Pakistan in the export sector remains very poor. In comparison, the figure for India is nearly $40 billion and Malaysia $80 billion.[181] The exports of both Singapore and Honk Kong are above $100 billion per year. Emphasize increasing exports on a high priority-basis. The realization that the most crucial aspect of the implementation strategy was that it shows an unwavering commitment to implement the reform in full. The military regime should initiate a reform agenda that should carry out the plan of the second Nawaz government, which had emphasized the following strategic directions:[182] (a) create a culture of export and quality in society, and including civil society institutions. Media institutions, professional associations, community development organizations, educational and research institutions, and NGOs, shall had to be involved in creating such a culture, (b) Ensure adequate supplies of raw materials for export industries on competitive rates, (c) Accomplish rapid institutional change for the creation of a supportive environment conducive to increased trade, (d) Focus on changing market conditions, trends and opportunities made available in the new global economy, (e)Promulgate an Export Insurance Scheme to safeguard new exporters, (f)Harmonize tariffs with ASEAN and develop a mechanism for exchange of information, (g) Explore ASEAN markets for non-traditional exports. The country may enter barter trade of some goods with ASEAN, (h) Pursue

---

[178] *Pakistan Observer*, June 1, 2001.
[179] See *Economic Survey 2000-2001* (Islamabad: GOP, Economic Affairs Division, June 2001), 1.
[180] *Pakistan Observer*, June 1, 2001.
[181] See Bottomline, *Asia week*, Nov. 17, 2000, 51.
[182] See unpublished report of the Planning Commission, Government of Pakistan, 1999.

aggressive marketing tactics, improve quality, price products in a realistic manner, and participate in trade fairs, (i) Better involvement of the Commerce Ministry in strengthening the trade sector. The ministry be fully aware of the implications of developments in the WTO regime and shall assist in better tapping the huge potential for trade expansion. It shall make the country better prepared to make use of the opportunities available. Simultaneously, steps were taken as part of an overall strategy, under Commerce Ministry guidance, to meet the requirements of WTO and be in a state of greater preparedness to deal with the concerns of our global customers, (j) More emphasis on increased trade in services and making better use of special treatment currently available to Pakistan as a developing country, (k) Incentives provided to export industries to increase value-added production. Increased emphasis on Total Quality Management and productivity shall become the topmost priority in Pakistan's production and service sectors, (l) Establishment of more Export Processing Zones (EPZs) in the country like in Lahore and Rawalpindi in proximity to the newly set up industrial zones. Organize of the EPZA along modern and professional lines in order to provide better services to foreign

16. Increase Foreign Direct Investment (FDI). There has been an actual decline in FDI in 2000-20001. The GOP's finance minister says that it is because of the economic sanctions, IPP issue and "unpleasant relations" between Pakistan and international financial institutions.[183]There was a decline of 70% over 1999-2000 fiscal year's level, bringing it to $150 million in the first three quarters of 1999-2000. [184] In 1999, it amounted to around $600 million, which constituted 0.21 per cent of FDI global flows ($4.7 trillion). Experts agree that Pakistan can increase FDI inflows only if its policy of offering incentives is consistent with its macro-economic policy, taxation framework, a consistent investment policy, besides establishing a framework for property rights and dispute settlement.

17. Discipline the government departments, as far as its own billing obligations are concerned. For example, the total debt of the two power utilities - WAPDA and KESC - to the federal and provincial governments has crossed $2.4 billion. "This exceeds the government's proposed development expenditure budget for financial year 2000 of $1.940 billion, i.e. the debt of the sector is 1.25 times of the government's development budget," said a report of the Asian Development Bank (ADB). The net liabilities of WAPDA as on June 2000 amounted to $1.4 billion, while KESC carried $631 million of net debt, said the report that is submitted to the federal government in December. Foreign exchange reserves are at $1.48 billion only. India, in comparison, has reserves of over $36 billion.[185] Pakistan had to meet the foreign debt liability of $4.5 billion by end of the 2000-2001 fiscal year.

---

[183] See speech of finance minister, Shaukat Aziz while presenting the Economic Survey 2000-20001 on June 16, 20001 in *Pakistan Observer*, June 17, 2001.
[184]See editorial, "lies and damned lies", *The Friday Times*, vol. Xiii, no. 15, June 8-14, 2001, 1.
[185] For the figure of India only, Ibid.

18. Meet revenue targets. The GoP has consistently failed to meet its revenue targets. The 2000-2001 fiscal year's thrice revised target of Rs 406 was also not met. Only Rs 302 billion were collected in the fiscal year.[186]

19. Plan for the rise of per capita income from the current $495 to a reasonable level, say $1,000, must be achieved in a reasonable time. This could only happen when domestic savings are adequately mobilized towards investments in economic and social development, retirement of substantial portion of domestic and international debt which should then reduce the severe debt servicing costs in the state budgets, and restoration of Pakistan's international financial credibility.

20. Adequately strengthen the financial and fiscal systems, create a favorable investment climate to attract foreign investment, and improve resource allocation mechanisms. Financial sector reform included giving greater autonomy and powers to the State Bank of Pakistan and the Corporate Law Authority, better monitoring and regulation of the banking sector by both the State Bank of Pakistan and the Finance Ministry, the strengthening of stock exchange regulatory mechanisms, better devices to mobilize savings by the institution of mandatory pension schemes, and the increase of Government savings through overall stringency measures pertaining to budgetary expenditure.

21. Satisfactorily strengthen the role of the Auditor General Pakistan (AGP) and application of additional resources for development of financial audit performance capabilities. A system of follow-up actions to hold individuals accountable for lapses and poor performance highlighted in AGP Annual Reports.

22. Increase spending on the social sector necessary for sustainable development of Pakistan.

23. Carry out an elaborate public education exercise to herald a strategic shift from consumption to investment.

24. Provide incentives to correct the abysmally low level of domestic savings in the country. Failed to increase the low savings rate. The figure was only 14.4% of GDP in fiscal year 2000-2001 Earlier in fiscal 1999-2000 it had been 15.2% of GDP.[187] In comparison, the figure for India is 22%.[188] The program should envisage a concerted effort for the mobilization of savings, including the introduction of a mandatory pension scheme, strengthening of financial institutions, strengthening of stock exchanges, the gradual reduction in state borrowings, and the encouragement of private savings instruments

25. Rebuild investor confidence shattered by past actions and in pursuing policies consistently and not changing them as frequently as done in the past.

26. Rightsize the GOP by the creation of a leaner and fitter civil service system. The Pakistan civil service system has about 3 million members, in comparison; the Indian civil service has in all about 8 million members. The recommendations

---

[186] *Dawn*, July 7, 2001,9.
[187] See Economic Survey 2000-2001, (Islamabad: Government of Pakistan, Economic Affairs Division, June 2001) in *Pakistan Observer*, June 17, 2001.

made in a number of reports suggest that the civil service could shed its weight to the extent of one-third of its present strength. Concerted efforts at restructuring the civil service have not been made yet. Economic problems require a reduction in GOP expenditures. Systematic efforts are lacking in this area. Steps have not been taken to curb the creation of new posts, abolish vacant posts in non-critical services, and to right size GOP departments.

27. Carry out a meaningful review of the functions of all public sector agencies, and federal statutory bodies. Some might need to be merged with other departments or even dissolved. In addition, the function of all urban Development Authorities like the Lahore Development Authority, and the Capital Development Authority need to be reviewed. Unnecessary duplication of efforts at this level is curtailed. Jurisdiction issues remain unsettled and control is clearly not demarcated. Functions of different agencies are not spelled out clearly. New posts should be created only when an assessment has been made on their relevancy in meeting the needs of critical sectors only. Consolidate in the functions of federal government. Cut the accumulated fat on the federal and provincial governments that has accumulated over the decades. End waste rampant in the bureaucracies. Anecdotal evidence suggested that billions of rupees could be saved because of strict measures.

28. Modernize the financial management system by completing and implementing international standards like PIFRA as planned in the second Nawaz government.[189] The intention of the system is to expedite the preparation of accurate financial statements in GOP agencies. The PIFRA system will fulfill the following four objectives: (i) Facilitate the maintenance of a complete and up-to-date set of accounts, (ii) Enable daily closing of accounts, wherever applicable, (iii) Provide for an improved management, budgeting, and accounting system, (iv) Enable timely preparation of the pre-audit annual financial statements, (v) To expedite the preparation of accurate financial statements in government agencies. A new financial management system to fulfill the following objectives:(i) Use of standard indicators on the performance of a Government agency, (ii) Facilitate the maintenance of a complete and up-to-date set of accounts, (iii) Enable daily closing of accounts, wherever applicable, (iv) Enable timely preparation of the pre-audit annual financial statements.

29. Bring a fall in real interest rates.

30. Increase development expenditure from 3% of GDP to a reasonable level of 5%.

31. Provide for a safe foreign exchange reserve position. As of June 20, 2001, the total foreign exchange reserves stood at $2.85 billion is very low.[190] In comparison the reserves of India are above $40 billion

32. Prevent millions to fall below the poverty line. The Social Development Policy Center's latest report indicates that 15 million more people could fall below the

---

[188] See Bottomline, *Asia week*, Nov. 17, 2000, 51
[189] See unpublished report of the Planning Commission, Government of Pakistan, 1999.
[190] *Pakistan Observer*, June 20, 2001, 11.

poverty line in the next three years if Pakistan was compelled to make a balance of payments adjustments in the short run due to severe foreign exchange reserves.[191]

33. National savings dropped by 1% of GDP from 13.7% in 1999-2000 to 12.7% during 2000-2001 year.[192]

34. Public investment declined by 0.2% and private investment by 0.7%.[193]

35. In 2000-2001, the spending limits have overshot by Rs 43 billion.[194]

36. There was a decrease of 2.5% in agriculture in the 2000-2001 year, as opposed to an impressive increase of 6.1 in 1999-2000 year.[195]

The Musharraf regime's achievements include, but not limited to, the following: [196]

1. On June 7, 2001 the National Economic Council (NEC), which is the highest decision-making body on economic issues approved a 4.5% GDP growth rate for next fiscal year.

2. In the Budget 2001-2002, approval was given to an Rs 130 billion PSDP, which was 7.9% over the budget estimates for 2000-20001 and 27.4% over the revised estimates for fiscal 2000-20001. The federal government's share is Rs 100 billion and the provincial governments' total share is Rs 30 billion only. Domestic funding is 60%, while donor funding is 40% of the PSDP. The GOP has allocated Rs 10 billion for the drought stricken areas, Rs 7 billion under the Khushal Pakistan program, Rs 3 billion for the devolution plan, Rs 5 billion for Northern Areas, Azad Kashmir, and FATA, Rs 4.8 billion for special programs like Karachi and Quetta water supply schemes and physical infrastructure for the police, Rs 9 billion for water related projects, Rs 13.8 billion for electricity power, Rs 21.6 billion for Transport and communication (Rs 13.3 billion for National Highway Authority, and Rs 6.3 billion for Railways), Rs 6.7 billion for fuels, Rs 2.7 billion for health and nutrition, Rs 1.1 billion for rural development, Rs 3.5 billion for IT, Rs 2.5 billion for Science and Technology, Rs 1.8 billion for population welfare, Rs 2.4 billion for education and training, Rs 0.7 billion for agriculture, Rs 1.6 billion for Physical Planning and Housing, and Rs 1.1 billion for planning, statistics, and research, Rs 0.3 billion each for industry and environment, and Rs 0.2 billion for mass media..[197]

---

[191] See report "A national Poverty Reduction Strategy and the Role of Donors" by SPDC in *Pak Observer*, May 6, 2001.

[192] *The News*, June 7, 2001, 12 and see Economic Survey 2000-2001 (Islamabad: GOP, EAD, June 2001), in *PO*, June 17, 2001.

[193] *The News*, June 7, 2001, 12

[194] Ibid.

[195] See Economic Survey 2000-20001 (Islamabad: GOP, EAD, June 2001) in *PO*, June 17, 2001.

[196] See *Pakistan Observer*, Dec. 17, 2000, *The Nation*, Dec. 17, 1999 and *The News*, Dec. 13 & 17, 1999, *The News*, Jan. 3, 2001 and also see and also Budget 2001-2002 (Islamabad: GOP, June 2001), *Pakistan Observer*, June 19, 2001, 1.

[197] *The Nation*, June 8, 2001, 10 and *Pakistan Observer*, June 8, 2001, 1& 11.

3. Approval of an Rs 304.2 billion three-year perspective plan. During 2001-04, Rs 86.1 billion will be spent on water related projects, Rs 81.2 billion for Transport and Communication (Rs 50.8 billion for National Highway Authority, and Rs 23.3 billion for Railways), Rs 47.2 for power sector, Rs 11.5 billion for fuels, Rs 12.9 billion for Health & Nutrition, Rs 47.2 for power, Rs 17 billion for Khushal Pakistan Program, Rs 11.5 billion for fuels, Rs 12.9 for health and nutrition, Rs 4.75 billion for rural development, Rs 13 billion for Information Technology, Rs 10 billion for Science & Technology, Rs 8.5 billion for population welfare, Rs 8.5 billion for Education and Training, Rs 5.7 billion for Agriculture, Rs 5.9 billion for Physical Planning and Housing, Rs. 3.6 billion for Planning, statistics and research, Rs 1.4 billion for industry, and Rs 1.2 billion for environment, and 0.8 billion for mass media.[198]

4. Approval for a 10-year perspective development plans. The 10-year perspective development plan (2001-2011) will have a total investment of Rs 1,553.9 billion, including public sector investment of Rs. 2.5 trillion and private sector investment of Rs 8.7 trillion. The aims of the plan are:[199] (a) Accelerating GDP growth, reduce unemployment, and alleviate poverty; (b) Financing growth increasingly by own national resources; (c) Contain external and domestic borrowing; (d) Improve competitiveness through promotion of productivity, efficiency, and quality; (e) Build human capacity for the long-term, conducive to sustainable development.

5. The allocation made for water is Rs 250 billion, transport and communication is Rs 332.4 billion, fuels is Rs 20.4 billion, health and nutrition is Rs 45 billion, rural development is Rs 34.7 billion, IT is Rs 27 billion, Science &Technology is Rs 24 billion, population welfare is Rs 34.1 billion, educating and training is Rs 29.5 billion, agriculture is Rs 20.7 billion, physical planning and housing is Rs 9.5 billion, planning, statistics and research is Rs 9.6 billion, industry is Rs 5.4 billion, environment is Rs 4.7 billion, mass media is Rs 2.8 billion, and social welfare is Rs 1.5 billion.[200]

6. Plan to build country's foreign exchange reserve to $4 billion in the next two years.[201]

7. For the first time, collecting Rs 392 billion in taxes without increasing the taxes and by broadening the base instead.

8. For the first time crossing the $9 billion mark in exports.[202] For the first three quarter of current fiscal year (July-march) exports increased by 8.4%, as opposed to 8.9% last year in the same period.[203]

[198] *Pakistan Observer*, June 10, 2001, 9.
[199] *Pakistan Observer*, June 8, 2001, 11.
[200] *The Nation*, June 8, 2001, 10.
[201] Ibid.
[202] Ibid.
[203] *The News*, June 11, 2001.

9. Lowering inflation rate to 4.7% in the first ten months of fiscal year 2000-20001. It was only 3.4% in the comparable period during 1999-2000, while it was 6.3% in 19998-1999.[204]

10. For the first nine months (July – March) of fiscal year 2000-2001 the large-scale manufacturing was up by 7.8%, up from decline of 0.2% in the comparable period of 1999-2000. Overall, manufacturing grew by 7.1%, as against revised estimates of 1.4% last year.[205]

11. Home remittances have increased by 16.8%, as against a fall of about 9% last year, and a fall of 31.5% a year earlier.[206]

12. The fiscal deficit was down to 5.3% in 2000-2001, as against 6.5% in 1999-2000 fiscal year, and 6.1% in 1998-1999 fiscal year.[207]

13. Foreign investment of $700 million in oil and gas sector alone.

14. Improved cash recovery position. According to international financial institutions, total size of stuck-up loans, including all the public, private and commercial banks, was still Rs 208 billion (about $4 billion). There must be a marked improvement in this area. The National Accountability Bureau (NAB) had recovered about Rs 56.7 billion, which was a good start.

15. Some restructuring the entire system of public finances by following good governance practices. Fiscal discipline, scientific mechanisms for checks and monitoring and judicious control over all state spending was a basic requirement of good governance in the financial area.

16. Launching of a Rs. 35 billion Poverty Alleviation Program.

17. Great progress in the Information Technology field. Rapid spreading of Internet connections across the country.[208]

18. Considerable improvement in the affairs of Pakistan Steel Mills, NHA, PIA, WAPDA and Railways.

19. Restructuring of the Central Board of Revenue (CBR) is a very high priority. Shaukat Aziz, the Finance Minister recently stated that the GoP aims at improving the tax system, broadening the tax base, and ensure better collection from the from the existing base. [209] Some steps have already been taken to document the economy strengthen the IT system, planned gradual integration of all the tax records, widening the tax base, and extending an across-the-board General Sales Tax. In addition, steps taken to eradicate the confusion and complexity in tax payment. The federal taxes shall be cut from the current more than twenty heads to just three (income, sales and customs). Reduction of 22 provincial taxes in Punjab to just seven. The revenue target for fiscal 2000-2001

---

[204] See Report of the State Bank of Pakistan (end of third quarter (March), fiscal year 2000-2001, *Pakistan Observer*, June 1, 2001, and *The News*, June 11, 2001. and also Economic Survey 200-20001 (Islamabad: GOP, June 2001), *PO*, June 17, 2001, 1.

[205] See Economic Survey 200-20001 (Islamabad: GOP, June 2001), *PO*, June 17, 2001, 1.

[206] See State Bank Report *The News*, June 11, 2001 and also Economic Survey 200-20001 (Islamabad: GOP, June 2001), *PO*, June 17, 2001, 1.

[207] Ibid.

[208] *Pakistan Observer*, Jan. 7, 2001.

[209] *Pakistan Observer*, May 25, 2001.

was Rs 435 billion, an increase of Rs 90 billion in actual receipts from 1999-2000 fiscal year. Total tax revenue collected I 2000-20001 was Rs 390 billion, up by Rs 43 billion from 1999-2000.[210] An increase of 11.3% in tax revenue in first five months of current fiscal year. An additional Rs 10 billion has been added resulting from the latest Tax Amnesty Scheme. This was ten times more than all such schemes in the past. The scope of direct taxes is being enlarged. For the first time, the Musharraf regime had decided to tax income from the farm sector in 2000.

20. Establishment of a new financial institution – Corporate Industrial Restructuring Corporation – to help solve the problem of sick industries.

21. Establishment of the Khushali Bank, a micro-credit bank modeled on the famous Grameen Bank.

22. Resolving the lingering dispute between Hubco and WAPDA. The country should save $1 billion due to the agreement wherein HUBCO has agreed to reduce tariff from 6.6 cents to 5.6 cents per unit of electricity.

23. Some strengthening of the role of the Auditor General Pakistan (AGP) and application of additional resources for development of financial audit performance capabilities. A system of follow-up actions to hold individuals accountable for lapses and poor performance highlighted in AGP Annual Reports. An adhoc arrangement under H. U. Beg, a veteran bureaucrat, has been made to streamline the work of the Public Accounts Committee responsible for the scrutiny and action based on the AGP reports. The committee has unearthed irregularities worth Rs 7 billion in Pakistan Steel, the biggest state enterprise, and is referring all corruption cases to NAB for further investigations. Similarly, it unearthed irregularities amounting to vast amounts in Pakistan National Shipping Corporation, another big state corporation

24. The initiation of a planning in strategic terms. The Planning Commission is working on a 2025 Plan broken up into segments that of five, ten, fifteen, twenty and twenty five years. Future Five Year Plans to be integrated in the 2025 Plan.

25. Downsizing of the government bureaucracy. The federal government shall cut by about 40,000 posts. In addition, some 45,000 employees of the Sindh government shall be sacked soon.[211] Merger of various departments in the provincial governments. For example, the forest, wildlife, traffic departments and some functions of other related departments in the NWFP government were to be merged into a new Department of the Environment.[212] The Musharraf regime has removed 2,586 federal officials. The provinces have imposed major penalties, which also include demotion to lower post, in case of 7,508 officials. The pace was unprecedented in history. So many officials had never been removed through legal means and established procedures.[213]

---

[210] *Pakistan Observer*, July 8, 2001, 12.

[211] *Pakistan Observer*, Jan. 7, 2001.

[212] *Pakistan Observer*, Jan. 6, 2001.

[213] *The News*, July 5, 2001.

26. Lowering of the maximum customs duty from 35 to 30% from July 1, 2001. Reduce tariff slabs from 5 to 4 with minimum duty on raw materials and machinery and maximum on finished goods.

27. Approval of separation of audit and accounting functions of the Auditor General Pakistan. A separate office of the Controller General of accounts shall be established for the preparing and maintaining accounts of the GOP, provincial and district governments. The Controller General will accredit all payments and withdrawals against approved budgeted provisions the creation of this office is in line with the principle that the authority that prepares the accounts ought not to certify the same as this creates conflict of interest. Thus, this development will provide transparency in the financial affairs of the GOP, provinces and district governments.[214].

28. The GOP intends to enact a law, which will limit the government borrowing to control debt.[215]

29. Various measures were taken in the budget 2001-2002 to strengthen the capital market that would fuehrer prop up the stock market, banking sector, and DFIs with extension in income tax exemptions on capital gains for another five years.[216]

30. Various development projects including the Makran coastal highway, Mirani, Gomal and other dams, and the development project for Gwadar shall be undertaken to beef up economic activities and create employment opportunities.[217]

31. Increase in the salaries of government employees, including defense personnel by an average of 17% to benefit 3 million salaried persons in the civil government and defense. However, the increase will be given on January 1, 2001 only. [218]

32. Decrease of duty tariff on 4,000 items to prop up industrial growth, and increasing duties on some items to protect local industry.[219] The SRO regime has been made transparent to provide a level playing field to all industries. The number of SROs was reduced from 120 to 60.[220]

In sum, the overall performance of the military regime in the year 2000 has been less than spectacular. Thus, the above facts support the conclusion that Pakistan's political economy remains in a crisis with no easy recovery in sight. However, the Musharraf regime certainly seems to be serious in its attempt to revive the ailing economy. Will it succeed? The success of the reform agenda depends upon many factors other than purely economic, including but not limited to, the political situation inside and outside Pakistan. Only time will tell whether the Musharraf regime is able to defeat the circumstance odds

[214] *Dawn*, May 17, 2001.
[215] *PO*, June 20, 20001, 11.
[216] *PO*, June 20, 2001, 11.
[217] Ibid.
[218] Ibid.
[219] Ibid.
[220] Ibid.

placed against it for achieving any meaningful victory. . The Musharraf regime should focus more on the revival of Pakistan's economy. The country's future depends on success in this area.

THE DEFENSE EXPENDITURE CONTROVERSY

Military spending is a controversial issue in Pakistan.

By all measures, the military spending in Pakistan is indeed very high. Pakistan's spending on defense is about 6% of GNP. On a comparative basis defense spending in relationship with GNP is still in the high category of country spending in the sector. Previously, the allocation for the 1996-97 budget for the defense sector was 4.2% of the projected GDP in 1996-97, up from 4.0% of GDP in 1995-96.[221] In the 1998 fiscal year, Pakistan's defense allocation was $3.3 billion, or Rs 145 billion, as compared to India's defense allocation, which is $9.8 billion. Pakistan's defense budget had increased by 8% from the previous year, which was Rs 134 billion. In comparison, India's 1998 defense budget is $9.8 billion slightly lower than $10 billion in 1997. India's defense budget in 1994 was $8 billion, which increased to $8.8 billion in 1995, then slightly decreased to $8.6 billion in 1996. The proponents of heavy defense expenditures had failed to make a convincing case especially when comparatively speaking the social sectors are so far behind in terms of resource allocation. Earlier, the Nawaz Government had decided to cut defense spending in the 1997 budget. The defense sector's allocation in fiscal 1997-98 was Rs 134 billion had decreased by 8% in real terms from the 1996-97 allocation of Rs 131 billion. Military spending is 29% of total current expenditure.[222] The defense allocation for 1999-2000 was Rs 142 billion, which is a staggering 45% of the total tax revenue. Subsequently, the defense budget was cut by the Musharraf regime by Rs 7 billion. The move was welcomed by both Pakistanis, and the international financial institutions that had given credit to the country. The defense budget for fiscal 2000-20001 was capped at Rs 131.6 billion, which was at the level of the revised spending in the 2001-2002 fiscal year. According to the Human Development Report, military expenditures as percentage of combined education and health expenditures in 1989-90 were much higher than some other Muslim countries, with the exception of Iraq. See following table:[223]

---

[221] "Federal Budget in Brief, Finance Division, Government of Pakistan", *Dawn*, June 22, 1996.

[222] *The Herald* (monthly), July 1997.

[223] See Human Development Report, 1992 in *American Journal of Islamic Social Sciences,* Vol. 12 No. 3, Fall 1995, 337.

Country	Military Expenditure as % of Combined Education & Health Expenditure
Pakistan	239
Saudi Arabia	177
Indonesia	143
Jordan	128
Iraq	511

Previously, Mahbub-ul Haq estimated that defense spending consumes 6% of Pakistan's GNP. Calculated on a per capita basis it costs $28 per year. The military expenditure is 125% of social spending on health and education. Comparatively our country carries a heavier defense burden than India, which spends only 3% of its GNP on defense. The comparative Indian figures for per capita cost is $10 and for the ratio of military to social spending ration is 65%. In aggregate term, India spends three times more than Pakistan. Objective analysis would indicate that both countries are spending far too much on defense and far to less on health and education. This situation has made them fall behind many African countries in terms of human development. The cost of military spending in terms of human development is very high. Since Pakistan's policy is based on reaction to Indian moves it would be impractical to expect that Pakistan would be able to unilaterally cut down its military expenditures, argues Mahbub-ul Haq.[224] He continues to argue that Pakistan is not deficit in enough resources to meet both development and military expenses. The problem is that we are managing them poorly. The country can raise at least another Rs. 100 billion yearly from proper collection of taxes, exchanging costly domestic debt against the sale of public assets, stern checks against corruption and embezzlement of public resources, and better quality control of public expenditure.[225] If the money is obtained than there can be a reduction of the budget deficit, finance the dilapidated social sector, and at the same time carry on with the current defense burden. We are not too sure on the premise of the argument. Mahbub-ul Haq wants all things to be set straight. We want it too. However, easier said than done! In the meanwhile, we must do what is best for the country now and not in the future. Pakistan must decide for itself based on its own requirements and the quickest way to achieve some of our national objectives. We simply do not need to ape anyone including our large neighbor. Benazir once claimed that one of the three major factors that have strained the economy was the heavy defense expenditure. The other two being the increasing burden of debts and the need for "economic democratization".[226] The proponents of heavy defense expenditures have failed to make a convincing case especially when comparatively speaking the social sectors are so far behind in terms of resource allocation. Pakistan is already spending three times more per capita on defense

[224] Mahbub-ul Haq, "Security without Starvation", *The News*, May 22, 1996.
[225] Ibid.
[226] "Federal Budget", *Dawn*, June 22, 1996.

than archrival India is. The total budget is much smaller, however. See table below for a comparison of Pakistan's military balance with India.[227]

	India	Pakistan
Armed Forces	1.2 million	587,000
Troops/1,000 citizens	1.1	4.4
Defense Budget (1996) (2000)	$8.4 billion	$3.8 billion
Per capita defense expenditure (1996)	$8.5	$28.5

The public, we ardently believe, desire a bigger defense cut. It needs to be pointed out that bigger state spending does not automatically mean better defense. Anecdotal evidence suggests that allocated money is wasted in the defense sector. The privileged and indulgent lifestyle of the military brass must also end with that of its civilian counterpart. After all, there is nothing special about the military in Pakistan. Politicians are afraid to criticize the military more out of displaced fear and myth than anything else is. Pakistan being one of the poorest countries of the world, as regards social well-being, cannot afford a big military. The fat on the military muscle needs to be cut as well. It is as simple as that. The people need to argue that the country really does not have a choice in the matter. We speculate that the caretakers are afraid to touch the defense sector. Such is the power of the Army in Pakistan. One of the basic principles of democracy is the establishment of civilian supremacy over the military. We urgently need to constitute this principle in Pakistan.

Ajay Singh argues, "The quest for military superiority has escalated into a dangerous, and expensive race in one of the world's poorest regions".[228] More money spent upon defense is not equivalent to better national security. The Pakistani military, like any other in the world, will always try its best to protect its allocations. We need to understand that this is normal politics between different bureaucratic structures. In our case, the matter is beyond inside politics and has become one of principle. The defense sector cannot be spared the belt tightening the caretakers have imposed on civilian government departments. The military must also share in the national hardship of resource constraints. Anything less is to be considered as unprincipled and should be condemned as despicable principle. We have to improvise and seek a better defense with less money. Maybe we really do not need such a large standing army just maybe a smaller military plus a better-trained reserve force like the one in Israel. Just maybe it can do the job of securing a better defense of the country. Alternate proposals of military structural reform cannot be dismissed without the required debate. Why cannot Pakistan achieve simultaneously the twin goals of better military preparedness with less money spent? The proposal cannot reject outright. As a sage once said, the business of war is too serious to be left for generals alone. In addition, Clausewitz reminds us that after all war are nothing but the continuation of politics by other means. The supremacy of the civilian order over that of

---

[227] Source: *The Military Balance 1996/97* and *Asian Strategic Review 1995/96*.
[228] Ajay Singh, "India's Fight to Keep Fit", *Asiaweek*, October 17, 1997, 36-37.

the military is a fundamental principle of democracy and cannot be compromised. No matter what!

The cost of military spending in terms of human development is very high. Since Pakistan's policy is based on reaction to Indian moves it would be impractical to expect that Pakistan would be able to unilaterally cut down its military expenditures, argues Mahbub-ul Haq.[229] Pakistan must decide for itself based on its own requirements of adequate defense. Pakistan can learn to do more with less. It simply does not need to ape anyone including its large neighbor. Benazir once claimed that one of the three major factors that have strained the economy was the heavy defense expenditure. The other two being the increasing burden of debts and the need for "economic democratization".[230] The proponents of heavy defense expenditures have failed to make a convincing case especially when comparatively speaking the social sectors are so far behind in terms of resource allocation. Pakistan is already spending three times more per capita on defense than archrival India is. The total budget is much smaller, however.[231] Previously, the second Nawaz government decided to cut defense spending in the 1997 budget. The defense sector's allocation of Rs 134 billion was decreased by 8% in real terms from the previous year's allocation of Rs 131 billion. Military spending is 29% of total current expenditure.[232] The public, we ardently believe, must call for a bigger defense cut. It needs to be pointed out that bigger state spending does not automatically mean better defense. Anecdotal evidence suggests that allocated money is wasted in the defense sector. The privileged and indulgent lifestyle of the military brass must also end with that of its civilian counterpart. After all, there is nothing special about the military in Pakistan. Politicians are afraid to criticize the military more out of displaced fear and myth than anything else is. The fat on the military muscle needs to be cut as well. It is as simple as that. The people need to argue that the country really does not have a choice in the matter. We speculate that the caretakers are afraid to touch the defense sector. Such is the power of the Army in Pakistan. One of the basic principles of democracy is the establishment of civilian supremacy over the military. We urgently need to constitute this principle in Pakistan.

A number of pertinent questions must be raised on the defense issue. Is defense spending adequate for Pakistan's needs or is it really too high? Why should Pakistan spend so much on its defense when the masses were living in such great misery? More importantly, do the people want a bigger defense spending? Lastly, does greater spending necessarily provide a better defense for the country? In other words, can Pakistan learn to live with less? Given the fact that poverty has grown enormously in the last two decades in Pakistan, the country must change its priorities from external matters to internal issues.

Previous civilian governments had shamelessly followed a policy of appeasement of the politically powerful Army interests. A fundamental change of direction is needed. The defense sector is further cut and savings realized should be transferred to education and health development. The social sector needs to be emphasized along with that of

---

[229] Mahbub-ul Haq, "Security without Starvation", *The News*, May 22, 1996.
[230] "Federal Budget", *Dawn*, June 22, 1996.
[231] Ajay Singh, "India's Fight to Keep Fit", *Asiaweek*, October 17, 1997, 36-37.

national security. Hunger, poor health and illiteracy pose an internal threat to the security of the Pakistani nation. The internal threat is as important as the military needs of the country. Given Pakistan's low level of development, we believe that the Pakistani public will be happier with a defense cut. It needs to be pointed out that bigger state spending does not automatically mean better defense. Pakistan should learn to do with less. However, the Musharraf regime was not expected to change Pakistan's priorities. It should be noted the world trend pointed towards lower defense spending. Today the number of military personnel is nearly 20% smaller than in 1988. By the late 1990s, known defense spending had decreased to about two-thirds of its level ten years ago, from 5.2% of the world's GNP in 1985 to 2.8% in 1995.[233] Pakistan spends a vast amount on its defense. The ratio of Pakistan's military expenditure as percentage of GNP is twice the average of global military expenditure.[234] Clearly, Pakistan is swimming against the tide. We need to cut down on defense because scarce resources are better utilized elsewhere.

TOWARDS SUSTAINABLE DEVELOPMENT: REFORM AGENDA

The meaning of development has changed over time. An interesting debate current in social science circles pertains to calculating the real worth of nations taking into consideration new set of standards. A recent thought-provoking report by the World Bank has ranked nations by what is known as "greener" set of standards. Traditional measures such as GDP have been downgraded and new weightage is given to national resources, education, social flexibility, environmental protection, and other assets of a country, which have been undervalued but can be significant instruments of long-term growth. The system has challenged conventional comprehension of development by looking at not only income but a country's wealth also. This approach expands the concept of wealth beyond investment and money. The new method gives the highest rankings to countries with small, comparatively skilled populations and national resources. The first in the list is Australia followed by Canada, Luxembourg, Switzerland, Japan, and Sweden. The USA ranks 12th on the list. Pakistan is not among the top twenty nor is it among the bottom 20 which includes India, Nigeria, Bangladesh, Nepal, Vietnam, Ethiopia, Tanzania, etc. The World Bank conclusions need to be stressed. Rich countries became prosperous because they followed a policy of investing more in human resources. Good environmental policies make sense because they are ultimately good economic policies and vice versa. Apparently, the World Bank is re-evaluating its policies regarding Third World development. Previously the World Bank has been criticized as being uncaring for the environment and the quality of life of the poor. Today the World Bank is trying to be more environmentally conscious and people-friendly. It recommends that the best way for a country to develop and grow is to change attitudes towards the

---

[232] *The Herald*, July 1997.
[233] *Newsweek* (Special Issue December 1999- February 2000), 68.
[234] *The News*, Jan. 2, 2000.

subject. Growth must not only be vigorous but sustainable also. The Nawaz Government must take a note and act accordingly. Betterment of the nation is not necessarily through a strong defense establishment but should actually mean healthy and well-educated people living in peace in neat and clean surroundings. Anything leas is a betrayal of the trust the nation has bestowed on its elected leadership. The Musharraf regime must take the lead in pushing Pakistan to a newer direction where the social welfare, health and education of the population are emphasized over the defense and national security of the country.

Currently, planners are obsessed with economic growth alone. Clearly, economic growth by itself did not make a better society. Meanwhile, social scientists are increasingly challenging the current development paradigm. What is real development? The debate pertained to the calculation of the real worth of nations taking into consideration new set of standards. A recent thought-provoking report by the World Bank had ranked nations by what is known as "greener" set of standards. Traditional measures such as GDP had been downgraded and new weightage is given to national resources, education, social flexibility, environmental protection, and other assets of a country, which had been undervalued but could be significant instruments of long-term growth. The system had challenged conventional comprehension of development by looking at not only income but a country's wealth also. This approach expands the concept of wealth beyond investment and money. The new method gives the highest rankings to countries with small, comparatively skilled populations and national resources. The first in the list is Australia followed by Canada, Luxembourg, Switzerland, Japan, and Sweden. The USA ranks 12th on the list. Pakistan is not among the top twenty nor is it among the bottom 20, which included India, Nigeria, Bangladesh, Nepal, Vietnam, Ethiopia, Tanzania, etc. The World Bank conclusions needed to be stressed. Rich countries became prosperous because they followed a policy of investing more in human resources. Good environmental policies made sense because they are ultimately good economic policies and vice versa. Apparently, the World Bank is re-evaluating its policies regarding Third World development. Previously the World Bank had been criticized as being uncaring for the environment and the quality of life of the poor. Today, the World Bank, to its credit, is trying to be more environmentally conscious and people-friendly. It recommends that the best way for a country to develop and grow is to change attitudes towards the subject. Growth must not only be vigorous but sustainable also. The Musharraf regime must take a note and act accordingly. To its credit, an elaborate environment policy had already been enacted. It remained to be implemented, however. Betterment of the nation is not necessarily through a strong defense establishment but should actually mean healthy and well-educated people living in peace in neat and clean surroundings. Anything less is a betrayal of the trust the nation had bestowed on the new military leadership. It must take the lead in pushing Pakistan to a newer direction where the social welfare, health and education of the population is emphasized along with the defense and national security of the country. Pakistan must re-think its overall priorities and direction. Why does it need to spend so much on defense while the social sectors stagnate? The Musharraf regime needs to immediately create a robust public, civil society, and a new private citizens' partnership. The creation of a vibrant civil society is an essential pre-condition for the country's progress. The NGOs have played a vital role in the provision of social services and eradication of poverty in various parts of the world and in various communities within Pakistan. There are over 10,000 NGOs in the country. The regime should desire to tap into their considerable expertise and resource base for the country's sustainable development. It should encourage them by providing financial support. The Musharraf Regime should establish a sound and transparent enabling regulatory framework for NGOs and CBOs. It should embark upon a process of debate, consultation and dialogue between itself and NGOs for the development of a policy framework for their proper functioning. To its credit, the Musharraf regime is aware of the need. Omar Asghar Khan, federal minister, has recently declared that no institutional reform policy, no matter how good it looks on paper, can be implemented without the active participation of the people. It can be hoped that the military regime will take the necessary steps to achieve this desired partnership. Even before the establishment of the local governments, the regime has instructed local officials to get input from the newly elected local government officials in some parts of the country. How should the Musharraf regime proceed? It should articulate a grand design and vision for Pakistan in the new century. The regime should follow the example of Franklin D. Roosevelt's "New Deal" initiative in 1932. According to this approach, the US federal Government undertook a massive job-creation program all over the country through a number of state programs especially set up for the purpose. The Musharraf regime must kill two birds with one stone. Build the local government infrastructure, and mitigate the rural-to-urban migration phenomenon. In addition, give an opportunity for the establishment of direct democratic practices at the local level. It is here that the future aspirants of political careers should receive their first training in democracy. It is important that mistakes of the past be avoided, rather than plan for boondoggles like the Yellow Cabs Scheme, Mera Ghar Scheme, Green Tractors Scheme, and the like. Instead, the military regime must go for massive infrastructure projects of small size, mostly in rural areas, that can produce maximum employment opportunities. The regime's efforts at decentralization and devolution must occur simultaneously with this grand infrastructure program. The purposes of the program are manifold: (1) to provide jobs, (2) stop rural-to-urban migration, and (3) establish the third tier of Government. The state should build local schools, hospitals, roads, parks, sanitation facilities, roads, and the like. Let the people through the District Boards decide what are their priorities. The Federal Government should only guide them with technical assistance. Comprehensive planning is the need of the hour. Stronger district government systems are a possible solution and a vital element of the programmed turnaround of the country Roundtable mechanisms at the regional level are to be established that should start anew the direct democracy experiment.

The Musharraf regime believed in creating a vibrant civil society, which it sees as an essential pre-condition for the country's progress. It is aware of the fact that NGOs had played a vital role in the provision of social services and eradication of poverty in various parts of the world and in various communities within Pakistan. Therefore, the new regime must encourage NGOs and provided financial support to them, especially those working to provide social services and in alleviation of poverty. It is fully committed to strengthen rural and urban grassroots level organizations that are pursuing community development initiatives. In order to improve and strengthen government's delivery of essential services a grand partnership with a number of NGOs and community-based organizations (CBOs) is taking place. Similarly, under the Literacy Commission, a number of NGOs be supported to reach the large segment of the population. In addition, these public organizations be involved in meeting immediate concerns of the population including hygiene, family size, health, sanitation and water supply.

The Musharraf regime acknowledged the vital role of NGOs in the development process, especially in provision of essential social services in remote rural areas. The regime must establish a sound and transparent enabling regulatory framework for them. It is encouraging a process of debate, consultation and dialogue between itself and the NGOs for developing the required policy framework. The NGOs be allowed to work independently provided their work does not fall beyond the requirements of the law and public interest. The regime should not try to control the NGO/CBO activity. It will however monitor the use of funds to ensure proper use in the public interest.

A vibrant civil society is an essential pre-condition for the country's progress. The Musharraf regime should recognize that the NGOs had played a vital role in the provision of social services and eradication of poverty in various regions of Pakistan. There are over 10,000 NGOs in the country. The regime should desire to tap into their considerable expertise and resource base for the country's sustainable development. It therefore encourages them by providing financial support. A number of NGOs and CBOs (community based organizations) will be greatly facilitated through initiatives like the Participatory Development Program and the Pakistan Poverty Alleviation Fund (PPAF). Under the Social Action Program II, the Government is developing public-private partnerships and had selected several NGOs as partners in its Participatory Development Program. The Program will fund several NGOs and CBOs for development of education and health services in the rural areas. Similarly, under the Pakistan Literacy Commission, a number of NGOs be supported to reach the larger segment of the population. In collaboration with some NGOs, several School Management Committees had been constituted for the administration of public schools.

The PPAF is a major initiative to reduce poverty and create economic opportunity. It will cater to the development of micro enterprises by facilitating easy credit to the poor through the establishment of outreach networks. Several NGOs be involved in meeting immediate concerns of the population including hygiene, family size, health, sanitation and water supply. Some NGOs had done excellent work in the area and needed to be supported more. The vital role of NGOs in the development process is acknowledged. The new regime is committed to strengthen rural and urban grassroots level organizations that are pursuing community development initiatives. In order to improve and strengthen delivery of essential services it is seeking partnerships with a number of NGOs and CBOs.

The Musharraf regime claims to attach the utmost significance to conservation and sustainable development. It is expected to promote actions to conserve the environment, reduce pollution, try to curb the wasteful exploitation and consumption of resources and energy. The regime is also expected to assure that sustainable development takes place from now on. Explaining the reason for Pakistan's backwardness, General Musharraf claims that: "During the last fifty years, the country could not march towards the path of development, despite availability of rich mineral resources. The past governments could have made efforts to remove poverty, but their wrong policies further aggravated the situation".[235] He vowed that his government will "make all out efforts to improve the deteriorating economic conditions in order to eradicate poverty and hunger in the country".[236] The military regime has planned to rectify the situation through a well-planned strategy. The poverty rate is planned to go down to 26% and the population rate to 2.1% by year 2003. The strategy says that increased public expenditure has the potential to reduce poverty by undertaking the following actions:[237]

1. Provide cash and food transfer to the most vulnerable and disadvantaged population.
2. Allocate more resources to the development of basic infrastructure needed by for farmers.
3. Provide micro-credit to entrepreneurs establishing labor-intensive small and medium industrial enterprises
4. Improve the efficiency and enhance the level of public expenditures directed towards safe water supply and sanitation facilities, basic healthcare and primary education.
5. The GOP launched the Food Support Program across the country on August 29, 2000. Under the program, monetary assistance will be provided to 1.3 million poor people. Under this program, 7.5 million people are estimated to benefit, said the General. He added that the newly set up micro-credit scheme - the Khushali Bank - will provide small loans of Rs 30, 000 to the poor and needy people at their doorsteps. Branches of the Khushali bank will soon be open in various parts of the country. General Musharraf said that the GOP is preparing a new scheme for proper utilization of Zakat funds worth billions of rupees. As a first step, Zakat amount to needy and deserving people had been increased from Rs 300 to Rs 500. The Khushal Pakistan Program's objective is to reach out to the rural poor and increase their well being through increased employment and income. Small infrastructure is being built in the rural areas like roads, irrigation drainages, storm channels, soil conservation projects, electrification, etc. The projects are being selected by local administrations with the assistance of government line agencies, including Agriculture Department. By end last year, a total of 6365 development schemes had been approved, out of which 3058 schemes had already been completed while another 2,476 are to be completed by the end of this year. The national program will provide jobs to about 0.5 million people.[238] According to General Musharraf, the decisions about utilization of money for development programs in previous eras are taken by ministers, MNAs

---

[235] *Pakistan Observer*, Aug. 30, 2000.
[236] Ibid.
[237] *Dawn*, July 26, 2000.

and MPAs "sitting in the cities and the people of the areas where the projects are located are not consulted. Now the system being introduced is such that the people of the districts will utilize the amount on their own through their own elected representatives". The system will be very effective for the people, he added. In this system the government, institutions will be "under the control of the people through their elected representatives".[239]

Although a good beginning had certainly been made, a lot more needs to be done to eliminate poverty in the country. Given the immensity of the crisis, the present GOP measures, though in the right direction, are pitiably short of the required level of state intervention. The poorest of the poor in Pakistan deserved better treatment.

THE "NEW DEAL" PROPOSAL

How should the Musharraf regime proceed? It should articulate a grand design and vision for Pakistan in the new century. The regime should follow the example of Franklin D. Roosevelt's "New Deal" initiative in 1932. According to this approach, the US federal Government undertook a massive job-creation program all over the country through a number of state programs especially set up for the purpose. The Musharraf regime must kill two birds with one stone. Build the local Government infrastructure, argued for elsewhere, and mitigate the rural-to-urban migration phenomenon. In addition, give an opportunity for the establishment of direct democratic practices at the local level. It is here that the future aspirants of political careers should receive their first training in democracy. It is important that mistakes of the past be avoided. Rather than plan for boondoggles like the Yellow Cabs Scheme, Mera Ghar Scheme, Green Tractors Scheme, and the like. Instead, the military regime must go for massive infrastructure projects of small size, mostly in rural areas, that could produce maximum employment opportunities. The regime's efforts at decentralization and devolution must occur simultaneously with this grand infrastructure program. The purposes of the program are manifold: (1) to provide jobs, (2) stop rural-to-urban migration, and (3) establish the third tier of Government. The state should build local schools, hospitals, roads, parks, sanitation facilities, roads, and the like. Let the people through the District Boards decide what are their priorities. The Federal Government should only guide them with technical assistance. Roundtable mechanisms at the regional level are to be established that should start anew the direct democracy experiment. A true partnership between the important stakeholders is envisioned. Thus, the various state agencies should be brought together on one forum with locally active NGOs and CBOs. Remember that the state could not do it alone, especially in poor countries like Pakistan, where resources are scarce and the task immense. Therefore, it is even more important that collective efforts be made. Such is the

---

[238] *Pakistan Observer*, March 10, 2001.
[239] *Pakistan Observer*, Aug. 30, 2000.

immensity of the sustainable development task before the nation. A true partnership approach is urgently needed.

Genuine public-private citizens' partnership must be designed. The Musharraf regime should create a strong civil society, as an essential pre-condition for the country's progress. It is already aware of the fact that NGOs and CBOs had played a vital role in the provision of social services and eradication of poverty in various parts of the world and in various communities within Pakistan. The Musharraf regime should encourage NGOs and CBOs more and provide financial and technical support to them, especially those working to provide social services and in alleviation of poverty. It is fully committed to strengthen rural and urban grassroots level organizations that are pursuing community development initiatives. In order to improve and strengthen Government's delivery of essential services a grand partnership with a number of NGOs and CBOs is taking place. Similarly, under the Prime Ministers Literacy Commission, a number of NGOs are supported to reach the large segment of the population. In addition, these public organizations are being involved in meeting immediate concerns of the population including hygiene, family size, health, sanitation and water supply.

The Musharraf regime had already acknowledged the vital role of NGOs in the development process, especially in provision of essential social services in remote rural areas. It should establish a sound and transparent enabling regulatory framework for them. Also, encourage a process of debate, consultation and dialogue between itself and the NGOs for developing the required policy framework. Allow the NGOs to work independently provided their work does not fall beyond the requirements of the law and public interest. The regime should not control or supervise NGO/CBO activity. It should however monitor the use of funds to ensure proper use in the public interest. The poor in the country lead a terrible existence. They are becoming disillusioned with GOP promises of better days to come. Pakistan had become a tragedy in this respect. Certainly, more monetary resources must immediately flow to augment the share of national wealth received by the poor and lower middle-income classes to prevent them from sinking further down the economic ladder. Apparently, economic indicators provide enough evidence of Pakistan's poor performance in the most vital areas of social and economic development.

The quality of life indicators like education, health and nutrition showed no appreciable development. Poverty remained prevalent. In reality, the poor had become poorer. This confirms the observation that rapid growth in GNP and income does not guarantee a sufficient degree of fulfillment of the basic needs for everyone in the country.[240] The World Bank says that Pakistan's economic performance in the last two decades had been characterized by relatively fast GDP growth driven by an enterprising private sector, agriculture and cotton-based manufacturing. In 1988, the country began to reorganize its social and economic policies to promote private sector investment, energize public finances and improve its extremely poor social indicators. Pakistan made important advances in privatization and in attracting private investment in the energy

---

[240] K. Balasubramaniam, "Privatization of Health and Its Impact on the People of South Asia", *Dominance of the West Over the Rest* (Penang, Malaysia: Just World Trust, 1995), 170-71.

sector.[241] While it is true that the country had experienced continuous growth of the economy, it is also true that it suffers from gross inequitable distribution of wealth. The rich had become richer while the poor had become poorer. Available data indicates that the iniquity in the income distribution is getting worse.[242]This state of affairs is intolerable in an Islamic state that calls for social and economic justice. The assumption of capitalism is that as the growth of the economy brought national prosperity every one will benefit. The rising tide will lift all boats; they will have us believe. It bears repeating that a growing economy benefiting everyone is not necessarily the case. The old theory of "trickle down economics" had been discredited. Poverty is not reduced just because the economy is growing. The military regime could not ignore the very poor. The state could not abdicate its responsibility to its most hapless citizens. It is responsible to transfer wealth or, at least, afford decent economic and employment opportunities to the weaker segments of society. This is an Islamic requirement. Pakistan had failed to translate this ideal into practice, unfortunately. Progress and development must translate into better quality of life for not only a small elite but also the masses. Any thing less is unfair, deplorable and a gross injustice. The political parties must make the establishment of an egalitarian society a central plank of their election manifestos. Egalitarianism is a cardinal Islamic value and the military regime must embrace it wholeheartedly and practice it firmly. The continued practice of supply-side economics without immediate relief to the very poor should be taken as betrayal of public trust. The Musharraf regime must bring about real change for the better for the people of Pakistan. The continuation of past practices and usual status quo politics will be a disaster for the nation. The nation must believe in the establishment of an egalitarian Islamic order.

In the past, the state had been directly intervening to expedite social and economic development agenda of the country. This set up required little, if any, ongoing private sector involvement other than the discrete periodic dialogues. The new paradigm called for a fundamental change - institutionalizing private sector and civil society involvement in the planning and implementation process. Strengthen rural and urban grassroots level organizations that are pursuing community development initiatives. In order to improve and strengthen delivery of essential services, a partnership with reputable NGOs and community-based organizations is executed. A vibrant civil society is an essential pre-condition for the country's progress. It recognized that the NGOs had played a vital role in the provision of social services and eradication of poverty in various regions of Pakistan. There are over 10,000 NGOs in the country. The regime should tap into their considerable expertise and resource base for the country's sustainable development. It therefore encourages them by providing financial support. A number of NGOs and CBOs should be greatly facilitated through initiatives like the Participatory Development Program and the Pakistan Poverty Alleviation Fund (PPAF).

Pakistan's economy remains in a crisis with no easy recovery in sight. However, the Musharraf regime certainly seems to be serious in its attempt to revive the ailing economy. The success of its reform agenda depends upon many factors other than purely

---

[241] *Dawn*, Dec. 5, 1996.
[242] Ibid. 171.

economic, including the political factor. The military regime lacks a grand vision for Pakistan's future. More than anything else, the recovery of the economy requires a supreme political will and bold leadership. Unfortunately, General Musharraf lacks both.

In reality not much had changed in Pakistan over the years. As in the case of much of the developing world, Pakistan is a fragmented society that is most easily seen in the country's politics. In addition, several hundred families at the most had ruled Pakistan since independence. This is indeed a recipe for a political confrontation. A very low rate of literacy restricted flow of information across cultural divides, thereby perpetuating linguistic, ethnic and sectarian differences. Almost two-thirds of the country's labor force is employed in agriculture, with most of them earning a minimal standard of living. The development paradigm pursued so far had failed to better the lives of a very large segment of the country's population. What good is the development policy when it is not reaching every one? The question is why, and more importantly, what could the Musharraf regime do about rectifying the problem? In sum, the nation must question the old paradigm for its usefulness. Let the Pakistanis debate the issues anew. A new Islamic direction needed to be set. The Musharraf regime is expected to create a new Islamic paradigm of development and conservation. It is universally accepted that the participatory approach is embedded in Pakistan's Islamic value system. The modern participatory approach is nothing but the operationalization of the values of shura and ijma. In addition, this is widely seen as necessary for integrated sustainable development, especially at the grassroots level.

Chapter 5

FRAGILE POLITICAL SYSTEM

Pakistan has a federal and parliamentary system of government. The last constitution adopted in 1973 created this system. There have been significant changes since then. Since the death of General Zia in August 1988, the country has had four governments because of four general elections based on adult suffrage. Benazir Bhutto and Nawaz Sharif have taken turns at running the government. Pakistan's constitution has been amended several times by the legislature. The federation of Pakistan comprises of four provinces: Punjab, Sind, NWFP and Baluchistan.

Pakistan's federal system was relatively centralized. The principle of federalism in theory signifies division of powers between a national government and constituent units. Such a division was given in the constitution. The provinces are administered by governors appointed by the central government and local governments constituted by elected Provincial Assemblies and headed by Chief Ministers. There are also tribal areas administered by the federal government. Responsibility for the subjects of health, labor, education, agriculture, social welfare, industry and roads was entrusted to the provinces. However, principal power resides with the central government, which was headed by a premier. The head of state was the President, who was elected for a renewable, five-year term jointly by an electoral college composed of the National Assembly, Senate and the four provincial assemblies. The presidency was originally a titular post, but following the famous Eighth Amendment of March 1985, the office holder was given authority to dissolve the National Assembly, and appoint and dismiss the Prime Minister, the cabinet and provincial governors. The president, therefore, emerged as a dominant political figure. However, the comparative significance of the office had been eroded due to the Thirteenth Amendment of the Constitution.

The crisis of governance in Pakistan mainly stems from an inadequate, failing federal setup, and over centralization of power in the central government. Let us first briefly examine the federal structure of the country. Pakistan is designed as a federal state, which signifies division of powers between a national government and constituent units. Such a division is given in the constitution. The federal legislature consists of a lower house, the National Assembly, and an upper chamber, the Senate. The National Assembly has 207 members, directly elected for five-year terms by universal adult suffrage, plus 20 women chosen by the National Assembly and 10 separately elected religious minority members. The Senate has 87 members, elected, a third at a time, for six-year terms by provincial assemblies, and tribal areas, in accordance with a quota system. The National Assembly is the more powerful of the two chambers, having exclusive jurisdiction over financial affairs. To become law, bills must be passed by both chambers and must be approved by the President, who has the power of veto. The presidential veto may, however, be overridden by a simple majority of both houses. The chief of government is the Prime Minister, drawn from the National Assembly. Benazir Bhutto held, until nearly the very end of her tenure, additional portfolios of defense and finance.

THE NEED FOR A NEW FEDERAL STRUCTURE FOR PAKISTAN

The federation of Pakistan is comprised of four provinces: Punjab, Sindh, NWFP and Baluchistan. The federal design signified division of powers between a national government and constituent units. Such a division is given in the constitution. Is the design suitable for our contemporary needs? I am afraid, not. Given its large size, Pakistan has too few provinces to become a balanced federation.

In addition, Pakistan is unlike any other federation in the world where only one province (Punjab) has more weight than all the rest of the constituent units. Most importantly, the other three provinces (NWFP, Baluchistan and Sindh) resent this occurrence. Punjab dominates the country as the erstwhile Russian republic dominated the Soviet Union before 1989. The current dispensation makes for a troubled relationship between the constituent units of Pakistan. Therefore, the imbalance must be immediately rectified. Comparative analysis indicates that the number of constituents units in a federation does have an important impact upon its effectiveness and operation. The fact that Switzerland has 26 cantons, Germany has 16 landers, Austria and Belgium each have nine provinces; Brazil 22 provinces, Egypt 26; France 21, Indonesia 27; Iran 23; Iraq 18; Japan 47; Nigeria 19; Malaysia 14, Turkey 67, Canada has 10 provinces, and the USA 50 states does explain different overall performance. [1] Recently, the Russian federation adopted a new constitution that has 89 constituent units. Federal systems are suited for either very large countries or ones, like Pakistan, that have numerous ethnic, cultural and linguistic cleavages. Analysts point out that a study of Belgium, Spain, Russia, India, Canada, Yugoslavia, Czechoslovakia, and South Africa indicates that the most significant factor behind the establishment of several federations is linguistic, ethnic, religious or racial strains, real or potential. Pakistan has too few provinces for its size and is a glaring exception in this regard. The Malakand tribal belt is unlike cosmopolitan Karachi, and the Potahar region in northern Punjab is dissimilar to the Seraiki belt in the south of the province. Hence, a new formula for federalism needs to be adopted. Pakistan will not be the first or the last federation to change its setup. India did it so can we? From only 12 provinces at the time of Independence, India has gone up to 27. It must be realized that

---

[1] Franz Gress, Detlef Fechtner & Matthias Hannes, *The American Federal System: Federal Balance in Comparative Perspective* (New York & Paris: Peter Lang, 1994), 207.

all countries evolve new political structures to solve their conflicts and that there is nothing sacred in the current federal setup of Pakistan. If by discarding the current setup we are able to lessen our problems of governance then we should not hesitate to incorporate the necessary changes. In addition, there seems to be an increasing consensus in the country for changing the current federal structure. Several nationalist movements have sprung up during the years. Nationalist parties protest of being deliberated ignored in the present setup. The Seraiki Qaumi Movement claimed that there were over 37 million Siraikis in Pakistan and some 25 million reside in Bahawalpur, Multan, Dera Ghazi Khan and Sargodha divisions alone. Previously, the Siraiki Suba Mahaz in Bahawalpur, the Jag Siraiki Party, Siraiki Qaumi Inqalabi party, Siraik Qaumi Tehrik, Pakistan Siraiki Party (PSP), Siraikistan National Front, Siraiki Mazdoor Mahaz, and Siraiki Inqalabi Council have demanded for the creation of a separate Siraiki province in Punjab. Similarly, there has been a talk of a Potahar province in northern Punjab, and a Hindko province in the Hazara area of the NWFP. The Muhajir Qaumi Movement has also talked of a Karachi province, that would be Muhajir dominated. It seems that the very idea of further division of Pakistan is anathema to the military government. It fears that this move may lead to the very disintegration of the country itself. In this notion, the military is surely mistaken. There is nothing sacred in the current dispensation of Pakistan that cannot be changed for the better of the nation. In fact, all other provinces resent the domination of Punjab and therefore it is time to break it up. We need to further break up other provinces also to achieve the desired balance. Let no one province dominate the federation in the future. Therefore, it has been proposed that at least fifteen provinces be created in Pakistan instead of the current four. This proposal appears very reasonable and we wish to strongly recommend it. Under the new federal scheme the Punjab province can be split into five; Sind into three; NWFP into three; Baluchistan into three; and FATA Northern Areas and Kashmir can be consolidated into the fifteenth province. The breakup of the federation into smaller units must necessarily be initiated from the Punjab for obvious political reasons. [2] This measure is politically very difficult for any government because of deep-seated fears of national disintegration. These fears are unfounded. We strongly urge the Musharraf Government to take the bold step of breaking up Punjab in the initial phase. The political costs of this move are indeed high. However, this year presents a historic opportunity that must not be missed. Only the Musharraf government can take such a courageous step given its virtual control over the entire country.

The breakup of the federation into smaller units must necessarily be initiated from the Punjab because of its heavy domination of the country's politics. This measure is politically very difficult for any government because of deep-seated fears of national disintegration. These fears are unfounded, however. We strongly urge the Musharraf regime to take the bold step of breaking up Punjab in the initial phase. Only the military regime can take such a courageous step given the unique circumstances. Many eminent

---

[2] "An Analysis of Pakistan's Transition towards Democracy: Performance in the First Half Century", *National Development and Security* (quarterly) Vol. VI No. 2, Nov. 1997, 136.

Pakistanis, like Khursheed Mahmood Kasuri, Altaf Husain leader of MQM (Haqiqi), Shahid Javed Burki, have already proposed more provinces to be created in Pakistan.

In addition, there seems to be an increasing consensus in the country for changing the current federal structure. The increase in number of provinces must necessarily accompany decentralization and devolution of power to regional and local levels of government. Pakistan suffers from an over centralization of power in Islamabad. Provinces should be granted greater autonomy and devolution of power must necessarily take place immediately. A highly centralized government is increasingly becoming unpopular in the minority provinces. The constitution of Pakistan should be modeled on that of Canada where the federal government is weak in comparison to the provinces. The federal government of Pakistan must retain only a few clearly spelled out powers in the Constitution. The country needs a looser federal setup because of its great diversity both social and economic. Provinces must have greater control over their purse strings and should have the freedom to allocate a greater bulk of their resources, as they deem fit. Jurisdiction over a number of subjects from the Concurrent List of the Constitution of 1973 can be permanently transferred to the provinces. It is about time that we stressed the principle of federal restructuring. The details of provincial autonomy should be worked out now. The Musharraf regime has shown some movement in this regard. This is commendable. Much more needs to be done though. The whole matter of increasing provinces and greater devolution can be settled through a national referendum held for the purpose. The referendum can be held by the end of this year. If most Pakistanis want the change then the Musharraf regime should duly incorporate it. However, we are afraid that given the very low political capacity of the Musharraf regime it will not agree to the proposal. That shall be most unfortunate for the country.

REFORM OF THE CONSTITUTIONAL AMENDMENT PROCESS

The constitution amendment process is too simple in Pakistan. A two-thirds majority in the National assembly can pass such an amendment. We propose to make the process more difficult and slower. In addition, the federating units must be involved in the process as this is a principle of good federalism. Along with the National Assembly, the Senate is required to pass the amendment with the same requirement of two-third majority. This would complete the first phase. In the second phase, the provinces pass the same amendment by two third majority as well. A successful passage of the amendment at both the federal and provincial level is required. The point is to make the process more cumbersome so that more time and deliberation occurs. After all, there is nothing more important than the constitution or its amendment.

REFORM OF THE PARLIAMENTARY SYSTEM OF PAKISTAN

It is universally agreed that the performance of the parliament has been extremely poor in the last few years. Pakistan urgently needs some fresh and bold initiatives for reforming the failed system. We propose the following reform measure for adoption.

Term Restrictions

A good way is to make sure the parliament gets fresh blood to serve it is to impose restrictions on the number of consecutive terms a person may serve in it. This proposal is under study in the USA and makes sense in our case. Maybe the maximum number of terms that a person can serve is limited to two or at the most three. This restriction will encourage more participation by a greater number of younger hopefuls. The Constitution needs to be amended to make this happen.

MOVE TOWARDS A PRESIDENTIAL SYSTEM

A presidential system of government is preferred over the current parliamentary type. The disadvantage of a parliamentary system is that the prime minister becomes too powerful with no real check and balance operating in the system. Since the executive and the legislature are fused and the majority party leader, who is also the prime minister, dominates both wings of government. Since the executive was already dominant in Pakistan's case a powerful prime minister like the one Nawaz Sharif could rightly be accused of "elective dictatorship". Power corrupts and absolute power corrupts absolutely sages have warned for centuries. Adhoc policy-making had failed before and will fail again. The powers of the executive need be counter-checked by the legislature and judiciary. Sharif was not the only prime minister who was being criticized for behaving like a dictator at one time Margaret Thatcher of Britain was also criticized of being the same. With the fusion of the legislature with the executive, a powerful prime minister has too much power, which was not healthy and should be clipped for the sake of the country. Only a presidential system of the American type can solve the problem of too much power in the hands of one person. Therefore, we recommend the presidential system be adopted in Pakistan.

Another drawback of the parliamentary system is that the premier is restricted in the choice of his cabinet team. It is not necessary that the best talent in the country is available only in the National Assembly or Senate. One of the reasons that Nawaz has a mediocre cabinet is because of this restriction imposed upon him. No such restriction is imposed on the president who can scout for talent all over the country. Of course, MNAs and Senators will not be able to become ministers in the cabinet. The purpose of the parliament is to legislate. For once, let us demand that our MNAs and Senators do what they are elected to do in the first place - legislate. The race for becoming a federal minister has become absurd at times. A case in point being the last round witnessed in the ranks of the Muslim League recently. The legislature must be able to provide a proper check to the executive, which can only be expected in the presidential system. In the parliamentary system, the chief executive is the premier, while the head of state is the president. Why have this duality of leadership? Pakistan can get rid of the presidential system and adopt something more suited to its needs. In a presidential system, the tenure of the president and the elected legislature is fixed which means greater predictability and political stability. The counter argument given is that democracy is functioning well in countries like Britain, Japan, Germany, India, Canada and Australia. A number of them, including Japan and Germany, are even considered as showcases of rapid economic development and are politically stable. What then does it mean to suggest that Pakistan go presidential? If these countries can achieve success then Pakistan can also. Why not? In addition, the presidential system is slow and cumbersome because the legislature and executive share power cross check and balance each other. Time is wasted in the process when things are simpler and speedier in the parliamentary system. For example, the time taken for legislation is far less in a parliamentary system then in a presidential one. We believe that there is much merit in the arguments. It is true that some parliamentary systems are functioning very well and are indeed the pride of the world. In the defense of the presidential system, we wish to state that it is indeed tedious and slow but that is precisely the point. It should be slow because there is nothing more important then legislation. In addition, the very ease with which major constitutional amendments are being passed in Pakistan today does not give a good feeling. It was being done too easily, which was not right. Hence, the charge of dictatorship being leveled on Nawaz Sharif. Pakistan can avoid this type of situation if it switches to the presidential type system. Lastly, we prefer the presidential system simply because it is closer to our Amir-ul-Momineen Islamic model. Remember the traditional Islamic model of government envisages a clear-cut authority figure as paramount leader of the country. A duality is not acceptable. The presidential type of government system is definitely much closer to Pakistan's Islamic legacy. The people of Pakistan should adopt it for no other reason then the Islamic legacy one. The Pakistani nation should try to be as close to our traditional culture and roots as logically possible. The Islamic ethos needs to be developed by the people and government of the country.

Why has Pakistan not adopted the presidential system? Undoubtedly, the current parliamentary political system has many disadvantages as compared to its presidential rival. However, one has to appreciate the counter-argument given in favor of retaining the parliamentary system. The people preferring the parliamentary system argue that one of the greatest advantages of the parliamentary system is its in-built basic flexibility. Weighing the pros and cons of the debate we have cast our vote in favor of the presidential type system. Most importantly, supporters of parliamentary system argue that the system has taken deep roots in the country and were the preference of Quaid-i-Azam. The point is well taken. Does that mean that Pakistan is forced to retain a system, which has clearly failed? Why cannot Pakistan try something that works? Why cannot the Pakistanis strive for something better for the future? It can also be argued that an abrupt switch over is neither desirable nor called for. It is suggested that we gradually shift towards our desired presidential system. The way to begin is to directly elect the premier. This is being done in Israel and we feel that the Israeli innovation makes sense for Pakistan. The Israelis directly elected their premier for the first time mainly because they wish to have the government lead by a person having national support. In the current system in Pakistan the leader of the majority party gets to form the government but he or she does not represent the national will because he or she has been elected in a National Assembly constituency just like other members of the parliament. The head of government - the premier - must represent the supreme will of the people and not the political party. The election of the premier will take place simultaneously with the National Assembly elections. If the premier and the majority parliamentary party are form different, political parties then a deadlock might result. In such a case the prime minister will not get the political support she or he requires to built a strong cabinet government. In the French variant of PR, the president not the premier is directly elected and not at the same time as the National Assembly. He can dissolve the government and call for new elections if he or she deems fit. It has happened in France once. Their system is best characterized by "presidential-premier" parliamentary system where the president is more powerful than the prime minister is. In Pakistan's case, we wish to create the opposite of the French case. It is the premier who is the head of government and the president the head of state and the prime minister's office is the most powerful in the country not that of the president as in the case of France. We can characterize our new system as "premier-presidential". Whether we want to hold elections simultaneously for the premier position as in the case of Israel or hold it at a different time as done by the French (for their president which in our case would be the premier) remains to be looked into further. To have a National Assembly elected at a different time then the head of government (our premier) will give more continuity to the system and may be the preferred. In addition, the country can save money by discarding the presidency. Currently, the total budget of the presidency is more than Rs 1.6 billion per annum something a poor nation like Pakistan can ill afford.

REFORM OF THE ELECTORAL SYSTEM

President Farooq Legahri promulgated the Representation of People (4th Amendment) ordinance on December 5, 1996. Among other things, defaulters were barred from contesting the upcoming general elections and defections were banned. The ordinance requires from the candidates to assure that he or she will not change or defect his or her party and shall follow a Code of Conduct issued by the Election Commission. Political parties will have to submit before the Election Commission the receipts of election expenditures. Parties are allowed to spend a total sum of Rs 30 million on the elections. Candidate for the National Assembly can spend a maximum of Rs 1 million while a candidate for the Provincial Assembly is allowed to spend a maximum of Rs 600,000 only.[3] The issue of campaign finances is a thorny one to say the least. There is a lot of public concern about the factor of money in politics, especially spending in elections. Spending vast amounts of money, if available, in financing election campaigns cannot be easily checked. The limitations imposed by the ordinance to check campaign expenditure are a good beginning. The phenomenon of "vote-buying" can hardly be controlled by official spending limits. Vote buying has been reported in India and Thailand and definitely is a problem in our country. However, what else can be done about containing the problem? Realistically speaking, not much! It is difficult enough to enforce the new spending limits. The stipulated limits on campaign expenditures are not easily enforceable. Practically speaking, we cannot impose any meaningful check preventing candidates from spending money or supporters of these candidates of assisting them in countless material ways. Despite the foreseeable difficulties, an audit of election expenditures is a welcome requirement of law.

THE ISSUE OF PARTY DEFECTIONS

The recent Fourteenth constitutional amendment has taken care of the endemic problem of defections, which had corrupted politics in Pakistan. The measure makes sense and will end "horse trading" finally. Issues Not Resolved by the Representation of People Ordinance

THE PHENOMENON OF INDEPENDENTS

The Fourteenth Amendment has failed to tackle the thorny issue of Independents. The phenomenon is encouraged in Pakistan's Simple Plurality (SP) or "first-past-the post" (FPTP), single-member constituency system. These candidates win elections because of "personalism" and are immune from any kind of discipline. Their political alignments are always shifting. Technically they never defect simply because they never belonged to any party. These politicians bank upon and support localized loyalties because the system allows it to happen. Subsequently, Independents tend to view national politics from a local angle even more than other representatives do.

THE DEBATE ON THE MERITS AND DEMERITS OF THE FPTP AND THE PROPORTIONAL REPRESENTATION ELECTORAL SYSTEM

Pakistan's current FPTP system is in vogue in India, Great Britain. New Zealand and the USA, among other countries. This system is the most commonly practiced voting system and is the easiest and the simplest to understand. Currently, the SP electoral

---

[3] *Dawn*, Dec. 6, 1996.

system is used by 87 countries.[4] The frequent use of SP does not necessarily mean to suggest that it is the best electoral system. In Pakistan's case, it has not worked very well. This is not surprising given the numerous defects in the FPTP electoral system and that is precisely why most democracies have discarded in favor of Proportional Representation (PR). For example, Japan and New Zealand have already moved towards the PR electoral system. The FPTP system is increasingly coming under attack in Great Britain and India and there preference is being shown for PR. We first highlight some important shortcomings of FPTP system and then proceed to advocate a PR type as replacement. The FPTP system has resulted in the following developments, which when taken together, are responsible for serious failures in Pakistan's political system.

The most serious defect of the SP or FPTP system is that it is inherently unfair. There exists no true relationship between electoral performance of a political party and its strength in the parliament. As a result, in countries with two major parties, such as New Zealand and Great Britain, third or fourth parties tend to win disproportionately lesser seats than votes.[5] The Musharraf regime desires to reform the electoral system of Pakistan. It has indicated that the country might switch over to the Proportional Representation type system. The current FPTP system is increasingly coming under attack, as it is being responsible for serious failures in Pakistan's political system

A serious point of public debate after the 1993 general elections in the country was over PPP's formation of government. It was thought "unfair" that with 41% of the vote cast in favor of PML the party was in Opposition as opposed to the PPP which got only 37% votes. This is not the first time that a party which did better in terms of votes cast in the general election s was denied power simply because it got less seats. This happened twice in Great Britain, and several times in India. Recently it happened once again in India's last general elections. The BJP was able to form a government, though for only 12 days, even when it's share of the popular vote at 20% was less that of Congress at 28%. The unfairness of the SP or FPTP electoral system is obviously apparent. In Great Britain, people are expressing their frustration at the SP system. In a recent poll 71% agreed with the statement: "The voting system produces governments which do not represent the views of most ordinary people."[6]

The FPTP system of elections gives greater significance to the individual candidate as opposed to the political party. The result is that these individuals once elected dictate terms for remaining in the party. Elections are less of an exercise of choice among competing party platforms but instead become more of a measure of the candidate's popularity in the constituency. All types of ethnic, linguistic and biradari connections sway the voters. Most significantly, elections become personality oriented instead of being issue oriented. Political parties, instead of selling their programs and policies try to measure constituencies in terms of primordial ties and search for candidates that best fit in that calculation. Consequently, parties tend to become collections of individuals, who can leave at their convenience. Hence, the SP or FPTP system assists in the maintenance

[4] J. Denis Derbyshire & Ian Derbyshire, *Political Systems of the World* (Edinburgh, UK: Chambers, 1989), 90.
[5] Ibid., 89.

of the superiority of the social structure over the functioning of the political parties. Not only does the existing electoral system weaken party ideology, it also leads to nepotism in the body politic. The candidate who wins based on local popularity keeps himself enmeshed in "pork-barrel" politics - attempt to bring resources to the constituency. The voters begin to visualize their parliamentary representatives as guardians of local interests as opposed to national interests. In this type of sectional competition, the party becomes secondary. Consequently, party loyalties are weakened further. The FPTP electoral system promotes a two-party system such as that of the USA and Great Britain. It is said that the two-party system offers clear choice to the electors and that minor parties tend to amalgamate with the two established major parties. Thus a third political party in Great Britain and the USA has little chances of coming into power. Consequently, the political system stabilizes, it is argued. The assumption is that coalition politics, which is a resultant of PR electoral system, is inherently unstable and therefore undesirable. Is that true? Evidence from a comparative analysis of stability of political systems indicates that this is not necessarily true. Coalition politics is a norm in many European countries and in Turkey, Lebanon and Israel, among other countries. Many of these systems are considered politically stable. Is Italy that has had governments last a year or two, at the best, since the end World War II to be considered as unstable? What about the political stability of Norway, Netherlands, Germany, Switzerland, Belgium, Finland, Luxembourg, Denmark and Iceland? In the 1987-88 lower chamber elections, 13 parties won seats in Switzerland, 11 in Belgium, 9 in Finland, 8 in Denmark, and 7 in Iceland. Previously, the United Front, which was a coalition of 13 parties, has formed a government in India and the Likud in Israel had formed a coalition with several small parties. Coalition governments work successfully elsewhere and apparently, they can do so in Pakistan. Strong political party systems are required.

In short, the strength of the political system depends upon the strength of the party system. It is essential to opt for an electoral system, which assists in the strengthening of the party system not weakening it. The main strength of the FPTP system is its simplicity not its fairness or sophistication. We must discard it in favor of something that works. There are alternates available.

Alternate Proposal

The Proportional Representation (PR)-Party List system is fairer as it secures a close relationship between votes cast and seats won. Thus, a party winning 20% of the vote cast is entitled to 20% of the seats in the Assembly/Parliament. Currently, 32 states employ list systems. They are: Austria, Belgium, Cyprus, Denmark, Finland, Greece, Iceland, Italy, Luxembourg, Netherlands, Norway, Portugal, Spain, Sweden, Switzerland, Turkey, Brazil, Colombia, Indonesia, Israel, Lebanon, Paraguay, Peru, Sri Lanka, Uruguay, Venezuela, and others. Overall, list systems have a tendency to favor multi-party coalition politics. The problem of a pure PR system, where no "cut off" limits is

[6] Marr, *Ruling Britannia: The Failure and Future of British Democracy*, op. Cit., 23.

imposed is that "hung" parliaments may result, as in Israel, giving minor parties a disproportionately greater influence over the arrangement of the government than their voting strength would normally allow. List systems can be doctored by specifying a "cut-of" point of percentage votes to be won below which very small political parties get no representation at all. If this is not done then essentially any political party, whatever its size, will have a chance of winning at least one seat and the assembly will be destabilized as a result. The size and nature of the "cut-off" threshold can vary greatly. In Germany it is 5%, Sweden 4% and as low as 2% in Denmark. A much tighter "cut-Off" is used deliberately in some countries as to favor the larger parties. The most prominent example is Turkey where the "cut-off" is 10% i.e., political parties need at least 10% of the popular vote to secure entry into parliament.

Critics of PR in Pakistan argue that this is exactly what they fear. Sectarian, ethnic and regional parties would not allow the composition or smooth working of any government. It is true that we do not wish to have too large party splinters in the national and provincial assemblies. The question is how many is too many. What is a good number of parties to be fashioned in our parliament? Maybe up to ten. The Turkish "cut-off" at ten percent of national vote as requirement to enter the national or provincial assemblies can be incorporated so as to eliminate smaller extremist or ethnic, sectarian parties.

The Additional-Member System (AMS) and its variants are currently practiced in Germany, Guatemala, South Korea, Mexico, Senegal and Japan. In the AMS system, two votes are cast on Election Day, one for the candidate and the other for the party. Half of the candidates will be elected on the SP or FPTP system and the remaining half on the Party List basis, to make the membership of the assembly accurately reflect the national vote. Hence, the Party List is introduced to correct any unfairness in the SP or FPTP system. Mexico, South Korea, and Japan have partial AM systems. Only a quarter of the Congress in Guatemala and a quarter of the National Assembly in South Korea are elected on AMS basis. Mexico has a partial AMS setup where two-fifth of the 500 seats in the Chamber of Deputies, are filled proportionately from minority parties' list. The upper chamber of the Diet in Japan has also been elected by a variant of AM since 1982. A national-level PR fills 40% of the seats in the chambers.[7]

The Additional-Member System (AMS) is also being discussed. It has been proposed that the National Assembly seats be either increased by a half or alternatively reduced by a half to incorporate the Party List system. Taken together the result would be the desired AMS electoral system. Meanwhile, the PR proposal is already under active consideration by the Musharraf regime. Representatives of various political parties, including the Jamaat-i-Islami and others in the Milli Yakhjehti Council (MYC) have proposed change in favor of AMS electoral system.[8] The regime is also considering discarding the plurality electoral system in favor of the majority one, as practiced in Australia.

What is the most suitable electoral system for Pakistan? We propose that Pakistan adopts the AMS system as practiced in Germany. This system combines the two PR and

---

[7] Derbyshire & Derbyshire, *Political systems of the World*, op. Cit., 94.
[8] *The Nation*, April 3, 1996.

FPTP into one. However, the military regime would most probably retain the FPTP system.

THE ISSUE OF TIMING OF NATIONAL AND PROVINCIAL ELECTIONS

It has been widely suggested that the National and Provincial Assembly elections be held on the same day.[9] It is argued that same day elections will be easy to handle and will be less expense. There is no evidence to suggest that there is indeed a definite advantage in holding elections on the same day. It is certainly not required nor a necessity that national and provincial governments be formed at the same time. Staggering of elections is done to ensure greater continuity of government. There is a lot of merit in the logic. We propose that the five-year life span of the National Assembly be continued as it is but that of the Provincial Assemblies be decreased to four instead of the present five. Thus, future elections will take place with a year's gap. While the National Assembly will be elected in 2002, the provincial assemblies should be elected in 2001. Deliberate overlapping will assure stability and lack of interruption in government. A less turbulent political system will thereby result. This would be conducive to greater political stability. The change of the election timetable will require an amendment of the constitution. The GOP must immediately take the initiative to get secure this change.

EQUAL OPPORTUNITY IN STATE MEDIA

The electronic media in the country is dominated by the Government. Political parties have demanded equal time on it.[10] This is a perfectly legitimate demand and should become law. Reasonable equity in media access and coverage is a universally accepted requirement of democratic societies.[11] Complete control of television and radio broadcasting by the government is not only bad politics but also unfair. The people know better. Government propaganda becomes incomprehensible and stale and, more importantly, the public resents it. This destroys the credibility of the state-controlled media. Some flexibility of approach, sense of toleration and fairness is shown to all political parties and groups, including the defeated ones. In this way, the Government can win over the wary public opinion. Let political leaders be invited to express themselves openly. This means political opponents also. The public demands fairness even for the fallen enemy. It would be the proper thing to do. A better-informed public is crucial for the success of any democratic political system. In addition, this is also an Islamic imperative.

---

[9] Ibid.
[10] Ibid.
[11] Derbyshire, *Political systems of the World,* 105.

THE ISSUE OF ELECTION FRAUD

Election fraud is not new in Pakistani politics. We need to be more vigilant against such abuse. Earlier, many parties, had recommended that the National ID number of each voter be registered in the electoral list and that it be required by law that the ID card be produced at the polling booth. In addition, many were considering the proposal that election results should be on the spot.[12] Both proposals seemed reasonable. Some sort of identification check was sensible in order to minimize election rigging. Announcement of results in the district office of the Deputy Commissioner by the District Election Commissioner could be arranged without much difficulty by the Election Commission. Since the first demands, these recommendations have been accepted by the Election Commission.

REVAMPING THE ELECTION COMMISSION

The EC is a Constitutional body, in accordance with Article 218 of the Constitution.

It constitutes of a Chief Election Commissioner (CEC) and two members who are judges of a High Court.

The CEC is appointed by the President.

The function of the EC is:

"To organize and conduct the election and to make such arrangements as are necessary to ensure that the election is conducted honestly, justly, fairly and in accordance with law and that corrupt practices are guarded against".

Under Article 219 of the Constitution, the CEC is responsible for:

(a) Preparing electoral rolls for election to that National and Provincial Assemblies and revising such rolls annually.
(b) Organizing and conducting election to the Senate or to fill vacancies in the House or the Provincial Assembly
(c) Appointing Election Tribunal.

Organizational Structure

The EC has its secretariat in Islamabad and offices in the entire provincial capitals.

The EC is responsible for preparing detailed guidelines for the polls to be conducted for each National and Provincial Assembly constituency. The guidelines cover areas such as:

(a) Setting up of polling stations in public buildings (segregated on basis of gender)

---

[12] *The Nation,* April 3, 1996.

(b) Assignment of voters to a polling station (normally 1,200) and ratio of booths to voters (maximum number four).

(c) Appointment of polling staff, which includes a presiding officer (BPS grade-17) who presides over each polling station and his assistants (BPS 16 and 17). Other polling officers are drawn from the state teachers and clerical category.

(d) Preparation of election material (official marks, stamps, stationery packages, placards, posters, banners, etc.)

(e) Appointment of Judicial Officers in the elections. Each district has a District Returning Officer who is a District and Sessions Judge. The District Returning Officer. The Returning Officers are appointed from the judiciary also (Additional District and Sessions Judges and Civil Judges).

(f) Role of the Armed Forces (assistance in supervision).

(g) Candidate nomination (qualifications).

(h) Scrutiny of nomination papers and disposal of Appeals

(i) Allocation of symbols for political parties

(j) Printing of ballot papers

(k) Ceiling of Expenses (Rs 1 million for a National Assembly seat) and Rs 600,000 for a Provincial Assembly seat. Each candidate has to file a return of election expenses incurred. In addition, each candidate has to maintain an account of expenses for the elections.

RECENT REFORM MEASURES

On May 10 2000, General Musharraf stated that his government was committed to empower the EC in a substantial manner so that it becomes a "completely autonomous and independent body with all necessary powers and resources befitting its status and functions" and that all future polls held under its authority be "completely transparent, free, fair and credible" [13] He said that his regime desired to enable citizens from the lower and middle-classes to participate as candidates at all levels of elections in the country. Therefore, it was essential to "formulate" and "enforce" regulations that would significantly "reduce" the role of money in influencing lection outcomes. General Musharraf also said that it was the objective of the EC to "facilitate the emergence of candidates with character, integrity and competence in place of disrepute individuals with large financial resources who have traditionally been elected to office despite being elected to office despite being defaulters and corrupt". [14]

General Musharraf announced the following reform measures for strengthening the EC [15]

[13] *Pakistan Observer*, May 11, 2000.
[14] *Pakistan Observer*, May 11, 2000).
[15] *The News* May 11, 2000.

- The autonomy of the CE has been strengthened by giving it more administrative and fiscal autonomy.

Specifically, It was to be disassociated from the Ministry of Law and Parliamentary Affairs. Previously, the CE was a subsidiary of the said ministry. The Rules of Business, 1973 were to be amended for the purpose.

The Chief Election Commissioner (CEC) given financial and administrative powers to bring the office at par with that of the Chief Justice of the Supreme Court. The CEC shall have full powers to sanction expenditures on any item from the budget allocated, to create new posts, and abolish old posts, upgrade or down grade any post.

- The EC was now responsible for holding Local Government elections also (previously the provincial governments were in charge).
- Fresh electoral rolls on basis of 1998 census. NADRA to assist the EC in the task.
- The CEC shall be able to stop unnecessary transfers of officials on the eve of elections. Previously, influential candidates tried and often got away with having officials of their own choice posted in their electoral constituencies to facilitate personal victory. Now the CEC will "ascertain if such transfer were made on a malafide basis and shall, if necessary, cancel such orders." The News May 11, 2000
- Speedy trial of election petitions. Retired judges of the High and Supreme Courts to be hired for the purpose on a one-year contract basis.

Another related development is that the EC is seeking to make intra-party elections mandatory for all political parties.

As pointed out elsewhere, one of the most important factors of the failure of the country's political system was the failure of its political parties. It seemed that democracy, as a value was never really internalized by the political parties themselves. Apart from some minor exceptions, no party actually practiced internal democracy. They only preached it. The hypocrisy and logical contradiction was obviously all too apparent. What was good for the goose was not good for the gander. Democracy was espoused all the time yet it was never really practiced within the party structures themselves. If the EC is able to have its say then it will be a real advancement for the cause of democracy in Pakistan. Most probably, the Musharraf regime will accede to the demand.

Previously, many in Pakistan had demanded that the Election Commission should be further strengthened by giving it statutory autonomy and by bringing it under the administrative setup of the Judiciary. It is also a requirement of democratic practice, universally recognized, that the campaign and vote counting should be supervised by an impartial administration, with an independent body being available to adjudicate in electoral disputes.[16] The Election Commission in India has done a reasonably good job

---

[16] Derbyshire, *Political systems of the World,* 105.

given the complexity and size of India's election exercises. It was also felt in Pakistan that a powerful Election Commission, acting fairly, is indispensable for the success of the election exercise. In future also, foreign observers are invited on government expense to authenticate fair elections. Elections should not be only fair but seen and believed to be fair. The lesson of the 1977 general elections in Pakistan should not be lost by us. The Musharraf regime, to its credit, has acted upon the demand to make the Election Commission a powerful institution. Briefly, there is real progress on this front. Previously, the EC lacked teeth and was not considered as being assertive or influential. Now things will definitely change for the better. The Musharraf regime is serious. However, the real test of the military regime is whether it shall itself respect the autonomy given to the EC.

Issue of Adequate Checks and Balances in the Political System

Pakistan also suffers from a weak checks-and-balances system that has led to abuse of power. Today, in Pakistan, for all practical purposes, we have shifted towards a presidential system instead of the earlier parliamentary system. The development is commendable. A presidential system is more suited for our purposes than a Westminster parliamentary type. Our Islamic legacy points to a powerful single office of the Emir, or Khalifah. There is no need for a fragmentation of power at the highest level as is the case in a parliamentary system. We have here both a premier and president, which is unnecessary. In a parliamentary system, a chief executive can become a "dictator". Many premiers have been accused of having dictatorial tendencies, such as Margaret Thatcher and Indira Gandhi. The only difference between a dictator and a strong leader is the ideological perspective of the person making the evaluation. Opponents paradoxically perceive what supporters see as "strong leadership" as "dictatorship" - simply meaning that you might agree or disagree with the accusation of dictatorship on the grounds of your own ideological moorings. If you are for the chief executive, then you will look up to him as a strong leader. On the other hand, if you oppose him, for whatever reasons, then you will think of the person as a dictator. The point is that it all depends on individual preferences and that the notion is relative. Only a strong presidential system with a built-in system to check abuse of executive power can possibly work in Pakistan. We must improve the quality of the Cabinet. A move towards a permanent presidential system will take care of the mediocrity problem in the Cabinet. Personal failure of ruling MNAs has hurt us the most. Very few of them are capable of handling the affairs of state. Yet, they filled the ranks of the Cabinet. This is done at the cost of the nation. In a presidential system, we can scout for the best talent available. That is a necessary condition for the revival of democracy. Recently, General Musharraf said that he is "completely committed" to the timetables for elections in 2002 given to him by the Supreme Court of Pakistan and that he "cannot visualize staying on beyond that deadline". [17] He also talked about the need for "checks and balances" on any future chief

---

[17] *Pakistan Observer*, July 28, 2000.

executive to prevent him or her from abusing power. The quality of politicians needs to be improved, as they have been a "dismal failure", said the General. The Plan is a good beginning in that direction. Let us adopt the presidential system in Pakistan, as it is more suitable for our requirements. General Musharraf should become the president of the republic immediately. President Rafiq Tarar must also resign at once.

Later, the military regime needs to revamp the National Assembly and Senate. This is very essential for the future working of the political system. Strengthen the two institutions because their performance up until now has been less than satisfactory. Require that the Senate be popularly elected. Let an equal number of Senators be elected from each province. End Presidential Ordinances and require that all laws, even if of an immediate nature, be passed by the parliament. Provide full media coverage for the proceedings of the parliament to educate the citizens. Strengthen the committee system to oversee the business of the federal government. Have a minimum education requirement for MNAs and Senators. Get rid of the Thirteenth Amendment, which is meant to stifle dissent within the ranks of the ruling party. Pakistan has suffered from the results of this heavy-handedness on the part of earlier ruler. The people should not let it happen again. Let people in parliament speak their mind. After all, the people elected them for that very purpose.

Issue of Strengthening the Political Party System

The regime needs to revamp the political party system. We badly need strong political parties that can deliver what they promise. Currently, it is totally beyond the capability of any one individual to deliver results. He or she cannot even comprehend the complexity of the age, let alone find appropriate solutions. Therefore, teamwork is a necessity. Groupthink can possibly work where a single individual might easily fail. Political observers suggest that Pakistan has a weak political party system. It has been argued that political parties are weak simply because they are never given a chance to take roots in Pakistani political soil. Pakistan has been ruled by the military for nearly half of its history. There are two significantly long spells of military rule: General Ayub Khan's (58-68) and General Zia's rule (77-88). Both are commonly considered as failures. General Musharraf's current military rule has interrupted the growth of the system yet once again. There is some reason in this argument though. The counter-argument is that the military intervened only when the country is/is threatened from within and that the Army is/is a reluctant ruler of Pakistan. It is also true of General Musharraf's seizing power in October 1999. Nevertheless, the military has cast a long shadow on the political party system in Pakistan. Most political parties owe their existence to the Army's Intelligence services. Such is the power of the Army that its support is widely thought to be indispensable for the establishment and continuation of political parties in the country. An underlying authoritarian culture in Pakistan makes this significant for politics. In other words, the democratic institutions of which the political parties constitute one significant element have never established themselves as they have done elsewhere, say, as in India.

Political parties, with very few exceptions, are undemocratic establishments where "personalistic" politics are the norm. Leadership is not chosen in democratic fashion nor is internal democracy practiced in any significant manner. There is mere lip service to democracy. Once in power they act(ed) with authoritarian impulses and weakened internal democracy even further. Moreover, patronage politics and massive corruption in party ranks have eroded popular faith in the party system itself. Most seriously, parties in power have failed to deliver according to the expectations of the people, including their own ranks. Disenchantment with the two parties ruling Pakistan for more than a decade - the PPP and PML - is at an all time high. Politics as a notion by itself has a disreputable ring to it owing to the scandals of the main political parties. Popular perceptions about politicians as such are negative, at least now more so than earlier on. People felt that things had grown from bad to worse in the last period of civilian rule from 1988 (after Zia's death) to 1999 (when General Musharraf took power in October). Pakistan has witnessed a criminalized form of politics since 1988. The political leadership has failed to come to the country's rescue. No doubt, there is great failure in the governance style of Nawaz Sharif and Benazir Bhutto. They have both developed circumspect personalities. Mediocrity, sycophancy, mismanagement have wreaked havoc with the administrative machinery of the state. Pakistan's failures are obviously greater than those of its rulers are alone. After all, the people of Pakistan chose them as their leaders and therefore should share the blame for their failures. It is a universal maxim that you get the leadership you deserve. The Prophet Muhammad (peace be upon him) also taught this maxim. Political parties have a vital function in democratic governance. A political party is simply an aggregate of groups holding similar views that aspire to gain power over the state machinery to implement their priorities. They offer the public clear choices in the elections and are accountable to it. Upon winning elections, political parties form governments to implement their manifestos. Political parties offer the public the means with which to participate in the political process. They serve as channels of communication between the people and government leadership. Political parties assist in recruitment of candidates for elections and canvass for them.[18] Different parties can have different priorities but they have one thing in common: the appreciation of politics as the art of the possible. Parties help to select candidates for elections, campaign for them, and provide winners with the support necessary to bring in tangible reform. Parties also help recruit members, articulate a program, and try to propagate it throughout the country. Thus, party politics is extremely important for a healthy democracy. Most importantly, local politics is the platform for entry on the higher levels. Future party leadership is nurtured at the local level. All strong political parties sponsor or have adjunct think tanks to do research and provide like-minded intellectuals some space to use their abilities. The above account is theory only. The reality, however, in Pakistan is quite different. The tragedy is that Pakistan's political parties, with very few exceptions, do not come close to the requirement. No wonder they are ill prepared to implement their agenda. The required

---

[18] Phil Cocker, *Essential Topics in Modern British Politics and Government* (London: Tudor, 1994), 73-73.

personnel are simply not there for the optimum use by the party. Hence the failure. This has occurred for a host of reasons, which need not detain us here.

POLITICS AT THE CROSSROADS: THE CHALLENGES OF ETHNIC NATIONALISM

Pakistan is heterogeneous society composed of several distinct ethnicities. The country has witnessed ethnic activism for some time. When national institutions falter due to lack of binding authority or a coherent ideology, ethnic activism results. In addition, in ideological vacuums, people fall back on their ethnic identities as witnessed in Yugoslavia and the Soviet Union. Much like religious affirmation, ethnic identity also contributes natural solace to such societies, which are suffering from segmentation of polity and fragmentation. Ethnicity is to be understood as a politics of inequality. Ethnic identity is invented by minorities on basis of different color, language or religion.[19] Nationalism is a sense of belonging and shared history and culture. Anderson argues that nationalism is an imagined political community. An important factor shaping nationalism can also be "forgetting history, or even getting history wrong", according to Ernest Renan. Nationalism, as a political doctrine takes the establishment of a state as a given right under the guiding principle of national self-determination. One can have a nation without a state like the Kurds or Palestinians but a state cannot exist without a nation. A nation-state is simply a nation having a political sovereignty in the form of a state. There is a fit here unlike the case of a stateless nation. A state can achieve national integration thorough consensus politics. A majority cannot overrule a minority easily. The opposite case is also prevented where a minority vetoes a majority. A democracy having representative and responsive institutions is geared towards the politics of consensus and is strengthened by a strong civil society. Ethnicity in the case of democracies emerges as an integral part of society. In such a case, ethnicity is not simply an anathema to centrist, particularistic and monopolistic tendencies. The dividing line between ethnicity and nationalism has blurred.[20] In democracy, a certain balance is in order. Unfortunately, in the case of Pakistan a majority, the Bengalis in the Eastern wing, rebelled when its political aspirations went largely unmet by the ruling establishment. Hence, the successful secession in 1971. History may repeat itself in Pakistan.

The Puktunkhwa Issue

Earlier in the country's history there was talk of Pakhtunistan being separated from Pakistan and uniting Pathans across the Durand Line in Afghanistan. The National Awami Party (NAP) led by Wali Khan was implicated in the venture. Independent

---

[19] Malik, *State & Civil Society*, 175.
[20] Ibid, 176-78.

Pakhtunistan never materialized. The successor of the NAP is the Awami National Party (ANP) and is a coalition partner of the current PML Government in NWFP. The party is demanding that the name of the province be changed to Puktunkhwa. The Pakistani establishment still does not seem to have learnt its lesson from history. We must be fair to our minorities and accede to their legitimate political demands. A case in point is the name change of the NWFP. Historical failure at national integration has created a strange and bizarre attitude among our ruling elite. They live in perpetual fear and insecurity. What else can explain the reluctance on the part of the elite in changing the name of NWFP? It seems to be a reasonable demand. However, many Pakistanis oppose the idea without giving any sufficient reason. After all, the British Raj vanished a half century ago and with it went its fabled Northwest Frontier. NWFP is the name of a location only while Punjab, Baluchistan and Sind are the lands inhabited by the Punjabis, Baluch and Sindhis respectively. What is wrong with a name change anyway? If the people feel strongly about it then it is not right for any one else to obstruct it in any manner. This will only accentuate our perpetual feelings of insecurity as a united nation. In fact, Pakistan is not yet a wholly mature nation and is unable to meet the challenge of meeting politicized ethnic political forces. The Musharraf regime must adequately meets these challenges as they have a profound influence on the country's future. Contemporary political science literature is full of accounts of countries imploding from within because they were largely unable to meet the challenges of sub-nationalism or ethnic conflicts. Sri Lanka and Yugoslavia being a case in point. It is widely believed that the rise of sectarianism and ethnic political forces has added a new chapter to our tragic history.

The Case of the Muhajirs

Muhajir nationalism has waned even though the MQM is a coalition partner in the current Sind government. Earlier, Nawaz Sharif had made a deal with the party before it agreed to join the coalition government. People were hopeful that the "dark days" of PPP rule were over and that Karachi would come back to normal. In mid-1995 Benazir had sent in the paramilitary to regain control of Karachi. Some 2,000-3,000 people had been killed in the city. Police atrocities and extra-judicial killings were widespread. It seemed that the MQM had been defeated and Karachi came back to normal for a while. Today violence and killings have returned. Over the three months in the summer of 1997, some 350 people had been killed. The MQM has made a number of demands on the Nawaz Government. These include: compensation for the victims of extra-judicial killings; the release of thousands of MQM activists from jail; jobs to be kept open in state corporations in the red and on the way to privatization. Nawaz Sharif has not delivered and the violence has erupted again. It seems that nobody has much of a solution to the Muhajir problem.[21] The problem of identity is real for the Muhajir. Their quest for Muhajir nationalism to be treated at par with others in Pakistan is not unprecedented. A distinct ethnic identity for the Muhajirs is a very subjective feeling. You cannot stop by

---

[21] See the *Economist* Aug. 16, 1997, 16.

force a section of the populace in acquiring a new means of perceiving their own identities vis-à-vis others. In addition, perceived grievances by minority groups are heard and allowed to be freely vented in democracies. However, this did not happen in Pakistan. Political problems can only be settled through negotiation, bargains and compromises and not with force. The lesson went apparently unlearnt in Pakistan for so long. What is the solution? We believe that Pakistan should follow the method of neighboring India and carve out more provinces based on ethnic and linguistic criteria. This will help contain regionalism or ethnic nationalism at the provincial and local levels. Elsewhere, we have recommended a separate Karachi province meant to be Muhajir dominated. We also realize that this is not possible right now.

In the previous democratic era, the two parties other than the PML and PPP that counted were the MQM and ANP. The MQM represented the Muhajirs of urban Sindh, especially Karachi and Hyderabad. The Muhajirs are the Urdu-speaking migrants who found themselves outside the primary four ethnic divisions – Punjabi, Pathan, Baluch, and Sindhi – of Pakistan. They perceived that Muhajirs were being denied political space in Sindh. Their political sensitivities were later exaggerated into full-blown ethnic nationalism and a demand for a separate province for the Muhajirs. Successive governments employed violence to contain the increasingly violent demonstrations of the MQM. The military and the para-military were used to curb MQM's violent politics and "terrorism". Several hundred have been killed over the years. The polarization between Muhajirs and non-Muhajirs (Sindhi and Punjabi) has not been gulfed. However, MQM has lost its support because of its violent tendencies. In addition, Altaf Hussein, the leader of the MQM had been in exile in Britain for several years. Resultantly, his hold on the party has weakened.

The ANP was the successor of the earlier NAP that had once ruled the NWFP during the Zulfiqar Ali Bhutto era. It was led by Wali Khan son of Badshah Khan who had gained fame for his populist politics and the "red shirt" movement before Partition. Wali Khan's NAP was a left-of-the center political party that had a stronghold in Mardan, Charsadda districts in NWFP. Currently, Asfander Wali was leading the party. He was the son of Wali Khan. The party had supported the renaming of the NWFP to Puktunkhwa after the term Pakhtuns, another name for Pathan. The renaming of the province was a controversial issue and was opposed by the mainstream political parties and the non-Pakhtuns in the NWFP itself. For example, the people of the southern Hazara district do not agree to the re-naming of the province to Puktunkhwa. They felt discriminated against in the northern Pathan areas. Currently, the party received a blow when its leadership was involved in corruption cases pursued by the Musharraf regime.

Both MQM and ANP have suffered politically for various reasons. The heyday of ethnic politics in Pakistan seems to be over. A new chapter is opening in the country's history. The Musharraf regime is going to promote a new style of politics in the country. It envisioned a clean political system as earlier corruption had weakened it considerably. It can be safely predicted that the above-mentioned political parties will suffer setback in the next general elections because they have been discredited for various reasons.

At the cost of both PML and PPP, other political parties shall gain ground. Today, political parties worth mentioning are:

1. Jamaat-e-Islami
2. Millat Party
3. Tehreek-i-Insaaf
4. Pakistan Awami Tehreek
5. Tehrik Jafria Pakistan
6. Jamiat Ulema-e Islam
7. Jihadists entities (Harkat-ul Ansar and Dawat al Irshad)
8. Sunni Tehrik

1. The Jamaat-e-Islami

The Jamaat-e-Islami (JI) was the biggest Islamic party in the country. In addition, it is perhaps the best organized and most disciplined political party in the country. Maududi founded it in 1942 in Punjab. The party had displayed street power on more than one occasion. It had a strong, relatively speaking, presence in the urban areas of Pakistan. The party had never had much success in electoral politics and was not expected to be capturing more than a few parliamentary seats in future elections. However, it had disproportionate political weight than its electoral success would suggest. This can be explained by the fact that the party sees itself as more of an Islamic movement with a global agenda than a political party in Pakistan. Its network has now spread to North America (ICNA in the USA and Canada) and Britain (Islamic foundations). The party has a think tank – the Policy Institute in Islamabad headed by an eminent scholar. It also has links with several parties or Islamic movements in the Middle East, namely the Muslim Brotherhood based in Egypt and Sudan. The party's public relation exercises are comparatively sophisticated. Over the years it has built a modern media service.

The Jamaat has consistently advocated the cause of Islamic "revolution" in Pakistan. It believed that the Islamic Ummah was united by religion. There was no separation between politics and religion in Islam. It had been consistent in its demand that the Shariah (Islamic law) was the guiding framework for all activity, economic and political. An Islamic "revolution" was legitimate but within the framework of the political system. The Islamic movement would usher into an Islamic state through disciplined activism. The movement would gradually take over the state apparatuses when the party itself comes into power.

2. The Millat Party

The Millat party was founded a few years back and was headed by former president, Farooq Ahmad Legahri. It has not contested elections so far. A close associate of his, Javed Jabbar, was now in the Musharraf cabinet. The party was supportive of the direction the military regime was taking. Now that the PML and PPP had been discredited, it was expected to do well in the coming elections. Ideologically it was centrist with emphasis on reforming the political and economic system of Pakistan.

3. Tehreek-i-Insaaf

Ex-cricketer Imran Khan founded the Tehreek-i-e Insaaf some years back. The party stands for youth, reforming the system, Islamic moderation, clean politics and end to exploitation and corruption. It contested the 1997 elections for the first time. It did not win any seat, however. The party was expected to do well in the coming elections.

4. Pakistan Awami Tehreek

Allama Tahir ul Qadri founded Pakistan Awami Tehreek (PAT) a few years back. Tahir ul Qadri had an academic background in law and about a decade ago, he established the Minhaj ul-Quran Islamic Institute in Lahore focused on Quranic Studies. Today there were several Minhaj ul Quran branches in the country. Qadri has written several books on Islamic subjects. Later, Qadri had ventured into politics by establishing the Pakistan Awami Tehreek. The PAT relied on the earlier religious network established for launching its political activity. It was a small but well organized political party.

5. Tehreek-i Jafria Pakistan (TJP)

The TJP was a very small political party of the Shiites in Pakistan. It was favorable of Iran and believed to have links with the Iranian clergy. It believed in Islamic egalitarianism and social justice. It was well organized. The current head was Sajid Ali Naqvi considered a moderate. The TJP was a sworn enemy of the Sipah-i-Sahaba, the extremist Sunni organization. The two had opposed each other and several hundred killings had resulted from these clashes since the late 1980s.

6. Jamiat Ulema-e Islam (JUI)

The JUI was a sectarian Islamic party based on the Debandi maslak (school of thought). It had influence in NWFP and Punjab. Today it was a regional player in NWFP where it had once been in power in a coalition government in the 1970s. It as expected to win a few seats in its stronghold. The influence of the party was not from its electoral position but from its network of Islamic seminaries, known as madrassahs, running into the hundreds throughout the country. Some of these seminaries were imparting quality Islamic education. Others were more involved in sending volunteers for jihad in Afghanistan. The party has close links with the Taliban ruling Afghanistan.

7. Jihadists Entities

Harkat-ul Ansar: A tiny Jihadists organization labeled as "terrorist" by the USA. The organization aims to liberate Kashmir from the Indian military yoke. It is also very anti-American and is suspected to have links with Jihadists in Afghanistan and elsewhere. The organization does not have any political aspirations yet. It was currently active in Punjab.

Dawat wal Irshad: A tiny Jihadists organization active in Punjab. Involved in the liberation war in Kashmir. The Dawat had grown impressively during the last few years.

Hizbullah: the newest entity established by a retired major general Ansari, who had been once accused of trying to overthrow a civilian administration while in service.

Pakistani Taliban: Supporters of the Taliban ruling in Afghanistan.

ISSUE OF REFORM OF THE LEGAL AND JUDICIAL SYSTEM

The section envisages some reform measures for Pakistan's judiciary. If enacted, the performance of the judiciary will definitely improve. We highlight the most significant issues as it pertains to the functioning of the judiciary in the country.

I. Appointment of Higher Judiciary

The issue of appointment of higher court judges, which had led to a confrontation of sorts between the deposed PPP government and the Supreme Court, stemmed from the inadequacies in the Constitution itself. No matter who has the final say the president or the premier the fact of the matter is that the Executive seems to have an upper hand on the appointment of judges. Article 177 of the Constitution reads: "The Chief Justice of Pakistan shall be appointed by the President, and each of the other judges shall be appointed by the President after consultation with the Chief Justice". Emanuel Zaffar argued that based on "Sharif Faridi v. Federation of Islamic Republic of Pakistan" judgment the consultation between the President and the Chief Justice and judges of the Supreme Court, and Chief Justice and judges of the High Court be "meaningful".[22] For the laypersons, the language of the Constitution seems to be straightforward on the issue. The term "consultation" means just that and cannot be contrived to mean a sharing of power. The Supreme Court does not agree, however.

We strongly believe that the Constitution needs to be amended because the executive should not be allowed to control judicial appointments of the higher courts. It is recommended that we follow a variant of the example of the USA Constitution where the President initiates the process by nominating a person to sit on the higher courts and the Senate confirms the appointment. This can only take place if a vacancy happens to occur. Thus, the executive and the legislature share powers of appointment. In our case, we can modify the requirements of the USA practice. The business of appointing judges to the higher courts is simply too important for the Supreme Court and the executive to handle it among themselves. We have to build into our political system a complex interaction of checks and balances so that not even the judiciary and executive - two out of the three basic wings of government - dominate a crucially important process such as selection of higher judiciary. We should allow the chief justice of the supreme court and the prime minister, not the president, to jointly nominate a person to the higher courts and then have the National Assembly, not the Senate as in the USA, to ratify the appointment. The process should follow the USA practice of careful scrutiny of the candidate and interview by a powerful National Assembly committee. This committee's recommendation should then be voted on the floor of the house. The point is to make the process of appointment of higher judiciary difficult for any one, or for that matter two wings of government, to dominate on their own or even jointly. We in Pakistan have a long way to go in strengthening our judiciary to the place it rightly deserves in an Islamic society. The cardinal characteristic of the Islamic political system is that it emphasizes the rule of law and justice above everything else. A beginning must be made immediately to complete the process of making the judiciary independent of executive dominance. The public must demand an amendment of the constitution to see it through. A powerful and independent judiciary is also indispensable for the protection of citizen's rights, especially rights denied by the government itself. Denial of civil rights by police and other executive apparatuses is a stark and unfortunate fact in Pakistan. We know that gross human rights violations happen all the time and that there is a long history of abuse, especially by the state itself. A consensus exists on the importance of Pakistan's legal/judicial system to economic development. The GOP is committed towards a quick and fair administration of justice in the common citizen's favor. The system of the administration of justice has been [sic Ed.] such that it should inspire confidence in the ability of the courts to administer justice fairly and impartially. The existing system is being improved to remove inadequacies and delays in the dispensation of justice. The Ministry of Law is conducting a study, with ADB assistance, to analyze ways to improve the efficiency and capacity of Pakistan's legal and judicial system. Key priority areas for legal reforms are given as hereunder:

(A) Judicial Administration

The GOP is alleviating problems existing in the organization, administration, procedures, policies, human resources, and financing of the judiciary. It is revamping and strengthening the governance and administration of the court system. The GOP is carrying out a plan for the establishment of an elaborate Court Information System.

---

[22] *The Constitution of the Islamic Republic of Pakistan*, first ed., Vol. I, (Lahore: Irfan Book House, n.d.), 540-41.

(B) Legal Education and the Legal Profession

The GOP is addressing the human resource needs of the legal profession and the judiciary. It is implementing the strategy by establishing new institutions to promote professionalism in the judiciary.

Training programs to be conducted by various public sector training institutions not only cover skills and knowledge but also emphasize on work ethics and values, such as, personal, leadership, professional and religious values. All government training institutions will inject elements of values and work ethics into their training curriculum.

ISSUE OF PARLIAMENTARY GOVERNMENT

The theory behind parliamentary government is that the nation freely elects its representatives to sit in Parliament, out of which an executive government is formed which is accountable to it. The theory goes on to argue that the government could only remain in office as long as it commands the support of the Parliament. The reality is a little different.

Once a government is in power, it could almost automatically assume that it will be able to carry through its major policies. To some extent, therefore, cabinet government could replace parliamentary government or, some will say, Prime Ministerial government. Recently, we had a Prime Ministerial government in Pakistan. Nawaz Sharif had become a dictator. The question is why did it happen. Is it the fault of the man alone? Alternatively, is it because of the shortcomings of the system in which he is only one part? In other words, is it systematic failure or not? We believe it is not only the man's fault but also the failure of the system. A premier becoming overly ambitious and domineering is not unique to parliamentary systems of government. In recent history, other powerful political figures had also been able to create this type of parliamentary government. Margaret Thatcher and Indira Gandhi are both successful in creating a Prime Ministerial form of government. The two leaders are accused of "elective dictatorship" by their detractors, but at the same time, are thought of as "strong leaders" by their supporters. The point is that perceptions about the office and the incumbent could go both ways – from a thinking that it is exactly needed in the circumstances to the opposite to that of thinking that the office had become too centralized and that it is bad for the country. It depended upon individual perception and ideological moorings. Remember that the parliamentary system is flexible enough to allow great positive changes in short time as undertaken by successful Prime ministers such as Tony Blair of Britain. However, the system had some disadvantages, the chief is that the legislature is subservient to the executive. In fact, the executive and legislature is fused. The party that attains the most seats in the recent general elections gets to form the government. The cabinet wears two hats – they are members of the parliament as well as the head of the executive. In a presidential government, the legislature checks the power of the executive like in the USA. Members of the legislature could not serve on the cabinet. The legislature had independent basis of support then the president. The president is the only elected official representing the nation; all others represent either their states or even smaller geographical constituencies in the states. The presidential system, as practiced in the USA, had many admirers. It may be slower but that is what is needed. Serious, open, and maybe somewhat slower deliberation is a prerequisite for good policymaking. We do acknowledge that excellent political systems are present in the parliamentary type also. Britain, Germany, Japan each had excellent working parliamentary systems that are the envy of the world. The debate rages on in political scientists' circles on whether one is better than the other is. We must try to find out what suits us best. We had pointed out elsewhere that the parliamentary system is suitable for Pakistan. An American political system – with clear checks-and-balances and separation of powers- is the preferable government system for Pakistan.

In the last civilian government critics argued that the Parliament had become the obedient servant of the PML (N) leadership but this had not stopped the usual "wheeling and dealing" though. The critics are wrong on this one. Whether the Pakistani Parliament is actually subservient is debatable. Thus, argument that the Parliament is weak institution in Pakistan is only a partisan view and relative. However, we do concede that we need to strengthen it. Among other reasons, this is needed for the sake of good governance in Pakistan. Some suggestions given to improve the working of Parliament:

1. Members should be better paid. They are paid far less than many countries in Europe, USA, Japan and even some other Asian countries.
2. Working facilities are poor in comparison with legislators of some advanced countries.
3. Research backup facilities are almost non-existent. For good legislation, the Parliament must have its own research capabilities like the USA's Congressional Service.
4. The intellectual level of the parliamentary debates is of low quality and need to be improved. Maybe a refresher three-month course for parliamentarians is arranged, at least for the newcomers, to aquatint them with the work of parliament like done in the USA. The JFK School of Government catered to the need.
5. The Question Time and privilege is abused often, which must be stopped. Question time could become more significant if it is used less as an arena for political point scoring and more as an opportunity for making the government account seriously for its policies.
6. The government ministers performance, with some exceptions, is unsatisfactory. They for the most part are not prepared to handle the issues or give sufficient explanation of government policy. They are asked to brush up their performance in the parliament.
7. The parliament should sit more frequently. The working of the parliament is deficient, among several other reasons, because of this fact.
8. The committee system in the parliament needs to be strengthened and become more effective, particularly the Public Accounts Committee, and Human Rights committee. This will put a dent on embezzlement, mismanagement and

corruption in the bureaucracy and will decrease human rights violations by the police itself. It is well documented that the police, like in many Developing countries, is itself the worst violator of human rights. Police abuse is a harsh fact in Pakistan. Exposure will help eradicate it.

9. An academic qualification for legislatures may be prescribed.
10. The accountability of legislators needs to be independent, credible and not guided by political expediency.
11. Actions need to be taken against political parties not following 1962 Political Parties Act.

The issue of decentralization and devolution has attracted considerable attention lately. Out of seventy-five developing countries that have a population of more than five million, sixty-three developing countries are engaged in decentralization. Many countries consider decentralization as an extremely promising process of solving various problems and employing existing potential.[23] People everywhere are demanding a greater share in power than ever before. Decentralization is a global trend and local governments have been empowered in many countries in Latin America, Asia, and the Middle East and Africa. Europe and North America already have a tradition of decentralized structures in many countries. The question to be asked is why is this happening? It is at the local level that people contact government Departments for meeting their every day life needs. For ordinary people the federal government is far away from their own every day life experiences and their needs. The local level matters most for the individuals and their families. In several countries, with centralized systems, the local level has been neglected. Despite allocation of money and many attempts of reforms, several governments have not been able to provide quality and consistent services at the local level required to improve the standard of living of the people. Kalin gives four reasons for strengthening local government. They are:

- A local body is more accessible and quicker in response. Local services and programs can be more easily adapted to a specific local need.
- The allocation of GOP resources can be done most efficiently the responsibility for each outlay is given to the level of government, which is the most close to beneficiaries.
- Local development assists in reducing costs. If the locals feel that the money is theirs then the local people are more likely to be watchful over expenditures and to utilize money more efficiently. In addition, it provides more opportunity for public contributions to augment a local project
- Development programs undertaken with public participation permits for adaptation to the specific needs of the locals. People are ready to give money if they are able to participate in the decision-making process and feel that the specific project benefits them directly. Involvement of locals increases sense of

---

[23] Marco Rossi, "Decentralization – Initial Experiences and Expectations of the SDC", *Decentralization and Development* (Berne: Swiss Agency for Development and Cooperation", 1999), 14.

ownership and responsibility for the program. The public becomes stakeholders in the success of the program. Therefore, they are more likely to invest their resources and time into advancing the goals of the program. In turn, these assists in producing superior outcomes rather than if the development programs are decided from distant government agencies. Thus, beneficiaries who possess ownership of a program are also more likely to ensure sustainability. The fact that the locals are involved in the early planning encourages careful monitoring and protection of the results of the planning exercise. The federal government lacks knowledge about local problems and needs. They do not understand differences in local needs and conditions because the knowledge happens to be thinly distributed across the entire community, which is not available to the central planning agency. Even the greatest central planning agency cannot decide whether, in a particular local village case, improving the irrigation system or expanding schooling is more significant at a specific time. Only the local government can decide these things.

From the perspective of the ordinary people what do we do that will make a real difference in their lives? How do you bring them the fruits of good governance in a most effective manner? We are strongly convinced that we could do this by creating an effective third tier of government. The concept of decentralization refers to the devolution of both responsibilities and resources to relatively independent and autonomous sub-national authorities that are accountable not to any central national leadership of the country but to the citizens of the region and/or community. Some times decentralization is confused with deconcentration, which implies something quite different. Deconcentration occurs where central governments have sought to devolve power not to independent, autonomous local governments but rather have tried to create administrative structures through which they remain able to maintain control of what are essentially national government programs at the local level. It is important to contrast the two concepts. An important element of the movement to decentralization has involved the organization and enhancement of governmental units beyond those of the national government. This has meant the strengthening and, in some cases, even the organizing of both local governments and intermediate levels of government (regions, provinces, states, etc.). Either simultaneously with this, or shortly thereafter, many countries, especially in Latin American have witnessed the emergence of issues of fiscal decentralization - especially in terms of revenue sharing, national grants in aid, and various types of privatization. Finally, this has also meant the encouragement and organizing of citizen participation, neighborhood groups, and local grassroots community organizations in both rural and urban areas.

The current movement to decentralization has been fueled by disillusionment with the administrative and policy-implementing capacity of highly centralized governance systems. This has especially been the case in terms of efforts to promote economic development activities through centralized planning. One consequence of the reaction against such centralism can be seen in the efforts of the principal international economic development agencies to energetically promote national decentralization strategies. Some of the national donor agencies such as the U.S. Agency for International Development (USAID) have become even more aggressive in such efforts. There are several benefits derived from organizing government structures in a decentralized fashion. The most important such benefit is the fact that decentralized governance serves to fragment and disperse political power. Secondly, decentralization serves to create additional civic space. By generating more focal points of power, civil society organizations can develop and find sustenance in inevitably more venues. This is important in terms of the promotion of democracy because it adds to the buildup of non- state focal points of power within a society. Such focal points of power can work to increase accountability of state officials. Given the significance of civil society organizations in this regard, they receive greater attention from international donors. Thirdly, it provides more options for citizens seeking a positive response from the state. Alternative levels of governance provide more options for individual citizens seeking delivery of public services. Fourthly, it provides for diversity in response to public demands. Fifthly, it provides citizens with a greater sense of political efficacy. In general, citizens tend to respond positively to government that is nearer to them. Sixthly, decentralized governance provides the opportunity for more efficient local economic initiative. Highly centralized governance systems tend to concentrate both economic and political power in the capitol. Very often, this concentration acts against the interests of other communities within a country. In highly centralized power structures, distant communities often have difficulty in creating the environment that can facilitate economic development. It promotes sustainable development. A local government is easier to get to and quicker in response. Local programs can be more easily adapted to particular local requirements. Efficient allocation of government resources can happen when the responsibility for each outlay is given to the level of government, which is closer to beneficiaries.

Local development helps in decreasing expenditures. If the local people perceive that the money belongs to them then they shall be more likely to be attentive over expenditures and to utilize money efficiently. Moreover, it provides greater opportunity for citizen contributions to supplement a local project. Citizens are ready to give money if they are able to participate in the decision-making process and feel that the specific project benefits them directly. Thus, the public becomes stakeholders in the success of the program. The fact that the local people are involved in the early planning of the development programs supports better monitoring, evaluation and protection of the program outcomes. Local governments matter most for the daily requirements of the common people. From the perspective of the ordinary people what do we do that will make a real difference in their lives? How do you bring them the fruits of good governance in a most effective manner? We are strongly convinced that we could do this by creating an effective third tier of government. This tier has to be provided sufficient resources and capacity to meet public needs. One consequence of the reaction against such centralism can be seen in the efforts of the principal international economic development agencies to energetically promote national decentralization strategies.

The third tier of government was that of local bodies/government. Local government institutions In Pakistan were weak largely because of their particular history, and the disinterest and the apathy of the federal and provincial governments. Effective links with government and the communities, which though had been a part of the cherished goal of the local government institutions, had been missing. Devolution of authority by government to this lowest tier had yet to occur. In Pakistan, an elected local government tier was missing for the time moment. An initiate taken by the previous Nawaz Government was ended by the new military regime. Previously, after a lapse of several years, elections for local governments were held in Punjab in 1998 in which the PML (N) swept all but a few seats in the province. The local governments were starting to function in Punjab in mid-1999. Elections were also held in Baluchistan in 1999. No elections had taken place in NWFP and Sindh. The Musharraf regime suspended all local governments and desired to revive local governments after restructuring in 2001. The earlier Local Bodies institutions were based on various Local Government Ordinances. They were essentially a reorganization of Ayub Khan period's Basic Democracies scheme. The idea was to provide the locally elected representatives an opportunity to serve for their constituencies. The local government system in Pakistan consists of representative institutions, which exist at the level of district and union councils for the rural area, and at the level of municipal corporations, municipal committees and town committees for the urban areas. The population size of these areas determined the exact nomenclature of these councils. In every district, depending upon the size of the district in terms of population, there were town committees, district councils and union councils running local bodies institutions.

The term local government, as applied in Pakistan, was misleading because it was really only another form of decentralized government. Although local councils had been elected in the past, they were subject to the will of the provincial governments, who had abolished them like done in Punjab. This was in line with the concept of local government in Great Britain but unlike that in the USA. The model of local government in the USA was far better than the one in Britain. Firstly, American local governments had constitutional protection given to them. Neither the federal government nor the state governments could abolish them like in Britain. We need to give Pakistan's own local governments that constitutional protection in order to make them effective.

Local governments were concerned essentially with providing services for the local communities like Municipal services, primary education and health care, These services were obviously very essential and local governments were given elected councils so that the citizens could had open access to them and get the services they desire.

Local problems were best handled locally. Islamabad should not interfere in the domain. It could only create unlikely problems like what was happening now. Undue delay was caused because Islamabad or the provincial capital was involved in affairs that were too mundane for their level. We need to apply the subsidiary principle in government. The principle simply says that decision-making should happen at the lowest level possible. In other words, decisions should not go to an upper level (provincial government, or even worse the federal government) than necessary. Decentralization was the only way out to solve governance problems in Pakistan. Acute centralization and lack of delegated authority at lower levels had created a mess of government in the country. Some indications point to a positive change.

Urgency to decentralize both government administrative and development services. This was needed to improve the equitable access and quality of public services. Political power needs to be decentralized so that it was accountable and responsive to the citizens.

The Musharraf regime envisaged nothing less than re-inventing the administrative machinery in Pakistan. This requires research, experimentation at various levels. The challenge was to develop a model to what works and was practical at the local-level. The third tier of govt. was vital from democratization and development. It had to be rebuilt after a lapse of several years. We need to ensure adequate provision of public services at the local level also. The people themselves were the stakeholders of the whole effort. It bears repetition that all previous plans suffered most, not at the policy-level, but, at the implementation stage simply because the people were not involved in the decision that were significant to them. We believe strongly that the past top-down approach needs to be modified with a vital bottom-up segment duly incorporated. Citizens had the right to participate in all significant decisions affecting their lives. Democracy demands it.

The basic issue of decentralization was the transfer of power to the grass root levels in the form of local government, so that if there were local level problems the community should be able to sort them there and then. The local government in fact was local development. The existing local government was a misnomer because it lacks the essential ingredients of a government the ability to administer justice and impose taxes

The issue of decentralization and devolution had attracted considerable attention lately. Out of seventy-five developing countries that had a population of more than five million, sixty-three developing countries were engaged in decentralization. Many countries consider decentralization as "a highly promising method of solving their many problems and using available potential"[24]. Advancement of local development could be full of promise when it was coordinated with the expressed needs of the citizens. Decentralized structures of government offer advantageous circumstances.

The comparative nearness to the citizens permits the naming of relevant local problems that were considered of being of high priority. These problems were included in a development program and solutions were found in partnership with local organizations. Such a methodology had a dispensation for adequate groundwork and dynamic participation of affected local people in the implementation phase.

People everywhere were demanding a greater share in power than ever before. In several countries, with centralized systems, the local level had been neglected. Despite allocation of money and many attempts of reforms, several governments had not been able to provide quality and consistent services at the local level required to improve the standard of living of the people.

---

[24] Marco Rossi, "Decentralization – Initial Experiences and Expectations of the SDC", *Decentralization and Development* (Berne: Swiss Agency for Development and Cooperation", 1999), 14.

LOCAL GOVERNMENT: LESSONS LEARNED FROM EXPERIENCES OF OTHER COUNTRIES

Most countries had local government of some kind. However, very often they do not perform even the few functions delegated to them. The common problems were:

1. Local governments were more often than not incompetent of in coping with assigned tasks because of lack of capacity. Therefore, local institutional capacities must be built, without which no efficiency and fairness in service delivery could be achieved. Enough attention must be paid to institution building when pursuing a decentralization strategy. It was obvious that an improvement of the legal framework in itself would be insufficient and must be accompanied with specific plan of actions to build appropriate institutional structures. In addition, if the democratic process of decentralization was to be successful, then it must be accompanied by sufficient in local monetary resources. Every one agrees on this basic fact.

2. In a situation where local governments were given large powers without accompanying resources, then failure could be dramatic. The central government was in the position to blame the local government for the failure.

3. In the case of unclear delimitation of powers and overlapping of activities between the local government and other governmental levels cause problems or even paralysis. This results in the public's loss of faith in the all the governments.

4. Lack of accountability and transparency breeds corruption. This was particularly true when information about state accounts was not accessible to the public, and there was no legislation to that clarifies the authority and responsibility of the different institutions involved in the local governance process.

5. Excessive control by the higher levels of government causes delay. Planning procedures were very complicated and slow that leave no opportunity to local governments to prioritize. Very often, local governments must get approval for all expenditures undertaken above a minimal level. In such a situation, local initiative was warped. Some important proposals under consideration were:

1. Security

The Constitution should be amended to give proper constitutional security to local government. The current constitutional provision for local government was extremely weak. In fact, it was hardly more than a mention in passing and no more. Local governments had to be protected from future dissolution and suspension in order to ensure continuity. Local governments could not function properly if their very existence was in jeopardy.

2. Sufficiency of Resources

For the democratic process of decentralization to be successful, a sufficient amount of monetary resources had to be provided. Every one agrees on this basic fact. Therefore, adequate resources were made available. This requires a guarantee of financial autonomy. Guaranteed income by transfer of a portion of provincial as well as federal revenue collections.

3. Autonomy

There should be no excessive control by the higher levels of government. Planning procedures to be simplified and made quicker. Provide many opportunities to local governments to prioritize. Local governments would not be required to get approval for expenditures undertaken above a reasonable level. Local initiative was to be encouraged. Therefore, the possibility of independent deployment of resources was increased. The Musharraf regime provides necessary support for tackling the issue.

4. Transparency Accountability

As lack of accountability and transparency breeds corruption. The most significant role by local government institutions was to regulate the services of the line agencies and create a system of dual accountability by becoming truly representative bodies. This could provide support to local governance through active participation of communities. The main strength of these institutions would come through their active role, maintaining their credibility, which would provide them a status, respect and thereby they would be able to effect change and influence local level institutions including government. These institutions could go a long way in improving the local conditions by creating awareness among the masses at the grass roots and extending their help to control and better manage resources, and participate in development programs. Therefore, information about state accounts was accessible to the public.

5. Clear Delimitation of Powers and Jurisdictions at the Local Level

No overlapping of primary jurisdiction between the local and other higher governmental levels. Demarcation of municipal, development and other functions, especially in urban areas to be undertaken on a priority basis. For example, in Lahore all agencies like WASA, LMC, TEPA, LDA would come under the Lahore Municipal Corporation under the control of the Deputy Commissioner. After local government elections, it shall come under the elected Lord Mayor.

6. The Principle of Subsidiary was Practiced

Decisions were taken at the lowest level possible. Recognize Local Government as an effective third tier of administration. Transfer local functions and ensure financial autonomy to Local Governments. Protect the infringement of their authority by higher levels of governments.

Effective decentralization requires strong local government. Moreover, local governance capacity depends highly upon local revenue raising capacity. Absent the ability to raise revenue, local government will inevitably remain in a dependent and vulnerable state and decentralization will be meaningless.

Strong local government also requires effective local law making capacity. Central governments must give regional and local governments a great deal of discretionary authority in terms of the passage of various kinds of laws, statutes, and regulations. Absent this authority, local governance is not likely to flourish.

Meaningful decentralization requires strong support from national government policy makers and institutions. This may take the form of enabling legislation as well as legislation providing local units of government with the capacity to act autonomously and independently to provide needed services regulate local activities and raise the revenue necessary to adequately fund local services.

Even the most permissive and supportive national government, if acting alone, cannot adequately insure meaningful, vibrant decentralization. Clearly there has to be significant local demand and local concern for the development and maintenance of a decentralized governance system. The reality is that the leaders of most centralized government are not, in truth, anxious to give up either resources or the authority to control them. For political purposes one may frequently hear national leaders speak of the need to encourage decentralization, local government capacity and citizen participation but the reality is that too often such statements gain meaning only when there is pressure from the local community to carry them out.

There is no one best way to structure a decentralized governance system. Those countries which have adopted decentralized governance systems reflect significant variation in terms of both the formal structures of sub-national governance and with regard to what services are carried out at national, regional, local or community levels. In general, there is a tendency to devolve education and health services to the local level, but even in these areas, there is much variation. In fact, in almost all cases, the organizational structuring of the institutions of sub-national governance (and the resolution of the issue of what services will be carried out at what level) is a product of citizen demand, local history, administrative capacity, institutional self-interest, perceived efficiency and political negotiations. Moreover, these decisions, once made, are almost never set in stone. In truth, adjustments are frequently being made between the central and the local governments on these matters.

LOCAL GOVERNMENT IN PAKISTAN

Pakistan has a highly centralized system, in which the local level had been grossly neglected. Despite allocation of money and many attempts of reforms, several governments have failed to provide quality services on a regular basis at the local level. Primarily, the GOP activity had been directed from above instead of from citizens' demands from below. Local governments serve a very important function in the administrative system of any country. Local governments are concerned essentially with providing services for the local communities like municipal services, primary education and health care, These services are obviously very essential and local governments are given elected councils so that the citizens can have open access to them and get the services they desire. Local problems are best handled locally. Islamabad should not interfere in this area. It can only create unlikely problems like what is happening now. Undue delay is caused because Islamabad or the provincial capital is involved in affairs that are too mundane for their level. We need to apply the subsidiary principle in government. The principle simply says that decision-making should happen at the lowest level possible. In other words, decisions should not go to an upper level (provincial government, or even worse the federal government) than necessary. Decentralization is an effective way to solve governance problems in Pakistan. Acute centralization and lack of delegated authority at lower levels have created a mess of government in the country. Some indications point to a positive change. The regime claims that the past top-down approach needs to be modified with a vital bottom-up segment duly incorporated in the development strategy. Accordingly, there is a need for an effective third tier of government backed by sufficient resources to meet public needs. The principle of subsidiary is to be practiced wholeheartedly for meaningful results. Thus, the regime realizes that decentralization and devolution of power is essential for the efficiency and effectiveness of public service. In addition, the development of the third tier of government is vital for democratization and public welfare. Although at present an elected local government tier is missing, things will change soon as elections are scheduled beginning this December. The Musharraf regime needs to decentralize and devolve power in a planned manner. Some experimentation is necessary. Failures are inevitable given the lack of capacity at the lower levels of government. The capacity at the local level is very inadequate. It will take time, resources, and great attention to build it. Having built some capacity, the regime intends to begin the Army-to-Civilian transfer of power process with elections at the lowest level first, proceeding gradually to the national level. It shall stagger elections for the purpose. Elections at the local-level are to be held by May 1999. This is to be followed by provincial and then national elections. National elections are to be held last by 2002. No date has been given for provincial and national elections yet. The regime needs to do this exercise in phases by gradually consolidating gains at the lower level and then proceeding upwards at the next higher level. There is an urgent need to decentralize both government administrative and development services. This is needed to improve the equitable access and quality of public services. The challenge is to develop a practical model at the local-level the country. To analyze the reform agenda requires some general theoretical understanding of the concepts of local government, decentralization and devolution of power. Moreover, a historical background of local government in Pakistan and the context of the reform plans are also required. From the perspective of the ordinary people what do we do that would make a real difference in their lives? How do you bring them the fruits of good governance in a most effective manner? We are strongly convinced that we can do this by creating an effective third tier of government. This tier has to be provided sufficient resources and capacity to meet public needs. Unfortunately, this tier is missing for the moment in Pakistan. We will soon have local governments functioning in Punjab. For the common person in Pakistan, like elsewhere, the local government is critical and it is the level that he or she interacts most and his most frustrated. The third tier of government will help fill a large gaping hole in the availability of state services to the people. The term local government, as applied in Pakistan, is misleading because it is really only another form of decentralized government. Although local councils have been elected in the past, they were subject to the will of the provincial governments, who have abolished them like done in Punjab some years ago. This is in line with the concept of local government in Great Britain but unlike that in the USA. The model of local government in the USA is far better than the one in Britain. Firstly, American local governments have far more constitutional protection given to them. Neither the federal government nor the state governments can abolish them like in Britain. We need to give our own local governments that constitutional protection in order to make them effective.

The basic issue of decentralization is the transfer of power to the grass root levels in the form of local government, so that if there are local level problems the community should be able to sort them there and then. The local government in fact is local development. The existing local government is a misnomer because it lacks the essential ingredients of a government the ability to administer justice and impose taxes. There are some constitutional, administrative, financial, political and professional aspects of decentralization and devolution.[25]

1. Constitutional Aspect

The constitution provides a concurrent list, which tends to favor the Federation and does not guarantee the flowering of provincial autonomy. There is no devolution beyond the provincial tier of the government despite the fact that the constitution does provide for the institution of local government. The constitutional provision regarding the Local Government is inadequate and has to be reviewed.[26]

---

[25] Ibid.
[26] Ibid.

2. Administrative Aspect

The tasking to the government has to be reviewed drastically and must be rationalized by relating the provider to the right level of the government. The time-old recognized competence of the attached departments is not being honored adversely affecting both the decision making and implementation processes.[27]

3. Financial Aspect

Because of administrative weaknesses, the decisions are not taken at the right levels and even if they are, the activities are not timely funded.

4. Political Aspect

The interface between the political and bureaucratic levels of administration has been provided in the rules of business but no such interface is envisioned in the context of Local Government. This interface must be clearly defined and the Local government institution should be sufficiently empowered.[28]

5. Professional Aspect

Any patchwork regarding de-centralization and devolution will create more problems and solve none. These reforms have to be introduced in a comprehensive package covering functions of the government, the transfer of power to the attached departments, de-centralization of regulatory work and the internal delegation within the organization itself.

The GOP has noted that the consensus on decentralization, both inside and outside, government circles is strong. The Government shall implement the following recommendations:[29]

1. Local Government shall be recognized as a formal tier of the government and adequate constitutional protections provided. The constitution shall be amended in 2001 for the purpose.
2. There is a need to establish the management capacity at the local government level. For this training facilities shall be augmented. GOP shall provide the necessary facilities for the purpose.

---

[27] Ibid. 8.
[28] Ibid.
[29] Ibid. 8.

3. A pluralist approach to government is preferable. Each province is encouraged to try out various policy innovations at district level. The Government shall encourage innovation and creativity in the formation of Local Government.
4. Local Governments shall be protected from future dissolution and suspension in order to ensure continuity.
5. Restriction on dual membership shall be applicable.
6. Demarcation of functions, especially in urban areas. For example, in Lahore all agencies like WASA, TEPA, LDA shall come under the control of the Lahore Municipal Corporation. The LMC shall act, as the soul administrative unit as far as the city is concerned. The model of Lahore City shall be applied in other cities of the country.
7. Localizing recruitment of personnel for local governments.
8. The Provincial Government shall not interfere in the matter.
9. Establishment of district development committees.
10. Financial autonomy to be guaranteed.
11. Guaranteed income by transfer of a portion of provincial as well as federal revenue collections.
12. Apportionment of governmental work between the provinces and the Local Government institutions shall be unequivocal. Subjects like primary education, primary health care, communications, land revenue administration, local police, civic amenities, forest, farm to market roads, transport, local taxation and administration of justice etc. shall be transferred to local government.
13. Chairman of the District Council and Municipal Corporation shall be directly elected.
14. The election for the Local Bodies shall be held on party basis so that no political vacuum is created at the grass root level.
15. The District administration along with the line departments shall be changed into the Secretariat of the Local Government.
16. The Divisional tier of the administration shall be abolished.
17. Local government shall organize its own services within their jurisdiction and certain linkages can be provided between the Local Government and the Provincial Government in order to ensure a friction-free working of the system.
18. A system of checks and balances shall be introduced in the working of the local institutions so that the heads of the local institutions use their authority appropriately without coercion and intransigence.
19. Accountability shall be ensured so that the citizens understand the working of the government and its accountability systems."[30]
20. Planning capabilities at the local levels must be institutionalized.
21. Environmental protection shall be made the responsibility of the Local Government.
22. Local Government shall be empowered to levy their taxes on the one hand and receiving sufficient amounts from the Provincial/Federal pools on the other. This

---

[30] Ibid. 10.

measure shall ensure financial viability of the Local Institutions. In order to ensure protection to the Local Government institutions under constitution, the National Finance Commission shall be assigned the task of sharing the finances between all the tiers of government.

23. Local Government shall have the capability of creating revenues and jobs. They shall be allowed to commission their own projects on self-financing basis.

24. Regulatory organizations shall be de-centralized. Powers shall be conferred upon the operational levels as required.

25. The irking parallelism between NGOs and the Local Government institutions is undesirable and counter productive. The NGOs shall function within an integrated framework of the Local Government, so that an atmosphere of accountability is created and energies coordinated effectively. NGOs shall not become a substitute for a strong and formal representative system at the grass root level.

REFORM AGENDA

The regime had taken a new initiative of institution building at the local government level. It had allocated Rs 20 billion for poverty alleviation for a two-year period. The plan was to target money to infrastructure development through local government. The regime initiated a new program of local development through a decentralized mechanism of local Government. Under the new program, District Development Advisory Boards (DSAB) would be constituted throughout the country by January 31, 2000. Omar Asghar Khan, Federal Minister of Environment, Local Government and Rural Development explained that these boards had been constituted in recognition of the importance of public input and participation in identification, formulation and execution of development schemes at the district level.[31]Each board would comprise of ten to twenty volunteers from different bodies. Only persons having a reputation of social service and integrity would sit on these boards. Women would comprise of one-third of total board membership. Representatives of Village Development Committees and CBOs/NGOS would be members of the boards. The military regime was also strengthening the capacity of training institutions such as the National Center for Rural Development, Islamabad and Municipal Training and Research Institute, Karachi. These institutes would be required to impart training to members of the DDABs. It seems that the military regime was very serious about the plan. Therefore, a guarded optimism was in order. We hope the Musharraf regime succeeds in this experiment. Pakistan would definitely be richer for it. The people must extend cooperation for the venture.

Notwithstanding the apparent contradiction between a military regimes promoting democratic governance, we are convinced that the Local Government Plan 2000 (henceforth Plan) has revolutionary potential. We believe that the plan shall prove beneficial to the country, if properly implemented. The overall direction is correct and the "bottom-up" strategy is certainly workable. Meanwhile, the Plan is proceeding as per scheduled. A set of ordinances were promulgated in the Sindh, Punjab, and NWFP's Local Government Ordinances 1979 and the Baluchistan Local Government Ordinance 1980. In addition, the Islamabad Capital Territory Government Ordinance 1979 as duly amended. According to the 1973 Constitution, holding of local government elections is the responsibility of the provinces and the Provincial Election Commissions. As the Constitution is held in abeyance and the provincial assemblies are suspended, General Musharraf has ordered the Election Commission of Pakistan to hold local government elections in the country. For this deviation, the GOP needs to make amendments in the various clauses of the 1973 Constitution.[32]Other than a few minor problems, the Plan is indeed remarkable. We wish it be implemented not for the sake of the military regime but for the sake of the nation. Remember this is the most serious thrust at devolution yet. The people want real change in the country and the military regime has to deliver. Pakistan will be richer for the devolution exercise. Given the past grave failures of all governments in our history, the Musharraf regime must be given the benefit of the doubt. Unlike other military regimes, it seems to be sincere in turning around Pakistan. Remember this is the most serious thrust at devolution yet. The people want real change in the country and the military regime has to deliver. Pakistan will be richer for the devolution exercise. Although the military regime is flexible on the final shape of the devolution plan, there are many complex issues still to be worked out. The plan's briefness and lack of essential details is uncomforting. As the popular saying goes, "the devil is in the details" and the details are surely missing. Thus, the main problem with the NRB report is not what it contains but what it leaves out. In all fairness, the NRB faces a stupendous task well beyond its human capacity and limited means. Therefore, all the more reason for civil society and international agencies to lend a helping hand. The people owe the military regime their full cooperation because if it fails the country fails also. We really do not have much of a choice in the matter. You cannot wish away the regime any time soon. Therefore, make the best use of it and the opportunity provided to fill in the gap at this crucial juncture in our nation's history.

General Musharraf has repeatedly said that he was committed to transfer power from the federal government-level to the local-level and that the Plan was a significant step towards realizing the goal. He has said that the new local government system would help remove the lingering rot in the current system.[33] He added that he thought that the opinion o the public was significant because no Plan could turn out to be successful without public participation. General Musharraf said while his regime was ready to hold debate on substantive objections or reservations on the Plan; it would not be cowed down because of unreasonable opposition.[34]

---

[31] *The News*, Jan. 2, 2000.
[32] *Pakistan Observer*, Aug. 30, 2000.
[33] *Pakistan Observer*, Aug. 30, 2000.
[34] Ibid.

HIGHLIGHTS OF THE PLAN

The system shall be in place on August 14, 2001 though staggered elections, which began on December 30 and shall end by July this year. The first phase of the local body elections were held on December 30, 2000 in 18 districts across the country. Voters elected members for 956 union councils in the 18 districts. The turnout in the elections was about 46% and the ratio of candidates per general seat about 3, according to General Musharraf. The Chief executive was happy over the good turnout in the local government elections. He expressed his confidence that in the next phase of the local government elections "the people would participate with more zeal and vigor."[35] The second phase of the elections was held on March 21, the third by end of May, and the last in June 2001.[36] The voter turnout in the second phase was better than the earlier one. It is expected that the turnout in the third and fourth phases of local government elections will be even better. The elections were fair and there was no large-scale rigging reported. Most analysts were of the opinion that the program was unfolding satisfactorily. Although elections were being held on a non-party basis, all political parties were participating in them through fielding candidates of their liking. This was happening when officially many political parties were critical of the whole devolution scheme. Apparently, all political parties were afraid to leave the vital local government arena open to rivals in case of a boycott of elections. Thus, the election exercise had been successful in some ways.

- The electoral system is based on the FPTP simple-plurality system as in the past.
- About 200,000 new officials shall be elected at various levels.
- Elections are being held on basis of Separate Electorate
- Direct elections for union level only and indirect for tehsil and district.
- The election of the nazim and his deputy – the naib nazim – shall be held jointly on one ticket.
- The elected Nazim of the union council shall be ex officio member of the district council and likewise the Naib Nazim shall be ex-officio member of the tehsil council.
- There are 21 seats in each union council. There will be 16 general seats, 8 reserved seats for workers or peasants, and 2 minorities. Half of these seats will be reserved for women.
- There are 4,147 union councils in the country. Of them, 2,492 are in Punjab, 625 in Sindh, 668 in NWFP, and 362 in Baluchistan, and 12 in Islamabad.
- The tehsil council shall consist of 34 members who shall then elect a Nazim to head it. There shall be 25 general eats, five reserved for women, and two each for workers or peasants and minorities.
- There are 376 tehsil (Punjab –118, Sindh 87, NWFP- 58, and Baluchistan-113).

---

[35] Ibid.
[36] *Pakistan Observer, Jan.7, 2001.*

- Cities will be called city districts to be divided into towns, the equivalent of tehsil in the rural areas. The structures of the two shall be identical.
- There are 105 district governments in Pakistan. Punjab will have 34, Sindh 21, NWFP 24, Baluchistan 26, and the Islamabad capital district.
- An indirectly elected Zila Nazim and his deputy shall head the district administration. All thirteen departments shall work under him or her. A district coordination officer who shall be given tenure of service will assist him or her in this task.
- On the pattern of the National Finance Commission, there shall be a provincial finance commission for the purpose of resource allocation among the districts.
- The divisional tier will be abolished. There are presently 22 divisions in the country.
- Speedy justice shall be ensured at the local level through more courts and revival of conciliatory mechanism to preempt litigation
- The voting age is lowered to 18 years.
- The Constitution of the republic shall be amended to give adequate cover to the Plan.

STRUCTURES OF LOCAL GOVERNMENT

There shall be established a three tier pyramid-shaped structure of local governments (district, tehsil and union).

A. Union Council

Each Union Council shall consist of 21 seats headed by a Nazim (administrator) and his deputy (Naib Nazim). There are 4,147 union councils in the country. Of them, 2,492 are located in Punjab, 625 in Sindh, 668 in NWFP, 362 in Baluchistan, and 12 in Islamabad capitol territory. The Nazim and Naib Nazim shall be directly elected on a joint candidacy.[37]

The Nazim will automatically become a member of the Zila Council while the Naib will become a member of the Tehsil Council. The Zila Nazim and the Naib Nazim shall have to be educated to at least secondary school/matriculation certification or equivalent.

The composition of the union council is:[38]

---

[37] See para 68 of the "LG Plan", *Dawn* August 16, 2000.
[38] Ibid, para 66.

Total General seats	12 (out of which, 4 reserved for women)
Workers/peasants	6 (out of which, 2 reserved for women)
Minorities	1
Nazim	1
Naib Nazim	1
Total	21

The four women members of the union councils are to be directly elected. Each Union Council shall be divided into 8 equal zones and voters from each two shall elect a women candidate? Out of six reserved seats for workers/peasants in Union Council there are another two reserved for women. Similarly, voters from each four zones shall elect a women member. Women seats even if left uncontested and vacant will not be open to men and shall remain vacant until filled through yearly by-elections.[39]

The functions of the union council is to undertake local development and perform a myriad of public services such as finance, municipal, public safety, health, education, literacy, works, and justice.[40] Monitoring committees shall facilitate the work of the union council.[41] In addition, citizen community boards in both urban and rural areas and village councils in rural areas shall be established to facilitate the functioning of the union councils.[42] The union council may also form a local guard service, which will be registered with the local police station. The guard service shall be recruited and paid by the union council. The Public Safety Committee of the union council shall liaison with the guard service and the police station.[43]

B. Tehsil Council

The tehsil council shall consist of general seats equivalent to the number of union councils in that particular tehsil. In addition, 33% of these seats are reserved for women, 5% reserved for workers or peasants and 5% for minorities. The Electoral College for elections to these reserved seats shall be the union councilors of the tehsil.[44]

Each tehsil shall have a tehsil nazims and a deputy (naib-nazim) to be elected as joint candidates. The Electoral College for these nazims shall be the union councilors of the tehsil.[45]

There are 376 tehsils in Pakistan (Punjab 118, Sindh 87, NWFP 58, and Baluchistan 113).

The functions of the tehsil councils have been left vague. It is mainly supposed to be involved in coordination function between the district and tehsil levels. The Plan says that

---

[39] Ibid.
[40] See para 71 of the *Local Government LG Plan.*
[41] Ibid.
[42] See para 72 of the *local Government LG Plan.*
[43] See para 76 of the *LG Plan.*
[44] See para 48 of the *Local Government LG Plan.*
[45] See para 50 of the *LG Plan.*

through various committees it will monitor the performance of the tehsil administration and the tehsil-level offices of the district government.[46] There shall be a Public Safety and Justice Committees at the tehsil level.[47]

City District Administration

City district administrations shall be establishing in all four provincial capitals and Islamabad. These city governments shall provide centralized municipal services with additional capacity and resources. Public services provided include: water supply and sanitation, waste disposal and sewerage, transport, housing, public works, roads, river and riverine management, and streets.[48] City districts to be divided into towns to be further sub-divide into unions. The borders of the city district shall be demarcated as that of the tehsil.

Cantonments

At present, there are 41 cantonments in the country that can be categorized into three types:[49]

1. Those that have become geographically a part of the bigger cities like Lahore, Karachi, and Peshawar.
2. Small garrison like Bannu and Kohat
3. Large garrisons like Pano Aqil, Gujranwala, Malir, and Kharian.

There already exist local governments in these cantonments if the shape of cantonment boards. Nevertheless, the issue of integrating existing cantonments into the new city government system is to be reviewed.[50]

C. District

The district government shall compose of a Zila Council and the nazim and naib-nazim. There are 106 districts in Pakistan (Punjab 34, Sindh 21, NWFP 24, Baluchistan 26, and the Islamabad capital).

Zila Council

The zila council shall consist of union nazims. Each union council shall have a representative in the zila council. Each zila council shall have general seats equivalent to the number of union councils in the district. In addition, there shall be 33% reserved seats for women, 5% for workers or peasants, and 5% for minorities.

---

[46] See para 52 of the *LG Plan*.
[47] Ibid.
[48] See para 96 of the *LG Plan*.
[49] See para 100 of the *LG Plan*.
[50] Ibid.

The Electoral College for these reserve seats shall be the union councilors of the district.[51]

An electoral college composed of union counselors of the district shall elect the zila nazim and the naib-nazim as joint candidates. There is an academic qualification required for the two candidates. They shall have to be at least matriculates, or equivalent.[52]

The zila council shall have the following functions:[53]

- Legislative powers to levy taxes.
- Monitoring and oversight through a specialized committee system.
- Grant approval of budget and development schemes of the district administration.

Zila Nazim and Naib- Zila Nazim Duo

The zila Nazim shall provide political leadership for the development of the district.[54]

He or she shall be the executive head of the district administration. The district police shall operate under the zila nazim.[55]

The naib-zila nazim shall be the speaker of the zila council and will liaison between the zila nazim and the zila council.[56]

The zila nazim will present development plans and budget to the zila council for approval. [57]

The zila nazism's powers to fire state officials have been restricted. He or she is only able to transfer district officials after giving them formal warnings and that too after first consulting the District Coordination Officer (DCO). In such an eventuality, he or she will have to give the reasons of the transfer in writing.[58]

The Zila Nazim shall initiate the performance evaluation report of the DCO. The technical reporting officer of the DCO shall remain the provincial Chief Secretary.[59]

Removal from Office

The zila nazim may be removed from office by an internal and external method. The internal method shall be composed of a two-stage process:[60] First, simple-majority motion initiated in the zila council. Second, affirmative vote by two-third of all union councilors in the district. The external method shall be composed of three stages: First, a motion by the chief minister of the province stating the grounds of the removal. Second, a simple-majority vote in the provincial assembly. Third, confirmation of the governor in his discretion. The zila nazim may not be removed in the first six months of his assumption of office. Only one removal motion may be made in a year.

---

[51] See para 18 of the *LG Plan.*
[52] See para 20 of the *LG Plan.*
[53] See para 25 of the *LG Plan.*
[54] See para 23 of the *LG Plan.*
[55] See para 26 of the *LG Plan.*
[56] See para 24 of the *LG Plan.*
[57] See para 23 of the *LG Plan.*
[58] See para 26 of the *LG Plan.*
[59] See para 37 of the *LG Plan.*
[60] See para 22 of the *LG Plan.*

District or Zila Administration

A grade 20 official shall be posted as the DCO to coordinate the Zila administration. There shall be 12 offices each headed by an Executive District Officer who shall for the most part coordinate the work of the sub-office. There will be an internal audit office under the Zila Nazim. District officers shall head sub-offices at the district headquarters. Deputy District Officers shall be in charge of specific functions at the tehsil level.[61]

An incentive system shall be established to quickly reward good performance by the public servants. End user satisfaction shall determine the grant of these public service rewards. In addition, unsatisfactory performance of public servants shall be punished.

The revenue and magistracy shall be separate offices.[62] This action alone has diminished the power of the erstwhile Deputy Commissioner's office.

The provincial government shall still be able to post the DCO, District Police Officer, and District Officers to the districts.[63]

The following offices shall be established:[64]

- The DCO shall be responsible for coordination, human resource management, and civil defense
- Works & Services Department shall be responsible for housing, urban and rural development, water supply and sanitation, building and roads, energy and Industrial Promotion, and Transport
- Finance and Planning Department shall be responsible for finance and budget, planning and development and Accounts
- Agriculture Department shall be responsible for agriculture, livestock, irrigation and drainage, fisheries and forests.
- Health Department shall be responsible for public health, environment, basic and rural health units, child and woman health, and population welfare.
- Education Department shall be responsible for boys and girls' schools, technical education, and sports (educational institutions).
- Literacy Department shall be responsible for literacy campaigns, continuing education, and vocational education.
- Community Development Department shall be responsible for local government institutional development, community organization, labor, social welfare and special education, sports and culture, registration and cooperatives.
- Information Technology (IT) Department shall be responsible for IT development, IT promotion, and database maintenance. The districts shall have transparent information systems and the IT department shall develop the automation of government systems in each district. A large amount of public data shall be accessible by citizens through the new systems.

---

[61] See Para 27 of the *LG Plan*.
[62] See para 28 of the *LG Plan*.
[63] See para 32 of the *LG Plan*.
[64] See para 38 of the *LG Plan*.

- Revenue Department shall be responsible for land revenue and estate, and excise and taxation.
- Law Department shall be responsible for litigation, legal, and legislation.

Magistracy

Functions of District Administration:[65]

- Prepare budget and plans for submission to zila nazim, and upon approval by him or her and the zila council, shall carry out their implementation.
- Formulate district rules and regulations for approval of zila council
- Application of federal and provincial laws and regulations.
- Executive oversight of implementation of policies.
- Provide information and cooperation for monitoring of zila, tehsil and union council monitoring committees, and citizen community boards.
- Use of information from evaluation systems at various levels.

Finances

The district shall be having financial autonomy and sustainability.[66] A district finance system shall be established to fulfill the following primary goals:[67]

- Ensure the autonomy and financial sustainability of the local government.
- Finance the new structure.
- Increase public participation in the development activity by "fostering ownership through the incentive framework".
- Provide an increased level of funding for the development activity.

The three tiers of local government shall have tax collection machinery and will be given a specified schedule of local taxes for each level.[68] On the pattern of the National Finance Commission, there shall be a provincial finance commission for the purpose of resource allocation among the districts. A formula for fiscal transfers from the provinces will be devised and implemented.[69] The finance system at best is very vague at present.

District Ombudsman

The office is established to redress citizens' grievances. The District Ombudsman shall investigate matters and redress matters suo moto or on receiving a citizen complaint. It shall be selected and appointed by Zila Council.[70]

---

[65] See para 40 of the *LG Plan*.
[66] See para 142 of the *Local Government LG Plan*.
[67] See para 142 of the *LG Plan*.
[68] See para 143 of the *Local Government LG Plan*.
[69] See para 146 of the *LG Plan*.
[70] See para 41 of the *LG Plan*.

Judicial System

A common criticism of the judicial process in all regions of Pakistan is that it is cumbersome, costly, and time-consuming. The idea that everyone is equal before the law does not make practical sense if people are prevented, or dissuaded from going to the law courts by the sheer cost involved. Critics of the system argue that not only is the system costly it is also riddled with corruption, especially at the lowest levels. Anecdotal evidence suggests that these observations are largely accurate. The GOP needs to make the judiciary much more efficient in terms of cases adjudicated in a given year. Court cases have piled up, and the backlog of cases is formidable. Even the higher judiciary suffers from a high amount of caseloads and delay. The GOP also needs to increase the equality and effectiveness of our judicial system. The quality of judgments can only be improved by the recruitment of quality judges. You cannot have quality judgments by mediocre judges. This is most important at the highest level.

No work plan has been chalked for the district judiciary for the reason that, after the approval of recommendations by the National Security Council, they have been sent to the Chief Justice of the Supreme Court. He is now consideration them for implementation.[71] The previous NRB document of the Local Government Plan released in May 2000 has vague references on improving the working of the judicial system. However, the higher judiciary itself is engaged in the revamping of the system. Details are not known yet.

Recommendations to Strengthen the Regional Judiciary System

The GOP is considering major reforms in the subordinate judiciary. A report by Asian Development Bank on the subject, plus proposals submitted by provincial law ministries and bar councils, combined in a final document had been submitted to the Chief Executive. The said document contains the following proposals:[72]

- Resolve public complaints against negligent practice by lawyers through a formal Disciplinary Committee mechanism. The committee consists of a High Court judge and senior members of the bar.
- Control mushroom growth of private law colleges. Improve entrance requirements to law colleges. Require a written bar examination for permission to practice the profession.
- Establish National Education Council for the purpose.
- Advance promotion of subordinate judges. Half of the strength of the High Court should be judges elevated from the subordinate judiciary.
- Improve quality of subordinate judiciary. No appointment of Additional District and Session Judges from the bar.
- Tighten entry requirements for civil judges. Only advocates with a minimum of 2-4 years are eligible for appointments as civil judges.

---

[71] See para 43, *Local Government Plan.*
[72] *The Friday Times*, June 21-27, 2000, 4.

- Reduce the time-period for the decision of a case by reducing the number of appeals granted under normal case litigation
- Improve the salaries and other benefits of the subordinate judiciary.
- Appoint a Judicial Ombudsman with all the powers to redress the genuine grievances of the litigant public and lawyers community against the judiciary. The Ombudsman is given powers to recommend action including termination of services of judicial officers.
- The improvement of physical infrastructure of the court systems. Provide better housing facilities to the officials.
- Recruitment, promotion is based only on merit alone. No other consideration is made, especially in the selection of the higher judiciary.
- The bifurcation of the judiciary and the executive should be enhanced. For a proper functioning of the judiciary, it must be separated from the executive and not be dominated by it. Otherwise, the cause of justice cannot be served.
- The number of courts is inadequate to serve a growing population. Therefore, a bigger court system is established.
- Laws may be simplified and Islamize gradually. A hotchpotch of laws, Islamic, British, traditional cannot be effective, especially if they cover the same subject matter. Laws need to be consolidated under the rubric of Islamic law, to the extant possible.
- Selection of higher judiciary is made more difficult and pain-staking process than at present as in most developed countries. An elected public body be also involved in the ratification of nominations for higher judiciary positions cleared by both the executive and the higher judiciary itself. The intention is to get the best people to be appointed as judges. The ratification process in would involve interview sessions open to the public, as in the USA.

Highlights of the Electoral System

Election to be held on a non-party basis.

Separate electorate to be maintained i.e. separation on religious grounds.

Term of office is three years.

Very tough conditions have been imposed on candidates. The required qualifications for candidates are:

- Minimum age of 25 years.
- Enrolled as a voter in the locality.
- Good Islamic character, applicable for only Muslim candidates.
- Good reputation requirements for all other candidates.
- Is not in state service or dismissed from public service on grounds of moral misconduct.
- Is not a tax-evader?
- Has not been adjudged a willful defaulter of any state tax or due.

- Has not been convicted by a state court on grounds of corruption or misuse of authority.
- Has not been sentenced to imprisonment for more than three months.
- Has not failed to file the election expenditure returns required by law.
- Is a patriot?

These are indeed stringent conditions attached for election. Presumably, the Election Commission shall be responsible to ensure that the above conditions are met. The GOP neither has nor stated how these conditions shall be enforced.

APPREHENSIONS ABOUT THE LG PLAN AND PUBLIC REACTION

The direction of the LG Plan seems to be correct. However, there are still many complex issues to be worked out. The fog has cleared somewhat. Yet again, the details of the LG Plan are still missing albeit in some areas. Some issues are still left undecided, the most important being the announcement of a date for provincial and national assembly elections. Other less important issues are:

- The manner of interaction between the districts and the provinces.
- Financial autonomy issues. Exact working of the new provincial finance commission.
- Taxation issues. For example, nature and extent of formulas for direct grants from provinces and the federal government.
- Actual implementation of the rules and regulations pertaining to elections by the Election Commission

FUNDING OF THE LOCAL GOVERNMENT

Local governments are usually dependent upon higher level funding to meet their requirements. In some cases, they receive money for general functioning and in other cases; they receive money for a specific service the local government agrees to provide for a higher-level government (provincial or federal).[73] Much like its counterparts elsewhere, the GOP shall also make the following transfers:[74]

- Block transfer
- Matching grants
- Specific purpose grants

---

[73] Kurt Thurmaier, "Local Government Budgeting", *International Encyclopedia of Public Policy and Administration, op cit., 1301.*

[74] *LG Plan,* 60.

The details of these transfers have yet to be spelled out.

REFORMS NEEDED

Other than the block grants, the GOP should also make categorical grants in vital areas such as environment to augment the services in the field. The categorical grants are somewhat different then the specific purpose grants because they are given to a category of services and the local government has some leeway to spend them. They are situated in between block and specific purpose grants. These grants are not without attached conditionality, however. For example, the GOP shall give out directives or formulas to direct the Local Bodies and Rural Development Department to function in a desired way and more importantly to uphold certain minimum standards of service delivery. The GOP shall first prescribe maximum limits of air and water pollution tolerable. In collaboration with he Local Bodies Department, it also then measures the air and water in each locality to determine whether limits have been broken or not. The specified indicators are periodically checked by the department and reported to the GOP. The locality establishes a "need" when pollution levels exceed maximum tolerable limits. Only then, the funding is made for a specific program to clean up the air and water to the desired levels. It is up to the local administration to decide how the actual clean up shall happen and who shall do it and what cost and period. Thus, the GOP shall not interfere in the details of the actual working. The Local Bodies Department should be better equipped to carry out the task. The advantage of these categorical grants is that the while the GOP channels funds to areas of high priority for human development, the Local government controls actual spending without outside interference. Obviously, the GOP shall provide technical services for the purpose, as the Local government is not equipped to handle such highly technical tasks as environmental monitoring and clean up.

DISTRICT POLICE

The police service in Pakistan is notoriously corrupted, inefficient, and ineffective. General Musharraf claims that through new reform, measure the police would be purged of corruption and it would be converted in to an honest, people-friendly, and efficient department. He has admitted that the existing police force "failed to inspire people and earn them confidence" and that the police is regarded as "a highly inefficient, corrupt and a politically motivated department."[75] Nevertheless, the government is committed to ensure rule of law and good governance, says General Musharraf. He claimed that the regime would soon implement police reforms to "restructure the force to make it modern,

---

[75] *The News*, Aug. 29, 2000.

efficient and respectable".[76] The efforts are now in an advanced stage and that a comprehensive strategy regarding police reforms has been formulated which includes:[77]

- Recruitment and promotion on merit.
- Revised salary structures.
- Latest equipment
- Improved physical facilities
- Effective monitoring system

The police reform Local Government Plan has been jointly prepared by the NRB and the Interior Ministry and is expected to get the approval of the Cabinet very soon.

As regards the district-level police service, the Plan says explicitly that:[78] "law and order will remain a provincial subject. The provinces will be responsible for raising, organizing, equipping, training, and maintaining the police for the district in all respects". Thus, the control of the police at the district level shall remain the same as before. Locals, as far as possible, shall operate the district police, however.[79]

While on the one hand, it is said that law and order shall remain a provincial subject on the other hand, it is said that the district police will be exclusively responsible for the maintenance of law and order in the districts.[80] The province will maintain all police facilities but the districts may also add to them for the purpose of greater efficiency.[81]

The police will be restructured with the aim of providing it with proper remuneration, training, equipment, and accommodation facilities.[82]

It had been planned that the Assistant Superintendent Police (ASP) officers shall head the police station eventually.[83] Note that the ASP is the entry-level posting of a grade-17 police officer in the Central Superior Services (CSS) and is recruited through the standard FPSC examination system. Generally, the current Station House Officer (SHO) heading the local police station is a junior officer and not part of the CSS system. Among other reforms, the police have also been given protection from undue political interference. The LG Plan says that no police official besides the DPO shall be directly answerable to any elected representative, board, or committee.[84] One of the factors often cited for police ineffectiveness is the undue political interference in the normal working of the service. An attempt is being made to rectify the problem. Another factor cited is the untrained and sometimes barely literate SHO being in charge in the "thana" (local police stations). The culture of the Thana invariably has become notorious for bad behavior corruption and abuse. It might be somewhat improved when better trained and

---

[76] Ibid.
[77] Ibid.
[78] See para 101, *Local Government Plan.*
[79] See para 101, *Local Government Plan.*
[80] See para 102, *Local Government Plan.*
[81] See para 104, *Local Government Plan.*
[82] See para 106, *Local Government Plan.*
[83] See para 105, *Local Government Plan.*
[84] See para 103, *Local Government Plan.*

senior officers operate them. Meanwhile, a serious exercise is being undertaken right now to replace the 1861 police act with a new one.

There was an obvious duality in the Plan's district police service. In addition, there was an obvious apprehension that the nascent district governments shall be unable to handle the awesome responsibility of policing. Therefore, it is best left in provincial hands. This line of argument has apparently won the day in the corridors of power. People fear too much change happening too soon. The question remains whether the duality shall adversely affect the working of the district administration. It much depends on how ground events unfold in realty. Maybe there is smooth working of the system. In that case, current apprehensions may prove to be largely unfounded.

The Plan has some other checks on police abuse, namely:[85]

- District Public Safety Commissions to monitor police performance. The commission shall be composed of 8-12 members, half of whom shall be elected by the Zila Council and the other half to be appointed by the provincial Chief Minister on the recommendations of a selection panel consisting of: (i) A District and Sessions judge, (ii) A non-elected nominee of the Zila Nazim, and (iii) A non-elected nominee of the provincial Chief Minister. In addition, as far as possible, one-third of the members shall be women.

- The differentiation of functions in the service. For example, the function of prosecution shall not be part of the function of the police. Investigation function has also been separated from normal police duties. It shall be performed by a separate chain of command accountable to the District Police Officer. The investigation head is responsible to the police chief o the province through a Deputy Inspector General of Police Crimes Branch.[86]

- An FIR can also be registered outside the police stations (already being done in Karachi).

- Public oversight has been strengthened. The citizens' community boards and the Public Safety Committees at various levels shall monitor the performance of the district police. There shall also be a criminal justice coordination committee.

- A Police Complaint Authority to guarantee fundamental rights is also being envisaged. The PCA shall be established in all provinces and districts, if required. It shall consist of a chairperson and six members.[87] The chairman shall be appointed by the chief minister of the province whereas the Home minister of the province shall appoint the members upon recommendation of a list of candidates by the Public Safety Commission of the said province.[88]

- Each province shall have a provincial safety Commission (PSC). It will have 12 members, the provincial assembly will elect six, and the remaining six will be appointed by the Governor of the province in his discretion, from a list of

[85] See para 107, *Local Government Plan.*
[86] See para 102, *Local Government Plan.*
[87] See para 125, *Local Government Plan.*
[88] See para 126, *Local Government Plan.*

candidates given to him or her by a panel. The recommending panel shall consist of the following:[89] (i) A non-elected nominee of the Chief Minister of the province, (ii) A non-elected nominee of the Chief executive Chief Justice of the High Court, (iii) As far as possible, one-third of the independent as well as elected members of the PPSC shall be a woman, (iv) the commission itself shall select the chairperson of the PSC. The person shall serve the term on a quarterly rotation basis.[90]

DISTRICT LEVEL CRIMINAL JUSTICE REFORMS

The criminal justice system suffers from a number of flaws that need to be rectified. Some proposals submitted by the Good Governance Group (G-3), GOP in 1999 were already under consideration. These are: [91]

- Complete separation of judiciary from the executive has not yet taken place, in the light of the concept of separation propounded in the Constitution. For its efficient working, the judiciary is still dependent on the police regarding production of under trial prisoners on dates of hearing, service of summons, warrants, attendance of witnesses, submission of "challans" within reasonable time, completion of investigation of different case at various stages. However, progress has been made in the process of separation of executive from the judiciary. It is time that other essential changes in the system are affected without any further dilly dallying so that the people start getting the feel of a criminal justice system which is fair, less cumbersome, relatively inexpensive and above all, efficient and effective.
- Special courts (ATA and STA) have not yielded the results which were expected from them although facilities provided to the said courts and the procedure which was to be followed by the said courts, was better and effective than that followed by the normal courts.
- Selection of the judicial officers is not on based on merit alone. There is no Federal Judicial Service established to ensure better functioning.
- The main reason for the delay in the disposal of criminal cases was due to the shortage of Judicial Magistrates. Presently, as many as 3000 cases are pending before the Judicial Magistrates. Given the backlog it is impossible for these officials to properly attend to these pending cases.
- Frequent changes in law have taken place and so a system be set up to ensure that all the notifications regarding promulgation of a new law and amendments of existing laws be all sent to the judicial officers.

---

[89] See para 128, *Local Government Plan.*
[90] See papa 128, *Local Government Plan.*
[91] District Level Criminal Justice Reforms, unpublished report, G3, Planning and development Division, GOP, 1999.

- The present judicial system is in vogue for almost one and a half-century and time-tested one. It is fully understood by the people and generally approved of. Appropriate reforms and changes may be allowed but drastic transformation of the system is most unwarranted.

- It is obvious that the criminal justice system can only perform effectively and efficiently if the components of the system act in concert, not if the agencies involved exercise their broad discretionary powers in an uncoordinated fashion, at times even acting at cross-purposes to each other.

- The strength of judicial magistrates should be suitably raised so that there may not be more than 250 or 300 cases before any single judicial magistrate. No vacancy of a magistrate should be left unfulfilled for more than one month and there should be a magistrate at the Thana level. In Baluchistan, there should be a magistrate at sub-divisional level, irrespective of the number of cases.

- No retired judge at any level is re-employed and no serving judge is posted against an executive post.

- Wasting police time by lodging false complaints/FIR's may be made a distinct offence, as is the case in most western countries, including Britain. Simultaneously, exemplary punishments may be meted out to policemen resorting to harassment. Inconsiderate, wanton and willful prosecutions must end. This will help enhance the efficiency as well as fairness of the system.

- Retirement age of judges may be enhanced for clearance of heavy backlog of cases.

- The system of summons process serving is improved.

- Imposition of time limits for investigations/trials in different types of cases. Excessive deviations from standards should be made accountable.

- Time limit for submission of "challans", in certain cases, may be fixed as 30 days. The old scales of punishment by fines should be reviewed.

- Arrangements for the pre and in-service training of judicial officers and court personnel are made on a priority basis.

- Investigating branch of police should be strengthened for timely submission of "challans".

- Witness protection programs are introduced, both for security and as an incentive to those volunteering evidence against hard-core criminals.

- A reasonable mandatory period for disposal of cases at the trial and appeal stages is fixed in consultation with the higher judiciary. Frequent adjournments on flimsy grounds are disallowed.

- No useful public purpose is served by sending those criminal cases to the trial courts, which do not meet the "beyond reasonable doubt" evidence standard. To make the system more efficient and to put scarce resources to optimum utilization, it is critical that subject to effective checks and balances, the investigators in consultation with the Public Prosecutors are allowed discretion not to forward cases that lack sufficient evidence.

- All summary cases and cases punishable up to one year imprisonment may be tried by Honorary Justices of Peace (JP) sitting in collective benches, not by professional judicial officers who should be exclusively tasked to try serious offences. This maybe on the pattern of Lay Magistrates as in Great Britain
- With a view to resolve the problem of backlog and ensure quick disposal of cases the GoP should increase the number of judges and judicial officers.
- Parallel judiciary is done away with. The present judiciary consulted for speedy trials not pre-sentenced trials, whose judgment on appeals are reversed being faulty and without substance.
- Trial and sentence in absentia be permitted. Right of appeal to all those convicted as such is allowed on surrendering within a stipulated period.
- Meetings between police officers, magistrate and session judges be conducted monthly and strictly enforced by the High Courts.
- With a view to ensure checks and balances, civil and criminal work is separated at the level of Additional District Judges/Additional Session Judges. The office of District and Session Judges be strengthened such that be may not be entrusted trial work, except when necessary. This would encourage specialization through rotation. All special courts at District level are merged with the District and Sessions Judges who should be the sole officer responsible for supervision of administration of justice at district level. However, the functions of the district and Sessions judge should vest in the same person.
- Panel of lawyers to represent those who cannot afford it, this assistance can also be sought from bar associations and human rights organization.
- Induct qualified and capable lawyers as public prosecutors at the district level. These officials will direct the investigations in a professional style and thereby strengthen the cases in such a manner that it leads to conviction in court.
- There is a need for organized and methodical arrangements of supervision and control by the high courts over the functioning of subordinate courts. The cases of corruption, inefficiency and in-proficiency must be noticed and appropriate punishments awarded. Similarly, the district magistrates must exercise strict control over the functioning of executive magistrates under his control. There should be a system of reward and incentives in the shape of giving special increments, preference in promotion or choice of posting for judges/magistrates whose performance is exemplary.
- An independent research body may be established to constantly monitor and analyze the crime statistics and suggest ways and means to enhance the efficacy of the system. The organization to encourage and sponsor all crime related research in major universities.
- Investigation and prosecution cadres should be separated from general police.
- A complainant should be given the alternative remedy of getting the FIR registered with the concerned Illaqa Magistrate if it is not registered by officer-in-charge of the police station.

- Departmental action should be taken against the police officer who dies not record FIR or who conducts faulty investigation and the result of the proceedings should be conveyed to the concerned court.
- The officer-in-charge of police station that records FIR should be sufficiently qualified in law. The investigating officer should be a law graduate.
- Law regarding submission of "challans" may be strictly followed so that chances of reinvestigation are reduced.
- The courts should encourage out of court resolution of cases through mediators with the consent of the parties except in cases of Hudood, cases in which minor and lunatic or a Government is party.
- Law may fix time limit for decision/disposal of criminal cases subject to fixation of number of cases.
- Uniform laws should be applied all over the country including FATA and Islamabad Capital Territory.
- As a prerequisite in the process of any meaningful reform process, the political leadership of the country at all levels should state as a matter of fundamental policy than an effective, independent, socially responsive and publicly accountable, democratically controlled yet politically neutral police is crucial to the development of civil society and stable democratic institutions.
- A fundamental change in Police Act, Rules & Regulations, Procedural and other laws is required to shift the perception of police as a hostile, coercive and repressive force to one that is based on the police as a community organizations functioning on rules of law.
- Police are transformed from a reactive to proactive organization. The police must function based on a Mission Statement as required by the other government agencies. Proper planning must be incorporated in the reform process.
- Police are restructured to have unified command with financial and operational independence. The recommendations of previous Police Commissions and reviews are considered.
- The police service is immediately de-politicized. All officials with strong political leanings are fired. Recruitment, postings, transfers and career development is on merit only.
- National Training Policy is formulated with Mission Statement for training emanating from National Mission Statement. Strategy for implementation of training policy is advised.
- There must be job description for each rank/post. Training is imparted according to the Job Description.
- Civil society groups can concentrate more on helping combat crime. The problem of endless postings and transfers will be controllable. Civic groups want to work with the same set of people and do not want to deal with different officers all the time.
- The police service recruitment, training, promotion – the entire service will be decentralized and under local control. Thus, instead of a Punjab Police we will

have a Lahore police, Multan police, etc. These different police services will be independent of each other and will not interfere in each other's work.

- The primary coordinating agency would be a federal agency. In other words, we are trying to bypass, to some extent, the provincial governments. We are localizing police because this is the best way to control crime.

- The training of the police services needs to be revamped. Better-trained police officers can only come about if we have better qualified recruits. The educational level of recruits in the police forces will have to be increased from what it is today. The thanna culture is messed up because of illiterate policemen, among other reasons.

- The investigation aspect of police work needs to be stressed. Investigation is a technical specialty requiring specialized training. It should be separated from the normal police work. Police beatings and other torture in our police stations are common and must end. Confessions through torture should not be admissible in court.

- State prosecution needs to be revamped. It is wholly inadequate. A powerful federal Advocate General office should be created with its counterparts in the provinces.

- The civil service, with all its shortcomings, is the glue that is holding the government together. Therefore, it cannot be discarded for only partisan political reasons.

- The compensation of the entire state service employees needs to be increased. An honest state service is not just a function of good intentions and ground facilities but also monetary compensation. For example, the civil services of Hong Kong and Singapore are honest because they are better paid. That we do not have the resources to increase salaries is a lame excuse. We do not have a choice in the matter. Penny wise and pound-foolish policies defy logic and common sense. Effective government is a function of satisfied and contented officials and is not possible otherwise. Simple as that. Moreover, this principle of good governance is accepted universally. No one has yet challenged its efficacy.

In May 2001, Moinuddin Haider, Interior Minister said that under the Plan, the police would work under the elected representatives who would be responsible for the maintenance of law-and-order at the district level. He added that the Plan would ensure the transfer of power to the representatives' of the people and good governance in the country.[92] In June 2001, the Interior Minister announced that GoP has decided to create an independent prosecution service with the aim of improving efficiency by reducing unnecessary clogging of the courts and by ensuring that only those cases are sent to court, which has a reasonable chance of conviction. In addition, Police Complaint Authorities are being established to ensure proper conduct of the police officials. The Public Safety Commissions are being established at various levels to ensure that the police can function

---

[92] *Dawn*, May 17, 2001.

without any outside pressure. The setup of the police service in the major cities is going to be changed. He emphasized training of the police officials in a single police academy.93 There has been a lot of talk about police reforms in Pakistan. In reality, reform plans are seldom implemented. The people hope that this time things will be different though.

JUDICIAL SYSTEM

A common criticism of the judicial process in all regions of Pakistan is that it is cumbersome, costly, and time-consuming. The idea that everyone is equal before the law does not make practical sense if people are prevented, or dissuaded from going to the law courts by the sheer cost involved. Critics of the system argue that not only is the system costly it is also riddled with corruption, especially at the lowest levels. Anecdotal evidence suggests that these observations are largely accurate. The GOP needs to make the judiciary much more efficient in terms of cases adjudicated in a given year. Court cases have piled up, and the backlog of cases is formidable. Even the higher judiciary suffers from a high amount of caseloads and delay. The GOP also needs to increase the equality and effectiveness of our judicial system. The quality of judgments can only be improved by the recruitment of quality judges. You cannot have quality judgments by mediocre judges. This is most important at the highest level.

No work plan has been chalked for the district judiciary for the reason that, after the approval of recommendations by the National Security Council, they have been sent to the Chief Justice of the Supreme Court. He is now consideration them for implementation.[94] The previous NRB document of the Local Government Plan released in May 2000 had vague references on improving the working of the judicial system. However, the higher judiciary itself is engaged in the revamping of the system. Details are not known yet.

---

[93] *Pakistan Observer*, June 1, 2001.
[94] See para 43, *Local Government Plan.*

Chapter 6

DYSFUNCTIONAL PUBLIC SERVICES

Pakistan faces an acute crisis of governance. Problems with the administrative setup include: poor planning, waste, mismanagement, inefficiency and the absence of a work ethic. Malfunction is the norm not the exception in the bureaucratic structure of the country. Overlapping of jurisdictions and the absence of clear-cut demarcations of authority and administrative control has wrecked havoc with government performance. Independent observers agree that the overall performance of the Government of Pakistan is poor or lackluster at best. The gap between policy-making and policy-execution is wide partly due to the politicization of the bureaucracy and the generally low quality of state personnel. Government restructuring is haphazard and ill planned. During the second Benazir rule, the Prime Minister's Secretariat seemed to be the only functioning institution in the Government. Over-centralization of powers in the hands of the prime minister had also made matters worse. We believe that this has happened because of the arrogance and egocentric personality of Benazir. She wrecked the efficient and orderly working of the government at all levels. The government apparatuses are still in a mess with no easy solution in sight. A careful study of the problems of governance may yield insights of what is wrong in government and why?

Government performance is not as expected because of some existing structural flaws and bad working practices acquired over time. Honesty, integrity, and hard work are not sufficiently rewarded. Political interference in normal routine affairs of the government services is unprecedented and hurts performance. We strongly believe that state employees do need the security of tenure in order to resist such unwanted political obstructions. This does not mean to suggest that sloppiness, disregard, and poor work habits should be tolerated. They should not. Strict disciplinary action is taken against all such employees who indulge in these practices. All we are suggesting is that outright dismissal of state employees by political heads without due process of law be made impossible. Nothing less that a constitutional amendment is needed to ensure this development.

Pakistan suffers from a crisis of governance. The efficiency and effectiveness of government departments are getting worse not better, with very few exceptions. The need for re-engineering the system of governance is being felt by many in Pakistan. It is unanimously agreed that the existing system is failing to deliver the services demanded by the public. Every one acknowledges this stark fact. Perhaps, never in the history of Pakistan has public perceptions been so negative about the bureaucracy. Problems have piled upon each other with no quick solution in sight. Obviously, there is some hyperbole in the print media that adds to public frustration and anger at government agencies. Nevertheless, public frustration is real and increasing. To its credit, the regime has somewhat stemmed the tide of bureaucratic malfunction. The newly set up National Reconstruction Bureau (NRB) is working on a practical plan to overhaul the entire administrative machinery. The work of the NRB suffers from being a somewhat closed affair. It has been asked to ensure that unnecessary duplication of government tasks would end. Thus, the military regime is moving in the right direction. Lack of accountability has resulted in corruption of horrendous proportions, threatening the very basis of our society. The term "Ehtesab" has been abused to an extent that it has lost its meaning. There is thus a need to reestablish faith in the process of accountability. No one disagrees with the General on the observation. However, the question is what the military regime intends to do about the problem? It hopes to tackle fundamental problems in a systematic way. It is a given that the revamping of the civil service system has become necessary for a quick revival of the economy. The civil service system in the central government needs to be restructured for the purpose. The performance of the state bureaucracy is not as expected because of some existing structural flaws and bad working practices acquired over time. The Musharraf regime should pursue civil service reforms in all earnest. What is wrong with it? The civil service has an overly centralized organizational structure. It is slow, ineffective, rigid and unimaginative. Discipline is lax and rules were not evenly enforced. Internal mechanisms of accountability have weakened over time. External accountability via parliament and legal system has become ineffective. With time, professionalization has eroded. Politicization of the civil service and political interference has reduced the effectiveness of state machinery. The bureaucracy has simply not kept up with the modernization trends in other advanced countries. Pakistan faces a crisis of weakening state capacity and poor public sector management. There is a crying need to increase effectiveness and efficiency of its administrative system. What is the problem with the bureaucratic setup?

Even after more than about fifty-four years of independence, the civil service has not been able to come out of the shadows of the colonial era. Colonial administration focused on law and order, the extraction of taxes, and export of primary commodities. The social and economic needs and desires of the 'native' population attracted minimum concern. Power is vested in the hands of a small elite. Although, the colonial legacy varied from country to country a common set of features can be identified: ambiguity about the roles and relationship of politicians and public administrators; a tradition that senior civil service appointments should be allocated to generalist administrators, rather than to those having technical background; relatively high level of non-salary compensation for middle and senior level officers (for example free or highly subsidized housing); limited consultations with the public and little recognition for a role for the media; a reluctance to provide information to those outside of the administration; an emphasis on written communication and processing paper; an undue emphasis on the role of the office, rules and procedures rather than accomplishment of assigned tasks. To some extent, the colonial style of administration is still in vogue in Pakistan. Thus, we are behind the times. This state of affairs is tragic. Several previous attempts at reform failed to make a difference. Red tape and mal-administration is now legendary in public administration. The requirements of the contemporary era dictate the need for establishing an effective and efficient public administration. Pakistan has a weak administrative apparatus. Problems with the administrative setup include poor planning, waste, mismanagement, inefficiency, and the absence of a work ethic. Malfunction is the norm and not the exception in the bureaucratic structure of the country. Overlapping of jurisdictions and the absence of clear-cut demarcations of authority and administrative control has wrecked havoc with GOP performance. Independent observers agree that the overall state performance is poor or lackluster at best in all regions of Pakistan. The gap between policy-making and policy-execution is wide, partly due to the politicization of the bureaucracy and the generally low quality of state personnel. The State restructuring efforts have been largely haphazard and ill planned. Nearly all the state apparatuses are still in a mess with no easy solution in sight. All observers also agree that bureaucratic red tape in the civil service is legendary. People are sick and tired of administrative inefficiency, unresponsiveness, and arrogance.

The World Bank, among others, has noted that the country faces problems, which includes the waning effectiveness and capacity of public institutions and weakness of local governments and other civil society organizations. These factors have severely reduced the effectiveness of public expenditures, undermined macroeconomic management, debilitated the environment, and worsened the other structural problems.[1] The efficiency and effectiveness of GOP departments are getting worse not better, with very few exceptions. It is unanimously agreed that the existing system is failing to deliver the services demanded by the public. Every one acknowledges the stark fact. Perhaps, never in the history of Pakistan has public perceptions been so negative about the bureaucracy. Problems have piled upon each other with no quick solution in sight. Obviously, there is some hyperbole in the print media that adds to public frustration and anger at government agencies. Nevertheless, public frustration is real and increasing.

The need for re-engineering the public service system is being felt by many in Pakistan. State performance is not as expected because of some existing structural flaws and bad working practices acquired over time. Honesty, integrity, and hard work are not sufficiently rewarded. Previously, political interference in normal routine affairs of the government services has become unprecedented which badly hurt state performance. The existing state system in all regions of Pakistan has failed to deliver the myriad services demanded by the public. A careful study of the problems of governance may yield insights of what is wrong and why? However, a detailed analysis is beyond the scope of the present study. The Musharraf regime is prepared to launch a major institutional reform initiative to introduce accountability in the administration. It is keen to provide information that is previously denied to the public. This wais to ensure accountability and transparency in its administrative system. The regime realizes that the on-going and

---

[1] *Country Brief: Pakistan* (World Bank web page).

planned interventions have to be designed and implemented within a strategic framework of reform initiatives. The military regime realizes the immensity of the problem. It is now in the process of studying the problems in some organized fashion. Thus, a beginning has been made. This should have been done years back though. Nonetheless, it is never too late. To its credit, the military regime has somewhat stemmed the tide of bureaucratic malfunction in Pakistan. Nevertheless, much more needs to be done. We are actually racing against time. Given the dismal state of affairs, a reform process must be immediately initiated. The military regime's main objective should be to urgently train government officials who can help create the conditions that shall assure Pakistan's appropriate response and adaptability to new and unforeseen changes looming across the horizon. For the operation of an effective, efficient, and responsive public service, a wide range of reforms is needed. Several civil service reform commissions have done valuable work in the past. They may be urgently reviewed to find out what can be done immediately.

A low level of accountability and discipline has created a mess in the government public sector. Officials are not fulfilling their trust with full responsibility. Tasks are not completed efficiently in accordance with relevant laws and regulations. At the same time, public servants are not adequately accountable to the relevant authorities for their performance. The integrity and credibility of the civil service has fallen. Thus, the service is no longer considered as the ultimate trustee of public and national interests is. It is important that the credibility of the service be restored. In the quest for excellence in the public service, the regime requires that a culture of innovation, creativity, and efficiency be inculcated in all state agencies. These organizations were required to review and update procedures and regulations that were obsolete and implement effective work systems to ensure that their outputs satisfy customers. The public service must fully recognize the role played by a culture of excellence, creativity and innovations in the quality improvement effort and towards increasing public satisfaction. The Musharraf regime was fully committed to the concept of individual recognition. Besides individual recognition, the regime should also give due recognition to public sector organizations through various awards. This recognition would act as a motivator for others. These awards should represent the higher recognition by the regime to organizations and individuals that had successfully implemented innovations. At the same time, all ministries, departments and statutory bodies, in their efforts to encourage their staff to strive towards excellence and be continuously innovative and creative, establish their own individual systems of recognition. This indicates that the values of excellence had been successfully institutionalized in the culture of the public service. The scheme consists of giving awards for individual excellence. The Musharraf regime envisaged nothing less than re-inventing government in Pakistan. A tall order indeed. This required research, experimentation at various issues from developing a model to what works and was practical level. The Musharraf regime should aim at creating public services that not only fulfills the demands of common man but also was also capable of meeting the requirements of the coming century. A wide range of reforms and re-engineering of the public service was required. The task was not easy, however. The implementation of the reform program required comprehensive planning and a reasonable gestation time. The main emphasis was to be on improving, standing mechanisms and finding more effective ways of enforcing these mechanisms. It bears repetition that all previous plans suffered most, not at the policy-level, but, at the implementation stage simply because the people were not involved in the decision that were significant to them. It was reiterated that no valid design of a good governance model could be created that possibly might last very long. Such was the pace of change in our lives. Good governance was a very complex issue. The isolation of citizens from the significant process of government policy-making needed to be ended. Improvement in governance was not something new to Pakistan. Since independence, as many as 26 commissions and committees had looked into the issue. While recommendations of these committees and commissions did make a difference in some areas, structural flaws needed to be addressed. The Musharraf regime recognized the need to increase effectiveness and efficiency of its administrative system. Lack of timely, reliable and accurate information was considered as constraint in efficiency of government operations.

The GOP's bureaucracy is inefficient, ineffective and unresponsive to public needs. The GOP wishes to set right the many ills afflicting the state machinery. For the purpose a reform strategy has been formulated that contains an important element of rightsizing the country's bureaucracy. Many feel that the government system of Pakistan has become bloated. The World Bank and Asian Development Bank (ADB) have underscored the importance of governance in GOP's development agenda. Recently, Nicholas Stern, Chief Economist of the World Bank said that corruption is a symptom of bad governance in Pakistan and the World Bank says it is very concerned about the phenomenon. The World Bank also wants the GOP to focus on the implementation of reforms. He said the very comprehensiveness of the GOP's reform agenda "presented challenges and risks in its implementation. Establishing priorities and careful sequencing of the reform is crucial. In the agriculture sector, Pakistan's farmers needed stability, sound governance, and good infrastructure, said Nicholas Stern.[2] The Asian Development Bank, in particular, has linked offer of soft loans to good governance practices in the decision-making mechanisms of the GOP. Delays occur and projects are not properly implemented because of such bad practices, says the ADB.[3] In a recent visit to Pakistan, some senior World Bank officials have called for a speedier implementation of the GOP's structural reforms program. The World Bank has also asked for the "building internal as well as external support for reforms through more thorough and sustained communication both at home and abroad".[4] In the quest for excellence in the public service, the regime requires that a culture of innovation, creativity, and efficiency be inculcated in all state agencies. These organizations are required to review and update procedures and regulations that are obsolete and implement effective work systems to ensure that their outputs satisfy customers. The public service must fully recognize the role played by a culture of excellence, creativity and innovations in the quality improvement effort and towards increasing public satisfaction. The Musharraf regime envisaged nothing less than re-

---

[2] *Dawn*, April 1, 2001.
[3] *Dawn*, Mar. 28, 2001.
[4] *Dawn*, Mar. 27, 2001.

inventing government in Pakistan. A tall order indeed. This required research, experimentation at various issues from developing a model to what works and is practical level. The Musharraf regime should aim at creating public services that not only fulfills the demands of common man but also is also capable of meeting the requirements of the coming century. A wide range of reforms and re-engineering of the public service is required. The task is not easy, however. The implementation of the reform program required comprehensive planning and a reasonable gestation time. The main emphasis is to be on improving, standing mechanisms and finding more effective ways of enforcing these mechanisms. It bears repetition that all previous plans suffered most, not at the policy-level, but, at the implementation stage simply because the people are not involved in the decision that are significant to them. It is reiterated that no valid design of a good governance model could be created that possibly might last very long. Such is the pace of change in our lives. Good governance is a very complex issue. The isolation of citizens from the significant process of government policy-making needed to be ended. Improvement in governance is not something new to Pakistan. Since independence, as many as 26 commissions and committees had looked into the issue. While recommendations of these committees and commissions did make a difference in some areas, structural flaws needed to be addressed.

During the second Nawaz Government the Good Governance Group, (G3) is established as "a point for the development and implementation of good governance reforms agenda".[5] The G3 held a number of meetings in 1998 and 1999 for the purpose. Provincial administrations are also engaged in number of initiatives for the promotion of good governance and institutional reforms. These initiatives had strong support and commitment of the federal government. Close inter-linkages between the NRB and the provincial governments are expected in the future in the form of counterpart good governance unit at the provincial level.

There was critical need to reengineer the services and training of public officials in order to meet the challenges of the 21st century. The existing arrangements have to be reordered in order to attract qualified personnel. The GOP recognizes the urgent need to improve the skills of the public service personnel in order to improve the country's international competitiveness. It lays particular focus on those dimensions of Personnel management weaknesses are accentuated by problems of finding the right man for the right job. In sum, Pakistan needs to desperately modernize and up-grade training institutes and set higher training standards.

The Musharraf regime acknowledged that implementing the new training emphasis could mean a sizeable investment, not only in money terms, but also in time and personnel resources. However, it was confident that it was an investment, which would yield benefits for state organizations. The regime believed that effective actions in the training area would lead to a more professional public service. The regime believed that an overall change towards better performance was needed if the public service was to meet the challenge of continuous improvement in an increasingly fast-changing world. A new program for training and development across the public service was being launched.

---

[5] Ibid. 4.

In order to build quality human capital, a program of action for training and development across the public sector had been initiated in the areas of health, education, science & technology and IT. Earlier, the Nawaz Government had made an allocation Rs 50 million for 1999-2000 for the project. The Musharraf regime, to its credit, carried it forward in an even bigger way.

THE PROBLEM OF OVER-LAPPING JURISDICTIONS

The Pakistani Government has to carry out an elaborate exercise to identify all areas where there is overlapping of any sort and try to correct the problem. For example, there are a number of intelligence and investigative agencies in the country, namely: CID, BI, and FIA, Special Branch in the civilian sector and the ISI and MI in the Army. Why do we need so many intelligence agencies? Surely, we can eliminate some of them with no bad affect on the security of the country. We need only one Federal Agency and only one counterpart provincial agency in each province. In addition, the Army's two agencies can be consolidated into one.

We have a Federal Shariah Court and Council of Islamic Ideology at the national level, which are both performing similar functions of Islamization. We recommend that the Council of Islamic Ideology be disbanded. The federal Shariah Court be merged with the High Courts as its separate existence is totally unnecessary given the fact that the country's constitution demands upholding of the Quran and Sunnah as a matter of normal procedural government practice.

Earlier, the caretakers had planned to consolidate some Development Finance Institutions (DFIs) like the NDFC and RDFC, PICIC, and IDBP etc. Nothing came of it though. Previously, the second Nawaz Government had also announced that it plans to merge a number of organizations. The RECP and CEC can be merged with the Trading Corporation of Pakistan as once planned by the even earlier caretaker government of Moeen Qureshi.[6] However, this move was never undertaken.

THE GOVERNMENT MUDDLE: WHO IS RESPONSIBLE FOR WHAT?

In some places, we have another problem of not knowing which agency is responsible for what service or function. The classic case is that of Lahore. A multiple of agencies WASA, LDA, and MCL are the city's providers of various services. The problem is that they often disagree among each other and shift responsibility. There is no clear demarcation of responsibilities and such confusion is nothing but a consequence of this state of affairs. It is advised that all the agencies be under the direct control of the Lahore City Government to be headed by an elected mayor with a clear overall responsibility for the affairs of the city. The city of New York has a single unit of

---

[6] *Dawn*, Dec. 5, 1996.

government responsible for the whole city under an elected mayor. This is no small government as the budget of the city exceeds $32 billion. The mayor being the chief executive of the city is clearly in-charge and responsible. We must copy this American model for our cities as well. Management of cites and towns are not the only problem of confused jurisdiction. There are other examples as well. Management of airport premises is a case in point. Here again there is a conflict among various federal agencies, mainly the ADA and ASF on who is supposed to do what. Bad governance by previous regimes had resulted in the breakdown of the service delivery system. The public service did not have an adequate responsive mechanism to cater to the needs of the society. The Musharraf regime should make a public sector performance oriented, efficient, effective and responsive to public needs. It also wanted to build a collaborative mechanism of governance between stakeholders and citizens. The regime must aim at creating a public service that not only fulfills the demands of citizens but also is also capable of meeting the requirements of the coming century. A wide range of reform and re-engineering of the public administration system is required. The new regime should carry out the task with great earnest. The implementation of the reform program will involve comprehensive planning and a reasonable time. The main emphasis will be on improving standing mechanisms and finding more effective ways of enforcing these mechanisms.

The Musharraf regime recognized the need to increase effectiveness and efficiency of its administrative system. Lack of timely, reliable and accurate information is considered as constraint in efficiency of government operations. The Musharraf regime is prepared to launch a major institutional reform initiative to introduce accountability in the administration. It is keen to provide information that is previously denied to the public. This is to ensure accountability and transparency in its administrative system. The regime should realize that the on-going and planned interventions had to be designed and implemented within a strategy framework of reform initiatives. The civil service system in the central government badly needed to be restructured for the purpose. We envisage nothing less than re-inventing government in Pakistan. A tall order indeed. This requires research, experimentation at various issues from developing a model to what works and is practical at the local-level. We wish to reiterate that no valid design of a good governance model could be created that possibly might last very long. Such is the pace of change in our lives Good governance is a very complex issue. We need to end isolation of citizens from the process of government. Pakistan needed to quickly change itself if it did not want to go down in the dustbin of history. Remember that this ability to adapt to changes in the global environment is seen as the most important determinant of national survival. Certainly, we do not wish to jeopardize our national future by taking wrong decisions today. For that reason, decision-making at the top of organizations must be democratically organized. For relatively simple tasks in a stable environment, authoritarian centralized leadership means that tasks are done faster and more effectively. However, where flexibility and openness towards new ideas and new tasks are required, tasks, which require a certain group loyalty, democratic structures, are far superior. Modern organizations and modern societies are organized analogously to the system of science. Gaining and distribution of information is the central activity of these organizations. Decision-making should be done within organizations by majorities and not by compulsion. Teamwork is the central characteristic of the democratic form of organization. Self-responsibility and self-initiative should be promoted.

Fortunately for Pakistan, there is some hope of a turn around. In an otherwise dismal and pathetic government performance, there are some notable exceptions like that of the IT thrust. Surprisingly, great progress has been made to introduce Information Age Government in Pakistan. This success was because of the dynamic leadership of Dr. Ataur Rahman, a distinguished scientist, who had been appointed as Minister of IT and Science & Technology by General Musharraf. This progress is testimony to the fact that there was tremendous latent potential yet available for exploitation by right people at the right positions. The facts speak for themselves. In the past, progress in the field was hampered because of the absence of a central coordinating agency. Recently, the GOP created a new IT Division and announced an IT Policy and Action Plan. The GOP will spend Rs 15 billion on IT this year out of which 60% would be spent on human resource development. The Action Plan is aimed at promoting extensive use of IT applications in government organizations and departments for improving their efficiency and transparent functioning. Also, to organize and facilitate public access to information about government activity. It shall also promote the widespread use of the Internet. On-line records management system is introduced in various departments like transport, police, education, health, etc. Improved records management systems will guarantee that a fast retrieval of records through "one-stop facility" is created for essential services. Make more and better use of the Internet. The IT Department should have its own web page. The Government of NWFP already has one. A number of pilot projects have been developed for "electronic government" in the three major state departments: police, justice and district administration. The new information system being introduced in the police department is going to link 1,300 police stations, the total across the country, into a single network of records. Thus, data regarding crime and other information will be instantaneously available all over Pakistan through this computer network system. Develop the potential of Internet in the country. Today there are 110 licensed Internet Service Providers in the country out of which 63 are operating. The number of users has climbed to 0.25 million.[7] The GOP has made remarkable progress in extending the Internet facility in the country. By the end of October 2000, the Internet facility was extended to 270 cities in Pakistan. By June 2001, the facility was extended to 400 cities and villages. The GOP is establishing Internet cafes at various district post offices and gas stations throughout the country. Two IT University are being set up in Abottabad and Lahore. In addition, three hours have been reserved on a newly set up education channel. Another virtual university is being established in Islamabad. [8] The GOP plans to provide a large skilled work force to meet the local and export needs. The GOP is set to launch projects like Government Online, Electronic Governance Project, and E- Commerce Network.[9] A number of pilot projects have been developed for "electronic government" in the three major state departments: police, justice and district administration. The new

---

[7] *The News*, August 27, 2000.
[8] *Pakistan Observer*, Aug. 28, 2000.
[9] *The News*, August 24, 2000.

information system being introduced in the police department is going to link police stations across the country into a single network of records. Thus, data regarding crime and other information would be instantaneously available all over Pakistan through this computer network system. The GoP is trying hard to develop the potential of Internet in the country. In this venture, it was quite successful. In addition, the regime was prepared to launch a major institutional reform initiative to introduce accountability in the administration. It was keen to provide information that was previously denied to the public. This was to ensure accountability and transparency in its administrative system.

THE ISSUE OF RIGHTSIZING THE GOVERNMENT OF PAKISTAN

The first problem to be identified is that of mushrooming of government ministries that is happening without any meaningful supportive logic behind the moves. The Benazir Administration had added nine independent ministries. The divisions constituted or approved by the Administration included: Statistics Division, Culture Division, Minorities Division, Federal Investigative Division, Aviation Division, Zakat & Usher Division, Maritime Division, Human Rights Division, and Intelligence Bureau. The Revenue Division was abolished. This was the controlling ministry of the Central Board of Revenue. It was placed directly under the finance ministry.[10] At the same time, the Benazir Government had indicated its resolve of trimming and revamping the bureaucracy in order to make it more efficient and economical. The Chatta Commission, named after MNA Hamid Nasir Chatta who headed it, was looking into the matter. Recommendations had yet to be made public when the Benazir government was dissolved. We believe that the said commission was mere eyewash.

Benazir had increased government expenditures instead of containing them. Waste, mismanagement and poor planning were the hallmarks of her not to glorious second term. For example, a full-fledged Ministry of Investment was especially established for the first spouse. The Privatization Commission was turned into another full-fledged ministry. The GOP was expanding without any good reason. Bureaucracies once created are difficult to dismantle. A separate ministry for human rights was not at all needed. The work could have been handled by the Law Ministry. After all, the whole issue of human rights was part of the larger picture of citizen rights, which was a concern of the said ministry. Unnecessary state expenditures were hurting the nation. Benazir was obviously not bothered. The question is why downsizing. The only way to boost sagging morale is to have a better-paid state service. In addition, the government services should be protected from undue political pressures and interference. Government servants are given tenure so that they can remain neutral.

The state should perform only vital functions and leave the rest for the private sector. Rather than cut government size the past civilian administration was adamant on increasing it notwithstanding its public pronouncements. The result of the frequent and ill-planned changes in the state setup was surely to add to the difficulty of future governments. We wish to point out that there is inherently nothing decisively wrong or bad in adding administrative structures to the government provided there is enough justification. In 1984, Italy had 28 ministries, Britain 22, Germany 17, while France had a grand 42.[11] Today Pakistan has a cabinet of 20, which is about the right size.

In Britain, Germany, France, and Italy new horizontal and control structures have been established alongside then traditional departmental hierarchical structures. All departments have a number of special advisory committees to help them in carrying out their administrative and legislative functions. Exceptionally significant are key ministries like education, finance, defense, public works, and agriculture. For the most part, they are committees with a legal status. They vary widely in sphere of action, composition and structure. A common element is the participation of consultants and civil servants from outside, usually acknowledged experts in their field or representatives nominated by major interest groups active in the particular area. These committees fulfill a very important function in supplying the government with advice and information on technical problems, above all as regards the preparation of regulations and legislation. It is natural that these committees become the focus of various interest groups.

Pakistan must learn from the European experience and develop entry points for outsiders in the decision-making process of the government. We must also institutionalize such public-private collaboration or at least exchange of views at a professional level. Thus, the advisory committees connected with the finance ministry must have representatives of the federation of chambers of commerce and industry, representatives of the agriculture lobby, independent scholars from academia, representatives of the stock exchanges, etc. The Health committee must necessarily have experienced medical professionals and, more importantly representatives of the Pakistan Medical Association, and the representatives of the pharmaceutical industry. The federation of journalists and federation of newspaper editors are strengthened in order to assist the ministry of information through their committee. In the education committee, the representatives of the federation of university staff associations, federation of teachers associations, etc. will render advice to the ministry. A new Federation of private schools management and another for the colleges and universities be established if not already done so. Committees including independent financial experts from the private sector can work with the Finance Ministry on a permanent and regular basis to render appropriate advice and analysis. A little of this exercise does happen but more is surely needed in the interest of sound financial planning. In short what we are advocating is an institutionalized form of shura, a permanent consultation, which is an Islamic injunction. We must further develop bodies to operationalize this Islamic concept in areas where none existed before. This would be strengthening civil society in the country something that is very crucial for the rapid development of Pakistan.

If Benazir had instituted this practice then she would not have been embarrassed by negotiating with the FCCI after the budget was passed and not before. By the time negotiations took place, the political and economic damage had already been done. The

---

[10] *The News*, October 7, 1995.

[11] Allum, *State and Society in Western Europe,* op. Cit., 358.

exercise should have taken place periodically throughout the year. Future governments must note that consultation is a cardinal principle of good governance. Representatives of the targeted populations of particular sectional interests must always be taken into confidence. Failure to properly consult on time can result in botched and unworkable policy.

Efficiency of government operations depends upon the civil service that is the core of any state administration. Highly trained and competent government servants are needed to carry out good and clean administration. It is indispensable that the employees of the civil service and other government departments be better paid than what is now the case. The Musharraf regime must gradually cut the size of the state bureaucracies and the savings realized can be utilized to create a better-paid and trained state service. The trend in the Western countries seems to point towards a smaller state bureaucracy. For example, in Britain the civil service strength was cut from 732,000 to 541,800 from 1979 to 1994. Further cuts are planned.

Many observers of the GoP had been arguing over the years that it had become bloated and needed to be cut down to size. However, only half-hearted attempts had been made to cut the GOP size. Earlier, the caretaker government of Moeen Qureshi (1996-97) reduced the number of governmental ministries/divisions from 46 to 34 made a notable attempt in this direction. The attempt to cut government size failed as the successor Benazir Administration decided to reverse the trimming of the federal government. The Nawaz Government supposedly desired to reverse the trend of ever-expanding government machinery. In 1997, Hafeez Pasha, then Deputy Chairman Planning Commission, claimed that it was the first time in Pakistan that the Government was putting all emphasis on reduction of non-development expenditures by reducing the number of divisions and ministries in the Pakistan federal government. Pasha was then heading a committee on downsizing, which had proposed reduction of ministries from 26 to 18. The committee had also recommended the merger of many departments and divisions. The IMF desired that the GoP remove at least 100,000 out of 275,000 state employees in order to achieve a substantial cut in the expenditure. Earlier, in 1997 the GOP had set up a Commission for Administrative Restructuring (CAR) to recommend measures for the restructuring and rightsizing of the civil service. The CAR had reviewed the staff strength of all federal ministries and divisions for the purpose of rightsizing, professionalization, and corporatization. However, Fakhr Imam, chairman, CAR did not report to the Cabinet until the ouster of the Nawaz Government in October 1999. The Musharraf regime was expected to utilize the findings of the report.

Bold measures were urgently needed to cut the size of the government. How many cuts were feasible? The regime is working on a plan to overhaul the entire administrative machinery. Unnecessary duplication of tasks would end. Merger of various divisions would be initiated immediately. A beginning is made with the merging of three divisions into one. The Water & Power, Petroleum & Natural Resources, Industries & Production divisions were merged into a new Ministry of Fuel & energy. The telecommunications division was transferred into the Science and Technology ministry and a new Information Technology division is to be established in the Science & Technology Ministry. In addition, the Gas Regulatory Authority (yet to be established) is to be merged with the

National Electric Power Regulatory Authority, NEPRA as a single regulatory of the energy sector. The regime has merged the Federal Chemical & Ceramics Corporation (FCCCL) and Ghee Corporation Pakistan (GCP) into the National Fertilizer Corporation. Most of the operating units under the FCCCL and GCP were to be privatized. The federal government has grown with time. Previously, there were 36 ministries/divisions with 17 federal ministers, ministers of state, and advisors running this huge setup.[12] Mergers of various divisions would be initiated immediately. A beginning is made when the military regime announced its intention of merging three divisions into one. Later it also decided to merge some federal commercial agencies.[13] For the sake of greater efficiency and effectiveness, the administrative machinery needs to be restructured. A number of divisions need to be merged. For example, merge the divisions of Education and Scientific & Technological Research into a new super ministry – the Ministry of Education, Science and Technology. The model to be adapted is that of Germany. An independent agency to be called the General Services Administration is to be created to take care of the entire housekeeping functions of the federal government. Economies of scale would be realizes in the procurement of essential goods and services. This new division essentially merges all current efforts in the area. No new recruitment is planned for the purpose. The statistics division would be merged into the Planning & Development Division. The Planning Commission would be upgraded into a full-fledged Ministry of planning to serve as another super agency responsible for strategic planning and development activity in the entire country. In addition to the established five-year Plan concept, a ten-year Plan would be introduced. The current Establishment and Cabinet Divisions are contained in a Cabinet Secretariat under the charge of the Chief executive himself. A new Ministry is created to be called Ministry of the Cabinet Office. The division of Parliamentary Affairs will be merged into this ministry. The newly set up ministry shall be the heart of the state. The Minister for the Cabinet Office shall be considered as one of the most influential persons in the military regime. The model to be adapted is that of Britain. In addition, a new ministry to be called the Ministry of Energy

---

[12] The divisions in the federal government are in alphabetical order: Capital Administration & Development, Aviation, Cabinet, Commerce, Communications, Culture, Sports, Tourism, & Youth Affairs, Defense, Defense Production, Economic Affairs, Education, Environment, Local Government & Rural Development, Establishment, Finance, Food, Agriculture and Livestock, Foreign Affairs, Health, Housing and Works, Industries & Production, Information & Media Development, Interior, Kashmir Affairs, Northern Areas and State & Frontier Regions, Labor, Manpower, & Overseas Pakistanis, Law, Justice & Human Rights, Narcotics Control, Petroleum & Natural Resources, Planning & Development, Population Welfare, Railways, Religious Affairs, Minority Affairs, and Zakat & Usher, Scientific & Technological Research, Statistics, Water & Power, Women Development, Social Welfare, and Special Education, Parliamentary Affairs, Privatization, Revenue.

[13] The Water & Power, Petroleum & Natural Resources, Industries & Production divisions were to be merged into a new Ministry of Fuel & Energy. The proposed ministry of Fuel and Energy had existed once before Partition but was later bi-furcated into Water & Power and Petroleum. The regime decided that the telecommunications division is transferred into the Science and Technology ministry and a new Information Technology division is to be established in the Science & Technology Ministry. In addition, the Gas Regulatory Authority (yet to be established) is to be merged with The National Electric Power Regulatory Authority, NEPRA as a single regulatory of the energy sector. The regime decided to merge the Federal Chemical & Ceramics Corporation (FCCCL) and Ghee Corporation Pakistan (GCP) into The National Fertilizer Corporation. Most of the operating units under the FCCCL and GCP were to be privatized.

by merging is created by merging the Divisions of Petroleum & Natural Resources and Water & Power. Create more regulatory authorities such as the Food and Drug Agency to regulate the entire sector of food and drugs. There is already a plan to create a Forest Commission to regulate our fast dwindling forests. One of the peculiar characteristics of our age was the near universal growth of the public sector reflective of an increase in expectations of government performance. The administration of the state had extended over diverse functions and activities both economic and social. Generally, state budgets had also increased as a percentage of GDP. Was that necessarily bad or good? It was hard to say. In West Europe state budgets increased from around 10% of GDP at the beginning of the century to about 35% in the 1950s. Budgets further increased to about 45% in the 1980s. In the countries of the former Soviet Union, the average government spending in 1992 was 45% of GDP but fell to an average of 29% in 1995. In Pakistan, the federal budget had also increased considerably over the decades. The federal government in Pakistan has grown with time. During 1998, there were 35 divisions in the federal government with 17 federal ministers, ministers of state, and advisors running this huge bureaucratic machinery. Today, the number has been reduced to 30 ministries/divisions. In the last few years, several attempts have been made at rightsizing the GOP. The military regime is working on a plan to overhaul the entire administrative machinery. Unnecessary duplication of tasks will end. Merger of various divisions has been initiated. The Musharraf government plans to devolve federal subjects to the provinces and reduce the total number of divisions to 17 only. In the future, the GOP shall consist of the following divisions:[14]

- Cabinet
- Establishment
- Communications and railways
- Commerce, industry, manpower, and overseas Pakistanis
- Information, culture, youth affairs, and women development
- Defense (including defense production)
- Finance and economic affairs division
- Foreign affairs
- Information technology and science& technology
- Interior, narcotics control, KANA and SAFRON
- Inter-provincial coordination
- Law, human rights, and parliamentary affairs
- Planning & development, statistics
- Energy (including petroleum and natural resources, and water and power)
- Privatization
- Religious affairs, minorities, Zakat and Ushr
- Revenue

---

[14] *The News*, June 24, 2001.

The Musharraf regime should realize that the on-going and planned interventions had to be designed and implemented within a strategy framework of reform initiatives. The civil service system in the central government badly needed to be restructured for the purpose

REFORM PROPOSALS

1. In Pakistan, the total number of federal government employees is 3 million. Presently, the GOP intends to cut about 40,000 jobs from its payroll. However, it needs to make more cuts in its total personnel strength. Ideally, the GoP should be reduced by a million or so in the next few years. The question was why downsize. A better-paid public service was the only way that Pakistan could develop at a decent pace.

2. Exchange of personnel between the private sector and the public sector should be encouraged. Rigid boundaries between the two sectors were not conducive to better mutual understanding and appreciation.

3. A system of performance contract with officers was recommended for heads of divisions and attached departments. The successful among them should be provided bonuses based on performance evaluated based on mutually agreed contract keeping in view the major targets to be achieved.

4. Secondments or deputation appointments be encouraged. This also included using private sector secondments in departments and state enterprises on an ad hoc basis to work on project teams. Such exchanges contributed towards better communications and a better mutual understanding of both the needs of the GOP and the business sector. However, just as importantly, they brought fresh insights, specialist skills and different attitudes into the process of government itself.

5. Performance would only improve if public servants were well paid. There was no consistency between the packages being offered by the public and the private sector. A comparative analysis of remuneration available would show consistent deterioration in real incomes of public sector officials. A balance would be achieved to attract professionals in the system and avoid perverse incentives for corruption. The Musharraf Regime realizes that without progress in this area all other efforts at reform of the public sector were doomed to failure. In 1999, the GOP had announced a 25% rise in basic salaries of all government employees and pensioners up to grade 16 and 20% increase for grade 17 and above. The total wage bill was estimated to be at Rs. 100 billion. Despite the recent pay increases; the public sector wages were still low. For the honest civil servants, survival had become impossible. It should be no surprise that corruption flourishes under such conditions. The GOP has already announced pay increases for federal and provincial employees ranging up to 50% payable on January 1,

2002. Still, an appropriate Cost of Living Allowance for the civil service is required in the next budgets.

6. There was an urgent need to ensure much longer tenures than what was being enjoyed by the officers of the Central Superior Services. The practice of designating an official as an Officer on Special Duty (OSD) purely as a form of punishment was a repugnant practice and needs to be eliminated.

7. The civil service was reoriented along certain specialization. These could include international trade, law and order, energy and transport, district administration, local government, economic administration, industrial management, management of environment, financial management, etc. Efforts were made to build a distinct ethos of the civil service. This was possible by encouraging officials of the civil service to formulate their own code of conduct and design their own rules, procedures and systems.

8. A trained and efficient intelligence service could reduce corruption. The FIA be strengthened to investigate white-collar crime and sophisticated corruption at the highest levels. Current investigation efforts were consolidated immediately, and unnecessary duplication of efforts was eliminated. The media could become an ally in the fight against corruption. A vibrant media helps control bribery by exposing graft in government offices. Therefore, the media's "watch-dog" function was promoted by rewarding investigative reporting. An awards scheme was formulated for the purpose. The panel of judges should included senior journalists of proven integrity.

9. The CSS examination system selected the best graduates through an open competition. However, much more needs to be done in the area. The exam was to be improved by making it more difficult, exact and relevant to the needs of the contemporary Civil Service. For the time being, encourage the best applicants from all backgrounds. In time, gradually increase the proportion of recruits with a scientific background, especially social sciences.

10. The centralization of functions at the highest level has rendered control mechanisms ineffective. Public management of local affairs and control of services received is now largely absent. Since centralization of functions have made control, management and decision-making non-participatory, the qualities of service deteriorated. Thus, public dissatisfaction has increased. The absence of representative bodies at the local level has created a vacuum in which even the failure of lower levels of governments is identified with central authority. Over centralization is compounded by failure to delegate. Confusion exists between line, staff, and house keeping functions in government agencies. Lower and middle levels of management are unclear about their responsibilities. Ministries have taken over decision-making from lower levels. It is now common to take minor decisions at the highest levels in the concerned Ministries. Consequently, areas of responsibilities are confused and it is not possible to identify the cause of a failure. Thus, responsible management at lower levels has vanished. Over-centralization has resulted in delays, inefficiency and dissatisfaction among the people as they struggle with a myriad nature of problems that affect their daily

lives. The traditional top-down model of management is discarded in favor of a team approach. Confusion over staff, line, and house keeping functions of Ministries and departments must end. For example, the Ministry of Planning & Development and Ministry of Finance are to function as policy-making agencies. They should not assume any line function, as they are staff agencies. Establishment, budgeting, planning, management and services are to be considered as general staff operations only. These agencies should avoid becoming involved in the detailed work of the line departments. House keeping functions may be reorganized in a central agency to achieve maximum efficiency. Economy of scale principle is applied. It is proposed that a General Services Administration be created for the purpose

11. Proper controls are established. A third party qualifying examinations shall become criteria of promotion of government officials. Accountability shall be introduced in exchange for flexibility with simultaneous increase in decision-making authority at various levels of hierarchy. There shall be periodical performance reports on organizations and a system of inspections based on regularly maintained record. The Government shall make efforts to instill higher productivity among the Civil Service personnel. Action is taken to improve the system, which includes training for all members of the Coordination Panels on Performance Appraisal and Salary Progression and a review of various sections in the Performance Appraisal forms to ensure greater emphasis on the work output.

12. The state auditing services need to be revamped. The Accountant General of Pakistan's annual reports have to become timely in future. For this the office of the Auditor General has to be strengthened. In the absence of the parliament, there is no proper mechanism to follow up the recommendations in the AGP annual reports. A beginning has been made. The Musharraf regime has made an adhoc arrangement where a federal public accounts committee headed by H. U. Beg, a very senior bureaucrat is reviewing audit reports of government departments. So far, it has unearthed irregularities in state agencies like National Shipping Corporation (NSC), Gwader fish harbor project, Port Qasim Authority, etc. The total amount of irregularities unearthed in just the National Shipping Corporation amounted to Rs 4 billion. The committee is referring cases of fraud and criminal negligence to NAB and a quarterly review would be conducted to ensure implementation of committee directives. [15]

13. Although state employees do need a security of tenure but this does not mean to suggest that sloppiness, disregard, and poor work habits should be tolerated. They should not. Strict disciplinary action is taken against all such employees who indulge in these practices. Nevertheless, outright dismissal of state employees by administrative heads without due process of law is also made impossible.

---

[15] *Pakistan Observer*, Nov. 29, 2000.

14. A system of performance contract with officers is recommended for heads of some autonomous agencies. The successful can be provided bonuses based on performance evaluated on the basis of mutually agreed contract keeping in view Plus, pay state employees well to attract talent.

15. Monetization of salaries to end injustice, wastage and abuse of power. Among others, this proposal has been put forward by the World Bank but the GOP is still reluctant to implement it.

16. Job description and terms of reference for officers must be provided. It should be monitored and made basis of promotions and benefits. In this reference, quarterly performance evaluation may be carried out, and provided to the officer concerned.

17. The ACR system is modernized. Design an appraisal system, which places emphasis on a more comprehensive, fair, and objective evaluation of annual work outputs and performance of civil service personnel. Work of an individual was measured in terms of time spent, quantity, and quality of outputs. Give detailed weightage for essential activities in different categories of employment. The ACR form is revised to suit the change requirements of various public services. Make the ACR available to the assessed. However, third party restrictions are still applicable (i.e., no other person will have access to the ACRs, other than the assessed).

18. Turn around the government bureaucracies soon enough. If left unintended, most institutions will crumble. Concentrate on a few vital institutions like the Advocate General, Election Commission, Accountant General of Pakistan, State Bank, and CBR, Military Intelligence services, and National Accountability Bureau (NAB) at the national level. Create a quality public service. Honesty, integrity, and hard work are not sufficiently rewarded. Moreover, sloppiness, and poor work habits are tolerated and no action taken against bad officers. Therefore, performance has suffered. Establish a new and better civil service by introducing new management techniques and organizational structures. In future, the staff would be better skilled and better trained. A wide range of reforms and re-engineering of the public administration system is required. The implementation of the reform program involves comprehensive planning and a reasonable gestation period. Emphasis is being placed not on creating new institutions but on improving standing structures and mechanisms, and finding more effective ways of enforcing these mechanisms.

Provide more information on the Internet. All current information sources on the computer network and Internet would be linked in a giant network - Federal Government Link (FGL) - for easy success. Provide numerous opportunities of doing business on the Internet in Pakistan. All current information sources on the computer network and Internet will be linked in a giant network - Federal Government Link (FGL) - for easy success. The setting up of the FGL will facilitate local and foreign businessmen and investors in obtaining information on various departments. A small service will be charged for this service. The FGL will provide an efficient and reliable information retrieval service. Thus, FGL will lead to a more open and transparent government.

19. Freedom of Information Ordinance must be promulgated immediately. Implicit in the right to free speech and press freedom is the freedom of information. The GoP record is not open to public scrutiny. Some of the GoP records are needlessly kept out of public view. Thus, the public right to know is hampered. The interim Government of Meraj Khalid produced a working document on the subject. It was not followed up later. The law may be based on the work of this period. A Freedom of Information Ordinance will do the following: -(a) Set clear rules and restricted standards on GoP document classifications. For example, the material printed in the Gazette of the GOP is marked classified. Such files need to be de-classified. (b) Consultations with civic groups to decide on what the GoP can withhold from public scrutiny. (c) Expand access to financial information to include personal financial information of senior public officials. All financial deals entered into by GoP

20. Management of development projects needs to be modernized. The civil service, which is the largest implementing machinery of the GoP, plays a key role in implementing development projects. Efforts to improve the management of development projects in terms of their planning, implementation and monitoring have not been successful. Delays, mismanagement and waste results. Focus should be on intergovernmental cooperation. Regulations and procedures are not streamlined.

21. House keeping functions of the entire federal government is reorganized in a central agency to achieve economies of scale. A General Services Administration is created for the purpose. It is instituted as an autonomous organization under the Establishment, Division

22. The regime's strategy at capacity building should mainly focus on management structures and personnel. The reform would ensure that the public services perform effectively, efficiently and responsively. The Regime resolves to create a performance-based and knowledge-driven system that was both efficient and effective. It would adopt a scientific approach to recruitment, advancement, remuneration, and evaluation of the public service.

23. The "Big Shuffle" dupe, a standard practice in Third World authoritarian regimes, must be discarded. The shuffle alludes to constant transfers of state officials, which creates great uncertainty, anxiety and apprehension in their minds. Officials have to endlessly maneuver to get next postings "fixed" or to stay in their place for long. Sometimes officials are punished by transferring them from place to place. Efficiency of all government operation suffers as a result. The Musharraf government has done its share of the shuffle, which needs to end now. The government servants deserve better. Appropriate legislation is enacted for the purpose. It is recommended that a Government Services Act be passed immediately to include the following provisions: (a) Prohibition of unnecessary transfers. A minimum period of three years service at a particular post should become law.

24. The principle of merit in recruitment and promotion of government servants be assured. All normal recruitment of government officers is through the several Public Service Commissions attached to various services. Explanation of service commissions follows: (a) Lower staff be also recruited directly by these public service commissions and not by heads of concerned departments or agency/corporations. Greater transparency and fairness must be ensured. All necessary measures are taken immediately. Justice and fair play is a basic Islamic value, which cannot be compromised under any circumstances whatsoever, (b) All quotas are banned, as they are inherently unfair and discriminatory. People from backward or rural areas and minority provinces do not have a claim for any job based on their domicile. Justice demands that all applicants be treated at par: rural and urban; backward areas and developed areas; and all provinces of the republic. The newly arrived at quota formula for Muhajirs in state jobs be scrapped immediately. The principle of merit is too fundamental to modern bureaucracies and cannot be compromised on any ground whatsoever. Political considerations are not acceptable as a remedy for past failures. The recent decision by the Lahore High Court upholding the principle is a welcome development.

25. Services to be established on a functional basis and not on superior or inferior basis. The Central Superior Services and the Pakistan Civil Service structures are amalgamated into functional ones. Thus we shall have an Accounts Service, a Police Service, a Revenue Service, a Medical Service, a Primary and Secondary Teaching Service, a University Teaching Service, a Foreign Service, a District Management Service, an Agriculture Service, a National Parks Service, an Intelligence/Investigation Service, a Secretariat Service, etc. All these state services shall be fully independent and will have their own organizational setups. They shall deal with all aspects of the administration of the particular service including selection of personnel and devising of appropriate career ladders. What this essentially means is that instead of a single Central or Superior Service there will be several of them on functional lines. Instead of a single recruitment agency like the Federal Public Service Commission there will be several of them. Promotion and transfers will remain within the preserve of a single service. Once a young entrant joins a particular service, he cannot move out of it except for a short deputation or another secondment. The purpose is to create a sense of belonging, an espirit de corps, and loyalty to a particular service. A career-ladder based on specialization, training and experience should be offered. The attainment of expertise and quality performance requires time and therefore proper training opportunities are available within each service. Performance and morale will improve with time when each service grows a distinct personality and culture. The most appropriate model is that of the USA government where government services are functioning not on horizontal superior-inferior basis but on vertically designed bureaucratic structures.

26. The finest officers should be posted as faculty members and heads of training institutions including NIPA, Administrative Staff College, and Civil Services

Academy. These institutions may be restructured to cater to current and future requirements. Additionally, LUMS, NUST, GIK Institute, all in the private sector, should be put to use for retraining of officers.

27. There should be strict enforcement of policy of promotion linked to successful training.

28. Corruption laws, departmental rules, E &D rules should be streamlined. In order to provide discipline in departments and to mete out minor punishments the powers of the Minister should be increased.

29. Reconsider the quota policy. All quotas, it is argued, are inherently unfair and discriminatory. People from backward or rural areas and minority provinces do not have a claim for a job based on their domicile alone. Justice demanded that all applicants be treated at par: rural and urban; backward areas and developed areas; and all provinces of the republic. The principle of merit is too fundamental to modern bureaucracies and could not be compromised. Political considerations are not acceptable as a remedy for past failures. Therefore, the quota policy should be re-examined.

30. The GOP should give a high priority to cost-effective, better-targeted training, which offers value for money. It should provide open and distance learning options offering flexibility. All departments should fulfill the requirement that the training and development of all employees be addressed. For many organizations, the major benefit of the approach should arise not from examining the roles and needs of senior management, but from focusing on the roles of the majority of their staff, and providing them opportunities to develop and grow in line with the organization's needs. The GOP should have a sharper focus on training and development that emphasizes: (a) Higher productivity, (b) More skilled workforce, (c) Better customer service, and (d) Motivated workforce

31. All government departments and state enterprises will set targets, quantifiable wherever possible, for improvement agency performance in these areas and monitor progress. These targets will reflect differing departmental functions and priorities. For the GOP will be looking to departments to ensure, through their action plans, that they are addressing each important area, as necessary. Progress against these indicators will be monitored centrally, drawing on information from departmental action plans as appropriate and from information collective centrally about the senior public service in the Establishment Division. The Musharraf Regime will monitor progress in this area not only because it is essential that key senior policy advisors and administrators rise to the challenge, but because it expects senior administrator to give a lead to the rest of the civil service.

32. All departments and state enterprises should keep their skill-base under continuous review and should act to recruit and develop staff to meet changing needs. There are four areas in particular where action is needed in pursuit of departmental objectives: (a) A sustained commitment to awareness training and development opportunities for senior staff to help them understand the environment in which they are working and keep pace with external

developments, for example in relation to scientific and technological change; (b) A flexible approach to recruitment particularly at senior levels, (c) The continuing development of a stronger managerial culture. More emphasis on professional management training and qualification. The new emphasis should be on developing awareness-training opportunities. An increased awareness of the context in which the civil servants work is important for staff at all level. The staffs in departments and state enterprises needed to understand better the impact of the services their organizations provide.

33. Formulation of work targets and responsibilities for each individual officer (a job description) is being formulated. The work target of every officer is being established through the mechanism of an open discussion between the supervisor and the officer to be appraised, like done in the Army. The annual work target of an individual is set only after the targets and performance indicators of the organization had been established.

34. Clear career paths be determined career planning be strengthened. The new approach assumes that civil servants are worthy of trust, are generally honest, capable and desirous of excellent performance and that the reason they are not able to do so is because of the dearth of appropriate rewards. Instead of emphasis on negative sanctions, the GOP should emphasize an elaborate incentive and reward system for promoting excellence in the public service. Thus, the priority is on the "carrot" side as opposed to using the "stick" side only. In addition, building trust is a fundamental value of any good governance system.

35. A competency and skills audit scheme is being initiated to determine the training needs of all the departments. A dialogue had been initiated with the corporate sector for incorporating their best management and human resource practices into the public service. The Musharraf regime should identify good practices and develop it further in other departments, wherever possible.

36. Make the civil service leaner and fitter. Eliminate inefficiency, malfunction, corruption, red tape, and procedural delays in state bureaucracies through incorporation of good governance practices. The professionalization of the civil service is promoted in great earnest. The personnel management system is modernized to create a more effective service. The civil service should evolve a professional performance appraisal system that better measures technical competence and the capability of officials. Hardworking dedicated and honest officers are rewarded while sloppy work is punished in a better-organized manner.

37. Instead of a single Central Superior Services (federal) have several distinct national services, as in other countries. For example, India had three such services, namely, the Indian Administrative Service, the Indian Foreign Service, and the Indian Police Service. Create a pilot National Education Service, Health Service on the pattern of Great Britain, a National Parks Service, and an Agriculture Service to be patterned after the USA model. The choice of these particular services is because of their fundamental significance in Pakistan's sustainable development agenda. Each professional service should develop its

own code of conduct and performance appraisal system. No one system could offer an all-time solution in this regard.

38. For all civil services, lateral entry at different levels is encouraged. These incumbents should be given contract positions. The lateral entry will inspire competition among the civil servants and allow the persons with ability to come in the civil services. It will also give opportunities to such people who either might had missed the bus earlier or might think of entering the civil service at a later stage for whatever reason. The GOP needs talent and therefore is flexible in recruitment.

39. Productivity and quality efforts be systematically monitored and evaluated. Towards this end, public sector agencies should implement their quality management programs in an integrated and systematic manner. The Quality Program operationalizes the reform strategy through the implementation of the following measures:

  i. MISSION STATEMENTS: Each department or state organization to had a mission statement covering its role, objectives, both short and long-term.

  ii. PERFORMANCE INDICATORS: All departments and state organizations to develop a set of performance indicators, both quantitative and qualitative, to assess organizational achievements. Institutionalization of the mechanism for review takes place gradually. Performance indicators applied are relevant, verifiable and suitable for each program and activity of the state organization. Suitable benchmarks are designed for the performance evaluation. Each department fixes explicit standards of service that could be reasonably expected from it. Actual performance against these standards is then monitored.

  iii. QUALITY CONTROL CIRCLES: All state agencies establish Quality Control Circles, wherever applicable. The management may be restructured, wherever required. All agencies and departments to formulate a Corporate Vision and Long Term Corporate Master Plan (2001-2010). All agencies submit a Comprehensive Annual Performance Evaluation Review measuring performance indicators reflecting, quantitatively and qualitatively, the sum total of achievements or failure, as the case may be, of predetermined targets.

40. Create District Management Information System units in the districts, which will carry information that will help the police and the line departments to improve their working. The idea behind this initiative is to enable the district teams to work more efficiently and effectively by having timely access to all information related to their specific fields. The GOP to furnish modern, efficient and appropriate means for business and citizens to communicate with government and to obtain services. Make GOP a learning organization by developing a modern mechanism to store and disseminate information. Establish a secure Intranet within the GOP. Provide onward links to provincial and local authorities. Establish a secure platform for the management of electronic GOP records. From 2001, individual taxpayers and businesses will be able to file income tax returns

to the CBR and register for GST etc., over the Internet. The GOP will give a special discount to businesses and individuals that file tax returns electronically.

41. All departments and state enterprises should report progress against above steps, and targets in their action plans. Progress across the public service will continue to be monitored by the Regime. The NRB, in association with the Management Services Wing, Cabinet Division, will promote and support best practices.

42. It is essential to break from the past and allow the staff better opportunities to realize their potential. For this to happen the public service had to be more flexible. Desired civil servants to had a new confidence that they could develop and manage their own careers, whether within the public service or outside it. The GOP is therefore looking to place a new emphasis on each individual member of staff taking responsibility for his or her own development. It is recognized that staff could not successfully take forward their development without real support, and that an unsupported approach will not be of benefit to their department or agency. An effective partnership between the organization and each staff member is required. The top management, the line manager and the individual should all be working within a cooperative framework, each with a clear role.

CITIZENS' CHARTERS SCHEME IN THE PUBLIC SERVICES

The concept of Citizens' Charters refers to an explicit written commitment by government departments and state enterprises providing assurance that they will comply with the declared quality and performance standards. The Citizens' Charters proclaim that citizens are entitled to accept quality service to be based on inter-related principles. All government corporations, agencies or departments at all levels of administration will be required to participate in the Citizens' Charter Program.

Citizens' Charters place emphasis on citizen demands for greater efficiency in public service delivery and their treatment as "customers" of the state agency. They emphasize the importance of exacting performance pledges from each government department. Essentially, they aim at bringing the state agency closer to citizens.

The concept had been successfully applied in Britain, France, Hong Kong, Malaysia. It is now being introduced in India also. These governments emphasized in their charters the importance of exacting performance pledges from each of its departments and holding them accountable for achieving the promised results. The concept of Citizens' Charters refers to an explicit written commitment by government departments and state enterprises providing assurance that they will comply with the declared quality and performance standards. The idea is that customers will have an idea and some expectation of what quality of service to expect from the Musharraf Regime. At the same time, government departments or corporations could use these Charters as an indicator in evaluating their own performance. The implementation of this concept masks the culmination of efforts to institutionalize a quality culture in the GOP services. Thus, the Citizens' Charter emphasized the "demand-side" as opposed to "supply-side" of public performance.

The Citizens' Charters proclaim that citizens are entitled to accept quality service to be based on six inter-related principles. These are: -

1. Setting Standards for Performance Related to Quality

Set, monitor and publish explicit standards for the services that individual users could reasonably expect. In addition, publish data on actual performance against these standards.

2. Making Sure Citizens Receive Value for Money

This principle, assuring that citizens receive value for money, is particularly radical inasmuch as it suggests that public services could and should be cost-out according to private sector measurements. Indeed, the driving precept behind the Citizens' Charter is "Value for Money"(VFM).

In the implementation of Citizens' Charters, service failures may occur. Standards might not be met or pledges in the charter remain unfulfilled.

3. Promoting Choice and Consultation with Citizens

There should be regular and systematic consultation with those who use the services. Users' views about services, and their priorities for improving them, should be taken into account in final decisions on standards.

4. Helping to put Things Right when there are Problems

If things go wrong, an apology, a full explanation and a swift and effective remedy are appropriate.

5. Being Open and Informative

Provide full, accurate, and readily available and easy-to-understand information about how public services are run, what they cost, how will they perform and who is in charge.

6. Showing Courtesy and Helpfulness in Dealing with the Public

Public servants should be courteous and helpful and normally wear nametags.

All government departments and agencies to formulate specific Citizens' Charters and to review the standards of quality services provided. It will be eventually evident that the Citizens' charter is instrumental in improving the quality of services, particularly in speeding up the delivery process.

The implementation of the Citizens' Charters concept requires actions on five key processes; namely:

(a) Formulation of the Clients' Charter.
(b) Promotion of Clients' Charter.
(c) Service Recovery.
(d) Monitoring.
(e) Evaluation & Improvement.

Formulation of Citizens' Charters

A Citizens' Charter must be well formulated to ensure its effective implementation. The process of formulation involved a number of steps, namely, identifying customers and their requirements, identifying major outputs, determining standards for such outputs, and preparing the Citizens' Charter.

The first step in this process requires departments or corporations to identify its customers and their requirements. The needs and requirements of customers are many and varied. Customers will generally demand goods and services that display quality characteristics such as reliability, safety, timeliness, courteous service and practicality.

Several methods are used to identify customers and their requirements. These methods included the use of dialogue sections, interview with clients, questionnaires and feedback information.

The concerned corporations or departments will then translate the requirements of customers in quality standards. In addition, standards of other organizations are also used as benchmarks. For example, the department of revenue could disseminate information on the charter to its staff as a preliminary step. A customer service committee will be established in each division to identify customer requirements specific to it.

These divisions could then prepare their respective Manual on Quality Standards that will then form part of the Organizations Charter. Below are given samples of Citizens' Charters that may be adopted:

Promotion of the Citizens' Charter

After the formulation process, promotion of the Citizens' Charter to the members of the organization will ensure that each member understands the contents of the Charter. This is to elicit their commitment to the service standards stipulated in the Charter.

The state organization also had to ensure that its Citizens' Charter is disseminated to the public. Promotion is done through posters and brochures. Signs are displayed in strategic places within the premises of the offices where they are visible to the public.

Monitoring:

The continuous monitoring of the Citizens' Charter is important to enable enterprises to evaluate their ability to fulfill the pledges made in the Charter. Mechanisms such as the Quality Control Circles could be used to monitor the performance of the agency. In addition, studying the weekly or monthly performance reports prepared by each division, unit or section within the agency could do monitoring. Channels to obtain feedback from customers on the quality of products or services rendered need to be established to re-evaluate the standards of products or services provided.

A large number of GOP agencies to establish their monitoring systems. For example, a state hospital in Islamabad, will monitor the quality of its output and services in relation to its written standards through a number of methods such as scrutinizing monthly reports, or hospital superintendent's report, reports of studies conducted, daily nursing report, minutes of meetings and the health department's report. In addition, the hospital will also establish various channels to obtain feedback from its customers such as suggestion boxes, information on the personal particulars of senior officers that is displayed at the lobby, inquiry counters and the direct submission of complaints to the said hospital's superintendent.

Evaluation and Improvement

In any dynamic environment, a continuous improvement is a requirement for organizational efficiency. Changes in technology, complexity in customer preferences and tastes, increases in operational costs and developments in knowledge, necessitate public sector corporations to review and modify their work processes, operations, strategies, and management policies.

Continuous improvement is essential in eliminating constraints that could hinder the smooth implementation of the Citizens' Charter. Such constraints included the non-compliance to quality standards as stipulated in the Charter, defective output outputs that are no longer strategic or preferred by customers and unproductive practices.

The implementation of the Citizens' Charter by departments or agencies had to be accomplished in a systematic manner and the standards contained in these Charters had to be realistic, practical and achievable. In addition, various mechanisms will be used to obtain feedback from customers to determine the degree of conformance of the quality standards as pledged in the Charters. The efforts undertaken by these government agencies in implementing the Citizens' Charter will soon prove the high priority the Musharraf Regime places on customer satisfaction.

The Annual Report on the Implementation of the Citizens' Charter

Government corporations, agencies or departments at all levels of administration will be required to prepare their Annual Report on the Citizens' Charter. This report will focus on three main areas, namely, service standards that had been set in the Charter, the level of standards achieved and future commitments towards the Citizens' Charter. The objective of this report will be to enable government agencies to monitor their success in implementing their respective charters and to take more effective action to ensure quality in service delivery. In addition, these reports will enable the evaluation and monitoring of the status of implementation of the Charters in the public service as a whole.

The Chief Executive's Award for Quality

An important element of the Citizens' Charters approach is that it included incentives for performance and awards that recognize distinguished public service. A similar approach had been tried successfully in the USA and Britain. The Chief executive's Award for Quality is a symbol of high quality of a public service, which is indicated by:

- High service quality standards
- Independent validation of performance
- Continuous improvement in both quality and customer satisfaction

The award is issued to a limited number of government organizations that had attained high performance in improving service to their clients. Agencies could then use the Quality Mark on their stationery and public relations material for a period of three years. It will be considered a sign of great prestige.

NEXT STEPS

1. All ministries/divisions to formulate Citizens' Charters that fulfill the following requirements:

   (a) Set standards for performance related to quality
   (b) Provide full, accurate, and readily available and easy-to-understand information about how public services are run, what they cost, how they perform and who is in charge.
   (c) Promote choice and consultation with citizens

(d) Assurance that citizens receive value for money. Public services are cost-effective in accordance with private sector measurements.

The implementation of the Citizens' Charter by departments or agencies is accomplished in a systematic manner and the standards contained in these Charters are realistic, pragmatic and attainable. Additionally, different means are used to obtain feedback from clients to ascertain the degree of conformance of the quality standards as promised in the Charters. To reinforce effectiveness in the implementation of the Charters, all departments submit an annual report on the implementation of the Citizens' Charter. The "Charter Mark" scheme is introduced primarily as a symbol of public service quality, which is indicated by service quality standards, and continuous improvement in both quality and customer satisfaction. In the first year of the program, at least five departments or state enterprises should be awarded the "Charter Mark". By year, 2010 there should be at least 50 national charters and hundreds of local charters published by among others, local authorities, hospitals, police departments and schools.

REFORM MEASURES: THE ISSUE OF DOWNSIZING

One of the peculiar characteristics of our age is the near universal growth of the public sector reflective of an increase in expectations of government performance. The administration of the state has extended over diverse functions and activities both economic and social. Generally, state budgets have also increased as a percentage of GDP. Is that necessarily bad or good? It is hard to say.

In West Europe state budgets increased from around 10% of GDP at the beginning of the century to about 35% in the 1950s. Budgets further increased to about 45% in the 1980s.[16] In the countries of the former Soviet Union, the average government spending in 1992 was 45% of GDP but fell to an average of 29% in 1995.[17]

It is a worldwide phenomenon that states are expected to deliver more and more in terms of job security and economic well being of citizens. Nearly all over the world, the number of governmental departments or agencies has grown because of an enlarged state role. This happened in Britain, France, Germany and Italy, among other countries. In the USA the federal government employees some 3.12 million employees, only 3% of all gainfully employed civilians, but if local and state employees are added than the figure reaches 16%. The comparative figures for Great Britain and France for the early 1980s are lower at 6% and 15% respectively. The GOP like its counterparts elsewhere had also grown over the decades. The question is whether the increase in size of the state had benefited the people in terms of better services and more development of the country. Some are of the opinion that the GOP had become bloated and needs to be cut down to size.

---

[16] Percy Allum, *State and Society in Western Europe* (Cambridge, MA: Polity Press, 1995), 359.
[17] "Temporarily tight in Tbilisi", *The Economist*, Aug. 3, 1996, 70.

Efficiency of government operations depends upon the civil service, which is the core of any state administration. Highly trained and competent government servants are needed to carry out good and clean administration. It is indispensable that the employees of the civil service and other government departments be better paid than what is now the case. The military regime must gradually cut the size of the state bureaucracies and the savings realizes could be utilized to create a better-paid and trained state service. The trend in the Western countries seems to point towards a smaller state bureaucracy. For example, in Britain the civil service strength is cut from 732,000 to 541,800 from 1979 to 1994. Further cuts are planned. In Pakistan the total number of state employee's number some 3.5 million. The setup is the counterpart of the federal government at second level. The total number of provincial employees, according to the 1996 census, is 1.7 million, which is 61% of total government employment.[18] Today the Punjab government alone has 950,000 employees and is spending 60% of its resources on salaries.[19] How much reduction was desirable now? It is hard to say. Maybe the Musharraf regime should reduce the federal public service by a million or so in year or two. The question is why downsize. A better-paid public service is the only way to boost sagging morale. In addition, the government services should be protected from undue political pressures and interference. Government servants are given tenure so that they could remain neutral. The GOP's performance is not as expected because of some existing structural flaws and bad working practices acquired over time. Honesty, integrity, and hard work are not sufficiently rewarded. Political interference in normal routine affairs of the government services is unprecedented and hurts performance. We strongly believe that state employees do need the security of tenure in order to resist such unwanted political obstructions. This does not mean to suggest that sloppiness, disregard, and poor work habits should be tolerated. They should not. Strict disciplinary action is taken against all such employees who indulge in these practices. All we are suggesting is that outright dismissal of state employees by political heads without due process of law is made impossible. A constitutional amendment is needed to ensure this development.

The state should perform only vital functions and leave the rest for the private sector. Rather than cut government size, the previous civilian administration is adamant on increasing it notwithstanding their public pronouncements. The result of the frequent and ill-planned changes in the state setup is surely to add to the difficulty of future governments. There is inherently nothing decisively wrong or bad in adding administrative structures to the government provided there is enough justification. In 1984, Italy had 28 ministries, Britain 22, Germany 17, while France had a grand 42. In the case of Pakistan, the second Nawaz Sharif Government had a Cabinet size of more than 80, which is extremely large. The total number of effective ministers was only 19, however. General Musharraf has a Cabinet of about 20.

The GOP's bureaucracy is inefficient, ineffective and unresponsive to public needs. The GOP wishes to set right the many ills afflicting the state machinery. For the purpose a reform strategy has been formulated that contains an important element of rightsizing

---

[18] *Dawn*, May 24, 1999.
[19] *Dawn*, Dec. 22, 2000.

the country's bureaucracy. Currently, the issue of rightsizing is causing anxiety in the bureaucracy, both federal and provincial. Many inside and outside the GOP feel that the government system of Pakistan has become bloated.

It is a worldwide phenomenon that states are expected to deliver more and more in terms of job security and economic well being of citizens. Nearly all over the world, the number of governmental departments or agencies has grown because of an enlarged state role. This happened in Britain, France, Germany and Italy, among other countries. In the USA the federal government employees some 3.12 million employees, only 3% of all gainfully employed civilians, but if local and state employees are added than the figure reaches 16%. The comparative figures for Great Britain and France for the early 1980s was lower at 6% and 15% respectively.[20] The Government of Pakistan like its counterparts elsewhere has also grown over the decades. The question is whether the increase in size of the state has benefited the people in terms of better services and more development of the country. Some are of the opinion that the government of Pakistan has become bloated and needs to be cut down to size.

There have been sporadic attempts made in the past to cut the bureaucratic machinery of the GOP. The caretaker government of Moeen Qureshi (1996-97) reduced the number of governmental ministries/divisions from 46 to 34 made a notable attempt in this direction. The attempt to cut government size failed as the successor Benazir Administration decided to reverse the trimming of the federal government. It added nine independent ministries. The divisions constituted or approved by the Administration included: Statistics Division, Culture Division, Minorities Division, Federal Investigative Division, Aviation Division, Zakat and Usher Division, Maritime Division, Human Rights Division, and Intelligence Bureau. The Revenue Division is abolished. This is the controlling ministry of the Central Board of Revenue. It is placed directly under the finance ministry. At the same time, the Benazir administration had indicated its resolve of trimming and revamping the bureaucracy in order to make it more efficient and economical. The Chatta Commission, named after MNA Hamid Nasir Chatta who headed it, is looking into the matter. Recommendations had yet to be made public when the Benazir administration is dissolved. It was believed that the said commission was mere eyewash. The second Benazir Administration had increased government expenditure. Waste, mismanagement and poor planning are the hallmarks of her second term. For example, a full-fledged Ministry of Investment is especially established for the first spouse. The Privatization Commission is turned into another full-fledged ministry. The question is why create more bureaucracies without any good reason. Bureaucracies once created are difficult to dismantle. A separate ministry for human rights is not at all needed. The Law Ministry could have handled the work. After all, the whole issue of human rights is part of the larger picture of citizen rights, which is a concern of the said ministry. Unnecessary state expenditures are hurting the nation.

The second Nawaz Government claimed to reverse the trend of ever-expanding government machinery. In 1997, Hafeez Pasha, then Deputy Chairman Planning

---

[20] Austin Ranney, *Governing: An Introduction to Political Science*, 6th ed., (Englewood Cliffs, New Jersey: Prentice Hall, 1993), 303.

Commission, stated that it wais the first time that the GOP is putting all emphasis on reduction of non-development expenditures by reducing the number of divisions and ministries in the Pakistan federal government. Pasha wais then heading a committee on downsizing, which had proposed reduction of ministries from 26 to 18. The committee had also recommended the merger of many departments and divisions. The IMF desired that the GOP remove at least 100,000 out of 275,000 state employees in order to achieve a substantial cut in the expenditure. By carrying out the unpopular exercise, it would save the GOP about Rs 10 billion annually. Another estimate put the saving at Rs 15 billion. World Bank welcomed the Nawaz Government's commitment to retooling the public sector and carried out a study of civil service issues as a basis for helping the government design the reforms it had committed to under Policy Framework Paper. The report finalized in September 1998, covered the following five core areas which according to the World Bank required comprehensive reforms:

(a) Personnel and Wage Bill Management
(b) Improving Performance and Accountability
(c) Downsizing and Obtaining new Skills

The second Nawaz Government took some actions, including but not limited to the following:

- In state-owned financial entities, some 23,000 personnel are laid off and more than 650 non-performing branches are closed. A major cost reduction program was initiated with mandatory and voluntary retirement schemes in PIA under which 3,600 redundant employees left the organizations. Top management positions were also cut substantially. Cost cutting measures also included closing down of stations, outsourcing of functions, reducing operational wastage and increasing productivity.
- Sui Southern Gas Company also laid off 525 workers.
- The GOP announced a "Golden Handshake Scheme" in August 1997 to reduce the size of several government agencies. Only some 80,000 had applied for the early retirement scheme by October 28, 1997. The response had been poor. In October 1997, the Nawaz Government sacked some 7,500 employees of United Bank Limited (UBL), the second largest commercial bank in the country. Habib Bank Limited (HBL), the largest commercial bank in the country, and the huge Agriculture Development Bank of Pakistan (ADBP) announced its own retrenchment moves. The two banks retired 7,486 employees under their "golden handshake" scheme. It was believed that HBL's retrenchment scheme was in some ways less harsh than UBL. National Bank followed suit. However, a popular reaction soon occurred. Opposition parties then severely criticized the Nawaz Government. This reaction was very much expected.

CURRENT SITUATION

The federal government of Pakistan has grown with time. Presently, there are about 35 ministries/divisions with about 20 federal ministers, ministers of state, and advisors running the GOP's bureaucratic machinery. Like the earlier civilian governments, the Musharraf regime is also wary of carrying out the downsizing exercise for obvious political reasons. Throwing out people from jobs is never easy for any government, political or military. However, critics argue that some bold measures are expected by the military regime to prove its seriousness about reform. It is expected carry out these tough reform measures. Many believe that these measures, if carried out gradually and methodically, will have a positive impact on government performance. A guarded optimism is in order because it seems that the Musharraf military regime is serious about the matter. Meanwhile, the military regime is working on a plan to overhaul the entire administrative machinery. Unnecessary duplication of tasks will end. Merger of various divisions has been initiated. The NRB has given guidelines for administrative restructuring and developing a database on the pattern of the National Reconstruction Information Management System (NARIMS) and developed the scheme for a National Technical Resource Pool (NTRP). Current reform measures also include the merger of a number of divisions in the federal government. For example, the divisions of health and population welfare are being merged.[21] The military regime announced its intention of merging three divisions into one. The Water & Power, Petroleum & Natural Resources, Industries & Production divisions are to be merged into a new Ministry of Fuel & energy. The proposed ministry of Fuel and Energy had existed once before Partition but is later bi-furcated into Water & Power and Petroleum. The regime decided that the telecommunications division is transferred into the Science and Technology ministry and a new Information Technology division is to be established in the Science & Technology Ministry.[22] In addition, the Gas Regulatory Authority (yet to be established) is to be merged with the National Electric Power Regulatory Authority, NEPRA as a single regulatory of the energy sector.[23] The military regime had decided to merge the Federal Chemical & Ceramics Corporation (FCCCL) and Ghee Corporation Pakistan (GCP) into the National Fertilizer Corporation. The workforce of Pakistan Steel is reduced from 20, 534 to 14,900.[24] The provinces are also downsizing. The NWFP government plans to close the Agricultural Engineering Department and the Agricultural Development Authority.[25] Some 45,000 employees of the Sindh government shall be sacked soon.[26]

The GOP is working on a plan to overhaul the entire administrative machinery. Unnecessary duplication of tasks would end. Mergers of various divisions would be initiated immediately. A beginning was made with the merging of three divisions into one. The Water & Power, Petroleum & Natural Resources, Industries & Production

---

[21] *The News,* Jan. 9, 2000.
[22] *The Nation*, Dec. 17, 1999.
[23] *The News,* Jan. 1, 2000.
[24] *News,* Oct. 26, 2000.
[25] *The News,* Dec. 13, 2000.
[26] *Pakistan Observer*, Jan. 7, 2001.

divisions were merged into a new Ministry of Fuel & energy. The proposed ministry of Fuel and Energy had existed once before Partition but was later bi-furcated into Water & Power and Petroleum. The regime decided that the telecommunications division was transferred into the Science and Technology ministry and a new Information Technology division was to be established in the Science & Technology Ministry. In addition, the Gas Regulatory Authority (yet to be established) was to be merged with the National Electric Power Regulatory Authority NEPRA) as a single regulatory of the energy sector.1 The military regime had decided to merge the Federal Chemical & Ceramics Corporation (FCCCL) and Ghee Corporation Pakistan (GCP) into the National Fertilizer Corporation, which was to be privatized. The State Engineering Corporation, State Cement Corporation, and the Pakistan Automobile Corporation were to be privatized. The GOP approved a plan where the officer-staff ratio will be brought down from the existing 1:4.5 to 1:3.2 from 1 July 2001. It would be further reduced to 1:2.5 from July 2002. About 40,000 workers will become surplus in two years. However, there shall be no retrenchment. The Management Services Division is being transferred to the Establishment Division to mange the surplus pool. A voluntary golden handshake scheme has been approved. Those officials opting for the scheme would be given 36 months salary besides normal pensioners benefits. Ten Centers of Excellence and six Area Study Centers working in various universities are being handed over to them. All federal educational research institutions would be handed over to the provinces. The functions of the National Training Bureau are being entrusted to the Labor Division. The hotels owned by the Pakistan Tourism Development were also to be privatized. The Pakistan literacy Commission, Pakistan Environmental Planning and Architectural concern, the central Claims Organization of the Finance Ministry, National Film Development Corporation, and the fertilizer Import Department were also to be discarded. The GoP was considering reducing the total number of federal divisions from 35 to 21. It was expected that the GoP should be able to save Rs 2.5 billion due to the rightsizing exercise. It was also planned that the rightsizing plan would likely cut thousands of contract and daily wage employees from the public sector. Cuts will be made in PTCL, PIA, OGDC, and Sui Northern Gas, which had become bloated over the years. [27] It seems that finally the military regime was moving in the right direction and was expected to gradually cut the accumulated fat that had accumulated over the decades. A downsizing was an absolute must. End waste through corruption and mismanagement with an iron hand. Anecdotal evidence suggested that billions of rupees could be saved because of strict measures. Bold measures were urgently needed. Cut the size of the GOP to nearly half of its current strength. Create efficient and effective GOP machinery. Pay state employees well to attract talent. Surplus personnel from the federal and provincial governments were adjusted in the new local government setups planned. It was envisioned that most state employees would ultimately belong to the local government level, as in the USA and other Western countries.

The issue of privatization of state enterprises had attracted a lot of debate in the Pakistani media. It is a given that every government strives for and initiates experiments

---

[27] *Pakistan Observer, May* 29, 2001, 1 & 11.

to improve management of its numerous agencies and departments. This is essentially an integral function of the government itself. In Pakistan, there is an agency for the purpose - Organization & Methods in the Cabinet Division. The performance of the division, like others in the government, is also not up to the mark and hence reforms failure. Previous attempts at structural reforms had largely failed to deliver which led to governments opting for the privatization strategy. This, we believe, is done in haste. It had become a fashion these days to pontificate that privatization is the key to national economic efficiency, development and progress. Capitalist theoreticians will have us believe that the lesser the direct government economic activity the better for society. The slogan is let the free market operate unhindered by the strong hand of the state. This is clearly a myth. The philosophy was a favorite theme of the Benazir and Nawaz Sharif administrations reflecting their pro-capitalist bias. It needs to be stressed that unlike the private enterprises sector, the objective of the state sector is not just the profit or the supposed bottom line criteria but also the availability of other much needed societal services. In case of high unemployment and poverty, like in Pakistan, it is ultimately the responsibility of the military regime and not the private sector to provide decent jobs for the people. Where do the poor and underprivileged go if not to the State? The military regime cannot be cruel to these weaker segments of society. After all, the rich do not need state assistance only the poor do. In addition, the Islamic State accepts responsibility for assisting the poor as it once happened in the time of Umar, the second Khalifah Rashidun.

From available evidence worldwide, it is indisputable that the private enterprise sector is not necessarily more efficient than the public sector. There are many public sector enterprises in Pakistan doing splendidly well. For example, Fauji Fertilizer a subsidiary of the Fauji Foundation and the Pakistan State Oil are just two among others. On the other hand, numerous private corporations live to make money fast and easy and do not had any qualms of fleecing the public. The point is that outright privatization is not the answer to all problems of inefficient public sector performance.

Previously, the second Nawaz Government had carried on with the privatization policies of its predecessors though somewhat slowly. Then Pakistan was set to receive $1.6 billion loan facility from the IMF in which the GOP was committed, among other things, to overhaul the public sector and reduce non-development expenditures. As part of the Program, most public sector entities and financial institutions are to be privatized by the end of 1998. However, the program was further postponed until the end of 1999. The Musharraf regime is bound to follow downsizing of banks and sack a large number of employees because it is seeking financial and banking sector loans from the World Bank The World Bank had earlier expressed strong reservations on issues of weak governance, corruption and financial weakness of the banking sector. The World Bank believed that the Nawaz Government had embarked on a multi-year comprehensive reform program to increase growth and improve the balance of payments position. The bank is considering an assistance of $1.9 billion to Pakistan. The Musharraf regime seems to be committed to restructure the civil service and had recently taken an initiative in that direction It is expected to take tough measures to eradicate the disease crippling Pakistan's economic problems, which to some extent are due to the ills of the state banking sector. Recent efforts by the GOP to privatize are in the right direction and should be applauded. More needs to be done. The GOP planned to raise $10 billion from the privatization of state public enterprises.[28] However, the regime should be very cautious of prized national assets. The intended sale of Pakistan Telecommunication Corporation Limited, United Bank Limited and Pakistan International Airlines, Pakistan National Shipping Corporation, Habib Bank Limited, etc. will be carried out very soon. The people expect that the Musharraf regime will ensure a fair price for Pakistan's family silver. The regime's primary responsibility is towards the welfare of the people and not the sectional interests of a certain class. Any thing less will be considered as falling short of public expectations.

INCREASE AVENUES FOR GREATER PUBLIC INPUT

In Britain, Germany, France, and Italy new horizontal and control structures had been established alongside then traditional departmental hierarchical structures. All departments had a number of special advisory committees to help them in carrying out their administrative and legislative functions. Exceptionally significant are essential ministries like education, finance, defense, public works, and agriculture. For the most part, they are committees with a legal status. They vary widely in sphere of action, composition and structure. A common element is the participation of consultants and civil servants from outside, usually acknowledged experts in their field or representatives nominated by major interest groups active in the particular area. These committees fulfill a very important function in supplying the government with advice and information on technical problems, above all as regards the preparation of regulations and legislation. It is natural that these committees become the focus of various interest groups.

Pakistan must learn from the European experience and develop entry points for outsiders in the decision-making process of the government. We must also institutionalize such public-private collaboration or at least exchange of views at a professional level. Thus, the advisory committees connected with the finance ministry must had representatives of the federation of chambers of commerce and industry, representatives of the agriculture lobby, independent scholars from academia, representatives of the stock exchanges, etc. The Health committee must necessarily have experienced medical professionals and, more importantly representatives of the Pakistan Medical Association, and the representatives of the pharmaceutical industry. The federation of journalists and federation of newspaper editors are strengthened in order to assist the ministry of Information through their committee. In the education committee, the representatives of the federation of university staff associations, federation of teachers associations, etc. will render advice to the ministry. A new Federation of private schools management and another for the colleges and universities be established if not already done so. Committees including independent financial experts from the private sector could work with the Finance Ministry on a permanent and regular basis to render appropriate advice

---

[28] *The News*, Dec. 13, 1999.

and analysis. A little of this exercise does happen but more is surely needed in the interest of sound financial planning. In short, what is being advocated is nothing but the creation of an institutionalized form of Shura and Ijma, a permanent consultation mechanism. The creation of such a mechanism is a clear Islamic injunction. The Musharraf regime must further develop bodies to operationalize this Islamic concept in areas where none existed before. This will be strengthening civil society in the country something, which is very crucial for the rapid development of Pakistan. Consultation is a cardinal principle of good governance. Representatives of the targeted populations of particular sectional interests must always be taken into confidence. Failure to properly consult on time could result in botched and unworkable policy. Pakistan must follow principles of good governance to usher real progress and betterment of its society.

HUMAN RESOURCE DEVELOPMENT

Identifying the Problem

Generally, state institutions are plagued by red tape, corruption, and lack of responsiveness to the emerging needs of the country. There is lack of proper direction in most organizations. The departments had become too much routine bound, rule oriented and follower of antiquated processes and procedures. Over-centralization is becoming apparent. Rent seeking rules and regulations do not help the public, but sap its energies. The world is going through unprecedented speed of change. Bureaucratic indifference, mismanagement, slowness, and sloppiness are now legendary. People are sick and tired of bureaucratic red tape, unresponsiveness and arrogance of the bureaucracy. State organizations do not have mission statements. Targets are not fixed. Clear responsibilities are not given. Hard work is not rewarded and sloppy work habits are not punished. There are no officially set performance indicators in the ministries and departments to measure organizational performance. Personnel management weaknesses are accentuated by problems of finding the right man for the right job. The efficiency and effectiveness of government departments are at an all time low. However, there are a very few exceptions to the general trend. Every one acknowledges this stark fact. Never in the history of Pakistan had public perceptions been so negative about the bureaucracy. Problems had obviously piled upon each other with no quick solution in sight. A systematic and comprehensive performance measurement system that is universally seen as vital to realize efficient and effective government operations is missing in Pakistan. In short, appraisal systems are ineffective at best and very irrelevant at worst.

Changes are required in enactment of new methods of management in Pakistan's government departments. There are no efficiency plans applied to government departments. Even reforms are not planned properly. Instead of reforms being an on-going process, they are on an adhoc basis. Thus, the system suffers immensely. The pressure to respond to change is increasingly being felt at all levels, including top management. It is widely recognized that there is an urgent need to raise the national skill base as the critical element in the drive to improve Pakistan's international competitiveness. It is being reflected in the Musharraf regime's recognition of the need for continuous lifetime learning for those employed in the public service.

There is a critical need to reengineer the services and training of GOP officials in order to meet the challenges of the 21st century. The existing arrangements had to be reordered in order to attract qualified personnel. The regime needs to create a performance-based knowledge driven system that is both efficient and effective.

Strategies for human resource development need to be overhauled immediately. Human resources are an organization's most important aspect. In line with this philosophy, the public service fails to adequately focus on human resources development. Career development, enhanced training, and performance appraisal systems are inadequate.

Continuity and change also set out demanding program of change. Increasing pressure on resources and demand for quality service had required a continuous improvement in the performance of the public service. This improvement had to be sought as the scale and pace of change accelerates in an increasingly competitive global environment. The public service must had foresight and vision, joined with knowledge and experience. Civil servants, not only need to keep abreast advances in science and technology and other relevant fields, they must also deepen their comprehension of change. The public service will therefore need to make better use of its employees. More widely, civil servants need greater computer skills to handle the data associated with these advances, and the important changes in accounting practice to be introduced. Better management skills will ensure that necessary change will be implemented efficiently and quickly.

For proper development, appropriate knowledge base and management skills had to be acquired. Countries, like Japan, had arisen because of attaining excellent management skills. For Japan, lack of capital or even physical resources did not pose an insurmountable obstacle on the path of development and prosperity. The ability to skillfully manage existing resources is the key to success. Pakistan is deficient in good managerial skills. The Musharraf regime must meet this vital requirement. Only then will Pakistan's dreams come true. This is not going to be easy. We must note that what works elsewhere is not necessarily suitable for us. It might work, and then it might not. We could only find out by trying it after some careful analysis. Experimentation of various models is the key to Pakistan's success.

Personnel management had become a critical area that needs to be emphasized. In the public as well as private sector, efficiency requirements demand change. Personnel management weaknesses are accentuated by problems of finding the right man for the right job. Some major areas of weaknesses had emerged as problems had surfaced in the fields of economic, debt, financial, project management, and tax administration. Operational excellence requires efficient management. Human resources are an organization's most important aspect. In line with this philosophy, the civil service fails to adequately focus on human resources development. Career development, enhanced training, performance appraisal systems are inadequate. Training must be a continuous learning process. Knowledge and skills of officers need to be continuously upgraded.

Training does not enable civil servants to cope with increasing job demands and to achieve greater levels of performance. Other than the training in CSS academies or military services, the training of departmental officers is largely insufficient.

The pace of technological change means that there is an ever-increasing need for the public services to be fully aware of development that may impact on their future work. This is particularly true for development in engineering, technology and science and technological understandings enabled individuals to be intelligent workers. They could better see potential for improving working practices and service delivery. Awareness training also improved understanding of the international environment in which staff work. In addition, a proper appreciation of the significance of core values of the public service is to be kept in the forefront of the minds of civil servants.

The Musharraf regime should recognize the urgent need to improve the skills of its personnel to improve the country's international competitiveness. To achieve excellence in the public service, a new approach will be implemented. It lays particular focus on those dimensions of capacity building that mainly focus on management structures and personnel. Significant effort and investment will be put into improving quality throughout the public service. There will be an ongoing focus on providing better service to customers, achieving standards, and increasing efficiency and effectiveness. Linking people management, process improvement, and value for money and service delivery will provide the new emphasis on training.

A comprehensive program for training and development across the public sector is to be developed. Integral to the new approach is the requirement that the training and development of all employees at all levels will be addressed. The costs of implementing the new approach will vary significantly between organizations.

The regime's strategy at capacity building should mainly focus on management structures and personnel. The reform will ensure that the public services perform effectively, efficiently and responsively. The regime should resolve to create a performance-based and knowledge-driven system that is both efficient and effective. It will adopt a scientific approach to recruitment, advancement, remuneration, and evaluation of the public service.

Stressed individual development so that each could recognize his or her relevance and value in fulfilling responsibilities in current jobs, or in extending their horizons so that they could confidently take up further responsibilities. This means that training and development must not only be strongly focused to meet the needs of departments and state enterprises but must also meet the needs of individual members of staff with different abilities, aspirations and potential. These individuals must, in turn, accept a matching obligation to commit themselves to a program of continuous development, and must be essential players in drawing up their own career and development plans.

ETHICS IN THE PUBLIC AND CORPORATE SECTORS

The military regime must establish a new and better civil service by introducing new management techniques and organizational structures. In the future, the staff will be better skilled and better trained. A more outward-looking approach, with greater concern for service users, is adopted. In seeking value for money, the civil service adopts a more business-driven approach. The regime should create a civil service where decision-making at the very top is democratically organized. It realizes that teamwork is the central characteristic of the democratic form of organization. Therefore, the Musharraf regime should promote it. In addition, self-responsibility and self-initiative will be promoted in great earnest. Fundamental to work excellence are basic values such as dedication, self-discipline, commitment, cooperation and moderation. The continuous practice of these virtues will invariably lead to greater productivity and quality in the workplace. Each civil servant should possess values that could help contribute and enhance their level of professionalism. Examples of professional values included being knowledgeable, intellectual and possessing skills in areas such as management, information technology and communication. Other equally important values included being creative and innovative, motivated, accountable as well as possessing a high sense of integrity.

In addition, the reform of the corporate sector is carried out simultaneously with that of the public service. The influence of the corporate sector had increased over the lives of people everywhere. A lot of material affluence had resulted by the dynamic activity of large business corporations. Citizen groups are demanding that earning profits is not enough that corporations need to be socially responsive as well. In other words, businesses are supposed to be more than moneymaking entities and turn into responsible corporate citizens. They must contribute their share towards the protection of the environment and promote sustainable development. Thus, more is expected from them than ever before. Some had responded positively. Corporations are to be guided by corporate codes of conduct to regulate their behavior. For example, the Conventions of the International Labor Organization protects rights of workers such as freedom of association, the outlaw of slave labor, child labor, and discrimination, and upholds the right of collective bargaining. Generally, the corporations are also expected to promote democratic values and governance wherever possible. The overall global trend points towards ethics becoming a key factor in not only the public services but also the corporate sector. Societal norms are changing everywhere pushing towards reform of corporate behavior.

Trust, responsibility, sincerity, dedication, cooperation and discipline are some examples of basic values that all civil servants should possess to ensure the smooth running of the administrative machinery. Within this context, a civil servant is expected to discharge his or her duties and responsibilities with sincerity, trustworthiness and cleanliness. Sincerity and trust are values observable through actions, such as in the judicious use of time, administering and spending public money according to set rules and procedures, avoiding excesses and corruption and completing work within prescribed time. Civil servants are required to show kindness, patience and a willingness to serve the public. Values that should be continuously emphasized in the public service included being polite, courteous, friendly, patient and fairness. These core values are the basis for the effective and efficient delivery of goods and services to the discerning public. It is desired that all civil servants give due priority to these values.

Train for Leadership

Attributes of a good leader do not entirely depend on absolute power, the ability to motivate, plan, develop and administer work and exploit the skills within the organization to achieve planned objectives. A leader should also possess positive work ethics and values in order to lead by example. Indeed, a leader of high moral values is one whose actions and behavior is seen to be fair, firm, courageous, responsible, reliable, noble and projecting wisdom.

Although western management gurus had been emphasizing the importance of exemplary leadership in the recent decades, it is however not a recent phenomenon. Islam had already enjoined its followers on the importance of leaders setting good examples in their deeds and behavior through the Al-Quran and Hadith of the Prophet, peace be upon him.

Inculcate Religious Values

In essence, religious values are the pillar and source of strength for all the other values. Holding firm to their religious beliefs will invariably acts as a factor that restraint deviation from good conduct and behavior. At the same time, it helps to facilitate the internalization of noble values. Promotion of Islamic values will be result in good practices and productive work ethics.

The Musharraf regime should desire to introduce an Islamic ethical paradigm in the country's corporate governance structures. What is exactly an Islamic ethical paradigm? Simply, a framework of knowledge and practices springing from the belief that God is perfect, wise, and caring towards all creation. Islam is eternal, universal and had been practiced completely at least once in the early period, and more importantly will be practiced again in the future. This much is the basic part pertaining to faith. From the faith, itself springs forth all human activity, knowledge sources, and national visions. In other words, Islam must guide everything under the sun, so to speak. A common belief among Muslims being that Islam is a complete code of life where the spiritual and the mundane could not be separated. The message of Islam covers every activity at both the individual and the societal level. In Islam material existence is not an end in itself it is the path towards God and His mercy. The religion emphasized individual and collective responsibility towards creating a righteous and just society. Hence, the cliché "Islam is the Solution" had become a common slogan for Muslims worldwide.

Value Structure

1. Hard Work and Honesty

The basic rule in Islam is to work hard and earn for yourself and your family. In fact, it is even preferred over retirement in the worship of Allah. The cardinal Islamic value is that of justice and fairness. The Quran commands:

"And the sky He had uplifted; and He had set the measure, that you exceed not the measure, but observe the measure strictly, nor fall short thereof" (55-7-9)

The Holy Prophet commanded that Muslim give a wage earner his due before his sweat on his brow dries up (meaning within no time)

Hard work is preferred in Islam. The Prophet emphasized pride in wages collected through work. He himself worked hard throughout his life.

Honesty and truth in dealings is a strict Islamic command. The Quran commands Muslims to be honest in their business dealings with others and not to cheat, or lie.

Muslims are asked to keep promises made and uphold contracts entered with other parties.

2. Social Justice

The Holy Prophet always emphasized justice as a cardinal Islamic value. In his tradition, the Khalifah -i Rashidun also emphasized justice in the early days of Islam.

3. Peace

The very word Islam comes from the root salaam meaning peace. The mission of the Prophet Muhammad is to establish peace in the world.

4. Human Dignity

Islam enjoins human dignity to irrespective to their religion, caste, creed, gender, or economic status. The welfare of humanity is a cardinal value of Islam.

In short, Islam calls for a society based on justice, truth, benevolence, security, peace, good neighborly behavior, and human dignity. The question is why these Islamic values are not seen in Pakistan's societies today. Why we did not live up to the golden rules of Islam? We will readily concede that Muslims had failed to live up to their own faith. This does not mean to suggest that Islam had failed only that it is never fully tries in contemporary times. What is the Islamic teaching about modern business practices? Earning money honestly, in accordance with the Shariah, is an act of worship in Islam. However, Islam will expect a strict code of conduct to be followed in this regard. What will be an Islamic Corporate Code of Conduct appropriate for our age? Any code so devised must be enforceable by the state.

THE NEW CODE OF ETHICS

In our rapidly changing world, universal standards had become ever more essential. Without them, it will be difficult to establish more practical and justifiable forms of governance. Keeping this in mind, the following value code is suggested for consideration:

- Justice and fairness to all
- Practice honesty in all business conduct. The creation of a corruption-free business environment.
- Be truthful in dealing with the tax authorities. Report actual income and expenditures
- Practice truth in selling. All deceptive claims by businesses must be curtailed. Meaning that advertisement claims should not mislead and deceive the public.
- Adopt clean business practices emphasizing the adherence of contractual obligations.
- Business activity that is environment-friendly.
- No exploitation of labor, especially child labor.
- Accountability, as a precondition of good governance in the corporate sectors also.
- Obligation of corporations to give back to the local community, i.e. contribute towards its development.
- Fairness, meaning that collusion and price-fixing is banned.
- Exorbitant profit seeking be curtailed in the name of fairness.
- Contribute to the common good.
- Consider the impact of their actions on the security and welfare of others.
- Promote equity, including gender equity.
- Protect the interests of future generations by pursuing sustainable development and safeguarding the global commons.
- Preserve Pakistan's Islamic cultural and intellectual heritage.
- Become active participants in the Musharraf regime's governance initiatives.
- Work to eliminate corruption.

STRATEGIES IN THE INCULCATION OF WORK ETHICS AND VALUES

To further strengthen its policies and programs on the inculcation of noble values, the regime should give due emphasis to the continuous implementation of strategies in the inculcation of work ethics and values. This should included the following:

(1) Training

Training programs are to be conducted by various public sector training institutions not only should cover skills and knowledge but also emphasize on work ethics and values such as personal, leadership, professional and religious values. All government training institutions will inject elements of values and work ethics into their training curriculum. These included punctuality in attending classes and meeting deadlines for assignments, developing team spirit and harmonious relationship through work groups, group dynamics and physical training. Activities on values and ethics are also integrated into all training courses.

(2) Take Strict Disciplinary Actions

The military regime should also institute new disciplinary proceedings against those who breach established work procedures, norms and values. Disciplinary action is developmental in nature, while reminding the guilty party on the accountability of his actions; it also acts as a deterrent to others.

The detailed disciplinary procedures of the public service will be given out in revised regulations for conduct and discipline in the public service, disciplinary board regulations, and proceedings.

The implementing the new training emphasis could mean a sizeable investment, not only in money terms, but also in time and personnel resources. The military regime should be confident that it is an investment, which will yield benefits for state organizations. The regime should believe that effective actions in the training area would lead to a more professional public service. The regime believes that an overall change towards better performance is needed if the public service is to meet the challenge of continuous improvement in an increasingly fast-changing world. A new program for training and development across the public service is being launched. In order to build quality human capital, a program of action for training and development across the public sector had been initiated in the areas of health, education, science and technology and IT. Earlier, the second Nawaz Government had made an allocation Rs 50 million for 1999-2000 for the project. The Musharraf regime must carry it forward.

EDUCATION REFORM

No nation can ever progress without emphasizing quality education is clichéd but true nevertheless. There is a broad consensus that, with few exceptions, the quality of education in state educational institutions had almost collapsed. The Musharraf regime must be cognizant of this fact. In addition, no nation can develop in a sustained manner without quality education. The world has moved forward from an era of Industrial Revolution to the Knowledge Revolution where brains not muscle power matters most.

Knowledge is also a cardinal Islamic value. The future belongs to the nations that have mastered the Information Revolution, so to speak. The world is changing quickly and unexpectedly, its also changing events. Where do we stand? Is Pakistan able to benefit from the Knowledge Revolution? Political scientists recognized that "information power" is becoming just as important as international affairs as country's military, economic, social and political strengths. If we fail at reforming our education system, we will fail to make Pakistan into the powerful modern Islamic State of our collective dreams. The military regime must act now.

The efficiency and effectiveness of Pakistan public educational institutions is getting worse not better, with very few exceptions. Every one acknowledges this stark fact. Decline in standards has not happened overnight, however. For the most part, we have failed in providing decent education in Pakistan The public education system is inefficient, ineffective and unresponsive to public needs. The GOP wishes to set right the many ills afflicting the education system. For the purpose a reform strategy has been formulated that contains familiar goals and methodology to achieve them. We have seen such talk in the past also. Once again more brick and mortar and the like. The only real change is the future localization of primary and secondary education and the emphasis on Information Technology. Will the Musharraf regime able to deliver quality education? More importantly, does it really understand the nature of the problems afflicting Pakistan education system? Unfortunately not. There is a consensus among scholars that the educational system is confronted with two basic problems.

Firstly, low expenditures. While the current fiscal year's defense expenditure amounts to Rs 170 billion or 6% of GDP, the total expenditure on education is only 8% of the total national budget or 3% of GDP. In comparison, most other developing countries spend much more on the education sector. This meager amount is insufficient for effective reform of the education system. More funds are needed for the purpose.

Secondly, bad governance at all levels has made the educational system mediocre and ineffective. In the past, many educational reforms have failed to deliver because of bad governance. Otherwise, good policies fail to deliver because of poor implementation. Very recently, the World Bank and Asian Development Bank (ADB) have again underscored the importance of governance in GOP's development agenda. Recently, Nicholas Stern, Chief Economist of the World Bank said that corruption is a symptom of bad governance in Pakistan and the World Bank says it is very concerned about the phenomenon. The World Bank also wants the GOP to focus on the implementation of reforms. He said the very comprehensiveness of the GOP's reform agenda "presented challenges and risks in its implementation. Establishing priorities and careful sequencing of the reform is crucial.[29] The Asian Development Bank, in particular, has linked offer of soft loans to good governance practices in the decision-making mechanisms of the GOP. Delays occur and projects are not properly implemented because of such bad practices, says the ADB.[30] In a recent visit to Pakistan, some senior World Bank officials have called for a speedier implementation of the GOP's structural reforms program. The

---

[29] *Dawn*, April 1, 2001.
[30] *Dawn*, Mar. 28, 2001.

World Bank has also asked for the "building internal as well as external support for reforms through more thorough and sustained communication both at home and abroad".[31] To carry out effective reform of the education system, the following elements must be incorporated in the new education policy:

The GOP must recast the education policy and make it more realistic to meet the challenges of the 21st century. A central plank of the new education policy approach should be the replacement of "catching up" (i.e. adding more assets), with "making things work" i.e. improving the efficiency and deployment of assets already on ground. In other words, a shift from planning to policy, from development expenditures towards recurrent expenditures, from the quantity of infrastructure to the quality and productivity of its services is required. In the earlier philosophy, the belief is to make new "things" (physical capital, institutions, and laws), and assume that productivity; quality, maintenance and operation will take care of themselves. The new policy should not take this for granted, and should not only to invest in new institutions, but also improvement, management, operation, and maintenance of existing ones. In other word, emphasis governance matters over everything else.

Modern organizations and societies are organized analogously to the system of science. Gaining and distribution of information is the central activity of these organizations. Decision-making should be done within organizations by majorities and not by compulsion. Teamwork is the central characteristic of the democratic form of organization. Self-responsibility and self-initiative is therefore to be promoted. A scientific bent of mind extolling research, analysis, and rationality is urgently needed.

Public backing for the reforms efforts have to be sought before any grand tinkering with the design is made. Without public backing of government initiatives, the chances of success are slim. Many reform efforts in the past failed because there is no institutional home for reformers. Corresponding support from civil society did not back the government efforts. Thus, the public should be involved as a significant stakeholder in the whole reform process. In the past, there had been several national reform efforts, some of which are overlapping at best, and conflicting at worst. Public perception had increasingly become negative.

The GOP should realize that without institutionalization and accountability, haphazard efforts are bound to fail. Many developing countries are trying very hard to improve efficiency, transparency and accountability of their personnel and administrative machinery. What are the causes of government failures? The issue is debated earnestly the world over. There are no "great men" any more. Men who always knew everything or could do everything better. Therefore, the main objective is to urgently train government officials who could help in creating the conditions that assured Pakistan's appropriate response and adaptability mechanism to new and unforeseen changes looming across the horizon. Pakistan must succeed imperative in its modernization of education venture. For the purpose, a strategic plan be formulated in the area of education

It be clearly understood by the GOP that ultimately it is responsible for the provision of quality education in the country. The contribution of the private sector, though

---

[31] *Dawn*, Mar. 27, 2001.

welcome, is not the solution for Pakistan education mess. The GOP should be cognizant of this fact when it plans to turn things around in the government educational intuitions on a high priority basis.

The efficiency and effectiveness of government educational institutions are getting worse not better, with very few exceptions. Every one acknowledges this stark fact. Decline in standards did not happen overnight. Pakistan has failed in providing decent education to its youth. The country's leadership must quickly turn things around. We can only fail at Pakistan's peril. Nevertheless, even now it might not be too late to grapple the monster of bureaucratic inefficiency and ineffectiveness. In fact, it is never too late. The regime must reform the entire education system as it has failed to deliver. Easier said than done! What should be the Musharraf regime's priority? Given scarce resources, what is the most cost-effective method of reform? There are neither quick fixes nor easy answers. Re-engineering government educational institutions must aim at an education system that not only fulfils the demands of today but also is also capable of meeting the requirements of the coming century.

A wide range of recommendations regarding reform of the education system has already been put forward. The implementation of these recommendations is problematic. It involves comprehensive planning and a reasonably gestation period. Main emphasis should be on improving standing mechanisms and finding more effective ways of enforcing these mechanisms.

Ultimately, the GOP is responsible for the provision of quality education in the country. The contribution of the private sector, though welcome, is not the solution for our education mess. The outright privatization of educational institutions is a betrayal of public trust and should be seen as an action on the part of the GOP to ignore fulfilling its fundamental duties. Therefore, outright privatization of higher educational institutions IS out of question. The Musharraf regime accepted its responsibility and is determined to deliver in accordance with public expectations. However, time will tell whether it succeeded or not. It should be held accountable for its own performance in this area.

Pakistan's education sector has been neglected. The facts speak for themselves. Consider the following:

1. Pakistan does not have a single world-class university.
2. Only a few private universities have an acceptable standard of education
3. The total research output from our universities and centers is extremely low and inconsequential by any international measure
4. Generally, the often-repeated promise to reform the curriculum has not been kept. Most of it is obsolete and needs to be immediately discarded.
5. The nation's education system is a weird mixture of several sub-systems exists with no overall direction or national integration. We have a triangle shaped structure with the elite private school system on top. For example, we have the of the "A" and "O"-levels type, elite public schools like Lawrence College, Ghora Gali and Atchison College, Lahore, military-type institutions like the public schools in Hasanabdal, military college, Jhelum, the one in Petaro, Sind, etc. Then we have the regular public school system having English as the medium of

instruction. In addition, we have the larger Urdu-medium public school system. The private education school system is further sub-divided into the bigger and expensive English-medium chains like Beaconhouse and then thousands of smaller, and less expensive, private schools with no meaningful state regulation. Some of them are little more than neighborhood schools imparting low quality education. The point is that the State has failed to regulate and supervise these school systems in the national interest.

6. The total adult literacy ratio is only 46.
7. Primary school enrolment is only 3.72(in millions)
8. Primary school enrolment is only 46(as percentage of all eligible) Middle school enrolment is only 4.35(millions)
9. Middle school enrolment (as percentage of all eligible) is only 46
10. Percentage drop out rate from primary schools is over 50%.
11. Higher education enrolment (as percentage of all eligible) is only 2.6 %
12. Total number of state universities in the country is 26.

Previous measures taken for improving the quality of education include:

1. Increased allocation of resources has been made to bring our education system at par with most developed countries in the region. The education budget has been increased by 106% in 1999-2000 from last year. Similarly, the budget of the state universities has been increased by almost 300% from Rs 166 million to Rs 458 million in the current fiscal year.
2. The private sector is being actively encouraged to come forward to help the GOP in providing much needed educational facilities, especially in the primary and secondary areas.
3. The main thrust is on the improvement of present facilities, to provide universal access to elementary education, and at the same time to fill the gap in adult literacy levels. The GOP put great emphasis on the advancement of elementary education. A new emphasis on non-formal education has been incorporated to raise the adult literacy level in the country. In addition, the NGO sector is being involved as partners in the cause. Relatively, substantial resources have been directed towards the achievement of the aim.
4. Pakistan curriculum is out of date and required major revision to cater to the needs of the 21st century. Academic experts are reformulating the curricula from primary to Ph.D. level so that by 2001 there is a single curriculum compatible with the best in the world.
5. A National Skills Development Program costing Rs 684 million had been launched to impart technical education to youth to meet essential market needs. Under the Program, 200 technical and vocational training centers are being set up in existing government high school facilities. These centers should work in the second shift. The facilities of these schools are under utilized, as they are lying idle in the afternoons. Another emphasis of the Program is on gradually shifting education from general to science subjects.

Education needs more attention of the Government. Pakistan can only become an Asian tiger if we stress augmenting our human resources. This is what was done by the previous "tigers" like Malaysia, Singapore and South Korea. Better-educated and trained workforce is needed to make a quantum leap into the 21st century that our leadership so earnestly desires.

Reforms undertaken by the Musharraf regime include, but not limited to, the following measures:

The GOP has approved Rs 21 billion expenditure for the "total reorganization" of the education system in the next fiscal year.[32] The GoP has approved a new plan, which aims at the following: [33]

1. Education reforms to benefit the masses,
2. Imparting of training and refresher courses for teachers,
3. Increase in salaries,
4. Renovation and standardization of the existing institutions
5. Institutionalize the establishment of colleges and universities in the private sector in order to "check the growth of substandard institutions under less educated people". An Authority shall be established for the purpose which would be empowered to "take action against the existing sub-standard and illegally established colleges and universities in the private sector'
6. Giving over ten federal Centers of Excellence and six federal Area Study Centers situated in various provincial universities, to the provincial governments. These autonomous institutions existing in Quaid-e-Azam University shall also be merged with the university. In addition, the Pakistan literacy Commission was also to be discarded. This action was a part of the rightsizing exercise of the GoP. The military regime is certainly moving in the right direction by taking this action.

REFORM PROPOSALS

The minimum of 5% of GNP is devoted to education sector as suggested by UNESCO.

The federal government should provincialize education. This means that drastic cuts are initiated at the federal level and a greater segment of the federal education ministry be provincialised. This exercise can be phased out over a period of a year or so. A downsizing was an absolute must. End waste through corruption and mismanagement with an iron hand. Anecdotal evidence suggested that billions of rupees could be saved because of strict measures. Bold measures were urgently needed.

Create efficient and effective GOP machinery. Pay state employees well to attract talent. Surplus personnel from the federal and provincial governments are adjusted in the

---

[32] *Pakistan Observer,* June 2, 2001.
[33] Ibid.

new local government setups planned. It is envisioned that most state employees would ultimately belong to the local government.

All state universities to become autonomous in the real sense. The current VCs are upgraded to be chancellors, i.e. the provincial governors be removed from the setup. Every university is provided with a permanent endowment to supplant the annual budget. In addition, the University Grants Commissions is abolished, as it serves no useful purpose.

The most important change, which is long due, is to change the education system from the British-type annual examination to the American-type semester system. The semester system is far more superior and has in-built flexibility something lacking in the annual system. We must not try reinventing the wheel. The American-type semester system has proved a roaring success in many Asian countries like Malaysia and some Arab Muslim countries like Saudi Arabia, Kuwait and Jordan. It must be noted that the class teacher is the best judge on the performance of his students. Let us allow him to do his job faithfully and to the best of his ability.

Immediately stop the bogus practice of private examinations where students memorize a few chapters from third-rate "key books" to get their degrees. It is both astounding and shameful that even MA degrees from a prestigious university like Punjab University can be had by this method. This is fraudulent to say the least. Evening degree programs on semester basis will be flexible enough to allow working students to complete their degrees at their own pace. These private degrees are adding to the already considerable disrepute of Pakistan's state universities and must therefore end at once. The tuition fees need to be increased considerably.

The federal government must introduce a sort-of "Pell grant" system as in the USA where the State guarantees education to all deserving. Basically, the federal government loans student money for his or her higher education based on need only and his parent's annual income. The money is repayable in generous installments only once the student graduates from the institution and gets a full-time regular job. In this way, poor students will be able to afford higher education in the country.

The pay structure of the teachers and professors need to be revised. If we want to become a great nation we must reward our teachers more than what we do now. After all, it is they who will train and educate the new generation, which will make all this happen. More public recognition of teaching is needed to attract talent to the profession.

University structures in Pakistan are in a mess. There is no recognition or appreciation for talent. Research is not supported nor encouraged. The libraries are inadequate and no other facilities like access to Internet and use of computers are provided to all faculty. Consequently, research suffers. Simply put, there is no incentive for a professor to work hard. Some individuals do work hard, attain excellence, and perform wonderfully not because of the universities but despite them. Meaning that there is nothing in our setup that would foster excellence in our teachers. This is a national tragedy. The excuse is lack of resources to reward hard work. We can earn money through a number of ways like starting evening programs and certificate/diploma classes to help generate resources. There is nothing stopping us from earning this money. The fee structure of the entire public-sector education system should be revised upwards.

Remember we have to raise the resources to bring any meaningful improvement in the education field.

The thrust of the State education policy should be to support private education in Pakistan. The rampant commercialization of education in the private sector needs to be checked immediately. There are too many fraudulent education organizations that hoodwink the public by parading their foreign (mainly USA and British) "affiliations". These affiliations are just marketing gimmicks. A powerful federal Higher Education Accreditation Agency is established to scrutinize all private education setups. Only those who meet minimum standards of proper teaching are allowed to continue others is immediately shut down. Assistance is available from international education agencies to help establish such Accreditation councils. We cannot allow this state of affairs to continue and drastic action in this regard is called for. Let education not be considered as a "get-rich quick" business. We owe it to our children.

The secondary and higher secondary education needs to be also drastically restructured. The American-type semester system is introduced at this level also. The Boards of Secondary and Higher Secondary Examinations are disbanded, as they are redundant in the new system. High schools should conduct their own examinations and should certify students themselves. A testing agency at the federal level should conduct tests to measure scholastic ability as an indicator of further education possibilities for our youngsters. College and university education should be meant for only the brightest and the most committed and not necessarily for everyone. The national testing would ensure this. Remaining students can be encouraged to learn professional trades in government polytechniques.

The language controversy must be ended. Let us simply leave it to the local administrations to decide what they want for their children. We should not be upset if some opt for local languages as medium of instruction instead of Urdu or English. If Pushto is used as, a medium of education in parts of NWFP, and Punjabi in parts of Punjab and likewise for Urdu, Sindhi and Baluchi then so much the better. We recommend that referendums be held at the district level to end finally the old controversy. Pakistan must be ready to become a multi-lingual society officially. People have the right to speak their mother tongue and to use it as a medium of instruction. English and Urdu can remain as a lingua franca for the whole nation. The principle of this politics is paramount: Let the people decide through their vote.

Strengthen the regulatory framework to encourage private sector investment in education. Involve local citizen groups in supervising the provision of these services.

The private sector is actively encouraged to come forward to help the GOP in providing much needed educational facilities, especially in the primary and secondary educational sectors.

It is recognized that while, primary and secondary education is a birthright of every Pakistani citizen. College and university education is not. Given the scarcity of resources, the GOP re-defines the role of higher education in the country. College education is a privilege that must be earned by attaining academic excellence at the higher secondary level. Not every one is ready for college. Nor can they be allowed to waste state resources. Therefore, a two-track system is being introduced, or improved if you may, the first is college leading to a bachelor's degree and the other is that of the technical institute leading towards a diploma or certification. Most students should be channeled into the second type of educational institutions.

The GOP cannot subsidize education at this rate. For example, the students in most of Pakistan universities and colleges pay only a fraction of the cost. The state picks up the tab. It is not fair because many students can afford to pay more yet the system does not demand it. Those who can afford to pay more are expected to pay their fair share of college or university education. Fees need to be increased while it must be guaranteed that poor students are not forced out of educational programs based on need alone. Every student, regardless of family income, should get an education, if he or she meets the merit criteria. The state should give a Student Loan to all eligible candidates to complete their degree programs. The loans should be repayable after the student graduates in easy installment spread over a long period.

The focal point or nucleus of the entire education system is the college or university teacher. Without good teachers, other things hardly matter. We have failed to honor the profession like Pakistan forefathers. Teaching is a very noble profession. The GOP should give it more status and recognition than at present. Only the best and the brightest should enter it. The GOP should make the teaching profession more attractive than at present. Teachers deserve to be paid much more for their services than at present. They should be held accountable for their performance also. Likewise, teachers must attain new skills and stress professionalism as a value. This should be in line with Pakistan Islamic heritage.

The highest priority should be in personnel management and training in the education cadre. Both should be revamped. Career advancement system needs to be reviewed. Merit should be the only criteria for advancement. It is too much dependent on length of service. The best teachers should be promoted faster. The criteria of promotion, other than service length, are rigid. Many such arcane rules stifle initiative and resolve of bright young instructors. The GOP should review the whole university promotion system and rationalize it. At present, it is too rigid with the most attention paid on years of service rather than professional competence. This is obviously stifling excellence in academia.

The existing system of recruitment in university/college teaching should be reviewed. Senior faculty should train new entrants in the difficult art of teaching. For example, a teacher is recruited to first serve as a Teaching Assistant with a senior faculty member before being allowed to be promoted to the post of a Lecturer.

State training institutes are also in bad shape and need to be revamped. The finest officers should be posted as faculty members and head of state training institutes.

Teachers that do not perform satisfactorily should be punished. Performance evaluation systems are not up to the mark. ACRs should not be kept secret from assesses. However, third part restrictions should remain in place. Student evaluations of teacher performance should be introduced. After all, who is a better judge than students who interact with their teacher the most in the classroom? In short, teachers should be held accountable for their performance in the classrooms. Therefore, better mechanism of control of teacher performance should be introduced. Sloppy work should not be tolerated in the future.

One of the criteria for promotions in the college teaching cadre should be a third party qualifying examinations.

There should be periodical performance reports on colleges and universities and a system of inspections based on regularly maintained database should be instituted. The federal Ministry of Education should be in charge of the program. The purpose is to foster uniformity of standards throughout the country.

More colleges should be given degree-awarding status like recently given to Government College, Lahore, Forman Christian College, Lahore and Kinnaird College, Lahore.

The BA degree course should be extended to four years from the current two. The BA Honors 3-year course should be initiated immediately, as already given in the GOP's education policy.

More evening diploma and certificate courses should be introduced to make full use of existing facilities. They could supplement the income of the educational institutions. More evening degree courses should be started also. There is a market for people desirous to pursue higher studies in the evenings. These people have full-time jobs and are not available in the daytime. The state universities should tap this student potential.

The concept of distance learning has immense scope in a country like Pakistan. The potential utility of Allama Iqbal Open University should be further extended. More courses for students inside Pakistan should to be provided. The current emphasis IS on providing education to Pakistani students in the Gulf region. A giant education network covering every nook and corner of the country should be established by the AIOU.

More community colleges of the American type should be started where admission requirements are less stringent and program lead to an Associate degree only. The time for completion of degree course requirements should be about half of the regular BA programs (i.e. two years). In addition, the community colleges provided avenues for a different clientele of students as the courses are primarily offered in the evenings and more importantly based on public demands. This is fundamentally the implementation of the continuing education concept. The very nature of the community college is best suited for providing education catering to regional priorities, cultural aspirations, and local needs. Thus, community colleges established in rural areas and in small towns should be better able to cater to the needs of the people in acquiring knowledge in the agriculture sciences. Similarly, community colleges in the big cities should cater to a different class of students with different demands and inclinations. The idea is to market educational packages according to local demand.

Student union activity should be banned. However, political activity of defunct student political groups continues unabated. Politics on campuses has ruined the academic environment and ambience of Pakistan educational institutions. Peace on campus should be guaranteed. Therefore, politics of any sorts is to be completed prohibited. All political parties, including the ruling Muslim League, should immediately dismantle their student wings. An All-Parties Pact is arranged for the purpose. All political parties and groups should guarantee the ban for at least ten years. After the period of the ban, the union activity may be restored, if deemed feasible. Pakistan needs to reinvigorate state institutions and should need some respite, calm and peace for a few years at the minimum.

The state universities and colleges should come up with a new program to increase their revenues by providing more services.

The mushroom growth of private educational institutions should to be checked by the Education Ministry. Teaching is an essential service not to be made into a moneymaking venture. The Islamic tradition had given teaching a coveted place in its hierarchy. Quality education is an Islamic imperative. The GOP is responsible to stop widespread fraudulent activity in the name of higher education. At the same time, genuine educational ventures should be encouraged. An elaborate technical process of national accreditation should be established. For this, the GOP should establish National Accreditation Council for the purpose. Top education experts and other professionals should man this council. The requirements of accreditation should be transparent and the process open to public scrutiny.

Merit should be the only criteria for entry in all types of educational institution. The GOP should gradually abolish all reserved seats after the stipulated constitutional quota protection period is over. The federal admission quota system should be reviewed as it contradicted the merit principle. The merit principle is a basic Islamic value that could not be compromised in any circumstance.

There should be a strong thrust towards science & technology in Pakistan education system. If neighboring India can excel in the area so can we. Everyone agrees that some of India's Institutes of Technology are reputed to be the best in the world. We need to compete with India in the field of education as we compete in the nuclear and military fields. In addition, we must recognize the enemy's successes in the education field and try or best to do something about it.

In order to bring all regions at par with each other in the field of education the GOP should concentrate on improving facilities in educationally deprived regions. Why cannot quality educational institutions be established in these backward areas? The GOP should provide much greater material incentives for students, teachers and administrators in these regions in order to improve educational performance. If quality education is available, the people from these underdeveloped areas should be able to find jobs on merit. Undoubtedly this should take time. Meanwhile, the GOP should push towards educational parity for all parts of the country. In a long-term plan, the backward regions should be given priority in resources.

The military regime should also institute new disciplinary proceedings against those who breach established work procedures, norms and values. Disciplinary action is developmental in nature, while reminding the guilty party on the accountability of his actions; it also acts as a deterrent to others. The detailed disciplinary procedures of the public service are given out in revised regulations for conduct and discipline in the public service, disciplinary board regulations, and proceedings.

The implementing the new teacher training emphasis could mean a sizeable investment, not only in money terms, but also in time and personnel resources. The State should acknowledge that it is an investment, which will yield benefits for all educational institutions. An overall change towards better performance is needed if the public education service is to meet the challenge of continuous improvement in an increasingly fast-changing world. Therefore, a new program for training and development across the public service is launched.

Education to become truly a provincial responsibility. This means that drastic cuts to be initiated at the federal level or alternatively a greater segment of the education ministry be provincialised. This exercise can be phased out over a period of a year or so.

The University Grants Commissions be abolished, as it serves no useful purpose.

All 25 state universities to become autonomous in the real sense. The current VCs are upgraded to be chancellors, i.e. the provincial governors be removed from the setup. Every university is provided with a permanent endowment to supplant the annual budget. The most important change, which is long due, is to change the education system from the British-type annual examination to the American-type semester system. The semester system is far more superior and has in-built flexibility something lacking in the annual system. We must not try reinventing the wheel. The American-type semester system has proved a roaring success in many Asian countries like Malaysia and some Arab Muslim countries like Saudi Arabia, Kuwait and Jordan. It must be noted that the class teacher is the best judge on the performance of his students. Let us allow him to do his job faithfully and to the best of his ability. Also, let us immediately stop the bogus practice of private examinations where students memorize a few chapters from third-rate "key books" to get their degrees. It is both astounding and shameful that even MA degrees from a prestigious university like Punjab University can be had by this method. This is fraudulent to say the least. Evening degree programs on semester basis will be flexible enough to allow working students to complete their degrees at their own pace. These private degrees are adding to the already considerable disrepute of Pakistan's state universities and must therefore end at once. The tuition fees need to be increased considerably. The federal government must introduce a sort-of "Pell grant" system in Pakistan where the government loans a student money for his higher education based on need only and is repayable in generous installments once he graduates from the institution and gets a full-time regular job. In this way, poor students will be able to afford higher education in the country.

The pay structure of the teachers and professors need to be revised. If we want to become a great nation we must reward our teachers more than what we do now. Quality education can only be provided by quality teachers. More public recognition of teaching is needed to attract talent to the profession.

University structures in Pakistan are in a mess. There is no recognition or appreciation for talent. Research is not supported nor encouraged. Simply put, there is no incentive for a professor to work hard. Some individuals work hard attain excellence and perform not because of the universities but despite the universities. This is a national tragedy. The excuse is lack of resources to reward hard work. We can earn money through a number of ways like starting evening programs and certificate/diploma classes to help generate resources. There is nothing stopping us from earning this money.

The thrust of the education policy of the Government should be to support private education in Pakistan. The rampant commercialization of education in the private sector needs to be checked immediately. There are too many fraudulent education organizations that hoodwink the public by parading their foreign (mainly USA and British) "affiliations". These affiliations are just marketing gimmicks most of the time. A powerful federal Higher Education Accreditation Agency is established to scrutinize all private education setups. Only those who meet minimum standards of proper teaching are allowed to continue others is immediately shut down. Assistance is available from international education agencies to help establish such Accreditation councils. We cannot allow this state of affairs to continue and drastic action in this regard is called for. Let education not be considered as a "get-rich quick" business. We owe it to our children.

The secondary and higher secondary education needs to be also drastically restructured. The American-type semester system is introduced at this level also. The Boards of Secondary and Higher Secondary Examinations are disbanded, as they are redundant in the new system. High schools should conduct their own examinations and should certify students themselves. A testing agency at the federal level should conduct tests to measure scholastic ability as an indicator of further education possibilities for our youngsters. College and university education should be meant for only the brightest and the most committed and not necessarily for everyone. The national testing would ensure this. Remaining students can be encouraged to learn professional trades in government polytechniques.

The language controversy must be ended. Let us simply leave it to the local administrations to decide what they want for their children. We should not be upset if some opt for local languages as medium of instruction instead of Urdu or English. If Pushto is used as, a medium of education in parts of NWFP, and Punjabi in parts of Punjab and likewise for Urdu, Sindhi and Baluchi then so much the better. We recommend that referendums be held at the district level to end finally the old controversy. Pakistan must be ready to become a multi-lingual society officially. People have the right to speak their mother tongue and to use it as a medium of instruction. English and Urdu can remain as a lingua franca for the whole nation. The principle of this politics is paramount: Let the people decide through their vote.

Strengthen the regulatory framework to encourage private sector investment in education. Involve local citizen groups in supervising the provision of these services

Effectively involve community organizations in delivery of education services in the localities.

Improve resource use through better management and inspections practices

Strive to create a culture of excellence that will demand a high quality of service, in both the private as well as the state-sector.

Sufficient allocation of resources should be made to bring Pakistan education system at par with most developed countries in the region. The education budget should be at least doubled next fiscal year.

The private sector is actively encouraged to come forward to help the GOP in providing much needed educational facilities, especially in the primary and secondary educational sectors.

Pakistan curriculum is out of date and required major revision to cater to the needs of the 21st century. Academic experts should immediately reformulate the curricula of the educational institutions.

A new institution had been created to foster a grand alliance for promoting the cause of education by bringing together on one platform teachers, administrators, parents and students. The educational alliance should open the doors for advancement of the recommended participatory approach of the new educational policy. The first national conference is held in Islamabad in June next, which should bring together about 500 stakeholders for productive discussions on the subject. The conference is held by the Education ministry with the collaboration of the Chief Executive's Secretariat to give it required importance. A strategy to implement the agreed reform agenda, because of the conference, should be then prepared by the Education Ministry. The consensus document should then be incorporated in its basic policy framework document. The educational alliance will be institutionalized at the provincial level in the next few months. Eventually, it should go down to the district level. This should become a part of the new educational policy.

Promote the participatory approach over every thing else. This shall help create an Islamic paradigm of educational development. It is universally accepted that the participatory approach is embedded in Pakistan Islamic value system. The modern participatory approach is nothing but the operationalization of the values of shura and ijma. In addition, this is widely seen as necessary for integrated sustainable development of quality education, especially at the grassroots level. The GOP should introduce a District Roundtable mechanism to bring together the government, civil society, and local community on a single platform for the purpose of evolving problem-solving strategies, which in Pakistan case is primary education. This is part of a wider exercise to strengthen direct democracy mechanisms in the country. Thus, there shall be 106 District Roundtables in the country.

Composition of Roundtable:

1. Federal Government (represented by the Planning Commission, Local Govt. and Rural Affairs, and Education divisions)
2. Provincial Governments (represented by nominees of the Chief Minister, particular district administrations, and the divisional commissioner)
3. Local Governments of the particular district Local research institutes, think tanks, state entities, NGOs and CBOs of repute.

Adopt the Institute of Development Studies, UK's Participatory Monitoring and Evaluation framework from similar ones employed elsewhere across the world. Thus, the method is essentially a generic one that can be adapted for our use. The steps in the sequence are:

1. Recognize who should and wants to be involved.
2. Explain participants' expectations of the process, and in what manner each group or person wants to contribute.
3. Define the priorities for monitoring and evaluation.
4. Describe the indicators that will provide the information needed

5. Submit plan on the responsibilities, methods, and timing of the collection of information.
6. Information collection.
7. Information analysis.
8. Decide on how the findings are to be employed and by whom.
9. Clarify if the PM & E needs to be sustained, and if so, how
10. Repeat of the cycle after every six months.

The PM & E approach created a communication channel between those in authority and those living as intended beneficiaries. It is recognized that development and conservation programs might be fundamentally challenged. Decision-makers must be prepared to respond accordingly. The purpose is to localize responsibility. Department experts need to increase their interaction with local communities to better understand their needs and priorities. In order to sustain the process we must plan carefully. Starting too big, too soon is a common mistake. Training is necessary and required at all levels.

While, primary and secondary education is a birthright of every Pakistani citizen. College and university education is not. Given the scarcity of resources, the GOP re-defines the role of higher education in the country. College education is a privilege that must be earned by attaining academic excellence at the higher secondary level. Not every one is ready for college. Nor can they be allowed to waste state resources. Therefore, a two-track system is being introduced, or improved if you may, the first is college leading to a bachelor's degree and the other is that of the technical institute leading towards a diploma or certification. Most students should be channeled into the second type of educational institutions.

The GOP cannot subsidize education at this rate. For example, the students in most of Pakistan universities and colleges pay only a fraction of the cost. The state picks up the tab. It is not fair because many students can afford to pay more yet the system does not demand it. Those who can afford to pay more are expected to pay their fair share of college or university education. Fees need to be increased while it must be guaranteed that poor students are not forced out of educational programs based on need alone. Every student, regardless of family income, should get an education, if he or she meets the merit criteria. The state should give a Student Loan to all eligible candidates to complete their degree programs. The loans should be repayable after the student graduates in easy installment spread over a long period.

The highest priority should be in personnel management and training in the education cadre. Both should be revamped. Career advancement system needs to be reviewed. Merit should be the only criteria for advancement. It is too much dependent on length of service. The best teachers should be promoted faster. The criteria of promotion, other than service length, are rigid. Many such arcane rules stifle initiative and resolve of bright young instructors. The GOP should review the whole university promotion system and rationalize it. At present, it is too rigid with the most attention paid on years of service rather than professional competence. This is obviously stifling excellence in academia.

The system of examinations should be reviewed. The annual system of examinations is unfair and too rigid and needs to be discarded. The semester system should be introduced in the universities. If it can work well in prestige institutions like IBA, Karachi, LUMS, Lahore and Quaid-i Azam University, Islamabad then why not elsewhere in the country? The semester system is inherently more flexible and adaptive than the annual system.

The MA "private" system should be discarded. The GOP should not permit the further devaluing of Pakistan degrees by this system. Private study of a few "key books" for a few weeks does fulfill neither the basic condition of student-teacher interaction nor the fulfillment of a regular MA degree. Designating an M.A. degree as "private" and therefore, much easily available is a shameful act. The GOP is itself decreasing standards by adopting such a method. Then why blame others for not valuing Pakistan degrees? For example, thousands of candidates sit for the MA private examination in Political Science each year, simply because it is perceived as the easiest way to get an M.A. Clearly, something is wrong here. The point is that the GOP must make higher education harder, a more meaningful experience, and not the opposite. It is hardly a wonder that Pakistani degrees are not being accepted overseas.

We believe that the Musharraf regime must carry the crusade for education reform. Unfortunately, it seems that the reform agenda is a low State priority. Pakistan can only become a powerful Islamic State when it has a world-class education system. Moreover, a sea change in public attitude towards education is also needed. Let us all join hands and strive with determination to make a real difference in this most vital field. We must act now. Otherwise, the future of this country is not very bright.

THE ISSUE OF CENSORSHIP OF THE INTERNET

The GOP should formulate its Internet censorship policy. Like elsewhere, the governance of the Internet is problematic for it. The pros and cons of cyberspace are being hotly debated the world over. As the use of the Internet has grown concerns about its uses and abuses have surfaced, and questions about whether and how governments might exert control over the "Net" inevitably have followed. Below are contrasting viewpoints and concerns about cyberspace. On the one hand are the Western libertarians who advocate free speech and are disdainful of any state intervention. These people are suspicious of government, disdainful of any censorship. Enthusiasts see the Internet as a sort of Utopia, not because everything on it is admirable, but because it is there at all. The Internet defies centralized authority; its mantra is "do your own thing".[34] Thus, everyone and anyone should be able to access the Internet with ease. This is the "great equalizer" of all times. On the other hand, are concerns about the control of the Internet? Theoretically, anyone could post information, but the reality is that government, corporations and academic institutions controlled the main content of the Internet. The ease with which it is possible to alter information or merely to shade the truth by selectively culling out unfavorable information is a real concern. The question is: who is the custodian of the

---

[34] Kegely and Wittkopf, *World Politics: Trends and Transformation*, 6th ed. (New York: St. Martin's 1997), 252.

world information? Although the Internet is supposedly available to anyone with a modem and the ability to use it, race, gender, income and age skewed the profile of users. Access is unlimited in theory, but the cost of the technology and the steep learning curve of the computer neophytes restrict it. If electronic communication were the future, what will become of the vast majority of people who can only stand by and watch the worldwide exchange of electrons?[35]

How will poor countries like Pakistan control the negative aspects of the Internet? A lot of filth and garbage in the form of pornography, violence and sex in songs are passed on the Internet like on TV and the cinema screen. What is acceptable in the West is not necessarily acceptable in the Islamic world. Islamic values are somewhat different than European. At least, Muslim countries cannot and will not allow the garbage in. These countries have the responsibility to protect their youth from the decadence of the Western culture. It does not mean to suggest that this is a blanket criticism of the West or the Internet. Only a part of it, the rest is admirable and to be copied. Islamic countries need to debate this aspect of the so-called Western cultural "invasion". Although the issue is legitimate, there is needless paranoia about it. The issue needs to discuss it in a dispassionate manner. The problem has a technical dimension. Governments cannot keep the garbage out in the first place even if we want to. Screen filters and censors can be circumvented. Islamic countries need to cooperate at the regional level to solve the problem. The ruling governments owe it to the future generations. The Musharraf regime should envision an Islamic world region as a prosperous and vibrant area but built on its own value-systems not on imported Western ones. Again, this does not seem to suggest that all of Western culture is debased and worthy of rejection. Certainly not. The Muslims need emulate some of its aspects. It is on the issue of Internet's impact on society that we beg to differ from the Western libertarian outlook. Muslims hopes that the West realizes that a very homogeneous (read Westernized) global society is not conducive to the progress neither of humanity nor for global peace. Diversity, in cultural practices, is admirable and therefore should be encouraged. Remember that there is no superior of inferior civilizations. They are just different. Let us develop in our own way in our own style. Let the Internet be censored by responsible governments.

AN AGENDA FOR POLICE REFORMS

The Musharraf regime should concentrate on reforming the police service on a high priority basis. The police service is notorious for its corruption, high-handiness, inefficiency and sheer ineffectiveness. The entire service system needed radical restructuring. During the second Nawaz Government, the following measures were to be undertaken for the purpose.[36]

---

[35] Ibid.
[36] See unpublished paper prepared by the Police Reforms Task Force, Government of Pakistan, 1999.

1. The police service is being transformed from a reactive to a proactive organization. It is also being gradually de-politicized. Today the country has a neutral and highly professional police service.

2. Recruitment, postings, transfers and promotion are on merit only. There will be a proper job description for each rank/post. A strategy for implementation of a new training policy is being formulated. Career development in the service is being linked with in-service training all levels.

3. Police organizations are being given necessary financial and budgetary autonomy. The police services are to be appropriated financial resources according to its enhanced role as an agency dealing with national security.

4. Police performance at the grass- roots level is being improved by the following actions: reorganization of duties on a functional basis, by clearly defining role and responsibilities of all individuals; discouragement of rampant transfer of investigations; improvement of technical capability of officers, fixing tenure of postings, rationalizing emoluments of officials, rationalizing the time scheduling of police officers, performance evaluation and strict discipline.

5. Community policing systems are being established. A pilot project has already been initiated in Abottabad. The Punjab Government is also going to introduce the system in the province.

6. Police services will be gradually decentralized to the divisional level. Eventually, Pakistan will have more than twenty police services. Independent local police services will perform better and be more effective at controlling crime. This viewpoint is based on the following assumptions:

    (a) The police service recruitment, training, promotion – the entire service will be decentralized and under local control. These different police services will be independent of each other and will not interfere in each other's work. Since the police officials are recruited from the local area, stay in it, know it well, therefore, performance will improve.

    (b) For the time being, the new police forces will be under the control of the DMG commissioners. Eventually, they will come under the control of elected officials.

    (c) People will have better access to the top police officials. Better service will increase citizens' support. Civic groups can concentrate more on helping combat crime. The problem of endless postings and transfers will be controllable. Civic groups want to work with the same set of people and do not want to deal with different officers all the time.

    (d) The primary coordinating agency will be a provincial government agency. The best way to control the crime spiral is to localize the police function and involve the public in a meaningful way. A case in point is the Punjab Provincial Police. It is simply too large an entity for effective management. The Punjab Police are in-charge of providing protection, police and security services to the whole of the province. The Punjab is nearly the size of France, Britain and Germany in population. It is like having a single Inspector General responsible for the whole of Britain, France or Germany. Simply put this will be tantamount to creating a unitary police service in a federal setup. This is a recipe for disaster and hence the very poor performances of the Punjab police. Punjab is too big and diverse a province for a unitary type institutional arrangement. It has been recommended that Punjab be divided into number of circles, maybe five, each with its own distinct and very independent police service. Instead of one, we will have five police setups. This will bring efficiency of operations. Shuffling of officers all over the province will be stopped forever. This "transfer business" has really hurt the moral of good officers. In sum, Punjab is too big for any one service to handle easily and in an efficient manner. This logic is applicable for other services also. We have already strongly advocated that there be at least fifteen provinces in Pakistan instead of the current four. Of all the provinces, the Punjab must be first demarcated into smaller units. This requires bold leadership. The GOP must make a move at once. The whole exercise will take several years and the sooner we start the better. Bahawalpur could be made a separate province. At least Bahawalpur must immediacy has a separate police service - a first step on the road of restructuring Pakistan's federation.

7. The training of the police services is being revamped. Better-trained police officers can only come about if we have better qualified recruits. The educational level of recruits in the police forces is being increased. The thanna culture is messed up because of illiterate policemen; among other reasons, National Training Policy is being formulated to overhaul the entire training of the police service.

8. The investigation aspect of police work is being adequately stressed. Since police investigation is a technical specialty requiring specialized training it will be separated from the normal police work.

9. The state prosecution arm is being revamped on a priority basis, as it is currently wholly inadequate. A powerful federal Advocate General office is being created with its counterparts in the provinces.

10. The Police Academy, Sihala will be given the same status as Pakistan Military Academy, Kakul. The same high professional standards will apply. Adequate finances are provided for the purpose.

11. A separate VIP duty section is to be established so that the regular work of the police staff is not disturbed unnecessarily.

12. Increase in the numerical strength of the police cadre.

13. The shift system is introduced with a maximum duration of 12 hours only.

14. Sufficient funds are allocated for modern weapons, transport system and crime detection laboratories.

15. Given the importance of the task of crime prevention, salaries are further increased for the entire police service.

16. Review of the rules, regulations and procedures of the police service. Improvements in the service include: application of merit principle in promotion and transfers; rationalization of time scheduling; community participation to

strengthen the service; revamping of training; provision of better equipment; crime fighting capabilities and inculcation of professional values in the police cadres.

17. The investigation aspect of police work is improved. Investigation is a technical specialty requiring specialized training.

18. Vehicle thefts are made a federal offense that cannot be bailed and with severe punishment since it linked with terrorism, smuggling, drug trafficking and gun running.

19. Police laboratories are obsolete and need to be modernized. Proper training of police officers to conduct criminal investigation is emphasized.

20. A National Vehicle Registration Authority is established. The pilot project establishing the registration agency in NWFP is replicated in other provinces.

21. Witness protection programs are introduced, both for security and as an incentive, to those volunteering evidence against hard-core criminals.

22. Honorary Justices of Peace sitting in collective benches may try all summary cases punishable up to six months imprisonment, not by professional judicial officers who be exclusively tasked to try serious offenses. The system be on the pattern of Lay Magistrates in Britain

23. The total strength of judges and judicial officers is gradually increased to resolve backlog and ensure quick disposal of cases.

24. A system of reward and incentives to grant special increments, quicker promotion, or choice of posting for all competent, hardworking and honest judges/magistrates.

25. The courts encourage out-of-court resolution of cases through mediators with the consent of the parties involved, except in some cases.

26. Uniform laws are applied all over the country, including FATA, PANA, and PATA and Islamabad Capital Territory.

27. The "supardari" system that allows recovered stolen vehicles to be used temporarily by various persons will be ceased. In future, such vehicles will remain parked on police station premises until the time their original owners take possession of them. Thus, damage and abuse of such vehicles shall be prevented.

NEXT STEPS

The Police Reforms Task Force met on August 31, 1999 and approved the following proposals:

(a) Inter-linking of all 1,300 police stations in the country in a computer network to share data and crime records. The network would provide the Interior Ministry officials to monitor and evaluate the performance of all police stations.

(b) Modernization and up grading of existing forensic laboratories. Setting up new facilities at the regional level.

(c) To increase operational efficiency of the police service the normal duty hours of an official shall be only eight hours.

(d) Equipping the police force with the latest tools and equipment.

(e) Revamping of across-the-board police training

(f) Special emphasis on employment of modern investigative techniques in police inquiries

A comprehensive action plan giving precise timetables, expenditures, and responsibilities was being prepared for Cabinet approval.

GOVERNANCE ISSUES OF LARGE CITIES

Big cities are potentially sensitive and their administration is highly inefficient. Urban areas in Pakistan need immediately attention of the Musharraf regime to resolve their myriad nature of problems. Rampant urbanization has put tremendous pressure on the government to deliver services to an increasing population. Social decay, crime, and loss of community feelings have resulted because of the inability of government to properly handle the situations. Shantytowns, around and in some of the big cities, are proof of a lack or proper planning to manage urban development. Problems have piled up and, if let unchecked, will prove explosive, politically speaking. The problems in all the cities differ only in quantum, but nature of the problem is the same. No large city has been able to develop a decent mass transit system; there is lack of discipline and chaos on the roads, etc. The Good Governance Group, GOP held a workshop on the subject in 1998 which came up with some key objectives of a reform strategy that include:[37]

- Users are able to select standards that are affordable and they are willing to pay for.
- Subsidies are eliminated and withdrawn in a stepwise approach.
- Tariffs must include recovery of capital costs, 100% of O&M costs, and full cost to install new system at the end of design life.
- It would be only after the above measures that the water & sanitation services can be provided on sustainable and replaceable basis.

There is a concern that the removal of subsidies would make the water not affordable to the poor. Subsidies are invariably abused whether in the developed world or under developed. The poor and needy shall be supported through independent poverty alleviation programs and social security networks, rather through provision of cheap and subsidized utilities and services.

---

[37] See unpublished report by Good Governance Group, Planning & Development Division, GOP, 1998.

UTILITY SERVICES

Utilities like public manage electricity, gas and telephone sector companies. Ordinarily, there should be no great problems in management of these utilities. However, lack of coordination of these agencies with the local bodies has added to the miseries of the people by digging the roads without proper repairs. Besides, the supply of electricity is far from satisfactory, mainly because of "Kunda Mafia". It has been in the news recently that there are about 100,000 "Kunda Connections" in Karachi and the KESC is obliged to remain silent. No action is being taken to curb this menace. The law-abiding citizens have to pay also for the electricity stolen through "Kunda Connections" and the big industrialists.

The possibility to privatize the distribution system after a public debate may be considered. In the short run, the officer in-charge of the zones is made responsible to control theft of electricity by maintaining the record of supply and consumption of electricity in the zone. The law enforcing agencies to control this menace must provide adequate support to them.

REFORM

How can the GoP conserve the natural environment and reduce pollution levels in Pakistan's human settlements? The town planners have a very important role in this connection, since they are responsible for not only planning of a new areas and improvement of existing slums but for the development control in cities and their rural hinterlands. The main problems identified are the following: -

- Inadequate water & sanitation services particularly for the poor.
- Affordability gap between the increasing cost and users' ability and willingness to pay.
- Lack of sustainability of services and unreliability of supplies.
- Use and adoption of inappropriate technologies.
- Contamination of surface water and ground water, with resulting health threats.
- Lack of standards and appropriate by laws.
- Ineffective monitoring, surveillance and enforcement of standards and by laws.
- Legal, administrative and social constraints.
- Lack of appropriately qualified management/technical/human resources.
- Insufficient involvement of users and the private sector.
- Centralized planning and management.
- Too many existing institutions with no clear-cut or well-defined distribution of responsibilities.
- Resource mobilization is poor
- Inadequate tariffs and pollution penalties.

Conditions of roads are poor. Capacity of roads is unable to take the load of increasing traffic. Road engineering is very poor. There is general congestion on roads. Time of travel is increasing in large cities. Conditions of public transport are poor. Over loading in public transport, is a perpetual problem defying solution? Risky and dangerous driving is on the increase. Ever increasing noise pollution. Lack of proper bus stands/stops. Lack of parking facilities. Lack of accountable administrative set up. Lack of consistent transport policy.

AREAS OF URGENCY

A. Revamping of Waste Disposal and Sanitation Facilities:

Current facilities are inadequate, particularly for the poor areas. Past measures have been mostly ill planned and short-term. In collaboration with multilateral agencies and NGOs, the GOP will formulate a long-term plan for the purpose. Care will be taken to provide affordable and sustainable services. Use and adoption of appropriate technologies will be guaranteed.

The GOP takes immediate action to provide adequate water and sanitation services in all urban areas. Efforts have been made to identify key issues at strategic level rather at tactical or operational level.

B. Augmentation of Water Resources

Pakistan is going to face acute water shortages in the next millennium. It needs to plan. Scarce water resources needed to be better protected. The contamination of surface water and ground water has resulted in threats to public health. In addition, the impact on the environment is catastrophic. Therefore, the GOP will undertake a long-term master plan for the purpose of development and protecting our scarce water resources.

C. Remedial of Institutional Inadequacies

The management of our urban areas lacked from many defects, such as: lack of integrated management; lack of standards and appropriate by laws; ineffective monitoring, surveillance and enforcement of standards; legal, administrative and social constraints; lack of appropriately qualified management/technical/human resources; insufficient involvement of users and the private sector; centralized planning and management; duplication of institutional work; and no clear-cut or well-defined distribution of responsibilities.

The problem of Pakistan's urban areas cannot be resolved without bringing in drastic changes in the present set up. The people should be allowed, supported and helped to participate in decision-making at the local-level.

D. Environment Protection Strategy

Environmental pollution is usually categorized into the following four types: air, water, solid waste, and noise pollution. The following are the main causes of the aforementioned types of pollution: -

(i) High Population Density
Concentration of a large number of people in a small area. For example, in the Walled City of Lahore, more than 100,000 persons lived in an acre of land. In planned settlements, the town planners will control the density of population through density zoning techniques, etc.

(ii) Traffic Congestion
The presence of a large traffic volume on narrow roads and streets. With population, the traffic volume has also increased in urban areas. For example, in Lahore, the number of registered motor vehicles has increased more than 8 times during the last 15 years, while the population doubled and length of roads increased by 30 percent only.

(iii) Dangerous Living Quarters
Development of industrial and commercial uses near living areas that may be hazardous to human health. For example, industries and workshops are commonly found in the slum areas of Lahore. Similarly, tanneries are located in the middle of residential areas of Kasur City, which are causing an increased incidence of cancer in the city.

(iv) Inadequate Waste Collection, Treatment and Disposal Sites
Current facilities of collection, treatment and disposal of solid, liquid and gaseous wastes are inadequate. For example, in Lahore, untreated industrial wastes and raw sewage are disposed off into river Ravi. The smoke and gases are also emitted out of industries without any treatment. Similarly, there is no proper system of domestic solid waste collection and disposal. More than 50 percent of solid waste does not reach the dumping grounds. Some of the solid waste is burnt openly and adds poisonous gases to the air. Tire burning during agitation is also an example of this practice.

The GOP should take immediate steps to conserve the natural environment and reduce pollution levels in our human settlements. The town planners have a very important role in this connection, since they are responsible for not only planning of a new areas and improvement of existing slums but for the development control in cities and their rural hinterlands. The following reform measures are to be executed to ensure sustainable development of urban areas:

Decentralization of Central Business District Functions: To remove congestion and concentration of traffic in the Central Business Districts (CBDs) of large urban areas, the future growth of cities should be planned according to Multiple Nuclei theory of land use zoning. It means that new local district centers should be established to reduce burden on the main city center. This will reduce movements (i.e. number of vehicular trips) to the existing CBDs and curtail the trip lengths considerably resulting in reduction in the fuel consumption, travel costs and travel fatigue. Local development authorities or municipalities can develop the new local district centers by purchasing land on market price. The additional money generated from this profitable venture can be used to finance the development of trunk infrastructure and open spaced.

Separation of Civic and Administrative Uses from Commercial Area: The new CBDs be planned in such a manner that adequate buffer zones in the form of parks and open spaces, are created between commercial/shopping areas and the civic and administrative uses. This will reduce concentration of traffic in the CBD areas resulting in reduced level of noise and air pollution.

Proper Zoning of City Lands: Haphazard and unplanned commercialization of urban areas should cease. Proper zoning and demarcation of land use for various purposes. Residential and commercial use of land should be clearly demarcated by city governments. Proper zoning of land should demarcate different uses, i.e. residential, industrial and commercial areas. All residential areas are separated from the other two. The industrial areas may be located with a suitable buffer of green areas between them and the other two. In addition, the change over of once designated residential areas to commercial use is stopped. In addition, violation of building regulations is strictly checked.

Provision of Open Spaces and Parks: In all new residential colonies and industrial areas at least 20 percent of the total area be reserved for open spaces and parks so that the air remains clean and healthy. For existing congested areas, small open spaces are procured by purchasing old, dangerous buildings and converting them into small open spaces through NGOs and CBOs (community based organizations).

Provision of Mass Transit System: In large metropolitan areas such as Lahore, Islamabad, Karachi, Peshawar, Hyderabad etc., mass transit system such as light rail, local bus etc. should be provided in a planned manner. The existing schemes for Lahore and Karachi are to be upgraded for the purpose and to serve as pilots.

Development of Housing for the Poorest of the Poor: The housing of the poorest of the poor have been neglected. The GOP should carry out the following measure:

- Regularization and improvement of Katchi Abadis and slums through self-help and public participation, as in Orangi Pilot Project model.
- Town planners in all cities are to be appointed for proper strategic planning and development.
- Micro credit schemes are initiated for home improvement and incremental housing construction. Provincial and local governments to streamline the scheme.

- More public-private partnership is formed for urban development. The model in Lahore is duplicated in all other provincial capitals, and Islamabad. The entities should have their own Board of Directors.

- The system of Urban Development Authorities like LDA, CDA needs to be reviewed. Unnecessary duplication of efforts at this level is curtailed. Jurisdiction issues remain unsettled and control is not demarcated. Functions of different agencies are not spelled out clearly.

- To help control the rapid urbanization phenomenon and to cater for future needs the GOP should undertake long-term planning of small towns in every region of the country.

- Efficient functioning of cities is primarily dependent upon appropriate local government structures. The mess created in all big cities is the result of an absence of elected local bodies over a long period.

- Local governments are made more independent and effective. These institutions are encouraged to become financially autonomous by generating their own revenues.

- A transport authority is established in every large city to properly administer an efficient public transport system. Wherever possible, a modern mass transit system is introduced. The use of cars in congested downtown areas is actively discouraged. The role of private transport sector should be clearly defined and regulated. Some improvement in this direction has been initiated in Lahore.

- Strict zoning of city lands is undertaken. Residential and commercial should be clearly demarcated. Stiff punishments for illegal use of residential areas for commercial purpose are meted out under new laws for the purpose. The notorious "Qabza" groups, land grabbers, must be eliminated finally.

- The mess created in all big cities is the result of non-functioning of elected local bodies. Therefore, Constitutional guarantees to be provided for continuous function of the local bodies.

The problem of water and sanitation cannot be resolved independently without bringing drastic and revolutionary changes in the present set up and the rethinking of the federal and provincial government roles and responsibilities. The private sector can be involved in the provision of services. The primary role of the city government is to restrict its activity to strategic planning and management. It can act as a facilitator rather than direct service provider. However, ultimate responsibility of city public services is to be shouldered by the elected city administration.

According to the Local Government Plan 2000, functions of state having direct impact on people shall be delegated to local government institutions. Functions like policing, administration, taxation, basic health and education, social services, water and sanitation, and other utility services such as power supply etc. shall be delegated to the local government institutions. The new local government institutions shall be truly representative and shall established in small manageable units having specific geographic boundaries. The people shall be allowed, supported and helped to make there own decisions at local level in a way most suited to their environment and local conditions. Clear overall responsibility to manage the cities is vested with city governments. A single unit of government is responsible for the whole city. All agencies providing various services to the city are brought under the direct control of the Nazim, elected by the city people. The nazim being the chief executive is clearly in-charge and responsible for the management of the city. He or she is accountable to the people. The concept of local self-government in true letter and spirit shall be the long-term objective. Full autonomy shall be given to municipal councils. Thus fully independent local government institutions without external influence to be able to increase revenues by levying taxes and having independent budgeting. In addition, there shall be established an efficient monitoring and evaluation system and management information system.

A citywide municipality shall be divided into self-contained - independent local municipalities or zones having independent taxation and budgeting and other revenue generation. City municipality shall be responsible for maintenance of trunk infrastructure and shall operate that on commercial basis - no profit no loss. The local municipalities shall be responsible for provision, operation and maintenance of local level infrastructure. They shall purchase the services from the city municipalities paying the true cost based on the quantity they consume. The local municipalities shall be able to select the standard of services and billing and rate fixing etc. The same can be in the long term applied to other utilities such as bulk purchase of power from WAPDA and Gas etc.

Focus on development of new small towns a plan construction of future cities as the population of urban areas is increasing very rapidly. Coordination between various city organizations may be institutionalized.

Currently, city management is weak and needs to be revamped. There is no clear demarcation of functions at the level of city government. This needs to be streamlined immediately. A multiple of agencies are providing services without proper coordination or even accountability. Proper demarcation of functions must be realized. The control of the cities is not vested in the hands of political representatives but only the bureaucracy.

Refuse collection services need to be revamped. Provision of refuse depots and bins and location of dumping grounds and incinerators should be properly planned in all cities. The local NGOs/CBOs will be involved in proper refuse collection and creation of awareness among people. The recycling and disposal of refuse be done in collaboration with the private sector companies, CBOs and NGOs. For example, a pilot partnership program is initiated between the CDA and the private sector outfit "Garbage Busters" in Islamabad. The model may be replicated elsewhere.

The problem with urban development authorities needs to be solved. Urban development authorities (LDA, CDA) need to be reviewed. Unnecessary duplication of efforts at this level should be curtailed. Jurisdiction issues remain unsettled and control is clearly not demarcated. Functions of different agencies are not spelled out clearly. An urban development cell is organized in the Planning Ministry for future planning. In addition, formulation shall be immediate. A review of Development Authorities is undertaken with the objective of solving jurisdictional issues.

PUBLIC PRIVATE CITIZENS' PARTNERSHIP

The Musharraf regime believes in creating a vibrant civil society, which it sees as an essential pre-condition for the country's progress. It was aware of the fact that NGOs had played a vital role in the provision of social services and eradication of poverty in various parts of the world and in various communities within Pakistan. Therefore, the new regime must encourage NGOs and provided financial support to them, especially those working to provide social services and in alleviation of poverty. It was fully committed to strengthen rural and urban grassroots level organizations that were pursuing community development initiatives. In order to improve and strengthen government's delivery of essential services a grand partnership with a number of NGOs and community-based organizations (CBOs) was taking place. Similarly, under the Literacy Commission, a number of NGOs be supported to reach the large segment of the population. In addition, these public organizations be involved in meeting immediate concerns of the population including hygiene, family size, health, sanitation and water supply.

The Musharraf regime should acknowledge the vital role of NGOs in the development process, especially in provision of essential social services in remote rural areas. The regime must establish a sound and transparent enabling regulatory framework for them. It was encouraging a process of debate, consultation and dialogue between itself and the NGOs for developing the required policy framework. The NGOs be allowed to work independently provided their work does not fall beyond the requirements of the law and public interest. The regime should not try to control the NGO/CBO activity. It would however monitor the use of funds to ensure proper use in the public interest.

A vibrant civil society was an essential pre-condition for the country's progress. The Musharraf regime should recognize that the NGOs play a vital role in the provision of social services and eradication of poverty in various regions of Pakistan. There are over 10,000 NGOs in the country and the regime should tap into their considerable expertise and resource base for the country's sustainable development. It therefore encourages them by providing financial support. A number of NGOs and CBOs would be greatly facilitated through initiatives like the Participatory Development Program and the Pakistan Poverty Alleviation Fund (PPAF). Under the Social Action Program II, the GOP was developing public-private partnerships and had selected several NGOs as partners in its Participatory Development Program. The program would fund several NGOs and CBOs for development of education and health services in the rural areas. Similarly, a number of NGOs be supported to reach the larger segment of the population. In collaboration with some NGOs, several school management committees had been constituted for the administration of public schools.

The PPAF was a major initiative to reduce poverty and create economic opportunity. It would cater to the development of micro enterprises by facilitating easy credit to the poor through the establishment of outreach networks. Several NGOs be involved in meeting immediate concerns of the population including hygiene, family size, health, sanitation and water supply. Some NGOs had done excellent work in the area and needed to be supported more. The vital role of NGOs in the development process was acknowledged. The new regime was committed to strengthen rural and urban grassroots level organizations that were pursuing community development initiatives. In order to improve and strengthen delivery of essential services it was seeking partnerships with a number of NGOs and CBOs.

The Musharraf regime should aim at establishing a sound and transparent enabling regulatory framework for NGOs and CBOs. It should embark upon a process of debate, consultation and dialogue between itself and NGOs for the development of a policy framework for their proper functioning. In the area of conservation, the Musharraf regime should enter a broad-based alliance with reputable international NGOs like IUCN- the World Conservation Union and WWF. The purpose of exercise was to chalk out a viable plan of action to protect the environment and promote conservation efforts. Similarly, in the area of sustainable development the regime must work with AKRSP, Sungi, NRSP, Orangi Pilot project, etc. The new regime must create Divisional Roundtables for Conservation and Development, as explained above. It would also seek collaboration in specific programs. For example, the Sindh Katchi Abadi Authority (an entity set up by the Government in 1987) could collaborate with UNDP, a district administration in Sind, and the Planning Commission, to work out collaboration for the purpose of development of a particular division. The purpose was to link the concerned officials of the entire government system - federal, provincial, district and local governments – with both international agencies like UNDP, WWF, IUCN, etc. and local NGO network. A similar initiative could be started in Peshawar division, NWFP where IUCN, Govt. of NWFP, UNDP, who were already working together for conservation and development.

NEXT STEPS

1. Create a vibrant civil society, as an essential pre-condition for the country's progress. For the purpose, encourages NGOs, especially those working to provide vital social services to the needy.
2. Strengthen rural and urban grassroots level organizations that were pursuing community development initiatives. In order to improve and strengthen delivery of essential services, a partnership with reputable NGOs and community-based organizations was executed.
   Who Would Do It?
   There was a need for establishing a sound and transparent regulatory and enabling framework for NGOs. The required NGOs legislation would cater to that need.
3. Encourage a voluntary adoption of a Code of Conduct for all NGOs respecting Islamic values.
4. Institutionalize a mechanism for a debate, consultation and dialogue between the NGOs and the regime. For the purpose, a policy framework in close consultation and collaboration with the NGOs was to be prepared.

5. A comprehensive national policy for NGOs was developed. NGOs should be held accountable for their activities. Registration process of NGOs would be simplified. There should be a simplification in the reporting format of NGOs that were small. Autonomy and independence of NGOs be preserved. In sum, the Musharraf regime must encourage NGOs to become partners in the development efforts.

6. An elaborate regional Roundtable mechanism in which NGOs play a very meaningful role.

THE SUSTAINABLE USE AND CONSERVATION OF RENEWABLE RESOURCES: A CASE STUDY OF PAKISTAN

Today, Pakistan faces an environmental degradation crisis of staggering proportions. All available evidence indicates that the overall situation of Pakistan's environmental challenges is very serious. Thus, the problem of environmental degradation in the country is getting worse not better. In addition, there is ample evidence to suggest that Pakistan has failed to stem the tide of environmental degradation in any significant manner. Despite the rhetoric, the GOP has miserably failed to ensure adequate protection and sustainable use of the county's natural resources. A recent official report says that resulting from increasing impoverishment and absence of any alternatives an increasing number of poor and landless persons are putting "unprecedented pressure" on the country's natural resource base because of their survival struggle. In the next few decades, the most pressing challenge shall come from environmental degradation, poverty, and lack of agriculture planning. Besides it will induce health hazards due to lack of access to sanitation facilities and clean water, indoors pollution from biomass stoves, severe soil degradation, and deforestation.[38] Among others, the World Bank notes that poor natural resource management and population growth have has a negative impact on the country's water, land, and agricultural resource base. Pollution and environmental degradation are having an affect on public health and agricultural productivity and other economic sectors. This is holding back economic growth. More or less, all surface water is being contaminated by pollution from agricultural runoff, domestic and industrial waste. Overgrazing, water logging, wind and water erosion, and salinization, have degraded almost 42% of the land in the country. Air pollution levels are escalating and are already above World Health Organization standards in Karachi and Lahore.[39] Some of Pakistan's natural resources like water for irrigation purposes and forests are facing increasing pressure. What needs to be done? Improvement of water courses, field water application as well as drainage are essential for making optimum use of the available water and preventing a decline in the productivity of the Indus Basin due to water-logging and soil salinity. The proportion of irrigated land in Pakistan affected by

---

[38] *The Nation, June 19, 2000.*
[39] Country Brief: Pakistan. Html, (World Bank Group Home web page, News, Publications, Topics in Development- Countries and Regions, IBRD | IDA | IFC | MIGA).

salinization is a high 35%, as compared to 15% in China and 15-20% in Australia. In Pakistan, irrigation is employed on 80% of all cropland and 40,000 hectares of this land are lost to water logging and salinity every year.[40] Another report says Pakistan faces a serious problem of salinity and water logging and that about 20-35% of the irrigated land is affected.[41] The wastage of irrigation water is about 20-30% mainly due to traditional methods of irrigation, undulated fields, application losses, and inequitable distribution.[42]

Overall, the forest sector is in bad shape. Pakistan faces a crisis because of a rapidly eroding stock of renewable resources. At the current rate of depletion, its forests are likely to last for another two to three decades. All available evidence indicates that the overall situation of Pakistan's environmental challenges is very serious. The problems of the environmental degradation are getting worse not better. Forests cover about 3 million hectares, which is only 4% of the country, according to one source.[43] The IUCN and USA sources indicate that area under forests is 4.57 million hectares which is 5% of the total land area of Pakistan and most of it is located in the north of the country.[44] Pakistan faces one of the highest rates of deforestation in the world, according to the GOP's Economic Survey 1999-2000.[45] No one doubts that forests are being rapidly denuded all over Pakistan for various reasons, including but not limited to, increased poverty and rapid population growth. The annual rate of deforestation is 0.4% in 1989-90, which contributed directly to the severe flooding in the early 1990s.[46] The PNCS document says that 7,000-9,000 hectares of land fall to deforestation each year, and the annual rate is 0.2%.[47] Primary factors that influence deforestation in South Asia, according to Middleton, are: Agricultural expansion, population pressure, fuel wood and fodder cultivation, and corruption.[48]

A recent World Bank review of environmental matters in Pakistan notes that poor administration of natural resources and rampant population growth have had a negative impact on the country's water, and agricultural land resources. Pollution and environmental degradation affect public health and agricultural productivity besides other economic sectors. This retards the GDP growth rate. Nearly all the surface water in Pakistan has been contaminated by agricultural runoff, pollution from domestic and industrial waste. Waterlogging, overgrazing, water and wind erosion, and salinization, have degraded about 42% of the land in the country. In Lahore and Karachi, the level of

---

[40] See Middleton, *The Global Casino- An Intro to Environmental Issues*, op. cit., 51.

[41] Derek Tribe, *Feeding and Greening the World: The Role of International Agriculture Research*, (Oxon, UK: Cab International, 1994), 67.

[42] Ibid.

[43] Anita M. Weiss, "The Society and its Environment", *Pakistan: A Country Study*, 6th ed., (Washington, D.C.: Federal Research Division, Library of Congress, 1995), 181.

[44] See The Pakistan National Conservation Strategy (Karachi: Environment and Urban Affairs Division, GOP and IUCN, n.d, 32-33, Also, the CIA's *The World Book, 1999-Pakistan* states that the total forest and wooded area is 5% only. See Fact <http: *CIA The World Book, Home Page, Pakistan.html*>.

[45] See *Economic Survey 1999-2000*, (Economic Affairs Wing, Ministry of Finance, Government of Pakistan), reported in *Dawn*, June 2000.

[46] Anita M. Weiss, "*The Society and its Environment*", op. cit., 89.

[47] See *Pakistan National Conservation Strategy*, op. cit., 32.

[48] Nick Middleton, *The Global Casino - An Introduction to Environment Issues*, (New York & London: Edward Arnold, 1995), 30.

air pollution is escalating and is already higher than World Health Organization standards.[49] In the face of daunting problems, there have been only a few notable environmental initiatives. The efforts of a few organizations like Agha Khan Rural Support Program (AKRSP), The World Conservation Union (IUCN), World Wide Fund for Nature (WWF), and the Government of Pakistan (GOP) have achieved some success in the field. The GOP had taken several steps to arrest further environmental degradation through a National Conservation Strategy (NCS) adopted in 1992, followed by an Action Plan for 1993-98. Later, provincial strategies were also prepared. The IUCN played a leading role in the formulation of not only the NCS but also the Sarhad Provincial Conservation Strategy (SPCS). In addition, the Chitral and Northern Areas Conservation strategies are also being prepared by its assistance. Though very ambitious, these strategies have received world acclaim and are considered as pioneers and role models in the developing world. A central feature of IUCN operational style is the considerable emphasis on undertaking the participatory and consultative approach to decision-making. Though tedious these approaches have been incorporated in all IUCN programming. The participatory mechanisms are also institutionalized by the AKRSP in the Northern Areas. This effort has also attracted worldwide attention for its high success rates. There are other success stories also. The point is that in an overall dismal scenario there is still hope. There is definitely a glimmer of light in an otherwise clouded sky. Environmental degradation has become a major challenge to Pakistan. According to a very recent report, the situation in Pakistan has become alarming. The report says:[50]

Pakistan's accelerated demographic growth and prolonged stay of Afghan refugees has led to acute pressure on local natural resources and is also likely to suffer disproportionately from climate changes and other global problems, like the green house effect, affecting patterns of agriculture, fisheries and forestry… As a result of increasing impoverishment and absence of alternatives, a swelling number of poor and landless people are putting unprecedented pressure on the natural resources base, as they struggle to survive…the most pressing environmental challenge in Pakistan in the next few decades will come from the lack of agricultural planning, environmental degradation and poverty. Besides, it will include health hazards due to lack of access to clean water and sanitation, indoors air pollution from bio-mass stoves, deforestation and severe soil degradation.

There is ample evidence to suggest that Pakistan is failing in its battle to protect its environment. The most serious issue in renewable resources management is Pakistan's rampant population growth. Today, Pakistan's total population is about 150 million, which ranks it as the seventh most populated country in the world. The population growth rate is a high 2.4% and it is estimated that by the year 2050 the population will have climbed to 300 million.[51] The stark reality is that unless the rate of its population growth is brought under control, Pakistan will not be able to provide for the basic needs of its teeming millions. Moreover, the scarcity of food and water might cause a crisis of public

---

[49]< *http://www.Country Brief: Pakistan/World Bank Group/ News/ Publications/ Topics in Development-Countries and Regions/ IBRD | IDA | IFC | MIGA. Html.*>.
[50] *The Nation*, June 19, 2000.

security making the country difficult to govern. This is already happening in the neighboring country of Afghanistan, where because of an unprecedented drought situation there is a serious scarcity of food and water that has led to the displacement of hundreds and thousands of Afghanis, many to Pakistan and some to Iran. In turn, these refugees have already creating an enormous financial burden on Pakistan because of which the GOP is not accepting any more Afghan refugees. Meanwhile, the provision of food inside Afghanistan itself has become a nightmare because of the on-going conflict between the ruling Taliban and the Northern Alliance. Today, Afghanistan is one of the most isolated and poorest countries of the world with rudimentary government to provide for the grief-stricken people of the country.

Pakistan faces a formidable challenge in tackling the twin problems of poverty and degraded environment. There is some recognition in the UN and other international agencies that much more needs to be done for countries like Pakistan. Elaborating on the concept of global goods, James Gustave Speth, Administrator, United Nations Development Program (UNDP) says:[52]

Sustainable human development cannot be achieved if we do not prevent conflicts, manage markets wisely or reverse the depletion of soils, energy, fresh water and clean air. Equity within and between generations is not feasible without an international system for identifying and apportioning environmental costs, for dealing with the destabilizing effects of weak financial architecture or for helping people everywhere to benefit from the accumulated stock of global knowledge. The responsibility for and the origins and effects of such challenges transcend national borders.

Given its present state of weakness, sustainable human development seems to be a pipe dream for Pakistan in the near future

Pakistan's forests are declining at a very fast rate. Forests cover about 3 million hectares, which is only 4% of the country, according to Weiss (1995).[53] However, the Pakistan National Conservation Strategy and US Federal Government documents state that forest cover is 4.57 million hectares which is 5% of the total land area of Pakistan and most of it is located in the northern part of the country.[54] Pakistan faces one of the highest rates of deforestation in the world, according to the GOP's Economic Survey 1999-2000.[55] Deforestation crisis continues deepens. An independent German research indicates that at the current level of extraction, the NWFP, where much of Pakistan's forest endowment is located, will loose most of its forest cover by 2025.[56]

Undoubtedly, forests are being rapidly denuded all over Pakistan for various reasons, including but not limited to, increased poverty and rapid population growth. The annual

---

[51] *The Nation*, July 13, 2000.

[52] See <http://www. UNDP/Forward/ Global Public Goods/. Html.>.

[53] Anita M. Weiss. (1995). *The Society and its Environment", Pakistan: A Country Study*, 6th ed. Washington, DC: Federal Research Division, Library of Congress, 181.

[54] See The Pakistan National Conservation Strategy (Karachi: Environment and Urban Affairs Division, GOP and IUCN, n.d, 32-33, also, the *<http://CIA/The World Book, 1999/Pakistan.htm>* states that the total forest and wooded area is 5% only. See *Fact Book Home Page, Pakistan.htm.*

[55] See *Economic Survey 1999-2000*, (Economic Affairs Wing, Ministry of Finance, Government of Pakistan), reported in *Dawn*, June 2000.

[56] See Editorial "Vanishing Forests", *Dawn*, Mar. 29, 2001.

rate of deforestation was 0.4% in 1989-90, which contributed directly to the severe flooding in the early 1990s.[57] The Pakistan National Conservation Strategy document says that 7,000-9,000 hectares of land fall to deforestation each year, and the annual rate is 0.2%.[58] Primary factors that influence deforestation in South Asia, according to Middleton (1995) are: Agricultural expansion, population pressure, fuel wood and fodder cultivation, and corruption.[59]

Pakistan suffers from a poor planning. There are no long-term measures for water conservation and efficient use of water through advanced irrigation systems. The GoP has taken no effective long-term measures to tackle the waterlogging and salinization menace afflicting the country. The proportion of irrigated land in Pakistan affected by salinization is a high 35%, as compared to 15% in China and 15-20% in Australia. In Pakistan, irrigation is employed on 80% of all cropland and 40,000 hectares of this land are lost to water logging and salinity every year.[60] Another report says due salinity and water logging about 20-35% of the irrigated land is affected.[61]The wastage of irrigation water is about 20-30% mainly due to traditional methods of irrigation, undulated fields, application losses, and inequitable distribution.[62]. Another report says Pakistan faces a serious problem of salinity and water logging and that about 20-35% of the irrigated land is affected.[63] The wastage of irrigation water is about 20-30% mainly due to traditional methods of irrigation, undulated fields, application losses, and inequitable distribution.[64] According to Federal Planning Commission sources, massive efforts to control the water logging and salinity have been undertaken since the 1960s. By 1999, about 60 drainage projects are completed at a cost of Rs 37 billion, yet six million acres of cultivated land is seriously water logged (i.e. the water table is less than five feet from the surface). Since 1978, the waterlogged areas have increased by 1.6 million acres despite the salinity control and reclamation projects (SCARPs).[65] According to the Ghulam Rasool, Director, Agriculture Research Department for Saline Areas, waterlogging and salinity have rendered about 15 million acres barren.[66]

Among others, the World Bank has noted that poor natural resource management and population growth has a negative impact on the country's water, land, and agricultural resource base. Pollution and environmental degradation are having an affect on public health and agricultural productivity and other economic sectors. This is holding back economic growth. More or less, all surface water is being contaminated by pollution from agricultural runoff, domestic and industrial waist. Overgrazing, water logging, wind and

---

[57]Anita M. Weiss, "*The Society and its Environment*", op. cit., 89.

[58] See *Pakistan National Conservation Strategy*, op. cit., 32.

[59] Nick Middleton. (1995). *The Global Casino - An Introduction to Environment Issues*. New York & London: Edward Arnold, 30.

[60] See Middleton, *The Global Casino- An Intro to Environmental Issues*, op. cit., 51.

[61] Derek Tribe, *Feeding and Greening the World: The Role of International Agriculture Research*, (Oxon, UK: Cab International, 1994), 67.

[62] Ibid.

[63] Derek Tribe, *Feeding and Greening the World: The Role of International Agriculture Research*, (Oxon, UK: Cab International, 1994), 67.

[64] Ibid.

[65] *The News International*, April 4, 2001.

[66] *Pakistan Observer*, Jan. 22, 2001.

water erosion, and salinization, have degraded almost 42% of the land in the country. Air pollution levels are escalating and are already above World Health Organization standards in Karachi and Lahore.

In addition, inadequate management of the deforestation crisis has deepened the crisis. An independent German research indicates that at the current level of extraction, the NWFP, where much of Pakistan's forest endowment is located, will loose most of its forest cover by 2025.[67] In the next few decades, the most pressing challenge shall come from environmental degradation, poverty, and lack of agriculture planning. Besides it will induce health hazards due to lack of access to sanitation facilities and clean water, indoors pollution from biomass stoves, severe soil degradation, and deforestation.[68] Among others, the World Bank notes that poor natural resource management and population growth have has a negative impact on the country's water, land, and agricultural resource base. Pollution and environmental degradation are having an affect on public health and agricultural productivity and other economic sectors. This is holding back economic growth. More or less, all surface water is being contaminated by pollution from agricultural runoff, domestic and industrial waist. Overgrazing, water logging, wind and water erosion, and salinization, have degraded almost 42% of the land in the country. Air pollution levels are escalating and are already above World Health Organization standards in Karachi and Lahore.

What needs to be done? Improvement of water courses, field water application as well as drainage are essential for making optimum use of the available water and preventing a decline in the productivity of the Indus Basin due to water-logging and soil salinity. The GOP must end the poor water management practices. Absence of an equitable water allocation or distribution formula by Indus River System Authority between provinces and within provinces. Essentially, this is a political task. In addition, the GOP should conserve Pakistan's natural resources. Inadequate protection and unsustainable use of the county's natural resources is seriously going to hurt the future generations of Pakistanis.

The creation of water users associations has already been successfully tried under various donor-assisted projects and the Pakistan Drainage Project is seeking to up-scale the approach to cover both irrigation as well as drainage. The Musharraf regime's devolution plan will greatly increase the impetus of this work by making it the concern of the district government. Maybe, privatization is less relevant to drainage and irrigation, which must be carried out on a scale beyond that of the individual land holding. However, it is possible that a system relying largely on direction from local landowners will work better than one involving "stake holders" with diverse interests. Again, we need to do more research to find out what best works for Pakistan. Local farmers should be able to organize themselves under the control of the local governments for creating efficient and effective irrigation and drainage projects. The impetus of creating such public organizations should remain with the local governments as the farming sector is very poorly organized yet. The very idea of forming a public water use association is new

---

[67] See Editorial "Vanishing Forests", *Dawn*, Mar. 29, 2001.
[68] *The Nation, June 19, 2000.*

in Pakistan. It will take some time to for the farmers of the country to acquire the required skills to mange their own affairs in regard to the optimum use of a scarce resource like water. Illiteracy in Pakistan's rural areas is extremely high now. With patient leadership and consistent efforts of the local governments, such self-help projects can be built for the farming community. The exact structural arrangements have to be worked out with the help of international agencies like the World Bank, which have some experience in the field. Now, only the principle of shared responsibilities between the local government and the farmers associations needs to be stressed. Remember, this is new to the farmers of Pakistan which have relied on the State to provide them with all their requirements, while their own role was limited to just putting in demands to the State for help. Most importantly, the State so far was not the local government but the provincial government sitting in far away provincial capitals comfortably away from the scene. Thus, great effort is needed to try out new methods of administering community affairs. Experimentation of organizational structures is therefore a requirement for our farmers and the new local governments.

To sustain natural resources, a country must have at least 20% of its area covered by forests. This figure, unfortunately, in case of Pakistan is extremely low at 4% only. The forest cover is further declining due to factors such as the timber mafia, lack of infrastructure, planning and implementation. [69] The GOP claims to attach significance to conservation and sustainable development of natural resources in the country. An action plan for implementing the National Conservation Strategy (NCS) is being prepared. The NCS had recommended several program areas for priority implementation. Nine of these Program areas relied on community organizations for their implementation. The NCS envisaged the GOP to provide a policy guideline, contribute monetary resources, and an enabling environment. Local governments and NGOs played an important role in community organization. The NCS states that the most significant role for local government was to develop a "working relationship" with community organizations.[70] It suggests that district development plans should consult these organizations so that their concerns are included in the plans. The NCS envisages the establishment of a two-tier structure at the district-level:[71]

The District Program Office: They will perform management and program planning functions, and provide village organizations with initial monetary assistance. Primary responsibilities include:

1. Coordination with federal and provincial line Departments, local government and NGOs
2. Monitoring and evaluation.
3. Project formulation.

---

[69] *Dawn*, July 5, 2001, 17.

[70] *The Pakistan National Conservation Strategy*, (Karachi: Environment & Urban Affairs Division, Government of Pakistan and IUCN - The World Conservation Union, n.d), 343.

[71] *The Pakistan National Conservation Strategy*, (Karachi: Environment & Urban Affairs Division, Government of Pakistan and IUCN - The World Conservation Union, n.d), 344.

4. Research training and development
5. Coordination and supervision of implementation of projects in the field

Technical Support Units (TSU). The most important function of the TSU is to assist in the formation of effective local government organizations as the main vehicle of development activity. Responsibilities shall include:[72]

*   Performing budget estimates and land use surveys.
*   Conducting surveys of physical infrastructures.
*   Information collection on the use and status of natural resources.

The NCS also suggested that the local governments, as per requirements, fund community organizations. The district councils will monitor the allocation of funds.[73] The implementation of NCS will remain problematic because of shortage of skills needed in five critical categories. The GOP realizes that it alone cannot carry out the huge task. Therefore, for the purpose of implementing the NCS, it seeks collaboration with international conservation agencies like IUCN, WWF; donor agencies like UNDP, UNIDO; and domestic NGOs like Sungi Development Foundation, Sustainable Development Policy Institute, etc. Obviously, the primary responsibility for the preparation of the action plan is with the GOP. It plans to take measures to curb the wasteful exploitation and consumption of natural resources. Much work needs to be done and done quickly. If the GOP wishes to promote the sustainable development of the country's natural resources then, among other things, its new decentralization plan needs to be effectively implemented.

Effective decentralization is synonymous with effectiveness, openness, transparency, accountability, and predictability. Therefore, immediate measures should be taken to institutionalize these values at the local government level. Given the comparative success of the consensus-building and participatory approach introduced in the field by IUCN, and the overall success rate of active community participation in realizing given goals in attaining environment policy goals, the introduction of a formalized mechanism is absolutely critical for further development. The whole idea is to institutionalize the partnership approach at the local level. This is also a part of the "bottom-up" strategy. Comparative research indicates that natural resources are best conserved when a participatory approach is adopted, which includes: [74]

1. The government and local communities join hands in developing the policy.
2. The local community is allowed to participate in the decision-making.
3. The local community has certain acknowledged rights to the natural resources under consideration.

---

[72] Ibid.
[73] Ibid.
[74] Mitchell Beazley. (1993). *Caring for the Earth: A Strategy for Survival.* Reed International Books in association with IUCN, UNEF, and WWF, 61.

The World Development Report 1994 notes that "consumer voice" mobilized through groups can become significant forces in reform and reorganization. These groups can impart feedback and monitoring to curtail abuses and hold government officers accountable to the public.[75] The IUCN has also noted that while there is raising pressures on forest resources and fiscal limitations on forest agencies, simultaneously another development has taken place. The quest for democratization and decentralization has emphasized the increasing demand by communities to get involved in the management of the forests themselves.[76] The report states:[77]

In the past, many forest-protected areas were established without sufficiently taking into account the needs of the nearby communities, or indeed their intricate knowledge of the forest ecosystems their livelihoods depend on. IUCN is working in a number of these areas to restore the balance between conservation imperatives and local needs. This is essential if forest protected areas are not to become symbols of oppression, to be torched during political upheavals or left without operating funds after the next election.... The Ban Khamteuy project helped convince the government to formally recognize customary forest use rights of indigenous communities in Lao PDR for the first time. The methodology developed by PROBONA for assessing external pressures on local forest use has been adopted by FAO. In Uganda, the natural resource management agreements concluded between the parishes around the Mount Elgon National Park and the Uganda Wildlife Authority are serving as a model for other protected areas.... In 1996, a multidisciplinary group of experts formed the international Working Group on Community Involvement in Forest Management (WG-CIFM) to draw and apply lessons from field experience with CIFM and to persuade governments and donor agencies to become more responsive to community conservation efforts. The Working Group brings together a wide range of stakeholders, including government and non-government community forest practitioners, policy makers, donors, NGOs, activists, and representatives from international organizations. IUCN facilitates the Working Group, as community involvement is key to its forest conservation program - advancing many of the objectives of the program. Why is CIFM the Third Way to Conserve Forests? Some conservation advocates believe there are only two ways to conserve forests. Setting aside forest in protected areas where use is forbidden or heavily circumscribed trying to ensure that market mechanisms and prices reflect environmental values.

More research needs to be undertaken to ascertain the possibility of copying the PROBONA methodology on forest management or the Uganda model for preserving protected areas in Pakistan. Most probably, IUCN has even better participatory models in its collective knowledge-house for our specific use. Experts have to further ponder on these issues. Meanwhile we can continue to explore the world for practical insights.

---

[75] *World Development Report 1994, 71.*
[76] *<http:// CIFM/seeking connections/coalitions for change/policy and practice/ profiles] [partners / main page/ contact.html>.*
[77] Ibid.

Another lesson for better renewable resource management can be learnt from the highly successful Joint Forest Management in Bengal, India. The story is: [78]

> Thanks to an unusual coalition of village communities and Forest Department officials. In this case, uncommonly progressive bureaucrats saw the traditional protection measures were not working and began negotiating with the villagers. The unusually motivated villagers formed their own Forest Protection Committees to help them negotiate…The foresters' union became concerned for the safety of its workers, and decided that cooperation with local people was the only realistic way of resolving the problem. The association began promoting dialogue between the frontline workers and the villagers through annual workshops and seminars in each region, and lobbied successive forest ministers for a more collaborative style of forest management. Finally, all three major stakeholders groups – villagers, government, and the frontline workers – signed onto the idea of Joint Forest Management. The moral of the story: the broader the coalition, the more likely its success in bringing about decisive change.

Pakistan too has its share of success stories. Perhaps, the best example of such collective action is that of AKRSP in the Northern Areas. Primarily, the success of the AKRSP stems from the respect that it commands in the area having made sustained efforts in introducing participatory management philosophy and innovative techniques in the field. The manner in which the AKRSP was able to harness the energy of countless village organizations for the purposes of sustainable development of natural resources is indeed impressive. Other organizations and the GOP itself must study the methodology and techniques introduced by AKRSP. Stringent efforts are made to replicate the model all over the country, if possible. The AKRSP model may be copied for attaining best results in the field. Privatization is less relevant, perhaps, to drainage and irrigation, which must be carried out on a scale beyond that of the individual land holding. However, it is possible that a system relying largely on direction from local landowners (as is the case with land drainage in the U.K.) will work better than one involving "stake holders" with diverse interests. More research needs to be undertaken on a suitable model for managing Pakistan's forest resources. Some consideration needs to be given to the possibility of diminishing the role of government in the administration of resources as an adjunct or alternative to decentralization of government management.

The IUCN has pioneered the Roundtable mechanism in the country. From the federal to the provincial level in not only NWFP but also Baluchistan, it has already gone further down to the level of the districts. Thus, IUCN is a trailblazer in this regard. The effort should now be to bring the mechanism to other localities, albeit in a more organized manner. The main purpose is to strengthen community participation efforts that will lead to strengthening of GOP efforts to manage sustainable use of natural resources. In addition, the Roundtable is to be institutionalized as a participatory dialogue process and not a stand-alone activity, i.e. it is by definition never complete or finalized. Even if a plan were finalized as such, it would be subject to further review, modification, evaluation, monitoring, feedback, and improvement. Technically speaking, a dialogue participatory process mechanism lasts forever. It is never ever completely finished for it

---

[78] "Forest under Fire", *World Conservation, (IUCN)*, 3-4/99, 22.

always continues. This is its main strength. The idea is to build as wide a coalition for positive change as possible and this takes time and sustained effort. In addition, the needs of different stakeholders are never constant and they perceptions of there need change with time. Hence, a Roundtable process makes sense and needs to be implemented.

Given the reality in Pakistan, another consideration is in order, which is specific to the country's situation. The key to the success of the participatory mechanism is the role of the department head who is the facilitator and coordinator of the whole effort. Research indicates that concerned state officials are not enthusiastic, with a very few exceptions, to the Roundtable concept. Therefore, participation should not only be mandatory but also rewarded by giving incentives to these officials for the purpose.

Through the Roundtable, we wish to institutionalize a mechanism for a true tri-partite partnership, which will bring together the Local Government, NGOs and CBOs, and international agencies. For this purpose the NGO sector must also be better mobilized to achieve maximum gain. The work of several good NGOs in the field needs to be studied further to find best practices and lessons to be learned. A detailed treatment of the subject is beyond the scope of this paper. Let it suffice that the NGO sector must also be streamlined and modernized along known principles of management applicable to the area. We have to first identify success stories in the field for the purpose. A few common sense principles can be easily derived for further applicability and duplication in other locations. More field research is needed here. A few common sense basics must be followed:

- The program should be able to mobilize households to form community organizations.
- Link the Voluntary Organizations (VOs) and Community Based Organizations (CBOs) with governmental services.
- Conduct a survey to identify priority community needs.
- Assist VOs/CBOs to acquire essential skills for use in their own development efforts.

BASIC INGREDIENTS OF AN EFFECTIVE ROUNDTABLE MECHANISM

The Environment Department before commencing the process shall work out a detailed strategy. Consultations should be all comprehensive, involving the full range of stakeholders. The timing of these consultations is very critical. They should not be held so early that no useful information is available, nor so late that all participants can do is reacting to proposals already under serious consideration. Ensure that local participation is not just tokenism, but should acknowledge involvement of community leaders as vital to the success of the department's goals. A permanent record is kept in the department, which is accessible to the public. An annual report is submitted by the head of the department to the district Nazim, the indirectly elected chief executive of the district, for further action and modifications, if needed.

Previously, the Pakistan Environment Protection Act, 1997 had established a Pakistan Environment Protection Council (PEPC) to be headed by the Chief executive and an Environment Protection Agency is to act as the executive arm. The Musharraf regime claims to attach the utmost significance to conservation and sustainable development. It is expected to promote actions to conserve the environment, reduce pollution, and the wasteful exploitation and consumption of resources and energy. The regime is also expected to assure that sustainable development takes place in Pakistan. The Musharraf regime intends to implement the National Conservation Strategy (NCS) as a high priority. Very recently, Omar Asghar Khan, federal minister for environment, rural development and local government said that the military government was "making strenuous efforts to fight out environmental threats. One has his own limitations and has to work keeping in view the available resources. However, progress in this regard during last year has been encouraging. We will appreciate to work collectively with community, NGOs and other stakeholders".[79] The same day minister also announced that the GOP shall start levying pollution charges on industries from coming July and that it will soon launch the National Environment Plan shortly.[80]

Obviously, translating policy into reality is not going to be easy. A beginning must be made, however. Notwithstanding GOP claims, little progress has been made in this direction. The implementation of NCS will remain problematic because of shortage of skills needed in critical categories. The new regime must realize that itself cannot carry out the task. Therefore, for implementing the NCS, it should collaborate with international conservation agencies like IUCN, WWF; donor agencies like UNDP, UNIDO; and domestic NGOs of repute. The primary responsibility for the preparation of the action plan will be with the GOP itself, however. It must plan to strengthen the capacity of civil society partners to find appropriate solutions to the nation's problems in the area. Little progress has been made in the field, however. In the area of conservation, the Musharraf regime should enter a broad-based alliance with reputable international agencies like UNDP, IUCN- the World Conservation Union and WWF. The purpose of the exercise would be to formulate a viable plan of action to protect the environment and promote conservation efforts. Similarly, in the area of sustainable development the regime must work with successful domestic agencies like the AKRSP, Sungi, NRSP, Orangi Pilot project, etc. The regime should also create regional Roundtables for Conservation and Development. It should seek collaboration in specific programs. For example, the Sindh Katchi Abadi Authority (an entity set up by the Government in 1987) can collaborate with UNDP, a district administration in Sind, and the Planning Commission, to work out collaboration for the purpose of development of a particular division. The purpose is to link the concerned officials of the entire government system - federal, provincial, district and local governments – with both international agencies like UNDP, WWF, IUCN, etc. and local NGO network..

The GOP must make a consideration of best practices in the area of conservation of natural resources. Lessons applicable to the local situation keeping in mind the concrete

---

[79] *Pakistan Observer*, May 15, 2001, 4.
[80] Ibid.

reality of low budgets and low capacity. In the past, many of the rural development projects failed because they were too complex for the public agencies to manage. The AKRSP's experience shows "that multi-component projects can be made to work, with synergy among their components, provided the institutional structure is appropriate."[81] AKRSP's "flexibility and grass-roots emphasis greatly contributed to the program's success."[82] The AKRSP has been able to introduce better farming inputs and better farming techniques, improved farmers organizations that led to a sizeable increase in general prosperity of the targeted population in the Northern Areas, a very remote and poor region in the northern tip of Pakistan. This development is widely acknowledged and praised. The participation by NGOs must become an integral part of the rural development. "Institution building through ownership can be used as a starting point for development. By involving the beneficiaries in every stage of their development, a foundation and relationship can be built for the future".[83] Discuss alternatives and possibilities of action.

Development of resources on an equitable and sustainable basis. This includes:

- Working out a mechanism to grant a fair share of the natural resource to the local people.
- Enforcement of rules and regulations pertaining to exploitation of the resources.
- Discussion of performance monitoring mechanisms for the sustainable use of the local resources.
- Discussion of the monitoring and evaluation mechanisms to be undertaken by the Department.
- Formulation of performance indicators for the Department.
- The possibility of developing partnerships with outside businesses, and development agencies, etc.

Like so many other developing countries, Pakistan today needs help of the international donor community. In fact, if the economy does not show significant improvement, overall poverty is projected to further increase in the current decade. More poverty shall translate into more pressures on the natural resources of the country.

The Musharraf regime needs to immediately create a robust public, civil society, and a new private citizens' partnership. The creation of a vibrant civil society is an essential pre-condition for the country's progress in the conservation area. The NGOs have played a vital role in the provision of social services and eradication of poverty in various parts of the world and in various communities within Pakistan. There are over 10,000 NGOs in the country. The regime should desire to tap into their considerable expertise and resource base for the country's conservation agenda. It should encourage them by providing financial support. To its credit, the Musharraf regime is aware of the need.

---

[81] Précis Number: 111, Operations Evaluation Department, 05/01/96, Agha Khan Rural Support Program: *Looking to the Future*, 1.

[82] Ibid.

[83] Ibid.

Omar Asghar Khan, federal minister has recently said that no institutional reform policy, no matter how good it looks on paper, can be implemented without the active participation of the people. It can be hoped that the military regime will take the necessary steps to achieve this partnership. Even before the establishment of the local governments, the regime has instructed local officials to get input from the newly elected local government officials.

NEXT STEPS

- Institutionalize periodic Roundtables mechanism in the district wherein the district government plays the key role of facilitator.
- Make efforts to invite representatives from all sections of the society, especially minorities and the disadvantaged.
- Information about activities in the field is disseminated through the press, public notices, etc.
- Set and agree on priorities through maximum public participation.
- Agree on monitoring and control mechanisms for field projects.
- Discuss project outputs and results in a free and frank manner.

The actual work of the Roundtable will be obviously grounded in the concrete reality of the district itself. Where the mechanism is very unfamiliar, much more effort needs to be undertaken to make the exercise fruitful. Most importantly, Pakistan can learn from others but must be able to fix its own problems in its own ways by applying corrective measures only as appropriate for the country. In addition, waiting for the new local governments to be grounded will take some time. The new local governments shall become functional on August 14, 2001, which is the independence day of Pakistan. The actual working shall obviously take more time. Meanwhile, the people can only wait for that to happen. The GOP, to its credit, has begun to institutionalize the Roundtable mechanism in the forestry sector in NWFP. We wish that every district should initiate the program. Any further delay would prove costly. Pakistan cannot afford to waste any more time. In sum, work at several levels is needed to make the Roundtable a success. Each individual partner must become better organized to make a real difference. However, the most important role in the Roundtable process is that of the local government. Without the GOP, taking the lead all else shall fail. We hope that within a year we shall have effective government machinery in place at the district level. Pakistan's conservation efforts depend upon the successful development of the local government system in Pakistan.

Meanwhile, a new forest policy is being formulated by the federal government. It highlights the need to conserve and develop the natural resources such as forests and biodiversity of Pakistan. The goals of the policy are:[84]

---

[84] Ibid.

1. Reduce political interferences in forestry and other environment departments.
2. Renovate and invigorate the institutions responsible for managing renewable natural resources and preparing and implementing policies.
3. To help evolve a consensus on key issues by holding a meaningful debate among all groups concerned and to agree on a shared vision and framework pertaining to forest policy.

CONCLUSION

Pakistan, after nearly fifty-four years of existence stands at historical crossroads. It continues to face a multi-dimensional governance crisis of immense proportions. The regime faces a serious governance challenge that cannot be easily overcome. The country's challenges and were being debated earnestly in the local media. In an age of scarcity, good governance has become the issue of today. Good governance is the major challenge of the Musharraf regime. In the race for reinventing government to make the most of the current opportunities, the GOP had been left behind. The Musharraf regime was desperately trying to turn things around, however. It was pursuing a cautious approach in tackling the complex issues. Reform is not easy. To achieve efficiency, effectiveness and fairness in public organizations fundamental change is required. In addition, these changes must be undertaken in such a manner that ensures the development process remains unhampered by lapses and shortcomings in present administration structures. Given the failure of all past governments, a very great majority of Pakistanis was still supportive of the military government. This speaks about their disappointments with the past political era and not about any great faith in the military itself. Nevertheless, the people of Pakistan are willing to give the military another chance. Pakistan has grave systematic failures and structural faults in its political and economic systems. These faults remained prevalent for too long. Therefore, the system has seriously malfunctioned as a result. The political and economic situation in the country can only be described as serious, if not dismal. The military government's reform agenda is an earnest attempt to pull the country back from the precipice. Attainment of the goals set forth in this agenda require serious and sustained hard work by all Pakistanis, with full commitment to building up social and economic strength, in an environment of peace and order. The Musharraf regime is trying to tackle the crisis in Pakistan's economy in a disciplined and systematic manner. However, tangible results are limited yet. Given Pakistan's fundamental crisis, the future seems to be bleak indeed. Unless and until the regime is able to augment Pakistan's resources and capacity in a formidable manner to turn the country around quickly, the country is destined to remain in a perpetual crisis of very serious dimensions. The Musharraf regime faces a serious challenge in reconstructing Pakistan's fragile political system. By the time it took power last year, the political system was seriously malfunctioning. Obviously, all the past rulers were responsible for the system's failure. That is certain. Undoubtedly the governance style of both Nawaz Sharif and Benazir Bhutto had wrecked havoc with the country's political system. The state had failed to deliver essential public services. Mediocrity, sycophancy, mismanagement had broken down the administrative machinery of the state. There was lack of direction that had resulted in complete confusion in the ranks of the governments. Incompetence, sheer callousness, and reckless attitude of the rulers had reduced the whole exercise of collective responsibility to a farce. Bickering over petty matters was the rule of the day. Both Nawaz Sharif and Benazir Bhutto had turned into egomaniacs and lived in a world of self-delusion. The scene at the highest level became comic, if not tragic. Cronies were awash with praise at their slightest "achievement". More and more state efforts were being made under their names. We had the Prime Ministers run a relentless election campaign from day one. It seemed absurd and uncalled for. It was not surprising that the coup was welcome news for the weary Pakistanis. Fortunately for the country, the times have changed. Today there is a more sincere and competent leadership at the helm of affairs in Pakistan. For its part, the military regime is desperately trying to turn around the country. In reality, not has been achieved so far. Given the regime's makeup, reforming the political, economic, and bureaucratic systems is a daunting task indeed. Although loosing popularity, the Musharraf regime faces no sizeable resistance yet.

Pakistan continues to be faced with a complex multi-dimensional governance crisis of staggering proportions. Undoubtedly, the Pakistani State is malfunctioning. Many would point out that poor governance is the primary reason of the failure. Pakistan still faces bad governance at every level. Pakistan was faced with a complex governance crisis. The country had stomached several periods of instability, corruption, and bad governance that lasted for more than a decade. According to popular perception, the state had failed to deliver and the poor people were suffering. During the period of the last civilian rule, national institutions had deteriorated in abysmal state of ineffectiveness and disrepute. The state failed to provide public security. Politics had turned extremely corrupt. Mafia had captured local power structures. The economic system had become unjust. There was intense poverty in Pakistan. The economy was in a recession. Unemployment was at an all-time high. The public was obviously very frustrated.

The Musharraf regime faced a number of daunting challenges, namely: economic crisis; increasing poverty and low human development; and failure of the development paradigm Although Pakistan is under military rule, the military leadership is still squeaking clean and committed. Pakistanis hope General Musharraf and his colleagues understand this vital fact of our age. Pakistan cannot fail in this venture. Previously, Pakistan seemed to be muddling through in its politics. Pakistan is a country where dramatic change is highly unlikely. Today the country faces a multidimensional crisis the most important of which was that of governance. Another failure was at successful nation building. The magnitude of the crisis was realized by most ardent observers of the country. Pakistan has not come up to the expectations of its own citizens and friends outside. More than a half century ago, it seemed that Pakistan was born to become a great, just, tolerant and prosperous Muslim country.

The Musharraf regime had promised to focus on rebuilding the economy, strengthening the federation, uplifting the masses, improving governance, and laying the foundations of true democracy. However, no timetable was given for the accomplishment of the task. It was commonly expected that the Army would rule the country for several years. How the Musharraf regime dealt with these challenges would determine Pakistan's future. The military regime's task of solving them was indeed very daunting. There were no easy answers to Pakistan's problems. However, proper planning, determination, and a single-minded resolve of the nation could see the country through the present crisis. A new era had begun in the country's life. Circumstances had put tremendous responsibility on the shoulders of the military regime. The nation hoped and prayed for its success. Given Pakistan's fragility it could not tolerate more rules of bad governance. The country would surely collapse if it happened again. Therefore, the Musharraf regime should not fail to deliver. A cautious note of hope is in order. Meantime, things were finally moving in the right direction. A cautious approach was being pursued by the regime. Maters were being handled cautiously. Having realized that there is no magic bullet or quick fix to Pakistan's governance problem, the Musharraf regime had decided to tackle the issue in a serious and systematic manner. Years of neglect are not easily ended. The central plank of good governance efforts is the reform of the public service system. However, public service reforms are notoriously difficult to undertake. The Musharraf regime had promised to focus on rebuilding the economy, the federation and building true democracy by primarily is focusing on governance issues. The Musharraf regime had promised to improve efficiency, transparency and accountability of their personnel and agencies. These issues were being debated earnestly in Pakistan. How the Musharraf regime deals with these governance challenges will determine Pakistan's future. In all fairness, the task of solving Pakistan's complex problems is indeed very daunting. There are no easy answers to Pakistan's problems. However, proper planning, determination, and a single-minded resolve of the nation could see the country through the present crisis.

The Musharraf regime faces a very serious challenge. The political and economic situation in the country can only be described as serious, if not dismal. Thee military government's reform agenda is an earnest attempt to pull the country back from the precipice. Attainment of the goals set forth in this agenda require serious and sustained hard work by all Pakistanis, with full commitment to building up social and economic strength, in an environment of peace and order. Given Pakistan's fundamental crisis, the future seems to be bleak indeed. Unless and until the regime is able to augment Pakistan's resources and capacity in a formidable manner and turn around the country quickly, we are destined to remain in a perpetual crisis of very serious dimensions. Therefore, the people of Pakistan hope and pray that the regime is able to turn things around soon enough. We have to chart our own destiny. In short, a new governance model has to be invented. Who shall undertake the vital task? We hope that Pakistan's rulers and intelligentsia shall rise to the challenge. Remember there are no great saviors or "a great general on horseback" any more. Men who always knew everything or could do everything better. Given the complexity of the age, a single leader cannot lead the nation to triumph. No single person can even understand the complexity, let alone have a solution for it. For modern societies, the concentration of power in one person or an uncontrolled elite is extremely dangerous. Since wrong decisions are more probable. Therefore, democracy is the best form of government. In the end, it needs to be emphasized that we do not have to reinvent the wheel. What is tried and tested must be implemented in all earnest. In addition, we have to be patient and work with determination as the district governments to be sufficiently grounded and working effectively will take a few years. Implementing the agenda is not going to be easy. In all fairness, the military regime faces a stupendous task well beyond its limited capacity and means.

The overall performance of the military regime in the first eighteen months of rule has been less than spectacular. The Musharraf regime is focused more on the revival of Pakistan's economy. The country's future depends on success in this area. The Musharraf regime realized that the most crucial aspect of the implementation strategy is that it shows an unwavering commitment to implementing the reform in full. The above facts support the conclusion that Pakistan's political economy remains in a crisis with no easy recovery in sight. However, the Musharraf regime certainly seems to be serious in its attempt to revive the ailing economy. Will it succeed? The success of the reform agenda depends upon many factors other than purely economic, including but not limited to, the political situation inside and outside Pakistan. Only time will tell whether the Musharraf regime is able to defeat the circumstance odds placed against it for achieving any meaningful victory. . The Musharraf regime should focus more on the revival of Pakistan's economy. The country's future depends on success in this area. Circumstances had put tremendous responsibility on the shoulders of the military regime. The nation hoped and prayed for its success. The Musharraf regime should realize that the most crucial aspect of the implementation strategy is that it shows an unwavering commitment to implementing the reform in full Given Pakistan's fragility, it cannot tolerate more bad governance. The country will surely collapse if it happens again. Therefore, the Musharraf regime was expected to deliver. Pakistan's future depends on this premise. Given Pakistan's fundamental crisis, the future seems to be bleak indeed. Unless and until the regime is able to augment Pakistan's resources and capacity in a formidable manner and turn around the country quickly, we are destined to remain in a perpetual crisis of very serious dimensions. Therefore, the people of Pakistan hope and pray that the Musharraf regime is able to turn things around soon enough. Given Pakistan's fundamental crisis, the future seems to be bleak indeed. Unless and until the regime is able to augment Pakistan's resources and capacity in a formidable manner and turn around the country quickly, we are destined to remain in a perpetual crisis of very serious dimensions.

LIST OF ACRONYMS AND ABBREVIATIONS

ADP	Asian Development Bank
AGP	Auditor General Pakistan
AGPR	Accountant General Pakistan Revenue
AKRSP	Agha Khan Rural Support Program
ANP	Awami National Party
CBO	Community-based organization
CSS	Central Superior Services
EU	European Union
FAO	Food and Agriculture Organization
FATA	Federally Administered Tribal Areas
FANA	Federally Administered Northern Areas
FGL	Federal Government Link
FIA	Federal Investigation Agency
FIR	First Information Report
GDP	Gross domestic product
GNP	Gross national product
GOP	Government of Pakistan
G-3	Good Governance Group
GST	General Sales Tax
IMF	International Monetary Fund
IUCN	The World Conservation Union
KESC	Karachi Electric Supply Corporation
MQM	Muttahida Qaumi Mahaz (formerly Muhajir Qaumi Mahaz)
MNA	Member of the National Assembly
NAB	National Accountability Bureau
NAFTA	North American Free Trade Area
NAP	National Awami Party
NCS	National Conservation Strategy
NFC	National Finance Commission
NRB	National Reconstruction Bureau
NRSP	National Rural Support Program

NWFP	Northwest Frontier Province (Sarhad)
OGDC	Oil and Gas Development Company
PAEC	Pakistan Atomic Energy Commission
PCA	Police Complaint Authority
PIA	Pakistan International Airlines
PIDC	Pakistan Industrial Development Corporation
PMDC	Pakistan Mineral Development Corporation
PML	Pakistan Muslim league
PPP	Pakistan Peoples Party
PPSC	Provincial Public Safety Commission
PSC	Provincial Safety Commission
PSDP	Public Sector Development Program
PTCL	Pakistan Telecommunication Company Limited
SDPI	Sustainable Development Policy Institute
SNGPL	Sui Northern Gas Pipeline Limited
SPCS	Sarhad Provincial Conservation Strategy
UK	United Kingdom
UNDP	United Nations Development Program
UNIDO	United Nations Industrial Development Organization
USAID	United States Agency for Internal Development
VO	village organization
WAPDA	Water and Power Development Authority
WWF	World Wide Fund for Nature (formerly World Wildlife Fund)

GLOSSARY OF ISLAMIC TERMS

Allah	Arabic for God
Amir	Chief, commander
Caliph	the Prophet Muhammad's successor ruler
Din	complete code of life
Fiqh	Islamic jurisprudence
Hadith	Oral or written account of the sayings or deeds of Prophet Muhammad
Ijma	consensus
Ijtihad	intellectual innovation according to individual capacity
Jihad	struggle in the name of Islam
Khalifah	Caliph
Khalifah-i-Rashidun	The Rightly Guided Caliphs, the first four caliphs of Islam (Abu Bakr, Umar, Usman and Ali who ruled from 630-62 AD)
Majlis	a consultative meeting
Madrassahs	religious schools
Shariah	Islamic law
Shura	consultation
Sunnah	practice of the Prophet Muhammad
Sultan	king
Ulema	plural of Aalim, Muslim religious scholars
Ummah	nation
Zakat	obligatory charity at the rate of 2-½%

REFERENCES

Agha Khan Rural Support Program (1996) *Précis Number 111, Looking to the Future* (AKRSP: Operations Evaluation Department)

Beazley, Mitchell (1993) *Caring for the Earth: A Strategy for Survival,* (Reed International Books in association with IUCN, UNEF, and WWF)

Bouckaert, Geert (1993) "Governance between Legitimacy & Efficiency Citizen Participation in the Belgium Fire Services". *Modern Governance New Government Society Interactions,* ed. by Jan Kooiman (London: Sage)

Central Intelligence Agency (1999) *The World Fact Book Pakistan* (Washington, DC)

Covert, Richard (1991) *In the Era of Human Capital· The Emergence of Talent, Intelligence and Knowledge as the World Economic Force and What it Means to Managers and Investors* (New York: Harper Collins)

Derbyshire & Derbyshire (1987) *The Business of Government* (Edinburgh: Chambers)

Government of Pakistan (various years) *Economic Surveys* (Finance Division, Economic Affairs Wing).

Government of Pakistan (2000) *Local Government Plan 2000* (Chief Executive Secretariat, National Reconstruction Bureau)

Government of Pakistan and UNDP (1998) *"The Effectiveness of Aid to Pakistan"* (Islamabad· Economic Affairs Division)

Government of Pakistan (n.d.) *The Pakistan National Conservation Strategy* (Karachi: Environment and Urban Affairs Division, GOP and IUCN)

Government of Pakistan (1999) *Strategy for Improving Governance* (Planning Commission; Planning and Development Division)

Government of Pakistan (1999) *D-8 Conference Report on Good Governance and Institutional Reforms.* February 20-21, 1991, Islamabad (Good Governance Group, Planning and Development Division)

Government of NWFP, Pakistan and IUCN (2000) *Sarhad Provincial Conservation Strategy* (Peshawar: IUCN)

Government of Pakistan and UNDP (1990) *The Effectiveness of Aid to Pakistan*

Gress, Franz. *The American Federal System*

Grindle, Marilee (1997) "The Good Government Imperative: Human Resources, Organization, and Institutions", *Getting Good Government: Capacity building in the public sector of developing countries*, ed., Marilee Grindle (Harvard Institute of International Development/Harvard University Press)

Hussein, Zahid Hussein (2000) "A Nation of Tax Resisters" *Newsweek*, July 17

Kaelin, Walter Kaelin (1998) *Legal Aspects of Decentralization in Pakistan* (UNDP Pakistan/Swiss Development Cooperation Pakistan office)

Kegely and Wittkopf (1997) *World Politics: Trends and Transformation*, 6th ed. (New York: St. Martin's)

Khan, Rashid Ahmad and Sohail Mahmood (2000) *Analysis of National Reconstruction Bureau's Plan for Decentralization and Devolution of Power and Responsibility* (Lahore: Punjab University, Department of Political Science)

Khan, Shahrukh Rafi. Ed. (1999) *Fifty Years of Pakistan Economy: Traditional Topics and Contemporary Concerns* (Karachi: Oxford University Press)

Kooiman, Jan (1993) *Modern Governance: New Government-Society Interactions* (London: Sage)

Mahmood, Sohail (1995) *Islamic Fundamentalism in Pakistan, Egypt, and Iran* (Lahore: Vanguard).

_____ (1985) *The Concept of Islamic State* (Lahore: Progressive)

Malik, Iftikhar (1997) *State and Civil Society in Pakistan: Politics of Authority, Ideology and Ethnicity* (London: Macmillan Press)

Middleton, Nick (1995) *The Global Casino - An Introduction to Environment Issues,* (New York & London: Edward Arnold)

Overseas Development Administration (1993) *Good Government, Technical Note no. 10* (London: ODA)

Rose & Evans, *"Pakistan's Enduring Experiment"*

Rossi, Marco Rossi, (1999) *Decentralization and Development* (Berne: Swiss Agency for Development and Cooperation)

State Bank of Pakistan (various years) *Annual Report* (Karachi)

Talbot, Ian (1999) *Pakistan: A modern History* (Lahore: Vanguard)

Todaro, *Economic Development,*

Tribe, Derek (1994) *Feeding and Greening the World: The Role of International Agriculture Research* (Oxon, UK: Cab International)

UNDP (2000) *"Forward"*, Global Public Goods (UNDP html. home web page)

UNO (1998) *Commission on Global Governance*

Weiss, (1995) *Pakistan: A Country Study*, (Washington, D.C.: Federal Research Division, Library of Congress)

World Bank (2000) *Entering the 21st Century: World Development Report*, 1999-2000 (Washington, DC: World Bank)

World Bank (1994) *World Development Report* (Washington, DC: The World Bank)

World Bank (1992) *Governance and Development* (Washington D.C.: World Bank).

World Bank (several years) *Country Brief: Pakistan*

World Conservation-IUCN (1999) *"Forest under Fire"* (IUCN: 3-4/99)

INDEX

D

E

F

G

M

N

P